ALSO BY ELIZABETH JANEWAY

FICTION

The Walsh Girls, 1943
Daisy Kenyon, 1945
The Question of Gregory, 1949
Leaving Home, 1953
The Third Choice, 1959
Accident, 1964

BOOKS FOR CHILDREN

The Vikings, 1951
The Early Days of the Automobile, 1956
Angry Kate, 1963
Ivanov Seven, 1967

NONFICTION

Man's World, Woman's Place; A Study
  in Social Mythology, 1971
Between Myth and Morning: Women Awakening, 1974

EDITED BY ELIZABETH JANEWAY

Women: Their Changing Role, 1972

Powers of the Weak

POWERS OF THE WEAK

Elizabeth Janeway

ALFRED A. KNOPF   NEW YORK   1980

THIS IS A BORZOI BOOK
PUBLISHED BY ALFRED A. KNOPF, INC.

Library of Congress Cataloging in Publication Data

Janeway, Elizabeth.   Powers of the weak.
Bibliography: p.   Includes index.
1. Social history—20th century.   2. Power (Social sciences)   3. Sex differences (Psychology)
    I. Title.
HN16.J35   303.3'3   79–3468
ISBN 0–394–40696–6

Manufactured in the United States of America

FIRST EDITION

INFERIORITY: *A value-bearing category that refers to the powers of the weak, countervailing against structural power, fostering continuity, creating the sentiment of the wholeness of the total community, positing the model of an undifferentiated whole whose units are whole human beings. The powers of the weak are often assigned in hierarchic and stratified societies to females, the poor, autochthons, and outcasts.*

Victor Turner,
Image and Pilgrimage in Christian Culture

Contents

Powers of the Weak

Power, Place, Process

Anyone who knows anything of history knows that great social changes are impossible without the feminine ferment. Social progress can be measured exactly by the social position of the fair sex (the ugly ones included).

Karl Marx

This is primarily a book about power, both as it operates and as it is seen to operate, in the world of events that is still "man's world." However it is also a book about women, and Marx's comment, in a letter to a friend, suggests why. Now as in 1866, the status of women illuminates the condition of society. My aim is to understand power, that ambiguous, menacing, much-desired quality whose accepted definition seems to me unsatisfactory. Is it a quality at all? Or is it, rather, a process that both reflects and produces "great social changes" in a continuing dynamic of human interaction? If so, it is driven by "ferments" which boil up in unexpected places while guardians of the superstructure are looking in another direction. Its "being" is "becoming." Its steady existence derives from ceaseless shifts in tensions, its balance is maintained by thrust and response, hope and frustration, and by the practical actions that grow out of confrontations and compromises among its myriad human components. In general, however, discussions of power take its nature for granted and ignore these shifting and busy components. I want to reverse these priorities and explore the dynamics of social change through the experience of some of its human data. Marx's comment suggests that the shifts in power that are an inevitable part of change can be studied by means of "the social position of the fair sex (the ugly ones included)."

It seems to me, indeed, that Marx was righter than he knew and that the position of women is not just a useful but a unique tool for the task at hand. If power is a process of human interaction, it takes place between interacting members of a relationship. We can name them most simply as "powerful" and "weak," in political terms as "rulers" and "ruled" or "governors" and "governed." But the step beyond applying labels isn't easy. What is the nature of these two entities? Conventional books on power tell us a lot about the powerful, for it is this side of the balance that they're concerned with, while the governed rest of us are pretty well ignored. That's natural enough if one accepts the usual definition of power as being a quality possessed by the powerful, but it won't do in the present case. To understand the workings of power as a relationship one must also consider the situation of the weak, the other, second, member of the process by which society at once exists and changes. And women are the oldest, largest, and most central group of human creatures in the wide category of the weak and the ruled. The adjustments that women have made to life over centuries spent as subordinate partners in a power relationship illuminate the whole range of power situations.

Indeed, even a negative assessment of the status of women is a product of social advance: it means that society finds us interesting enough to look at as separate beings, visible as an independent group. Of course, women have always been present in daily life, with designated roles and functions, but in the past it was the functions rather than the women that were perceived. Sometimes we have served as a means of exchange, "pumped out" (says Lévi-Strauss) from one familial group to link it with another and thus operate as a kind of social glue. Married, guarded, and warned to be chaste, our foremothers bore the sons whose legitimacy could be trusted, and who could then inherit property in legal and peaceful fashion. Obviously we have served other, sexual, needs too, and we have certainly used such needs to help ourselves when we could. But no matter how useful, or desirable, or even necessary we may have seemed from time to time, the meaning of female experience has been fed only rarely into the larger reservoir of valued social knowledge. Just fifty years ago George Bernard Shaw declared, in *The Intelligent Woman's Guide to Socialism and Capitalism,* that one might read a score of books on socialism "without ever discovering that such a creature as a woman ever existed." He was himself overlooking Engels's work, *On the Origins of the Family;* but that simply strengthens his point by demonstrating the epidemic spread of male blindness.

This blindness is not applied to women only. It is typical of a general tendency of governors to ignore the humanity, and even the presence, of groups whose lives fall within the category of the weak. So when we take the position of women as a tool for studying the relationship between rulers and ruled, our first lesson should certainly be that the experience of other governed human beings can't be ignored. No one considering the dynamics of power can turn away from reports and analysis of black life, of slavery, both ancient and modern, of hierarchical feudal societies, of conquest and rebellion and nationalist aspirations, of caste distinctions and class consciousness, of revolution and its aftermath, and of extreme repression in prisons and death camps. The methods and uses of governance and the resistance to domination have been touched on in many fields of study—political philosophy, history, sociology, ethics, anthropology, psychology, literature, and religion at the least. No student can hope to command this mass of material, though any explorer of power relations should try to be aware of it to the extent that strength and insight allow. What we need is a clue, a strand to follow, just such a thread as Ariadne gave to Theseus to guide him safely through the labyrinth where the Minotaur lived in darkness. Appropriately, that clue is the condition of women. It is paradigmatic of the existence of all the governed, of those whom their betters see and define as "other"; paradigmatic because women are present in all groups of the weak, which is not true of any other segment of the governed, but also—and more important—because the connotation of "femaleness" fixes women in an extreme position among the weak, a position which is significant by its *centrality* and by its *pertinence* for all other denizens of this realm.

Women are "different," that is, by being *more* different than are others of the governed. Because we are thus isolated among the weak, we exemplify the lesser but still essential isolation of all the weak. We have been feared for mythic reasons by those who hold the reins of authority, but so too have the rest of the ruled been feared, sometimes shamed by being likened to women and sometimes dreaded, as women have been, as deviant from normal humanity. These charges of abnormality make the weak incomprehensible to their rulers. Their conduct can't be predicted by the rules of the powerful and it is therefore felt as menacing. So it is with women's odd reactions and bewildering behavior, their incoherent outbursts of emotion. Labels of deviance will be used here as clues to the situation of the weak in general.

I don't intend to use these pejorative definitions of women in only one direction. If our condition is revealing of the situation of others, theirs can reflect the sociology and the psychology of women. Large-scale disorders of power affecting whole races and classes work themselves out in the daily existence which women guard, so that public and private events intermingle. Mental disturbances in troubled children throw light on female responses to repression. Such daily reactions serve as guides for analysis of overall behavior in wider areas: in the political arena, in the worlds of learning, of art, of philosophic interpretation. What women know, learned and relearned in our long sojourn in the country of the weak, is the geography of an uncharted territory of human existence. It is human existence, not female existence; nor has its looming presence been utterly unknown, simply repressed and suppressed, an Atlantis drowned not by accident but by subconscious purpose, whose influence still troubles currents and climate.

It is a commonplace today to say that looking at women means looking at half the human race, but more people say it than do it, I think. Like all generalities, it tails off without any specific recommendations for how to look and what to look for. What we need is a guide to the way in which this half of humanity connects with and affects the other, via differences and like-nesses. If women have a place in man's world, where does it lie? What's the geography? In recent years the female half of our species has begun to look about with more attention, for the simple reason that the rest of the world has begun to seem more accessible. Those who are motivated will learn, and the idea that one may be able to depart from the place assigned and walk about freely in a larger sphere is a powerful reason to spy out the land. And so a mist of inattention has lifted for us. Here is "insider" knowledge of what the governed know, more of it than we ever imagined. Here is an expanding view that doesn't seem to correspond with the old maps; or, to change my metaphor from one that is static for something suitably dynamic, here is evidence of an undiscovered planet whose mass disturbs the orbit of that which belongs to the powerful.

Having said so much about the usefulness of studying the circumstances of the weak, especially as exemplified by the position of women, my next step should clearly be a brief description of this position. I would do that at once if I could. I can't, and the reason I can't is the reason for writing this book. For there is no way to describe the position of women except in terms of current definitions of power, and current definitions of power are part of what I want to look at and question. So my attempt to outline the status of women is going to work out as a tussle with accepted ideas about the context of life in which we have a position. These accepted ideas can't be taken as neutral because they are part of the subject matter to be discussed. Contem-porary charts of the social world have been drawn up by the powerful without much regard for the ideas of the weak. They're based on events as seen by the powerful and interpreted by way of associations and connections that match the experience of the powerful. Our new discoveries are off the map.

All through this book, therefore, we shall be working with two views of the world. Not only are there discrepancies between them, but the ortho-dox frame of reference influences what the governed are able to see for themselves. The significance of what the weak are told is "really there" has been filtered through the heads of those who see their role as being in charge: in charge of public life, in charge of morality, and most important of all, in charge of deciding what's important. The position of women, as described by orthodox axioms of power, is certainly interesting and we should be aware of it, but it is not the position of women as women know it; a statement that also applies to descriptions of other groups of the weak. So a different description, one that takes account of what women have been learning about the position of women, has to challenge a number of axioms on which our current social mythology is based. I will be as simple and direct about it as possible, but part of my job is to question what seems simple and direct; an irritating procedure, but if we are to begin, then we have to start at the beginning. To begin, then:

If women's position in the past has been obscure, that's because the functions and occupations held to be proper for the female sex are not the same as those with which the powerful have been charged. Look back as we may, the view hardly changes. Mothers and wives and servants, food-gatherers and cooks, spinners and sewers, nurturers and scapegoats (along with the rest of the weak), women are necessary; but what this army of scurrying ants does is taken for granted, no doubt because it *is* necessary. The powerful don't have to argue; they just point. A close corollary to the necessity of this kind of life is that it's assumed to be unchanging; an assumption extended till very recently to the other ranks of the governed, sunk in repetitive labor, Kipling's "mere uncounted folk." Events only happen to the great. When women and others of the weak turn up in history, it's because somebody or bodies has been making some sort of trouble that has brought them to the attention of the authorities. The peasants rise, the slaves revolt, there is a prevalence of witches.

Even so, not all of these disruptions can have been recorded by keepers of annals. If protest was suppressed, its failure was enough to label it as unimportant. Besides, caution would surely dictate that keeping records of rebellions could be dangerous since it might inspire others among the dissatisfied to try revolt again, for themselves. These are rational reasons for neglecting the appearances on the public stage of women and the weak, but there also exists an element of unconscious defensive screening moved by precisely the impulse which defines "difference" as "deviance." Women, says orthodox wisdom, are not just different but specially, inescapably different. When these creatures behave oddly, that's part of their nature; it's built in. Divine power created them dissimilar, whether by taking them from man's side while he slept, in a second creation that was more afterthought than originating inception, or by bestowing on them smaller brains, more primitive instincts, and recurrent hormonal disturbances which prevent them from thinking logically; and anatomy, which is destiny, proves it.

This isn't merely a description, it leads to a conclusion; or does the conclusion evoke the description? Whichever comes first, such a judgment serves to set women aside and apart. Whatever we say or do can be dismissed as not relevant to the mainstream rest of human existence and especially to the administration of weighty public affairs. The private events of women's lives are held to be merely private and, therefore, neither useful for understanding normal operations, nor having any consequences in the real world of action.

This taken-for-granted assumption is one that must be questioned. True, humanity has long been accustomed to summing up (or reducing) male-female differences to variations derived from the physiology of sex; and since bodily difference has been inescapable—that is, until recently when transsexual operations began to be made—sex differences have been regarded as a kind of unarguable, primal cause of divergence among human beings. The physiology of sex is thus extended to become an absolute polarity, which marks women not just as different, but as separate. There can be no intermediate range between the genders, nothing equivalent to shadings of skin color or mixture of genetic groups to produce "mestizos." This is the sign that labels women's position as extreme. By it, we are cut off from power and, in addition, we are cut off from others of the weak. Our experience can never be applicable to the lives of others, nor can we regard our lives as representative of those of the rest of the governed.

The question raised here has a clear bearing on the status of women. If it's physiology that makes us separate, then we are separate forever, never to be assimilated into "normal" social processes, which must be reserved for nondeviants, who can only be males. We are not just outcast but "out-caste" and unabsorbable, more deeply untouchable than India's untouchables. Women may be better off here and now than there and then, or vice versa, but Marx was wrong in taking the position of the fair sex as a measure of social change, for it must always stand outside the processes that society sets up as ways of controlling events and managing the material world. The line drawn round woman's place becomes an impenetrable barrier. One part, the largest part, of the weak is divided from the rest.

Two questions at once come to mind. First, is the dogma of special difference true? Second, if it isn't, should it be read as an effort by the powerful to control and divide the weak? *They are the wrong questions.* They can be answered easily enough: first, No, of course not; and second, Yes, of course, though the process is unconscious. But neither answer tells us how to respond intelligently to the problem of sex difference by evaluating its meaning and its importance. What we are looking at, and what we need to understand, is the exercise of an enormously significant power: the great and valuable power to define the elements of our world and to declare how weighty, how urgent, and how pressing they are. In this case, the power to define, to connect, and to name assures us that male dominance stems from a bodily conformation which assigns to every human being an inescapable role, duty, and place in the world. The aggressive, thrusting penis symbolizes active, assertive power. The hidden inwardness of women's sex organs stamps the female as a passive receiver with the duty of shielding and nurturing.

If we want to dispute the conclusions drawn from physiology, we cannot dispute the facts; we are so made. What we can dispute, however, is the *significance* of this bodily disparity: that is, we can talk about importance. How important is the physical difference between the sexes in relation to the rest of life? Is it important enough to justify male dominance and to place women in a state of permanent apartheid?

From this beginning it's possible to make some progress because we are not trying to argue against dogma, but to judge the validity of dogmatic assumptions by testing them against actual experience. When we ask a question about experience, we see at once that a number of varying answers have been found. In some societies the roles of the sexes are strongly polarized. In others they overlap quite substantially. History, anthropology, and the events of our own lives tell us that social conditioning has a profound influence on the way human beings perceive and react to the effects that the sex they were born with has on the lives they lead. Gender identity and the proper behavior that goes with it have to be learned by young children. This behavior differs from culture to culture and is sometimes learned wrong; that is, inaccurately. Moreover, changes in the external world, in economic relations, in methods of production, in technology, in scientific understanding, in medical advance, in political institutions, in religious beliefs, in education, have all altered the ideas we carry with us about what each sex can and should do, because they have changed the limits of action and the opportunities open to us. Bodily differences, that is, have been interpreted in so protean a fashion that it seems impossible to draw precise inferences from them. Which can only mean that their importance can't be absolute or ultimate, however large or small it seems at any particular time. Q.E.D., women's experience is pertinent for others.

As a matter of fact, the particular experience of being labeled as deviant because of some bodily difference is itself pertinent to others. Sex is the most intensely stressed physiological fact that has been used to distance a group from power by ranking its members low, but it is not the only one. Skin color is so obvious that it doesn't need mention, but almost any kind of characteristic can be caught at and exaggerated, or even invented, as a mark of shame. Our media-aware society will be most conscious of the use of cartoons and caricature against Jews and Orientals in this century and against the waves of immigrants to the New World in the last: witness "Paddy, the Irish bogtrotter," with his Neanderthal brows and scruffy chin. The malnourished, undersized poor have always been targets. And where no physical trait can be found to act as a sinister stigma, something else will be devised. Clothing is an obvious way to label people by status and rank, and sumptuary laws tried to do this for centuries. Greater hostility required Jews to wear a yellow Star of David, branded slaves, and cropped the ears of criminals. In such a perspective the physical difference of sex takes a central place, but for a new reason: it seems as if any effort to keep the weak in their place had to be reinforced by imitating, or at least alluding to, the sex difference. Almost any physical difference will do as an analogy, and where it can't be found it will be invented, in an effort to recreate the permanent polarity of sex difference.

Symbolically, the metaphor that connects women with weakness is very widespread. "Boys don't cry, only girls cry" say our social norms, and in almost any corner of the globe men are habitually shamed for failure or cowardice or ineptitude by being compared to women. To show "inappropriate" emotion, to wince at pain, to hesitate or hold back from action are decried as effeminate, as "unmanly" acts, only proper for females. So the formula "To be female is to be weak" is also used in reverse: "To be weak is to be female." It is used thus by men themselves, spurring themselves and their sons on to engagement with the male role. Power and weakness are thus factored into masculine and feminine gender images quite explicitly. *Virile* men are decisive and forceful (say our dictionaries), and *feminine* women are passive.

It's true that some societies make an effort to gloss over the equation that male equals strength and power and female equals weakness and passivity by putting forward a doctrine of separate but equal spheres of action for the two sexes. With us, men are assigned to the public world and instructed to compete there for fame, success, status, all the attributes we commonly associate with power. The women attached to them participate vicariously in their achievements but are not supposed to pursue these goals independently. Women, instead, are granted a right to exercise power (usually labeled "moral authority") in the private sphere of woman's place, over children and other dependents, and to influence, to whatever extent possible, the men who also dwell there; though these men will naturally assume that their women don't have much sense about the world outside their private place, since they aren't supposed to roam abroad. However, the contribution that women make to family life, by emotional support, continuity of relationships, monitoring and easing friction, and (practically speaking) domestic skills and daily management of the living space—plus sexual accessibility, though that's not always mentioned—earns economic support and protection from men.

This is the traditional picture of what women's condition is and should be. Anyone who accepts it, male or female, is going to ask: "What's wrong with this arrangement? Isn't it what we should aim for, even if we have to adjust some of the working details from time to time?" But today it is not just details that require adjustment. Current versions of the ancient bargain are not only false, they are widely felt to be false, even by some of those who oppose the feminist push toward equality. The tradition that men are properly dominant over women is sometimes thrown overboard by antiwomen's-movement women, who declare that women are actually better off than men, as things stand now. Why men should put up with this imbalance is an unanswered question; it suggests that female antifeminists don't think much of male intelligence. But, in fact, if society offers women only a limited portion of a larger world where men move freely, it appears to be ranking our special place below the larger territory. If it thought us fully capable, why should it ban us at all? And how can good old-fashioned masculine logic maintain that the part of existence assigned to women equals the whole?

The root of these problems lies in faulty definitions. Power, being not a thing but a process of interaction among human beings, is simply not "divisible" according to any static principle. If the comfortable arrangement in which women's work at home is as much honored as men's activities outside, in which women's influence is equally decisive, exists today in some happy homes, that's not because power is divisible. Power can be administered in areas and departments, but its administrators still have to decide on the relative importance of one area as over against another: Which takes priority? Do we pay attention first to the demands of a man's career, or those of family life? The decision may be automatic—or it may be arrived at by conscious bargaining in a search for what's best for all; but it *is* a decision by someone within the relationship, and not a natural event ordained by immutable laws. By extension, then, a couple who have decided to live their lives according to the traditional pattern have made an agreed-on bargain on the basis of active choice, and the choice must be reinforced again and again.

Today that's not easy to do, for traditional marriages are becoming harder and harder to maintain, a trend that also needs to be assessed. Does it come out of "the feminine ferment"? Or is it because of "great social changes"? Or both? If so, how do they affect each other? Have the demands that appear to originate in the feminine ferment actually arisen because of great social change? Has change, as I believe, called forth responses which permit hitherto unused energy and unsatisfied aspirations to emerge as newly relevant to the matter at hand? Such creative potential is part of the human repertory; at least we must assume so if we're not to believe that evolution has come to a dead halt. It must lie latent within social groups who have been kept offstage in the past, just as it has demonstrated itself as present in the powerful men who have invented the world as it is. Of these distanced groups the largest and the least touched by earlier demands is that of women, who not only form a distinct group, but whose experience mingles with that of others among the deprived.

So women's experience, expressed in this ferment, is not just a measure of change but also a sensitive guide to the future. Unfortunately, we must then see resistance to women's demands as arising from fear of the future, fear of the changes that are already upon us; fear and anxiety in the ranks of the powerful. These are not healthy emotions. They do not bode well for the ability of our rulers to deal with social operations. That situation gives an unhappy topicality to my exploration of the dynamics of power via the experience of the weak with women as a basic reference point.

What form does this fear of change take? It is a fear of equality; that is, women's experience is exemplary here too. Because the traditional female image is labeled "weak," achieving equality with men is perceived, by women, as being a step up to a level of greater opportunity and wider horizons. What men perceive is the opposite: not a leveling up, but a leveling down for them. The greater the depth of the step down, the greater the fear and resentment. Men who are most anxious are those who believe most strongly that women are inferior and who see them primarily as objects of sexual desire and not as human beings. A great deal of overt machismo derives from the expectation that granting women equality will reduce men who are not explicitly members of the elite to the same status as women, and that means opening them to the treatment women should expect, including sexual treatment as women. The idea that feminists want to castrate men is one expression of this fear. A more realistic ground for it, as well as another bit of evidence that women's physiology does not constitute a different difference, is the sexual abuse that nonpowerful men have suffered in situations of deprivation—prison, for example. The underground sequence of emotional logic runs: giving women equality implies that nonpowerful men can be treated like women, right up to rape. We may hope that some men conclude that rape—that is, the natural combination of sex and violence—is wrong, but I am afraid that often the reaction is: equality is wrong because it invites violence. Judges, juries, police departments, and the press still find it tempting to assume that rape victims have done something to provoke attack.

The changing condition of women, then, is a response to social change, and it raises important questions about power that are hard to deal with as long as we accept our current definitions. Having said so much, we can see that what has been happening to women is a loosening up of the bonds of necessity that limited female activities in the past. Today we no longer need to spend our lives at childbearing, child-rearing, and related tasks—unless we want to. In the past a great deal of productive labor required physical strength that some women commanded, but many did not. And since sexual activity was hard to de-couple from childbearing, fertile women had to expect to spend a large part of active existence in bearing and rearing children. The medical knowledge that has made contraception a matter of course and the technology that has replaced muscle power with machines are part of the social changes which have widened opportunities.

How accessible these opportunities are in practice depends on the woman and her circumstances, but in theory very few slots are totally closed, and they are closed by custom and social opposition, not by physical inability. Now, merely theoretical opportunities certainly aren't good enough; but psychologically, the idea that one *can* do something, even if the doing is very hard and success unsure, is quite a different thing from the conviction that any such doing is impossible. Possibility lifts restrictions on hope and effortful planning. Of course, many women still follow traditional female patterns of living—or think they do, even as they add a paid job to homemaking and so give the labor force an unprecedented new shape; our world isn't that of the past, and traditions have had to adjust themselves. But women can also add new activities to old, or even set out on totally innovative courses, and move back and forth from one pattern to another; not easy, but possible.

These changes are not hard to see. What may be less obvious is how very new is any element of choice at all. It barely existed in the past, and that was true also for the rest of the great human majority of the governed, when custom bound serfs to the land, shepherds to their flocks, workers to their crafts, and the bourgeoisie to their enterprises. These were the fortunate. Choice was often a desperate dilemma in which the dispossessed sought a way to survive; and there are those who still live on such an edge.

If, for many women, change has increased choice, choosing still isn't simple. Part of the condition of women is a need to create new choices, not simply to react in predictable ways. On the face of it, enlarging woman's role offers an obvious option: move into the existing alternative of the male role or roles. Men, rather naturally, assume that is what women are about to do, and some certainly are. But not all women want to. Hesitation like this can suggest that women really liked their old status, and are unfit for active struggle in the public arena; or, even more simply, that these really are very odd creatures, whose motives can't be sorted out by familiar sequences of masculine thought. "What do women want?" cried Dr. Freud and did not stay for an answer. Well, what women want is a world that offers more than two choices—male role, female role, and nothing else. Add then to the condition of women a sort of creative doubt, an unwillingness to accept a view of the world which ignores an inner awareness of the need for more change still, and especially for the incorporation in this public world of women's experience.

The ability to add new perceptions, purposes, and goals to the dynamics of social interaction is not something that the powerful expect from any of the weak; but the powerful are wrong. Any existing culture can only reach and develop a certain amount of human creativity. The rest is suppressed because the terms of life don't demand its use, or are even hostile. In times of change, however, the old repertory of action will turn out to be insufficient; then the untapped reservoir of creativity belonging to hitherto overlooked groups and classes of society may be called on. The nineteenth-century Europeans who emigrated to the United States offer examples of creative energy. The country we live in today is very different from the one that the first of these incomers reached, so different that the smug description of our society as "a melting pot" is inadequate. The material that was to be melted has instead melted the pot of WASP sensibility and run out in veins and streams through our society. The internal migration of black people is having a similar effect, and Hispanics and Asians are already functioning as new centers of radiation. There seems little doubt that purposes originating in these groups will shift goals that may seem eternal but are merely traditional.

Almost as significant—and as obscure—as this untapped evolutionary potential is another element characteristic of the experience of the governed: the experience of *being* governed; that is, of being the second member in a power relationship. What the weak know about this process of interaction is considerable, for they've been involved in it for a long time. No doubt much of this knowledge is unconscious, for just as stereotypes define the sexes, so they attach themselves to the condition of being ruler or the condition of being ruled. The power to define guarantees that the stereotypes themselves are created by the powerful and reflect only their view of life. The self-image our rulers make for themselves holds them capable of analyzing and dealing with complicated political situations, and of arriving logically at difficult decisions. The poor and the weak, in the opinion of their governors, give themselves over to trivial daydreaming, and sacrifice future possibilities to the gratification of immediate wishes; any member of the elite will sadly agree. Most of the time the weak accept this opinion for reasons that will be explored later; here it's enough to say that the rewards of power seem hedged about with dangers and priced very high. But below their surface acceptance of this world picture and their place in it, the weak possess a latent appreciation of how power works in the everyday world, and especially of what happens when it works badly. Their own everyday lives rub the awareness into them. As for personal relations, whether in the family or in the world of work, those who are more rather than less dependent gain a working knowledge of the motivations of the powerful because they have to, in order to survive. Why, on the other hand, should the powerful study the weak? Few of them do.

What the weak don't know about the processes of the power relationship is their own strength. In this world, we learn by doing. When the governed shy away from conscious, purposeful intervention in the process of governing, they not only lose the opportunity to affect its outcome, they lose the chance to observe the working—good, bad, and indifferent—of both sides of the partnership. But though one may decline a position of power, one can't escape the effects of the process. There's no way to stop the world and get off; we're all here together, both those who shun power and those who lust after it. Whether the weak intervene or not, they are touched by the continuing dynamics of the political process. The input that they don't supply is not just lost; its absence allows other considerations to weigh more heavily and to unbalance the relationship. Reject the chance to act for your own good and the world will still trundle on, but it will do so according to the demands of other people.

If in time this imbalance becomes too severe, the governed will rebel, and now their past avoidance of power can hinder them seriously. In a period of breakdown a forceful, rising movement can overthrow the Establishment (any Establishment) and its goals in a burst of unplanned, angry energy. But changing overt goals isn't enough. If the old system of values and the old methods of rule are still taken to be the only ones that are effective, the same old pyramid of power will rise again. And when the weak habitually turn their backs on power because they accept the stereotypes that undervalue them, they permit their rulers to define proper processes of governing according to the experience of the rulers alone, so that it comes to seem that only one "right way" to handle power exists.

If there is one right way and only one, we haven't yet discovered what it is. In this book I am taking another tack in order to try to sort out some of the things that we know about living together, controlling the events in our lives, and operating the political process where private needs meet in the public sphere, which lie outside the stereotype—things we know but have forgotten, or have never brought centrally to mind. I shall be seeking this intuitive knowledge in the unexplored country of the weak. In a way, it's a social equivalent of the personal hoard of forgotten and repressed emotion and experience that each of us carries around and reacts to unaware which psychoanalysis probes. This is not to say that psychoanalysis, applied simplistically to public events, will return profitable answers or help us understand the sources of public pressures. Psychoanalysis is designed to probe individual motivations, and though such matters affect the public world, they are only a small part of it. Psychologic studies can be helpful, however, if they are used as analogues from which methods and areas for study can be adapted. Symbolically, a private unconscious corresponds rather well to the unexamined knowledge possessed by the governed mass of humanity: knowledge about the underside of social relations, about survival and endurance, about discontent and frustration, about the drive and the difficulty of coming together in resistance bands against unconscionable demands. In private the rational ego represses such awareness, in public the elite refuses to listen. These odds and ends of existence form a kind of public unconscious which is not beyond research and evaluation through methods that fit. As any troubled individual is more than the "ego identity" that knows its name and thinks it knows the course of its life, so any troubled society is more than the conscious elite who believe that they act for, and in the name of, the whole community. We can learn a good deal in the country of the weak.

In addition, what psychoanalysis tells us about the problems of individual existence, when it's applied to its own proper territory, can be extended to public situations that match up with private binds. These certainly include the experience of weakness, of vulnerability, fear of powerful others, and psychological efforts to cope with and control these terrors. Internal efforts won't control public terrors, but they do indicate the ways in which human beings react and respond to overpowering situations. Especially useful here are analyses, in classic form, of early childhood development, and what can go wrong in this area. Therapists of the individual patient now question overconcentration on this period, and they may be right. But for students of power relations, the start of life, the awakening of consciousness, the formation of character can be very enlightening. It is then, after all, when individuals acquire a repertory of responses for dealing with later situations. Those responses may be modified, but they are never entirely lost.

And it is these early responses to the world, unearthed by analytic methods, which influence social interactions among human beings, including power relationships. At the start of life, each individual is not all that individual. Each of us lives through an experience that is infinitely more similar, more common to all, than the years after, and *it is particularly similar in what it teaches us about power.* For all human creatures begin existence in almost total dependence, more dependent than our animal cousins. A shared "collective unconscious," such as Jung suggested, need not be derived from some theorized genetic memory. It follows equally well from the fact that human babies are born helpless and take a large percentage of their lives to reach maturity. During this period of growth, all of us learn a great deal about interaction within a relationship of power and dependency. Moreover, our position changes, for as we grow, we learn (or so one may hope) to take some of the uses of power into our hands: to formulate our own goals, to test them against the facts and the institutions that exist in the outer world, to bargain and negotiate and rebel and meet defeat and pick ourselves up and start over again.

Consequently I shall begin my attempt to understand the social identity of the second member of the power relationship—the weak and the governed—with a look at this relationship as we know it first, in the earliest months and years of life. As the position of women supplies a useful reference point within social history, so early childhood development allows us to trace the usual effects on the psyche of first encounters with power and dependence. Normal growth has been watched, and stages of development have been established. Equally useful are studies of the emotional disturbances of children, for where normal growth is largely interior and silent, disturbed growth is highly visible, because it's disruptive. Advances in medicine aren't made by studying healthy people only, and disorders of growth show up the process by telling us how it can go wrong.

When it goes wrong, students of childhood development declare, over and over, that something has also gone wrong within the relational connections to the rest of the world that are made by the child with, and through, other human beings. Growth is a process of learning about the world, how to respond to events, to predict them, to control them; and this is a process of achieving power. It takes place within the relationships that surround a child from its moment of birth; and because that's so, it seems to me impossible that the understanding of the power process, and any realistic use of it that connects individuals with the outside world, can be detached from a surrounding network of relationships. Anytime we think of power as being simply a possession of the powerful we are thinking inaccurately.

At this point one of my major guidelines, the experience of women, asks to be touched on again. There's no way to look at early childhood development without looking at mothering, at the first shaping relationship of life, and orthodox definitions of femaleness tie the work of mothering into the essential quality of being female. This is another bit of taken-for-granted doctrine that will have to be explored, and will be. Here I want simply to put aside our acceptance of standard gender definitions and bring up once more the touchstone question of importance: How important is the mother-child relationship? Ask anyone, male or female, and the answer will almost certainly be that it's enormously important, paramount in the development of children to healthy maturity. And in almost every case, as things stand now, the basis of such development is certainly in the hands of mothers; although, if we think for a moment, we know that it's perfectly possible for healthy children to be raised by other affectionate adults besides the natural mother. Adoptive parents have been doing it for a long time.

But let that be, for now. There are still two interesting omissions in this exchange on the importance of mothering. The first is that we don't ask: Important to whom? To the child or the mother? We assume that the child's need is the determining factor and that the mother will accept the child's need as overwhelming, as superseding her own purposes. Most women try to do that; but try or not, the mother's emotional investment in the relationship can never be as great as that of the child, whose whole being is absorbed in the looming maternal environment. But mothers are adults. Sometimes there are other children, and other adult relationships certainly exist. Mother-child symbiosis, it would seem, is naturally binding for the child, but not for the mother. For the adult member, there has to be an element of willed choice. Most women do will it, quite happily, but there is a fundamental emotional imbalance of payments in the situation. Even the most devoted mother expects something back. It may be demonstrated appreciation, it may be more affection than a growing child finds it easy to give, it may be submission to her authority. These things are part of a process between human beings, and no process is ideal. Children struggling to create an identity for themselves are perfectly capable of taking an adult's pleasure in their growing strength as an effort to share an achievement they see as their own. These things pass in the course of normal development and become jokes in memory shared by two adults, parent and child, but we falsify reality and its memory traces if we imagine they don't exist.

In fact we recognize their likelihood when we blame overpowering mothers for distorting the personalities of their children by the intensity of their devotion and their demands for reciprocal intimacy. But if the need of the child is taken as the only measure of a good mother-infant relationship, aren't we inviting such a response?

We fail, also, to ask what happens if this one-to-one relationship can't be sustained. Instead, the overemphasis on the mother's obligation implies that if failure occurs, it's her fault. She's accused of coldness, not giving enough, thinking of herself first. Undoubtedly breakdowns in the mother-child bond happen for reasons of emotional stress. They also happen when sheer necessity forces women to leave their children for economic reasons, because of ill health, because other duties make demands, or when their own lives have been so troubled that the emotional demands of mothering are traumatic. Doesn't that suggest that we are mistaken, on purely pragmatic grounds, when we emphasize the unique value of close care of an infant by the mother alone? What we are doing is turning a situation that's traditionally usual and desirable into one that's universally necessary. We say: Raising a child is primarily the concern of the mother, and also the primary concern of the mother—and we go no further; we don't even see that the two things aren't the same. Nor do we ask what happens when things go wrong and try to provide a socially supported fail-safe mechanism to take over if they do go wrong. We assign child to mother, mother to child, and imagine that that's sufficient.

It isn't, either for mother or child. Even when things go well, a one-to-one relationship needs supplementing. Great social changes have pretty well swept away the easy connections with networks of kin, friends, and neighbors that used to be available for support when needed, or simply as extensions and variations of the adult-child bond, and to temper the intense intimacy that develops when mother and child are alone for much of the time. Very little thought has been given to replacing these supports and connections with the rest of the adult world that supplement the central mother-child relationship, even though the isolation of modern nuclear families exacerbates the problem. It almost seems as if we are looking at an effort to deal with a real need by denying that it exists. In an individual, we would call that a neurotic reaction. What shall we say about it when we observe it in society at large?

In any case, we must see this condition as part of the position of women today: obligations to children and to family in general fall on us first, and they fall very heavily in an era when the strength and unity of small communities have been sapped. They are probably more onerous than they have generally been in the past. By means of the power to define, the woman's responsibility for family life is being exploited, in order to protect society from having to face family needs: if child-raising is the mother's business, then society doesn't have to be concerned with the problems that may arise here; and that means that when problems arise—and they certainly will from time to time—then neither mother nor child has anywhere to turn.

We shall see later what this bind can mean to a child and the particular disorders of the power relationship that it produces. For a desperate woman with a troubled child, trapped in a position where she cannot expect consistent help, it means escalating guilt, the guilt of a victim who feels she is victimizing another, and doesn't know how to stop. When society turns victims into scapegoats, it's operating badly—neurotically. When it sacrifices children in this way, it's operating horribly. And it happens out of inattention to the reality of the lives of the weak, which the weak themselves accept as befitting.

To look at the beginnings of life requires that we look at the human environment into which children are born and also at the surrounding structures and processes of power that condition this environment, if we are not to take for granted the very assumptions I want to question. How do these processes work, for powerful and for weak? What is the impact of their demands, and how can it be met? Are there means that the great nonpowerful bulk of humanity can use to monitor power processes and deal with their aberrations? A social contract between rulers and ruled, based on the consent of the governed, is an old idea and ideal. Is it anything more? Is the nature of the power relationship merely dominance and submission? Or are there abiding, effective powers of the weak which can enforce a social contract?

Any group that is moving closer to centers of power-use will find itself asking this kind of question. Women who are doing so now are very much aware of the problems that accompany this move: confusion over proper roles, proper goals, over appropriate means of judging the operating machinery of the world of events. Most of us think of these difficulties as peculiar to our time and our sex—"women's issues," which seem so stubborn and resistant to solution by customary procedures that invention is not just the child of necessity, but necessity itself. But the questions transcend time, and sex. If they seem to women to come out of woman's place—well, that's still located in the territory of the weak, and any answers will be useful there.

In the search for answers, women have some advantages. Freshness of vision is one. Things familiar and taken for granted in man's world are seen from a new angle. Second, women's lives are full of lessons in flexibility. That statement contradicts the orthodox view of women as conservative, conventional thinkers, and designedly so, for the view is based on old definitions of what it's important to think about. To consider philosophically matters of high politics, or abstract principles, hasn't interested women much for a simple reason: What could our foremothers do about these matters? Thinking in a vacuum, when you can't implement the conclusions you draw, invites frustration. But in everyday life women are prime experimenters and quick learners, pragmatically ready to accept or invent new ways to do things.

That brings me to the most significant advantage of all: women are deeply aware of life itself as a process. Any woman's history is a record of change: from seventeen to thirty-seven she will typically be a student, an earner, a wife and mother, and an earner again. If she combines all these jobs she is involved in a continuing process of accommodating one to the others and all to each. And then, these activities alter within themselves. The mother of a teen-ager is part of a different relationship, requiring different skills and activities, from the mother of a toddler. She has witnessed and participated in a long, slow process of growth and learning that has demanded a continual interaction with her own being. Some part of her knows, whether she can articulate it or not, that abstractions and obiter dicta don't always—don't often, perhaps—fit individual human situations, and that the options life offers are not confined to either/or dichotomies.

Among the processes that women learn in the changes of daily life are those that involve ordinary and ordered uses of power, which must be taught and demonstrated to children as part of helping them grow to responsible maturity. This teaching is done within, and by means of, relationships—by using the self as giver of love or withholder of praise, approving and disapproving, turning emotions into instruments while they are still felt, doubting yourself and knowing that, doubt as you may, you still have to trust yourself to do the best that can be done. Traditional wisdom holds that women are more aware than men of interaction and personal influence. If that's so, it's not the result of inherent biological differences; it's been learned—learned in order to ease things in families, to help children find the knowledge they need without overt instruction, to head off emotional collisions. It doesn't set women off from the rest of the weak, far from it. All the governed have to find room to live in a world they don't control. They come to sense the presence, and the weight, of others who live there. Because these others make the decisions and exercise authority that affects the governed, they are judged also in terms of competence and realism. Do they know what they're doing, or are they rash and willful risk-takers?

This view of power from below has been largely nonverbal, a kind of subliminal awareness that's expressed in behavior rather than words. The analytical vision of power, from Aristotle through Machiavelli, Hobbes, and the philosophers of the Enlightenment, of revolution, of Communism, has been directed to matters that concern the powerful: how to rule, how to seize a patrimony, how to justify a revolution, or create one. But that's only half the story, it's the eagle's view of power from above, sharp and definable but separated from ordinary processes of living.

To be content with this view alone is to agree that power belongs to the powerful as an attribute or a possession, a kind of magic wand that compels obedience. Such an appraisal leaves out the deeply grounded relatedness in which new human creatures find their own identities through the intervention of others, whose presence mediates and interprets the whole ground of reality. I shall try, in this book, to see how this vision of relatedness modifies our understanding of power. If it is a process of human interaction, it is much more than a static structure of dominance and submission. Instead, we must expect to find participants with different and separate interests, and differing amounts of authority, but each capable of influencing the other to some degree. We know pretty well how the interests of the powerful affect the weak. How do the interests of the weak affect the powerful? Are there actual sanctions within the social contract or is the term simply a bit of outdated liberal wish-fulfillment? Does all power tend to tyranny and all submission to impotence? Or are these extremes limiting cases, signs of breakdown?

How much can we discover by starting this journey of exploration in the territory of the weak?

CHAPTER 2

Origins, Births, Beginnings

Oh God, I could be bounded in a nutshell, and count myself king of infinite space, were it not that I had bad dreams.

Hamlet, *Act II, Scene II*

The power-process that children learn as they grow, which shapes their mature understanding of the uses of power, derives from their relations with the other human beings who surround them and interact with them as they develop. But the early development of human creatures can be understood in two ways: first as the journey through childhood, but also as the evolution of a distinct human species. Can we understand the first without considering the second? Or do we not have to ask ourselves what "healthy growth to maturity" can mean unless we have some conception of what it means to be human? Are we naked apes, imperial animals, or creatures just a little lower than the angels? Today the sociobiologists, probing for the dimensions and force of our animal inheritance, are busy at still another redefinition of the essential humanness of human beings. Any conclusions about what's normal—or what's possible, or what's desirable, or what's inescapable—in our behavior, including our uses of power, must factor in some sort of definition of who we are.

Heaps of data pile up, reasoned analyses proliferate, philosophers build systems. Here I shall simply offer something like a parable, an outline of what we can imagine in a long reach back, through our own self-awareness, to the ancestors who were present in the dawn of awareness. Their descendants, nearer ancestors of ours, left sketches on cave walls of momentary but profound experiences, painted or engraved by flickering light from stone lamps where tallow burned. They are evidence of the continuity of human mysteries. Can we find our way back past them to the earliest glints of consciousness, the first steps on the journey into the human condition, in the darkest of dark ages?—a journey that one authority calls "a qualitative leap forward"[1] within the process that another calls an "evolutionary continuity of mental experience."[2] It begins with the first sense of a self that is separate from its surroundings, and yet is present among them, hoping, fearing, and wanting.

This separation between self and not-self seems to me a crucial event of human experience. To make it the criterion of humanness does not deny that animals have mental experiences, use memory traces, and anticipate the near future. We know very well from our long association with other species that they can learn and adapt their behavior to new situations, that they dream, and that anticipation of suppertime will bring even the haughtiest of cats to the kitchen door. But to say that they act as independent selves is not the same as saying that they know themselves to be individuals, that they can abstract a steady identity from the flow of sensations and perceptions and reflex responses to exterior and interior stimuli. "Are animals aware of what they are doing?" asks Donald Griffin, and he answers that we don't know: what we have of affirmed, negative evidence "supports at most an agnostic position,"[3] while recent studies of communication among animals point to some kind of cognitive capacity.

But to be aware of *oneself* is something else. The mental states of animals seem to be sunk in the immediate context of their surroundings, so that they appear to react without any consciousness of a barrier between inner and outer experience. That division is central to human consciousness, it is part of our earliest memories—*ourselves as present*—frightened or angry or delighted or simply looking at the world, but also *there,* aware of inner and outer events, riding the line between. Awareness, said Descartes, creates identity: "I think, therefore I am."

For us today, old products of human evolution, that first bloom of awareness is mediated by the presence of others who are not only there, but who cross the line for us between inner and outer—cross it by language. They have been talking to us already, asking and answering for us, so that we grow within a specifically linguistic frame.[4] But in the beginning, before language, how could mind have spoken to mind? Common touch, mutual gaze, familiar smells and sounds, these worked to knot our animal foremothers and their young together in herd-comfort. But humans are set apart by that locus of bad dreams which our unique evolutionary experience has created: the great, convoluted brain-blossom that flowers atop its nerve-stem, bound within the nutshell skull. Somehow, at some first moment and then repeatedly, the increasing mental activity sustained by this growing mass of brain-stuff took fire in a new phenomenon: it became able to know itself, to feel itself feeling. This is the qualitative leap that humans have made. It not only separates us from the rest of the animal kingdom, it separates us too from ancient herd-comfort. We start in the warmth of common touch and the assurance of mutual gaze, and then we grow past them into individual solitude.

That must have been very frightening. Whatever we were to gain by knowing ourselves, we had lost a sense of commonality which assured us that we were connected with and part of others. Awareness put a boundary around the self, and by so doing it made other selves impenetrable and unpredictable, menacing strangers who had to be watched in wary alertness. Moreover, because the lone self could no longer reach them, it could no longer look toward a sure and taken-for-granted continuity of action. How could it shape a purpose, decide what to do next, or what to expect from the strangeness round about? Without the aid of easy communication, the past gets lost. Everything must be invented and reinvented.

Past commonality had produced simple laws that functioned as directions, and were unquestioned because no self existed to question them. "Move toward light," said the laws, "or toward warmth, toward food or the smell of sex." Change was possible, of course, and laws were adjusted and supplemented as the growing brain with its increasing neurons processed more experience and used it to flesh out instinct. In the space that was allowed it by time and physiology, behavior felt its way to effective patterns of action and response. Memory stored away reports from the outer circumstances of existence: spots where game abounded, where water was sweet, where the circling seasons could be trusted to bring food. As tracks formed in the outer world, in forest and grassland, they were paralleled by brain-tracks from nerve-end to nerve-end so that brain-use forced brain-growth.

Then, as awareness arose, memory would have been questioned, for the first time. F. C. Bartlett, in *Remembering,* speaks of the capacity of an organism "to turn round upon its own 'schemata' " as being "a crucial step in organic development. It is where and why consciousness comes in."[5] The schemata of memory, the old directions for action, came under scrutiny. Could they be relied on, were they always right? Memory itself was constrained to recall how it could fail or mislead and the times when its directives had led toward dry springs and barren land.

Memory was not being replaced, it was being supplemented by reflection. It had evolved, we may guess, to keep track of the "how" of things and supply its directions from this store: "Go here, do this, you will find safety, food, water." As long as memory could bring to mind relevant cues from the outer world, that was sufficient. But with the rise of awareness came a need to *choose,* to ask: "Why go here and not there? Why do this and not that?" By its questions the lone self was pulling out not just directions, but *explanations,* from the memory storehouse. Instead of self-justified programs for action, consciousness, faced with a need to choose among possible courses, was looking for ways to evaluate what it remembered.

Our ancestors—that is, we humans, our thinking selves—had come to the time for interpretation, when memory had to be searched for meaning. Choice was bringing a new necessity as well as a new freedom, for if one *can* choose, then one *must.* That means another step forward, for in order to choose, one must *judge*. The human journey had brought us to the place where we not only had to assign values to possibilities, but to think ourselves into the future, and consider the consequences of action. We were discovering, or inventing, causality. Time thrust itself forward as the self reached back for evidence from the past on which to base its plans. The three-dimensional world around us took on other aspects. Because time's arrow moved there, the world itself became continuous and possessed of a solid past. Because the inner self now planned the processes through which its needs would intervene in the world of action, both world and self acquired a future.

At that moment, human creatures must have needed to reach each other more than ever, for the load of past and future is too heavy for anyone to carry alone. Once upon a time the common herd-purpose had protected our ancestors from the menace of choosing, choosing *wrong*—and knowing it. If disaster threatened, they were ignorant; which would not save them from disaster, but would spare them incapacitating fear, panic fear of making any choice, fear that would ensure disaster. The isolation that consciousness brought with it had to be broken, so that one mind could reach another and profit from shared experience. In that sharing, one memory store, one capacity to plan, would supplement another; but—perhaps even more needed—emotions too could again resonate together and so gain a validity that was more than individual.

These, surely, were the needs out of which language arose as a means of reconstituting the lost bonds of commonality. The qualitative leap into consciousness was demanding another leap, the invention of a method for doing what touch and gaze and shared sounds had done before, and doing it now in an infinitely more complex and flexible fashion. Human language is not unique in the sense that we and we alone communicate with each other, for bees dance and birds sing and animals announce their whereabouts or warn of danger; but human language differs, rather as a hand differs from a paw. What it can do is so much more extensive that it does stand alone. It has been shaped by the human condition, and it has gone on to help fashion the human condition in an endless process of interaction. Language is the living web of connection by which each solitary, conscious self can reach other selves and so authenticate its own experience, by and within a network of relationships. *We cannot live as humans without it because we cannot live without relationships.*

The leap into consciousness separated us from each other. The creation of language brought us together on a new plane of possibility. And the vastness and scope of this creation indicate the potential range of human capabilities. If we could imagine and effectuate such a linkage, what may we not yet do by way of invention?

The origins of language have been much disputed. If speculation about them is anything more than an intellectual game, it has to be put in the context of our human need for connection. Suppose for a moment that we could not reach each other, that we were not simply bounded by the nutshell skull, but caught there irretrievably. Suppose that in the same events you and I discerned different patterns of meaning. That's far from unthinkable; it is exactly the context in which Hamlet, Prince of Denmark, found himself. How can you know the truth? Shakespeare asks us through him. Are parents murderers, mothers whores, is the beloved a deceiver? What do their actions mean, how can I interpret their words? What is dream, what is fantasy, what is reality? How can I ever know, bounded in the nutshell of my single identity? Unless I can weigh my words and your words together against their words (or vice versa) I can never understand the world, and without understanding I can't live in it.

Three things come together here. The isolation of the conscious self means that we can't use our new mental capabilities to establish an agreed-on meaning which will allow us to manage our lives unless we can reestablish the relatedness in which we once shared experience and took an accustomed place in a familiar world, as the animals do. We need others in order to trust ourselves. As the old mutuality vanished, our ancestors must have clutched at any old behavioral forms in the human repertory that could allow continued sharing. To me, the most convincing theory is that which Susanne Langer describes in "Speculations on the Origins of Speech," elaborating on an idea of an earlier thinker, J. Donovan, that speech might begin in festal ritual; specifically, in dance.[6] We know that animals communicate physically, as we still do by body-language, that threats were and are conveyed by gesture, by shaking fists, bared teeth, arm-wavings, posture confrontations. "Don't touch," "come here," "go away," "comfort me"; gestures can say all these things. Suppose they are done jointly—does not dance begin here, with copied gestures, together-movements, each "I" dancing out its need and its capacity to come together into a "We"? Accompany this with shared sounds and cries, and song adds itself to dance. Joint noises match stampings and turns. Out of jumping and shouting, miming threat and retreat, menace and submission, attraction and response, luring and mimicked flight, shared meaning is being created. Would not this meaning, reinforced by gesture, find repeated expression until, bit by bit, one meaning attached itself to a sound? Which was a message, if not a word?

However it happened, by some kind of repeated, active sharing, a new kind of community manifested itself which was not simply physical, but was *symbolic*, embedded in words and rituals that could break down or reach across the boundary that separated the solitary identity from its fellows. By this strange process, almost paradoxically, symbolic communication made it possible to establish that boundary even as it was crossed; for if we are to tell reality from fantasy, we have to know both what we share in the outer world, and where our solitude begins. If we can't do that, there's no limit to bad dreams—they spill out, they invade reality. Then we may be kings of infinite space—but the space is all within our heads, it is infinite only because it is closed to others, it cannot be shared.

And so we come back to power. Unless we can judge our actions and lay our plans on the basis of related experience, of common and shared reality, our lives can't be distinguished from our dreaming. To be "king of infinite space," to wield omnipotent power, is possible only in isolation, cut off and "bounded" from others; that is, in what we call insanity. The road to ultimate power, where nothing exists that can limit or oppose our will, is the road to solitary madness. *Finite* space is what we need, space that we can share, where we can agree on events and our own presence together, and so save ourselves from intergalactic nightmares and incomprehensible ghosts. We need *here* and *now* defined and touched by hand after hand, words understood, meanings corroborated, causality completing itself from known event to predicted result. Our common humanity finds shelter and strength in agreed-on reality. Tell me your mystery, and it will illuminate mine.

What a strange shelter it is, to be sure! How fragile it seems, this mosaic of individual selves that combine by symbolic gesture and language into a common artifact, a coral reef of social mythology, symbol built out of symbols. But how long it has endured! It is the product of our essential humanity, which can come to fruition only within the structure that it created from our individual identities in order to satisfy our need for connectedness.

My parable has a moral. The experience of isolation is built into the human condition as the result of evolutionary development, but individual consciousness must ground itself in community if it is to function at all. On this community depends our ability to understand the world and to live within it. Separation from total togetherness is, of course, part of normal growth; we are not herd animals, or social insects, and the establishment of a stable identity is a major aim of the maturation process in children. But too extreme a separation is dangerous, not only to the community, but to the individual self, which needs to be able to share and compare its experience in order to stay in touch with reality. If we imagine that power is a force to be taken up and used by and for a single individual, we are isolating this powerful creature from the rest of us in a way very dangerous for all concerned.

But that is not the only way that power can be used. Ordered power operates within society as a gravitational force that holds us together. Like language, it is a network that reaches everywhere and touches us all. If language is the technique by which we communicate with each other, power is the process by which we interact in order to implement the plans that we have made. They are no longer directed by instinct but must be framed by thought and communicated to others before they can be put in motion. In turn, the need to maintain social organizations that will operate competently fosters higher internal order in the planning, responding, communicating ego. So as the spiral of growth swings round, a higher level of consciousness and individuation appears. But it does not and cannot work alone. To achieve individual ends in the real world requires an effective political connection—a power relationship—with other individuals. That is, it requires social bonds.

When we turn from speculation on the origins of the human species to everyday child-raising practices, we find ourselves once again looking at a process of individuation that depends on relatedness, and which carries each human creature from a condition of total powerlessness toward a goal—not always reached!—of reasonable control over the external circumstances of life and comfortable, affectionate connection with other human creatures. Whatever we know of power begins here, as the self becomes aware of the line that separates it from not-self and then learns ways of dealing with the not-self, some more successful than others. This learning begins so early that much of it is unconscious, but the interest that our culture almost uniquely has come to take in childhood and maturation offers a great mass of material for study. In it we can trace the incidence and the effects of ordered and disordered use of power.

Until quite recently, the whole cycle of birth, growth, maturity, and decay was pretty much taken for granted everywhere. With us, scientific research has extended its ground from the physical world to individual and society. It's rather like a repetition of the first burst of individual awareness of self, but this time it is society that's becoming conscious of itself and its rules of behavior. Once upon a time newborn babies survived to childhood (or very often slipped quickly away, perhaps half before they were five years old), grew into youth and maturity, and declined into old age without much attention being paid to the process. Certainly there were approved methods of training the young, and often ritual ceremonies would mark stages in the course of life, but these directives and definitions were enforced for the convenience of society, in order to place its members in categories and deal with them in groups. Along with sex, caste, and class, age was simply a handy way to assign occupations, status, and proper behavior to members of society: there were appropriate roles that went with different age-grades.

Thus, until they were seven or so, young children had few responsibilities and received little attention. Almost everywhere they ran free from the time they were old enough to leave their mothers and toddle off after a gang of older children. It was a time for learning the imponderables of any culture, what can't be taught because they aren't consciously known, but which set standards of value and significance. Children picked up this knowledge at home and from each other; they picked it up from watching and listening to kinfolk and neighbors; they practiced what they knew in the interminable play, formal and informal, that is the serious business of childhood. They were present at festivals and celebrations and witnesses to the adult work that went on all around them. Even in the slave South, black children had their playtime, often shared with the children of their masters. "Children play inside yards and on the streets, and in open lots throughout the village so that, in effect, the entire central community serves as a play-ground";[7] so runs a description of an Okinawan village in the nineteen-fifties, but it could just as well describe a painting by Breughel.

As children grew older they began to share family and community occupations and to learn consciously by instruction and doing. By adolescence, boys and girls had been separated by sex and directed to the specialized roles that were going to occupy and order their adult lives until, in age, they drew together into a less differentiated group of more-or-less dependent old. Some of the old, of course, were honored for their wisdom; some managed to clutch at dominance and hold it in their grasp at almost any time or place. In some societies the old have been specially esteemed, perhaps out of a particular people's sense of their own dignity. In others they have enjoyed authority because they are thought of as unborn ghosts, and are feared and catered to in order to appease the supernatural force they will command after death. Most often, they are inexorably pushed aside. But at every state of life, society as a whole has tacitly supplied directives for proper ways of acting, and feeling.

The individual, personal meaning of this progression through life has not been totally screened by the social roles allotted to different age-grades. It has been celebrated in poetry and drama for the emotional experience that it provides, and the images and demeanor assigned to each of the Seven Ages of Man were surely built around a core of genuine feeling. But only very recently has the formation of the individual ego which lives out this life come under study as being significant *in itself,* as the result of a process that can and should be examined objectively and not simply in terms of social and cultural ideals. For our ancestors, the development of an ego identity in each of those ubiquitous, free-running children was part of a moral, not a scientific, question: how daughters and sons should be properly reared for known and specific aims, how their characters could best be formed to match the ideals of their parents' world and/or to provide them with a livelihood, how bad habits could be prevented and good dispositions trained. Children were human material to be shaped, and nothing more. We are still endeavoring to shape them, that's true, though with rather less certainty as to the goals we envisage; but with the birth of psychology and the social sciences, "early development" has also become an area for scientific examination.

Which is not to say that such science will ever be totally objective, value-free, but simply that what *does* happen as children grow has begun to be distinguished from what *should* happen. A sense of this difference increased slowly through the nineteenth century, until Freud's insistence on the importance of events in the lives of infants and children removed this field of study from the confines of educational policy. The case histories of Freud, his disciples, and his opponents made it clear that training the infant mind was a much more complicated matter than had been believed. Instincts weren't programmed into the brain but, on the other hand, no *tabula rasa* awaited overt manipulation and direct injunctions. Training was necessary, but training could backfire and produce unlooked-for results. In psychoanalytic patients, that is what seemed to have happened. Something quite unsuspected appeared to be going on within the psyche of the swaddled infant or the frolicking child, some welter of fears and desires. These could be influenced—but how? A need to know was felt. Certainly the moral question remained, and so did the pragmatic. Parents and psychologists both prefer normal to abnormal growth in children, but in order to foster the first and discourage the second, one had to have some idea of what was going on inside as the children grew.

Since that time an enormous amount of research and of thought has gone into the question of how a human creature develops, how impulses come together, how a central, coherent self is integrated out of wants and needs, fears and desires, frustrated anger and satiated content. Within this heap of data and among the theories that have tried to give it structure, there is a great deal that is relevant to an exploration of our concepts of power and its uses. Whatever we mean by power—and we mean a number of things, sometimes contradictory—one aspect or another of the idea turns up over and over in studies of human growth. Let me cite a few:

"The ego," writes Erik Erikson, "is an 'inner institution' evolved to safeguard that order within individuals on which all outer order depends."[8] So ego-formation is the evolution, often difficult, of order, which means *control,* an aspect of power, over both the interior world and its environment. Without fairly good control there can be no order, and we recognize ego-failure of a disjunctive kind.

"The period that extends from birth to the acquisition of language," writes Jean Piaget, "is marked by an extraordinary development of the mind. Its importance is underestimated . . . [but it] determines the entire course of psychological evolution. In fact, it is no less than a conquest by perception and movement of the entire practical universe that surrounds the small child."⁹ A *conquest* of the universe! That is certainly a vivid image of power.

The English analyst and pediatrician D. W. Winnicott saw this "conquest" of the world of reality as a triumph of *creativity.* "The baby creates the object, but the object was there waiting to be created."¹⁰ The perception of reality, that is, demands a real act of making on the child's part, what is created being the inner image that corresponds to objects and events and relationships in the external world. The component of power that inheres in this ability to create is clear, and Winnicott opposes it directly to *compliance,* which "carries with it a sense of futility for the individual and is associated with the idea that nothing matters and that life is not worth living."¹¹

Control, conquest, creativity instead of compliance—these are aspects of power that the child learns on the road from the utter helplessness of the newborn, and they are very early lessons. But the universe is not conquered alone, and the world that each of us has managed to create and has matched to experience took a hand in its own creation. It tended and trained us as the Powers-That-Be protected our infant selves, fed us, disciplined us, reacted and responded. The inner reality that we made for ourselves was mediated by others.

The need for the young of our species to learn is also part of our evolutionary heritage, and therefore part of our essential humanity. Where other animals are provided with many quite explicit instinctive patterns of behavior, the human creature has few. What we *can* learn and store, consciously and unconsciously, in the roomy warehouse of the brain is far more than any other living species; but so is what we *must* learn in order to become functioning adults. Clearly, what any one individual learns won't be exactly the same as what another learns, since learned behavior is much more variable than genetic programming. Nonetheless, learning isn't simply random. It's controlled both by physiology and by culture. There are distinct stages of learning that all normal children go through which provide one sort of order to the huge curriculum that is taken in as we grow. This kind of order is influenced by the time and the place and the background into which children are born. An example of the simplest sort of physiological growth is the development of vision. An infant under a month old can distinguish between a patch of all-over gray color and a pattern of black and white stripes, if the stripes are at least an eighth of an inch wide. At six months, babies can see a pattern (they prefer it to boring old gray) with stripes only one sixty-fourth of an inch wide. The physiological advance in sight can be tested.¹² What else the baby has learned in the same period is harder to determine, but it must be at least as remarkable; and both kinds of growth depend to differing degrees on the support and stability of the environment in which this enormously hard work takes place, for babies are anything but passive little bundles of flesh. They are making a world and creating a universe.

It's easier to see the effect of different kinds of environments when we turn to language learning. Just the same, there is a regular sequence of development here too. At two months, babbling infants use seven or eight sounds. By the time they're two and a half, toddlers are speaking intentional sense and, on average, have a battery of twenty-seven sounds and better than two hundred words at their command.[13] But there's a good deal of variation around this average. No doubt some is inherited, but there is clear evidence that babies who are born into an environment that talks back, that asks questions before they can be answered and answers for them, plays games and sings to them—these babies learn sounds faster and speak more at the same age than those who haven't enjoyed these relational advantages. Our common heritage as human beings lays down regular stages for development, but the speed with which children reach them and the richness of experience that accompanies each stage depend on the surrounding context of support and attention. In a deprived environment some stages may not ever be reached.

The cultural element in learning is greatest and most evident when we consider what it is that children are learning. Stages of growth are universal, but the content and the structure of what is imparted to the young are not. Thus, some proper way to enter and take part in power relationships is learned by children everywhere, it is part of the first curriculum; but the message and thrust of these lessons vary according to the lines of force within a particular society. Not only does the actual content differ, so does the ordinary interaction between adults and infants that conveys the message. Degrees of intimacy within a family, rules of deference to kinfolk, unconscious differences in handling girls and boys, time spent with adults and what's done during this time, early tasks and responsibilities given to children, all of this flavored by the status of the family within the community —these imponderables influence the way that different human beings, at different times and in different parts of the world, have understood the techniques and the significance of power-use and power-process.

To say that our concepts of power are class-and-culture-bound may seem neither very new nor encouraging. But there's another way of looking at this diversity if we see it as part of a larger process. It indicates that there is not just one right way to handle public interaction or arrange personal affairs. It suggests that our capacity to discover and try out different ways of operating in groups or in tandem is greater than we think. When we assume that the world as members of our own society and culture experience it is the same as the world experienced by others, we are not just being ethnocentric, we are limiting our own creativity. If, instead, we look at the variations between cultures as clues to the breadth of human imagination, the significance of what we see is a good deal more hopeful: this is still a plastic age.

For the variations between human ways of knowing and doing run very deep. To begin with the obvious, in a quick overview: there are many different languages that meet the universal need to communicate facts and emotions, and language patterns modify thought patterns, if only by directing the attention of their speakers to particular areas of experience and employing special ways of making references. Again, the kind of time perception by which Westerners now regulate their lives (or are supposed to regulate them) is extremely different from time as perceived by the clockless. Another variation occurs in our understanding of images: remote peoples, who are unaccustomed to pictorial representation of the world around them, find it very hard to make out what photographs record and have to learn to see what, for us, leaps to the eye. The ability to read not only extends the experience of literate cultures by giving their members access to the past, it adds a spatial component to expression. Sentences may start at a different corner of the page, depending on whether one is reading Chinese or English or Hebrew, but they move regularly up or down, to the right or to the left. Mundane as this seems, it has the unexpected effect of making "handedness" more important in a literate society than it is among those where illiteracy is normal.

Indeed the changes produced in human culture and ways of thinking by the invention of writing and the spread of literacy go far beyond the obvious. Jack Goody's study of these effects in *The Domestication of the Savage Mind* suggests that many differences which we think of as separating modern, civilized societies from those which we call primitive are better described as being due to literacy versus oral tradition. A written record not only preserves a fleeting moment of speech as it is, it also permits rereading and rethinking, what Goody calls "constructive rumination"; and not only by the speaker within the internal monologue of memory, but by other minds as well. Out of this can develop a tradition of debate and of criticism, where the ideas of philosophers and, in time, the findings of scientists can be compared and contrasted. "It is now possible," writes Goody, "to see why science, in the sense we usually think of this activity, occurs only when writing made its appearance and why it made its most striking advances when literacy became widespread."[14]

Barriers created by patois and dialect fall before literacy. Eugen Weber describes the process by which a pretty well unified French nation replaced a spread of territory occupied by inhabitants who payed taxes to a French government, but who were regionally diverse and regionally patriotic, separated by language far more than by custom. The spread of schooling under the Third Republic provided the motive force, later strengthened by the circulation of printed journals, enforced by wartime service, and by the twin tugs of urbanization and industrialization.[15] An author's creative work, however, changes toward individualization when it is freed from the elementary need for mnemonic. Once written down, it is *there*. Not only will it remain, it can be edited and revised. In the third volume of his *Gulag Archipelago*, Aleksandr Solzhenitsyn tells of the reverse effect on an imprisoned writer compelled to do without a record of his work. Composition was exhilarating, transporting, but memorizing a burden. He resorted to a rosary made for him by fellow prisoners, Lithuanian Catholics, deeply impressed by the piety of one whose prayers needed one hundred beads, each tenth bead being different, and the fiftieth and hundredth again distinguishable. With its help he "accumulated" twelve thousand lines before his sentence ended. "Even so," he writes,

> things were not so simple. The more you have written, the more days in each month are consumed by recitation. And the particularly harmful thing about these recitals is that you cease to see clearly what you have written, cease to notice the strong and weak points. The first draft, which in any case you approve in a hurry, so that you can burn it, remains the only one. You cannot allow yourself the luxury of putting it aside for years, forgetting it and then looking at it with a fresh critical eye. For this reason, you can never write really well.[16]

As Goody says (and Solzhenitsyn supplies, quite by accident, a remarkable example of exactly the point he is making), "The existence of the alphabet changes the type of data an individual is dealing with, and it changes the repertoire of programmes he has available for treating this data."[17]

Here we have just a handful of the instances that could be cited to show the range of ways in which human beings can interpret the world around them and construct an agreed-on "reality." *There is always more reality around than we allow for; and there are always more ways to structure it than we use.* A painter's world is different from a musician's, even when they have grown up in the same neighborhood. All these variations are evidence of the scope of the human repertory for dealing with the world around.

And, in addition, they have all been *learned*. They aren't programmed permanently into our genes. They can be modified, certainly within the same culture as circumstances change: the requirements for daily living in the rural America of our great-grandparents were quite different from the requirements that we must attend to. We have not made all the adjustments necessary, but we have clearly changed quite a few of our ideas and more of our habits. So when we consider the essential humanity of human beings, we can add to our individuality and to the network of relationship that sustains it a further factor: the ability to learn, and to go on learning.

CHAPTER 3

Name This Child

Even in the first volitional acts, which imply choices, a new dimension enters: the interpersonal (the you). From a philosophical point of view it seems almost a contradiction in terms: the first acts of volition are acts of obedience, or of submission to the will of others. Choice, this new portentous tool that emerges in phylogenesis with the human race, in the early ontogenetic stages requires support from others before it can be exercised independently. . . .

From a certain point of view, the history of humanity, subsequent to the primitive period, can be seen, in spite of many detours and regressions, as a gradual movement toward freedom, that is, toward less reliance on the support of the group and toward individual will. This act of liberation from the influence or suggestion of others has its ontogenetic representation in the negativistic stage of children, who, for a certain period of early childhood, refuse to do what they are told to do. By disobeying, they practise their newly acquired ability to will.

Silvano Arieti,
The Interpretation of Schizophrenia[1]

After all that theory, let us look at one small datum, the "ontogenetic representation" of "choice, [the] portentous tool that emerges in phylogenesis with the human race": here is a two-year-old saying "No." She says it with sheer delight, for she is starring in the classic role that embodies the "negativistic stage of children" and what she's enjoying is power, the effective right to refuse. She knows it, too. She is doing something in which her own swelling sense of her self takes part, for this is not just a turning away from activity, a shunning of the outer world. Saying "No" is a positive act and a liberating one, because it confirms the sense of ego-as-active-agent, of autonomy in which it's possible to say either "Yes" as an act of obedience or "No" as defiance, by one's own decision. But the choice is not made in an empty world. It is a response to another presence there, and if the response is agreement instead of disagreement, the "Yes" is offered in love to a loved and significant person. The "I" that chooses to obey, or not to obey, communicates the choice to a "You." The dimensions of choice are being learned within a relationship.

Two-year-olds saying "No" are confirming their presence in the world, and they do that by the sequence of refusal, followed by response from the human environment. Each step is vital. Without a sequential reaction, the child's choice is simply an expression of emotion that flows out into a vacuum. "No" demands an answer to the question, "Do you hear me?" which really means, "Am I here at all? Do I truly exist? And if I am, am I free to choose what I want? Do my wants matter?" The answer isn't always gratifying. A "terrible two" may seem very whimsical to a busy parent who, under pressure of time, will pick up this still-portable person and carry her off to where she belongs, by the parent's right of choice. In ordinary circumstances children have to expect that this will sometimes be the answer they get. Even so, if it can be understood as part of the sequence, as a response to their action, and not as simply the act of ignoring them, they will learn from the exchange. An irritated parent or caretaker provides more useful information of when to say "no" than does one who seems deaf.

But if the child's refusal to obey is habitually denied, her presence in the world is also denied. What she wants and means, what feels very real inside, is being mocked by what is outside, by the powerful human environment. She is being allowed no control, and even her desire for control seems to go unrecognized. When that happens, she will be forced into an attitude that is far more negativistic than the testing of reality that refusal makes possible. She will have to deny either her own interior emotions and her sense of self, or else she will have to deny the reality of the outer world where sharing of experience will validate her felt sense of life. It's a necessary part of normal growth for two-year-olds to be allowed to say "No" effectively often enough; enough, that is, to feel that they share some control over life with their powerful elders, those unpredictable creatures of outer space. Children can't take in the experience of external reality, and create adequate images of its workings in their own minds, unless they can interact with it, can see how their decisions affect what goes on out there. Saying "No" is not just a way of asserting oneself, but of *inserting* oneself into the ongoing process of shared activity as well. The experience of acting and the experience of sharing are central to the formation of a responsible individual with a stable sense of being. The "I" constructs itself by means of what it learns from the various creatures called "You" who represent the "interpersonal," the human, relational world. Without connections and responses from the interpersonal, the inner world can't be shaped into identity, and there will be no central being there.

A dawning awareness of self creates the need to choose, and active assertion that elicits response affirms the child's ability to do so.

A normal two-year-old, of course, is already vastly experienced in the first curriculum. If we turn to the scheme of growth as Erik Erikson has worked it out, we see that the muscle-flexing nay-sayer of two has successfully surmounted the first of the stages of development that Erikson calls "life-crises" and is busy dealing with the second. Though Erikson's definitions are conditioned by the assumption that masculine norms are valid for female experience, this is not particularly important in the early stages of life when there's a good deal of similarity in development. In each phase of growth, he feels, the individual is faced with circumstances emanating from the external world which must be coped with; and the solution, when found, must be absorbed and accepted by the developing self. If this isn't done—and no doubt it's never done with total success by anyone—the unresolved crisis will continue to plague the individual. It will hinder the successful conquest of difficulties inherent in later stages. Not only will failure to integrate an unresolved problem bind stores of psychic energy in an endless, neurotic involvement with the past, it will distort the individual's understanding of the outer world, so that later stages of growth are approached on the basis of false perceptions and expectations.

The first crisis is that in which an infant becomes aware that she and the world are not totally one. She learns that she is separate because her wants aren't automatically satisfied. A hungry child will eventually be fed by the Powers-That-Be, but before that occurs, she may have to wait, and must sometimes demand satisfaction. Will the outside world hear and respond? Will it respond soon enough? Can it be *trusted?* That is the specific character of the first crisis. It has to do with the regularity of the outside world in its answer to needs. An adequate response that supplies adequate satisfaction, in food and warmth and attention and affection, is assimilated into the developing ego as a sense of trust which, writes Erikson, "forms the very basis in the child for a component of the sense of identity which will later combine a sense of being 'all right,' of being oneself, and of becoming what other people trust one will become."[2] This trust in the world, and in one's place there as recognized by others, provides the psychic strength, or virtue, of *hope,* "the enduring belief in the attainability of fervent wishes, in spite of the dark urges and rages which mark the beginning of existence."

The hopeful baby, trusting the world, can now move on to the experiment of asserting her own will. Saying "No" both announces her presence and tests the outer world in order to learn how it works, specifically, to learn where the limits of assertion lie: What is it possible to *want* and also to *get?* If integration of the first crisis established a sense of trust and a belief that the world sees and responds to needs, the second refines the process of interaction by laying down boundaries. Learning to choose means learning that one can't have everything, and so had better discriminate among wants. Discrimination means giving something up; and so learning to assert one's will also means learning to control it; to use it instead of being used. Choosing teaches restraint by means of realistic evaluation: the power to refuse and limit one's own desires. The two-year-old nay-sayer, then, is almost ready to move on to the next stage of growth in which the will can be harnessed to a goal, and purposefulness will further reinforce identity by saying "I am what I imagine I will be."[3]

In following Erikson's stages of growth I have left aside (as he does) the tremendous achievement of the toddler in learning to talk. Lively, unobstructed progress through the language-learning process measures healthy growth, and it also demonstrates development of that essential human characteristic, the ability to use symbols. This capacity is central not only to communication but also to thinking, to the manipulation of symbols in the interior world. The images of the outer world, the signals we hear, and the warmth of touch take on meaning and come to stand for more than a particular bit of data or, as computer-folk would say, a byte. The whole structure thus functions as an interpenetrating system that joins the inner and the outer realities in which we live.

Current linguistic theory as developed by Noam Chomsky and his followers holds that the "deep structure" of language is inborn. We learn a particular vocabulary and set of grammatical formations, but the capacity to put words together in grammatical relationships that will be understood by others is given to humans at birth, as a fundamental potential of the species. Because we can manipulate verbal symbols within a shared framework, we are able to make statements that are not only comprehensible, but are also new. Bird songs and cries of warning, the directions of the bee-dance to a store of nectar, convey information about a particular event in the present, but they do so in prepackaged ways; though recent experiments with chimpanzees indicate that these near-cousins of humankind can learn to communicate symbolically to some extent.

Interesting as these attempts to evoke language-use among chimpanzees are, it's highly unlikely that they will do more than blur the line a little at the trailing edge of human evolution. Certainly animal communication exists, and if chimpanzees can express their emotions and needs by gesture and expression, it is pleasant but not enormously surprising that they can adopt other methods, supplied by interacting and trusted humans, for the same purpose: sign language as used by the deaf, computer symbols, and even small plastic objects of different shapes. What these symbols "mean" to the chimpanzees themselves, we shall have to wait to learn until they have learned enough to tell us; nor do we yet know whether they have begun to assimilate these new tools for communicating well enough to use them with others of their kind, if the use must be taught by the chimpanzees themselves. Domestication of animals has always involved teaching them to understand words and signs from us, and not only act on them, but supply some information in return. How much further inter-species communication can go with chimpanzees than that of shepherds with their dogs, or mahouts with their elephants, is still a question. At any rate, in the ordinary course of events, the manipulation of symbols in order to think new thoughts and to say new things is easy and omnipresent with humans, and humans alone. We are born possessing a biological potential to do this in a uniquely high degree, even if it's dimly present in other species.

But each child, in turn, must learn to use the language potential. A baby will babble, and her repertory of sounds will increase as she grows, but unless she lives surrounded by speaking human beings, who speak specifically to her in a relationship of mutual recognition and connection, speech will not come. In spite of the charming but fictional example of Mowgli, the boy raised by friendly wolves in Kipling's *Jungle Stories,* children abandoned in the wilds don't learn to speak. A few survivors of such exposure have been found, and prodigious efforts of training have occasionally been expended on them. Past a certain age, it appears that the ability to learn language atrophies. A few fragments may remain, and also some capacity to comprehend what is said. But even in the most recent case where scientific teaching and care combined, a deprived thirteen-year-old, isolated from the age of twenty months, is still far from normal in language use after five years of intensive work, and only rarely speaks at all. The stage of growth where language is easily acquired passes quickly, in the absence of human surroundings.[4]

There are other nonspeaking children, among the mentally disturbed. Mute, autistic, they seem to have lost their way before they could learn to use the potential for communication with which they were born. It may be that they have been caught in those early crises that Erikson describes and were overwhelmed before they found a world that responded in a trustworthy way. "Wild" children have lost physical contact with a community. Speechless autistic children seem to be missing emotional contacts with a supportive community whose responses normally work to develop understandable speech patterns. I shall be looking at some of these disturbances of growth in the next chapter. Here we need only observe that the ability to establish and maintain relationships and processes of interaction by language depends on related interaction in early stages of growth. Without such interaction the formidable grasp on power given us by language is beyond our reach.

Here we stand, as little children, staring about at a landscape where the pyramid of power looms large, and we find that we can't see it at all, it doesn't exist for us, unless there are those with us who describe and name what we see, assign values to the features before us, and assure us that what we see is there because they see it too. Human as we are, we can create our interior world only if other humans explain and authenticate the exterior world by means of common symbols, learned through relationships. Unless we can do that, we are not just powerless; we are not human.

. . .

So the child's first use of power, the ability to grow to maturity, is the product of relationships which sanction this use of power. It's my hypothesis that all ordered uses of power carry some flavor of this primary experience, and that enduring political structures, continuing social connections, and satisfying personal relationships all incorporate the need for such a sanction for the validation by others of the use of power. If this version of a social contract does exist, it's not because it's ordained by Divine authority, or by natural laws of morality, but because every human creature has spent the first weeks, months, and years of life within sanctioning "interpersonal" surroundings. Our very capacity to grow and to develop the special and essential traits of humankind depends on the presence of interacting folk, interpreters of the world who arrived here before us. We grow by climbing up the ladders toward maturity that these relationships supply. How, then, my hypothesis asks, can the ordered use of power *not* continue to bear the stamp of its origins, of mutual recognition and validation?

Even before children demonstrate their ability to interact with the human world by means of language, there's evidence of a tendency toward the invention and use of symbols; and it's linked with a reach toward something beyond the self, which can be controlled by the child. D. W. Winnicott, after years of practice as both pediatrician and child analyst, came to feel that the first sense of a split between self and not-self called forth a coping pattern in which the use of symbols was linked with an aspect of power that we would define, in later life, as ownership, or possession; as an acting out of the word "mine."

Winnicott thought of the space between the inner self and the outer world as being not just a boundary, but as an intermediate area across which the inner self built symbolic bridges. Without such connections, there would be no way to move outside the interior world of fantasy and bad dreams. This intermediate zone he named "transitional space," and defined as an "area of experiencing to which inner reality and external life both contribute. [It is] a resting-place for the individual engaged in the perpetual human task of keeping inner and outer reality separate, yet interrelated."[5] What adults know about the child's first reaction to this field where separation evokes attempts at connection is learned by the appearance of objects—real, physical objects—which the child uses as symbols of continuing, emotional connection to the surrounding not-self environment.

We know at once what he means: the battered teddy-bear that must not be lost, the armless, hideous doll, Linus's security blanket. Anyone who has ever tried to subject such a property to the alien adult black magic of washing it knows how much emotion is invested in its staying absolutely the same. Nothing must change if the beloved object is to function as a trustworthy safeguard on the journey between inner and outer reality, a journey made every time the baby drowses into sleep. In addition, Winnicott came to feel, there are transitional phenomena of behavior that can start even earlier in life, sometimes before the baby is four months old, and that are characterized by just this quality of *sameness,* of unchanged, ritual performance. A thumb-sucker always has a favorite thumb or finger, clutches and sucks at a corner of sheet or blanket with patterned gestures, so that the behavior takes on something of the continuing quality of an object.

This comforting repetitious behavior, these enduring and trusted objects, Winnicott called *transitional* not because they will be outgrown, but because they represent, they *symbolize,* the ability to bridge the gap between inner and outer reality. They are real and tangible, but what they mean is determined by emotion, they stand for something beyond themselves. "I think," Winnicott wrote, "that there is use for a term for the root of symbolism in time, a term that describes the infant's journey from the purely subjective to objectivity; and it seems to me that the transitional object (piece of blanket, etc.) is what we see of this journey of progress toward experiencing."[6]

The inescapable human need for early development of the capacity to symbolize is emphasized by recent studies of autistic children.[7] This disturbing mental and emotional deficiency is usually identified by symptoms of which the most important are an inability to achieve normal relations with other human beings, and severe problems in learning and using language. It is now hypothesized that what has gone wrong is the capacity of these children to create the interior symbols which correspond to outer reality, and thus to store and to use generalizations about the world based on past experience. These children seem able to function only in response to immediate, present circumstances. They are said to need "sameness" in the context of their lives, and we can see why. If they lack an ability to store up the past in symbols which give it continuity into the present and make the future predictable, life splinters into fragments. Everyone is a stranger, every change a catastrophe.

Normal children, then, are already taking the miraculous steps toward human connection as they clutch their beloved objects, which are symbols of continuity and therefore of their own solid identities, in their journey toward experiencing and managing the ever-present gap between subject and object.

What we also see of this journey is the use that the baby makes of the object. *It is a power-use.* This is the "first possession," cuddled, loved, and mutilated, under the child's control. When she is older, we will hear her remaking and acting out the experience of the power relationships that she has lived through, but the impulse to explore experience by rehearsing it is older than speech. If we ask what the object means, what emotions are invested here, they seem to combine power and relationships: comfort *and* control, continuity *and* the ability to reach out to the world around, to act as well as be acted on.

Perhaps the best analogy, from the adult world, is a fetish, which is, in the same way, a real object that can be owned and carried around, but which is also a symbol; and symbolic, specifically, of a bridge to still another imagined world, the supernatural. It is a possession that gives its owner a purchase on the mysterious powers of magic. It may be that the very earliest art we know had just such a function. These are the mobiliary figures from the Paleolithic caves and shelters, including the fecund fat "Venuses" found across Europe and Asia, and datable in some cases to thirty thousand years ago. Incised pebbles too, showing animal figures, must have served as lucky pieces for the hunter. Also suggestive of magic is the similarity between the patterned, regular behavior of the baby sucking a thumb and humming a repetitious, interminable droning tune as she falls asleep, and the ritual spells by which the supernatural is invoked—spells that must be performed with absolute exactitude, to the last world and gesture, if they are to be effective.

A further example of the ritual need for sameness is the insistence by older children on unvarying repetition in stories, read or told, the same stories that must be repeated without a word changed or an episode omitted. "Oh, not that again!" groans the bored parent, "let me read you something new!" But the old story is predictable, and to know what's coming also symbolizes control, power over the course of events. Moreover, old stories aren't all that old to a learning child. Analyst Ernest Schachtel points out that stories can be absorbed only slowly, for even the simplest deal with a number of objects or people or animals and, still more complex, with the relationships among them. They are charts of the unknown human environment, not simple entertainments or distractions. "For the young child to grasp and digest a story," writes Schachtel, "requires an amount of attention and of effort at understanding which the adult is incapable of imagining. . . . Only by repeated acts of focal attention, which at one time turn more to one part, at other times to other parts can the child very gradually come to understand and assimilate a story."[8]

It's easy for adults to lose any conscious memory of early childhood, though of course these experiences, including those of threat and of dependence, return vividly in dreams. But the need for time and repetition when one is learning something that isn't related to an existing knowledge structure—and the feeling of baffled helplessness that accompanies the effort— can be reproduced. We feel this when confronted with a strange language, and specific learning tests show how much repetition is normally required to set things straight. One simple test is to memorize a sequence of nonsense syllables. When reading-aloud is used as a means of instruction, as with the stories told to children, eight repetitions are needed to learn eight pairs of syllables.[9] To a child, the activities of the external world as presented in a story aren't nonsense—that is, they aren't irrelevant—but they are embedded in an undifferentiated matrix of presented experience, whose inner coherence must be sorted out from scratch. Before they can be used to create the inner images that match the real world, they have to be analyzed for meaning, and for relational fit.

"Any change in the story," writes Schachtel, "makes it elusive and frustrates the child's efforts to master it," efforts not only to memorize the complex fabric of the tale, but also to solve "the equally or even more difficult problem of finding his way in the puzzling distinctions between reality, representations of reality, possibility, and sheer phantasy."[10] Which is to say that the story functions as another sort of bridge between inner and outer reality. It is an implement to be used, and used in a similar way: as a means of control. This time the control is achieved by a gain in understanding of how things work, which allows better, more satisfactory interaction with the world across the transitional space, the world of events and objects and other living creatures. Specifically, understanding what goes on there allows the learning child (or adult) to predict what will happen in the future.

Now, prediction is certainly not the same thing as control, but it is not unrelated, either. At the least, it allows an individual to prepare for an expected event and to take defensive steps if it can't be avoided. Moreover, though one may not be able to control the event, one can do much to control one's own responsive actions. We can't control hurricanes, but we can bring in or secure movable objects, lay in supplies of food and water, board up windows—or flee. In the sense that learning the world improves one's ability to predict the future and act sensibly, knowledge is power; or, at any rate, it improves one kind of power-use.

Piaget is pointing to just such an advantage when he says that part of the task of growing up is the accommodation of the child's interior interpretation of the world to the world as it is; "as it is" here meaning "operates in this contextual relationship." Another authority on creativity in quite a different field is the art historian, E. H. Gombrich, who is really as much a philosopher and psychologist of art. In an essay, "Illusion and Art,"[11] he reflects on the value of accurate information not just for humankind, but for prehuman organisms. Learning to do things the right way (and here "right" means "in a way that will contribute to survival") is not just reacting by conditioned reflex like Dr. Pavlov's poor dogs, who salivated to no purpose when they heard the dinner bell ring, after being subjected to lengthy behavioral training. Indeed, instead of regarding this famous experiment as an example of purely mechanistic training, Gombrich wants us to include an element of useful, even rational, learning on the part of the dog. It had adjusted to associating the arrival of food with the bell, because at first this did occur. Then Dr. Pavlov changed the rules and, moreover, he confined the dog in an apparatus from which it could not move. If he hadn't done that, Gombrich suggests, the dog would have trotted off to look for food when it heard the bell. It would have used what it had learned, and if it didn't, that was because it was prevented from doing so. Plenty of dogs and other pets have learned to turn up for dinner at a whistle, or even the scrape of a knife as it cuts up their food. They are "conditioned" to useful behavior.

Surviving organisms, then, are those that can learn, that can scan the world for meaning and make an effort to interpret the evidence of their senses. They will certainly make mistakes that a totally conditioned creature might avoid—as long as its environment didn't change. But, Gombrich goes on,

> unless we concede the possibility of the animal making some kind of inference from evidence, we cannot envisage evolution ever getting on to the ladder that leads from the lower reaches of the soul to critical reason. . . . It is clear that in the condition of search the possibility of anticipating reactions must therefore be one of the greatest assets that evolution can bestow on an organism.[12]

What Dr. Gombrich is saying can be reduced to the familiar truism that knowledge is power; but he is adding one significant term, as his use of the example of Pavlov's dog indicates. Knowledge is power *if it can be implemented.* Without a connecting link of action, the knowledge we've learned can't affect the outer world. Normally little children are eager to learn. That's not just because they are praised for doing so. They receive another sort of positive reinforcement when their new knowledge supplies them with greater power to act for themselves, to control the world around, or, in Erikson's terms, to use the will in a purposeful way. They are, after all, physically small beings in an adult-sized, and adult-complicated, world. No wonder that power-to-act-autonomously seems attractive; though, as we shall see, it is conditioned by other needs as well, needs for support, affection, and safety within relationships.

The growth of a self, the creation of a secure identity, which is the first task that any child faces, is thus in very large part a process of learning to use power well, in a way that both serves the self and is acceptable to the human environment in which the self is growing. From the first of Erikson's life-crises, when the division of self from not-self is resolved by trustworthy response from the external world, successful growth is dependent on others. The individual self that is steady, centered, and competent does not develop by itself. The phenomena of the outer world can't be learned and then controlled, can't even be understood to exist in relation to the self, without authentication to the child of their reality and coherence, and that must come from others. In the same way, when the child acts, meaning is attached to the action only by the reaction of the world around. If, as Dr. Arieti states, the history of humanity can be seen as a gradual movement away from reliance on support of the group and toward individual will, the individual reproduction of this progress still begins in supporting and validating connection with others, and won't occur without it.

For creating a self is not an easy matter. It involves divining the difference between inner and outer reality, between fantasy and agreed-on finite events. "At the outset of mental evolution," writes Piaget, "there is no definite differentiation between the self and the external world. The self is at the center of reality to begin with for the very reason that it is not aware of itself." From this undifferentiated state, "the progress of sensorimotor intelligence leads to the construction of an objective universe in which the subject's own body is an element among others and with which the internal life, localized in the subject's own body, is contrasted."[13]

This is the hardest task that human beings face. How does the child manage it? Piaget's dedicated, lifelong study of the development of thought processes within growing children provides a kind of historical atlas of mentation. Within this development we see needs for control and autonomy at work. Thus, the ability to predict events is based on an assured knowledge of continuity in the external world. Piaget has documented the growth of the idea that real objects are permanent and exist on their own whether one is paying attention to them or not. Peekaboo games, balls that can be rolled away and recaptured, and of course those necessary "transitional object" bed-companions, all teach trust in the continuity of reality.

And they surely also reinforce the sense of a continuing individual self, a permanent "internal life, localized in the subject's own body." Another expert on childhood thought touches on just this anxiety in his own classic work, and then resolves it with humor. Lewis Carroll in *Through the Looking Glass* raises the philosophic problem of how to know what's real with his slumbering Red King, "crumpled up into a sort of untidy heap, and snoring loud":

> "He's dreaming now," said Tweedledee: "and what do you think he's dreaming about?"
>
> Alice said "Nobody can guess that."
>
> "Why, about *you!*" Tweedledee exclaimed, clapping his hands triumphantly. "And if he left off dreaming about you, where do you suppose you'd be?"
>
> "Where I am now, of course," said Alice.
>
> "Not you!" Tweedledee retorted contemptuously. "You'd be

nowhere. Why, you're only a sort of thing in his dream."

"If that there King was to wake," added Tweedledum, "you'd go out—bang!—just like a candle!"

"I shouldn't!" Alice exclaimed indignantly. . . .

Dear Alice, with her firm affirmation of the reality principle, has been a reassuring figure for over a century now. One reason she retains her popularity is certainly that the worries she responds to with such pragmatic good sense are universal. How *do* we know what is real, who is dreaming whom? In the earliest days of life, objects are ephemeral, fleeting impressions that come and go, and the baby can't yet reach out with controlled purpose even to touch them and make sure they are there. Fleeting impressions are also the stuff of dreams, images huge with terror and just as "real" in the emotions they awake in the dreaming brain as are the material objects of the physical world. How is the baby to tell which is which? It requires a long process of learning, for we know that even later on, much later in the time frame of childhood, vivid nightmares can convince a child that a dream-object may have withdrawn from waking view, but is somehow still present: the bear in the closet, the tiger under the bed, the horrid shape crouching behind the chair, all waiting till the light goes out again. Perhaps these terrors are only playing the peekaboo game, and are actually permanent. And mentally disturbed adults can assign reality to hallucinations, and imagine them permanently present, in the outer as well as the inner world.

So the continuity of existence that we often use to define the line between interior and exterior reality is not enough to do the job, in itself. Once more, what is needed is agreement from others, the validation of reality by a figure who says, "It's all right, you're awake now. You had a scary dream. Everyone does, sometimes. There's no tiger under the bed, I'll look behind the chair and in the closet; come see for yourself if you want. I'll be right here . . ." and so on. Here too we see that the ability of the individual to distinguish fantasy from reality grows out of experience that is authenticated by others. The world we live in is an agreed-on world. What the baby creates or constructs or assimilates is a structure that is shaped by what others say is there, and that includes the sense of her own existence.

In order to create a secure identity, the child invents a world. It is a world that already exists, an artifact invented over and over again, and of course it is an artifact that differs somewhat from culture to culture, and changes with the passage of time. It is never something that is handed to us whole for immediate easy acceptance. Unless we make and match interior reality with what we are assured is out there, we cannot function in either place. The deepest understanding of power and its uses is woven into the construction of a self, and this construction can take place only through the mediation of others, in established relationships. Like everything else we learn, we learn power this way.

So when I argue, as I shall, that power can be properly defined only as a relationship between or among human beings, and that consequently some sort of social compact for using it well not only should, but does, exist, I am basing my statements on the universal processes by which humans have become human, and do become human, in evolutionary and individual development. I also believe that this way of looking at power can give us clues for using it well. All too often, those who have gained ascendancy over others seem to regard power as a rather simple possession that can be used according to their own narrow purposes. And those whom they dominate too often seem to agree, and to behave as if their only guarantee of decent survival depended on the ethics and morality of the powerful; as if there were no way that they, the governed, could influence the outcome of events. To my mind, the roots of power lie in our very first relations with each other and the world around, and the growth to maturity that we have all lived through offers clues to its proper use, within a relationship that includes much more than simple dominance-and-submission. What we learn about power as children remains in our minds and it can be tapped for later use—if we will simply implement what we know by action.

CHAPTER 4

Lessons from the Dark Side

Individual and society are certainly beings with different natures. But far from there being some inexpressible kind of antagonism between the two, far from its being the case that the individual can identify himself with society only at the risk of renouncing his own nature either wholly or in part, the fact is that he is not truly himself, he does not fully realize his own nature, except on the condition that he is involved in society.

Emile Durkheim,
Moral Education[1]

The way that children learn to understand and exercise ordered uses of power within relationships is a central part of normal growth, the primary and earliest fashion in which the individual becomes involved in society. But of course growth doesn't always run a smooth course. Breakdowns occur, some minor, some very severe. I want to examine a few examples of these disturbances because I believe that they tell us a great deal about disorders of power and the effects of its misuse. Case histories of emotionally disturbed children, that is, are not just unpleasant reports on freakish accidents of nature or outbreaks of inexplicable illness. The breakdowns we shall be looking at exaggerate the stresses of ordinary life, but they occur at points of strain in the normal process of growth, strains that average healthy children also feel. In Erikson's vocabulary, these examples illustrate what happens when a life-crisis is not surmounted and integrated into the maturing individual.

In addition, these case histories tell us something about the efforts of children to cope with stress, and so they illustrate techniques of defense and survival that are available in the early periods of growth: the stages of life in which human beings experience the extremes of powerlessness and the start of effective control, learned through relations with others. The dependence of infancy is something we have all lived through, each of us alone, but all of us in ways that are much the same, for the first relationships of life have a good deal of similarity just because the helplessness of little children makes similar demands on parents for care. Of course, parental care differs in kind and in quality, but all human stories begin here and they begin, specifically, with the adequacy of adult-child relationships for healthy growth. When things go wrong instead of right, the defensive reactions of children throw light on social reactions to larger threats and traumas. No matter how bizarre the behavior of an individual child, the symptoms stem from common responses to common dangers within the human situation, responses that appear when power relationships tip out of balance.

Child analysts, in general, see the study of growth and its problems as valuable for understanding adult experience as well as the maturation of normal children. Erik Erikson, for example, has called his best-known work *Childhood and Society* and, in his foreword, describes it as dealing with "the relation of the ego to society." Within this overall involvement, questions of power are of great importance. "It is necessary to understand the basic fact that human childhood provides a most fundamental basis for human exploitation," he writes in his summing-up, and goes on to define and place such exploitation in a universal frame:

> Man, in the service of a faith, can stand meaningful frustration. [But] exploitation leads to fruitless rage: exploitation being the total social context which gives a specific frustration its devastating power. Exploitation exists where a divided function is misused by one of the partners involved in such a way that for the sake of his pseudo aggrandizement he deprives the other partner of whatever sense of identity he had achieved, of whatever integrity he had approached. The loss of mutuality which characterizes such exploitation eventually destroys the common function and the exploiter himself.[2]

Similarly, the analysts from whose work I draw these examples thought of childhood disorders as illustrating social disorders. Powerlessness can produce mental disturbances in children that are analogous to the destructive and disabling emotions found in deprived groups subjected to brutal political dominance. Bruno Bettelheim specifically relates the inner world of autistic children to the actual position of prisoners in Nazi concentration camps, seeing both groups as caught in extreme situations that call forth overwhelming fear and anxiety. These children "not only fear constantly for their lives, they seem convinced that death is imminent."[3] True, the child's conclusions reflect only the internal image of the surrounding environment, whether or not it is an accurate representation of objective reality, while for prisoners in the camps, the external world itself declared that "one's life was in jeopardy at every moment and that one could do nothing about it." Psychologically, however, Bettelheim views the reactions of children and of prisoners to extreme threat as following a similar course and calling forth similar patterns of behavior and thought.

In his comparison of such extremes, D. W. Winnicott saw political subjugation as producing the loss or enforced concealment of creativity, the characteristic human capacity to interact appropriately with the world across the transitional space between inner and outer realities. Children who have been unable to develop this trait are caught in straits as hazardous as those brought about by political persecution, for they do not know how to deal with change and novelty, and these of course are inevitable in any life. Where Erikson notes the loss of mutuality that goes with exploitation and Bettelheim the paralyzing effects of overwhelming anxiety, Winnicott is touching on another distortion, the loss of the power to imagine activities that connect the human being with the world around. In his own therapeutic experience, Winnicott found the creative insight of his patients very valuable indeed, and sought to enlist it in treatment. "It is not . . . my clever interpretation that is significant," he remarks, but rather "the moment . . . *at which the child surprises himself or herself.* "[4] In balanced and adequately satisfying human relationships, he tells us, this universal and essential gift appears and sustains individual identity in the very earliest forms of play; it then leads on without a break, by way of shared playing, to effective participation in adult activities, both within relationships and as ground for the great cultural creations that we call art.

The examples I use, then, were first written down and are now discussed not only for the light they throw on the process of human growth, but also for what they show about patterns of ordered human existence.

A breakdown is a kind of jamming. People get stuck. External reality refuses adamantly to respond to inner needs; its laws seem mysterious or punitive; creative insight is unable to imagine ways to deal with its caprices. In these case histories we shall see children who are desperate in the face of muddle and threat. Some have gone beyond despair to withdrawal in an attempt to ignore the vortices of hope and indecision and fear and anger which swirl destructively in the inner world of self, and exhaust the energy needed to reach across transitional space in order to merge one's life with events outside. We see how an ambiguous context of life can garble messages and prevent the creation of a coherent identity, how rigid rules can produce a compliant automaton instead of an eager child diving happily into the sea of experience. What these children are suffering from—and also what they are learning—are disorders of power.

They are profound disorders because they affect the very roots of personality: the capacity to assert one's will by choosing between "Yes" and "No"; the daring that can commit emotion purposefully to a future goal; the sheer physical control of nerve and muscle and the steady mental effort which teaches the competence that Erikson sees as the goal of the next step in growth; and most basic of all, the underlying trust in the world's responses to one's existence. Something has gone wrong on the way to easy use of these powers, and the wrong is due to faults in relationships. We are looking at images from a flawed mirror.

All sorts of accidents can happen on the journey from infant dependence to adequate adult control of life and self, but the most crippling of these result from repeated experiences of vulnerability and helplessness. The potential self with all its inherited possibilities reaches out in an attempt to learn and predict and assign meaning to events, and receives no steady response. Perhaps the mirror seems to show no image at all; no one present to cast a shadow on reality. Perhaps the image is terrifying: a monster child, a changeling (and we might remember how omnipresent in folk-tales are the changeling infants, left by fairies or goblins in place of human children. These creatures, says folklore, need not be loved or cared for. We are looking here, I think, at a very old justification for child abuse and rejection; that is, at a failure in relationships which is as ancient as it is terrible). Or, again, the child's efforts to be and to do may call forth responses that are overwhelming, too much for the baby to deal with. However things go wrong, there comes a time when failed efforts to connect with the world become too much to bear, and the child gives up. What follows may be retreat into solitude and the rejection of any interaction, or the child's behavior may become incoherent and disconnected, so that irrelevant gestures and inappropriate speech take the place of activity directed to a goal and language that communicates a message.

D. W. Winnicott gives an example of misdirected, uncentered energy in a report on a thirteen-year-old named George. Winnicott did not, in the end, take George on as a patient because he lacked the time that he came to believe would be needed for good results, while to offer the boy another relationship that ended in failure would, he felt, be disastrous. Before he decided, however, he conducted a fairly lengthy exploration of the situation both with the child and his family, for George was part of an apparently functioning family group. This report, then, is not a study of progress, but a snapshot of a child in a frozen moment of trouble. George was a potential, if not already an actual, delinquent, who functioned badly at school, who stole uncontrollably, who destroyed property (he set fire to chairs and smashed pianos), and lied continually though not, it seemed, for any conscious purpose, but simply because he didn't connect what he said with what he did. George, alas, sounds all too familiar.

Winnicott had worked out, over the years, a technique that allowed him to reach quickly a fairly deep level of the psyche without, however, giving the child any sense of intrusion or manipulation. He did it by setting up a "play situation" in which child and doctor both took part. Like all child analysts, he had toys available for the children to busy themselves with, but in the "squiggle game," his patients could enter, spontaneously, into an activity which the doctor shared, and which carried no threat of failure or possible blame. Such play situations—and Winnicott studied them extensively—are removed from the heavy reality of a world where terrible things can happen if you go wrong, and so they permit fantastication and spontaneous invention in which the self reveals its nature. One player drew a "squiggle," some kind of convoluted line, and the other then finished it and gave the image a name. Because it called on the child's creativity, Winnicott felt that the game supplied more illuminating material than formal investigations of the self based on Rorschach inkblots or the Thematic Apperception Tests, which offer standard pictures for interpretation. In the squiggle game, humor and fantasy were given free rein. As a result, children were able to present worries and remember dreams that communicated the unresolved problems troubling them, and could do it in a situation where guilt and shame were suspended. Winnicott took the evidence that children's problems were reasonably accessible as a good sign—though not because this gave him material to interpret, for it was not his understanding of the situation, but the child's, that would have a therapeutic effect. If the children could bring their difficulties to light, however, chances of their coping with them were good.

In George's case this did not happen. What did show up, both in the drawings he made and his interpretations of them, was his inability to connect one thing with another, the same inability that appeared in his unmotivated but persistent lying. He saw things in parts: heads without bodies, the claw of a crab but no crab—nothing complete. One squiggle of Winnicott's he elaborated and then called "a nothing." It followed his own drawing which he then completed himself of an image that Winnicott felt to be an iconic representation of the mother's breast. This symbol showed up frequently in these game interviews. It can be taken as a casting-back to the period of earliest dependency, greatest vulnerability—but also a period before hope had been abandoned. George named this image "a shadow, traveling fast."

George's sense of the transience of this mother-child relationship followed at once by a sense of nothingness, his inability to create whole creatures and, overall, his lack of involvement in the game (though he complied with the procedure)—all these Winnicott took as evidence that the boy lacked a center of being. Outwardly, George presented a personality that was conformist and compliant, giving no hint of his bad times; once more a lack of connection. At first meeting, in fact, he got on well with strangers, he rose to situations, and he could pass tests. In a single structured situation, that is, when there was no question of an intimate, ongoing relationship, the "false-self" that his family had helped him build (for their own sakes as well as for his own) could function. But George was never in control of his experience, his intentions, his will. "Often he says to his mother," wrote Winnicott, " 'I can't help it; I don't want to steal,' and he works himself up into a state of remorse; but *at the same time* he is stealing, and no one believes any longer in his remorse except as another kind of deception. He says 'I want help,' but at the same time he shows signs of that complete hopelessness about getting help which makes an individual avoid looking for it." Something had happened very early on to prevent George's will from gearing his actions to the purposes he expressed. There appeared to be no permanent presence dwelling within George's handsome, healthy body, no person there who was capable of countering the impulses that beset him with a strong assertive "No." Perhaps a teller of folk-tales would have recognized a "changeling."[5]

George's history is revealing. In the first place, he was an unwanted child. His mother had raised two other children, brother and sister, with adequate success; but the family was going through a bad stretch, including a near-bankruptcy, when she became pregnant with George. George's mother had kept things going by taking in several foster children for payment, but another baby would make that impossible, and what would happen then she didn't know. She therefore asked her doctor about getting an abortion. To obtain a legal abortion in England, two doctors must agree that it is necessary for the mother's health, and her doctors kept postponing their decision—until it was too late. "She therefore," Winnicott writes, "had to get rid of the foster children and prepare for a baby that she did not want to have, and she very much resented the way in which no-one had dealt with this matter in a logical way." It's a bone-chilling, everyday, matter-of-fact story; one sympathizes completely with the resentful mother—and then one thinks of the child, born into a situation where adequate response to his needs and joyful recognition of his presence just could not be given truly and spontaneously by the person whom society had designated to be responsible for him. It would be foolish to talk about blame. The problem arose because the social structure, while effectively forbidding abortion, provided no alternative or additional support for either mother or child, no backup mechanism to function in case standard procedures failed. So we had better forget about blame or sympathy for the moment and consider the result of this social contradiction. It was very bad for George.

He registered his disturbance by crying incessantly, all night and every night. As he grew he was constantly greedy for food, but when he took it he would hide it; it was not physical hunger he felt. His older brother and sister were protective and indeed concerned for George; in part, perhaps, because the presence of this changeling threatened their own identities. But they were too young to be of practical help, and in the interests of peace, they urged their parents to let George get away with things. So there gradually developed what can only be called a pattern of appeasing George, already well organized by the time he was two. "It is in this pattern that the family has managed to survive."[6]

But this pattern isolated George from the world. First, the not-self, exterior reality, was unresponsive to his early demands and seemed to ignore his existence. His constant crying, Winnicott judged, indicated his hopeless sense of "being nothing." It was an appeal for help, and when the appeal was not adequately answered, it became unappeasable. His screaming, then, his effort to act on the world, appeared to make no difference and bring no results. In the same way, his naughtiness was not punished. Nothing he did seemed to make contact with the human environment. He was being spoiled, but not in a way that answered his real needs and brought him real satisfaction. Significantly, and unlike his brother and sister, he neither found a comforting "transitional object" nor developed a regular form of transitional behavior as a trustworthy way to reach across the zone between his inner feelings and outer reality. He survived as a conglomeration of fragmentary impulses and reactions. The false-self did well enough at dealing with strangers; it had been trained in superficial public manners; but there was no centered person inside who could sustain a long-term intimacy or aim purposefully at a long-term goal. What was steadiest in George was the continuing, compulsive drive to destruction and stealing.

Winnicott believed that antisocial behavior like this indicates feelings of deprivation and represents attempts to reach out and snatch what the child feels to be both absent and owed. It can, in fact, be seen as an effort to communicate a need for help; and sometimes children in such quandaries can be given the help they want fairly quickly. Winnicott cites other cases where this did happen. But these children were much less divided and confused within themselves than George was, and possessing a central vision, they were able both to understand something of the situation that troubled them and to get a grip on it. They could reach the dreams that expressed the inner side of their worries, they could use the support of the doctor to confront unhappy experiences in the real world, and then begin to cope. There was someone inside who had been puzzled, or baffled, but knew what control was, knew how to respond to events. The elements of personality within George had never coalesced into such a "someone."

I have dwelt on George's situation at this length both because it describes a fairly familiar kind of disconnected character, one who doesn't match cause and effect, and seems at the mercy of momentary whims, and also because it has a good deal to tell us about power. It would appear, on the surface, that George had great power over his family. They allowed him to exercise his random gusts of willfulness, they bought him out of scrapes (and some of the scrapes were expensive), they did their best to deal with vagaries of behavior that he couldn't explain himself. But all of this did George no good. License was granted to him, but not as part of a continuing process of interaction between equals, interaction that held him responsible for what he did. And therefore he was not given validation for his actions: he was still a nothing. He could do anything—but the price was that what he did had no meaning.

The power that George's family allowed him, then, was powerful only to them. *They* had a steady purpose and a strong continuing relationship with each other; but the way in which they used this relationship to support George did not help him *because he was not included in it.* It's impossible, of course, to interpret their purpose at third hand; one may guess that they were trying to protect themselves from George by distancing him from the rest, and at the same time to protect themselves from guilt for doing so. Possibly George's destructiveness acted out, and satisfied obscurely, some hidden anger for the way things were, felt by the mother or the family as a whole. We can't know. But we can see that they handled George as if he were not a person but a distressing natural phenomenon, a spell of bad weather or some other unpredictable nonhuman force. So the family support was really a rejection of George-as-a-human-being and it thus left him outside, and at the mercy of any will-o'-the-wisp of emotion that overtook him.

There are various social metaphors that can be drawn from this personal tragedy. Some radical analysts, like R. D. Laing, see disturbed children as representing scapegoats who are victimized in order to preserve other structures or relationships that sustain more powerful members of a family. Whether or not this is true in George's case, he was treated as incompetent, and so not fully equal. That kind of treatment is repeated in social settings when groups of people who are "disturbing" the status quo are distanced from "normal" citizens and dealt with as if they were unequal and irresponsible. Sometimes these groups are viewed with hostility and loathing and treated as sacrificial victims, but that isn't always the case. They may be seen, more subtly, as dependents in need of benevolent help because they're incapable of looking after themselves. That pattern is closer to the treatment George received. It's hardly necessary to say that many societies, including our own, have fitted this image to women's proper role. Dependent groups in general have been, and are, treated in this way, from "the deserving poor" of Victorian times to welfare recipients today. "Good" is to be done to these people, but the good is never defined by its recipients. Such paternalism is self-justified in two ways: first, by the benevolence of the motives which those able to dispense charity identify within themselves and, second, by the unspoken assumption that those who are being helped don't know what they want and couldn't meet their needs even if they knew.

Now, in George's case this would seem to be factually true: he was not in control of any means that would supply him with satisfaction of his needs. And yet *the standard pattern of paternalistic care didn't work even in a family setting,* because George was simply its object, and was not involved in helping himself. Perhaps he could not have been; Winnicott judged that treatment was not impossible, but that "in practice the difficulties are immense" and would require "close collaboration with a boarding establishment . . . willing to give him full attention, or he would need to be taken over by a team orientated towards the total management of this boy and of others like him."[7] If this treatment worked, however, *it would succeed only if it elicited George's participation;* and the dim possibility of success that Winnicott discerned was based on his belief that the boy "has an idea that there could be a better life and that he could be a more real person than he is." Only if this faint spark of hope still alive within the child could be nourished from without would progress be made.

If the Parable of George has a moral, it's that good can't be done to people unless they are allowed to have a stake in choosing the good and effectuating the doing. All too often the "unintended consequences of . . . good works" turn out to be the diminishment of the liberty and the stature of those who are seen as requiring benevolent help. In a study of the rise of social services supplied by a well-intentioned, liberal state, Ira Glasser notes how easily administrators, sure in their own minds that their motives were good and their purpose caring, fell into paternalism. In doing so, they "embraced dominion [over people's lives] and persuaded themselves that . . . they were helping the helpless. [Thus] dominion became legitimate. . . . As a result, they infantilized those they intended to help."[8] We shall consider this attitude and its consequences later in more detail. Here, in the case of George, we can see that even in family situations, and desperate ones at that, parents who ignore the reality of the actual existential needs of a dependent will resort to ineffective strategies. They may know best, but they don't do good. Still less in the public sector, where paternalism is no more than a convenient metaphor, can benevolence and high motives be trusted to instruct the powerful in ordered use of authority, if the human presence of the beneficiary is ignored.

Bruno Bettelheim, who distrusts the efficacy of good intentions to the extent of calling one of his books *Love Is Not Enough,* supplies our next example. Paul, like George, had early known a difficult and unresponsive environment, and some of his reactions to it were very similar. Bettelheim took the case on, since in the Orthogenic School of the University of Chicago, he had available exactly the kind of establishment that Winnicott believed was necessary to treat George adequately. Paul too had been born into an unhappy—one might say disastrous—family situation. His father was immature and dependent on a family of origin that rejected both his wife and his child. Paul's mother was herself emotionally disturbed as well as being, like George's mother, under severe economic pressure. Paul spent most of his first years in rigidly controlled institutions, but this experience of minute-to-minute domination was broken by visits to his mother or his grandmother, and there, in extreme contrast, his life was almost without schedule. At six, when he was put in an orphanage, he was asked where he'd like to live. Said Paul, "I'd like a good place to eat [!], clothes, a nice house, like a bird house." With whom would he like to live? "All alone."[9]

Paul was a screamer too but, unlike George, he had never learned to present a calm face to the world. During his four years at the orphanage he was subject to spectacular tantrums, made several efforts to kill himself by leaping from a window, and finally attacked another child in what seemed a homicidal rage. At that point, the Orthogenic School (whose reason for existence is the attempt to deal with children suffering from severe mental disturbances) took Paul in. He was ten. Unlike George, who had at least lived all his life with the same people, Paul had a bad derangement of speech. His counselor reported that it was impossible to listen to him, or to take down what he said, without mentally sorting the words and reinterpreting them, with the help of his facial expressions and bodily contortions, for the possible hidden meanings. Again unlike George, Paul directed his antisocial behavior against people instead of property; but psychiatric examination revealed "not . . . murderous and depressive phantasies—as might have been expected— [but] emptiness, great flatness, instability of emotion, inability to relate, extreme detachment, and markedly infantile feeling and behavior."[10] This interior landscape is more like that which Winnicott perceived in George than the differences in their behavior would indicate. And like George, Paul was capable of acquiring some of the skills that children learn at older rather than younger ages. He was, for instance, good at math. Bettelheim hypothesizes that he could manage the logical operations of math because they were so distant from the highly charged emotional relationship he experienced with his mother; and we might wonder, too, whether the enduring, always-the-same, quality of mathematical processes might not have seemed reassuring, a mental "transitional object" which offered its own kind of permanency in a disjointed world.

There are other resemblances between the two cases. George took no pleasure in his game with Winnicott, and Paul had never learned to play either; also he was another greedy grabber of food. Bettelheim believes that greed can be understood as an almost universal symbol of felt deprivation, and made it a policy of the Orthogenic School to let children have all the food they want whenever they want it. Raiding the icebox means that in at least one way they can satisfy their wants by their own actions. In addition, there was evidence in Paul of the false-self structure that is both mask and defense, though it was not as developed as the one George displayed. Paul clung to repetition and routine as he had learned it at the orphanage, where it was of course the sign of a good obedient inmate, but he did so obsessively as if he felt that only rules, strictly observed, could keep his urgent desires in bounds. The impulse to set things on fire showed up, too; but here it was quite obviously an appeal for help, because he did it when his counselor was with him. He seemed, indeed, to be demonstrating this destructive urge as a way of reaching for a relationship with a person who could be trusted to keep him from going too far: "I'm doing this *in order to* get you to stop me." As with George, his antisocial behavior could be understood as a desperate appeal to the human environment to respond and show him that he really was present in the world, could really have an impact on it, could be seen and taken account of. Difficult as they are to deal with, these outbreaks indicate progress away from compliance and withdrawal.

Paul had a long, hard way to go. What he first communicated was a condition of profound isolation. His memories of past life were empty of human beings. He addressed no one by name. Receiving gifts at Christmas overwhelmed him. Writes Bettelheim:

> He had wished too long for the good things in life and been so deeply disappointed that when the good things came, they overpowered him, and he had to defend himself against their impact. We have seen this kind of behavior again and again. If frustration has been too severe, then satisfaction becomes too threatening to be really enjoyed. . . . It only evokes angry memories of past disappointment.[11]

Early and repeated denial of one's real and effective presence in the world, that is, makes it hideously difficult to reach out toward the relationships that, at the same time, one so desperately wants. To invest emotion in these connections, to believe them and trust them, seems—on the basis of past experience—to be an invitation to another rejection and further wounding.

Paul's progress was slow, but there was progress. It is part of the therapy of the Orthogenic School to allow children to regress to the period of life in which their problems developed, to act out their frustrated impulses, and then to help them redirect these urges by offering the understanding and validating responses that will allow the children, finally, to integrate them into a coherent self that can set up a permanent structure of control: a true, steady identity. Because the acting-out is both allowed and recorded, Bettelheim's case histories give valuable details on what has gone wrong and, of course, on the various therapeutic measures that work. They are maps of disasters overcome, and the mapping is made up of moments of daily living. Paul, for instance, was furious at the need to say "Thank you" or "Please," and thus to acknowledge the human environment that had failed to acknowledge him. He wanted, writes Bettelheim, "to rule the world," and he expressed this fantasy of absolute power, of being king of infinite space, again and again; though sometimes with one small mistake. He wanted, he said, to be "king of the universe," but occasionally he expressed this as "king of the university"; it was all the same to him. But, at the same time, he drew pictures of himself as "Mr. Nobody," like George, who drew "a nothing." We can see that the fantasy of omnipotence was put forward in opposition to the fear that he would be reduced to nothing; or that he really was nothing, and had no defenses at all *except* fantasy. Then, slowly, he became able to talk about his fears. This was a real advance, for now Paul-as-person was not totally swamped and possessed by fear. When, like some Dickens character, he muttered, "New, new, new. Change, change, change all the time. Don't like it. Don't like it at all," he was both distancing himself from fear (even if the self could not yet bring itself to say "I") and entering into communication with another person.

We need not follow Paul's case in detail, though we should note that, as he become increasingly able to cope with the world, he went searching for knowledge of the human condition and read voraciously in an effort to learn "how other people lived and worked and what their motives in life were." He was able, too, to extend his learning to his own past and retrieve memories that became steadily less terrifying and more comprehensible. Both processes were used to place himself for himself as a continuing person in a relatively sensible and steady world. In addition, his genuine talent for drawing won praise, and the expert knowledge that he built up in several special areas—he was fascinated by stamp-collecting and good at sports— gave him prestige that he slowly came to trust. In classes at the Art Institute he not only experienced success, but discovered that the "normal" boys and girls he was meeting had problems of their own, just as he did. He finished high school and went on to college in spite of some continuing difficulties in communicating. Doubtless there were permanent losses in the person he might have become, but he arrived at the relative human success of managing an independent and useful life. In short, the work done by the human environment to discover and respond to Paul's real and disabling troubles evoked his own efforts in his recovery. Good was done *for* and *with* Paul (not *to* him), using his own active support and participation. A continuing relatedness had given him a sense of both commonality and capability, in which he could live as an individual among other individuals, neither "Mr. Nobody" nor "King of the Universe." In growing up to find a human space of his own, Paul had put aside his grandiose fantasies because they were no longer needed. A world in which he was present proved to him that he had sufficient power to influence events and to get satisfaction and affection; and this, of course, is the usual sequence of events. The history of Paul's difficult journey merely illustrates the way to ordered use of power, both for interaction and for self-control, by pointing up some narrow squeaks that one child had lived through.

Another of the children Bettelheim treated, John, had experienced over-control in infancy rather than the disjointed and contradictory conditions that had confused Paul or the unresponsive and then falsely generous treatment that George had known. When John arrived at the Orthogenic School, he was in a truly infantile state, although he was actually five and a half. His infantile helplessness had been prolonged because he'd not been allowed to do anything for himself. He had even been force-fed as a regular procedure. Arbitrary rules and abrupt handling had ignored his own feelings and his outreach toward activity that would teach him the world by means of his own explorations.

There were physical reasons for this: John had had a bad mouth infection soon after birth, and had been hospitalized again, within a month, for a mouth injury. In addition, his parents clearly projected grave anxieties of their own onto the baby who was, like George and Paul, another unwanted child. All of this had the effect of making John see himself as an appendage of others, powerless in the face of the world. Out of the complex story of John's troubles, we can draw one illuminating instance of his reaction to being controlled by others, unable to act or even to will for himself. Bettelheim writes: "John could not stand . . . the threat of being overpowered; to ease his anxiety, to 'get it over with,' he immediately made himself the willing victim of aggression rather than endure his conviction that he would be overpowered anyway."[12] It was a sign of real progress when John dared to be angry instead of hopelessly compliant.

The moral of John's case for the larger world is so obvious that we may overlook all that it has to tell us. We know that groups of the weak, forced to comply with regulations laid down by those against whom they cannot hope to rebel, repress their anger. They are the Uncle Toms or, that ideal of Victorian womanhood whom Virginia Woolf labored to kill within herself, the Angel in the House. We can see that the ability to let anger out, to *show* hostility one way or another (John did it by spitting at his counselor), is indeed a mark of progress on the way to daring to act for oneself, according to one's own choice. But John's example, his active decision to become "the willing victim of aggression" takes us deeper into the experience of being powerless than does mere rational understanding of why the weak comply with demands from those in charge. It's only sensible not to show one's rage, for that would invite vengeance; and by definition the mighty have the power to defeat the weak. Defeat simply underlines one's weakness. So, to be angry is to invite defeat.

But *choosing* to become the victim goes further than that. It seems, in fact, an irrational action. Bettelheim interprets John's behavior in a way that may be too rational: to get it over with. Undoubtedly that motivation exists. But in addition, a fantasy element can enter here, and we find it doing so expressly in some attitudes assigned to femininity. To do what one is being forced into *as if* one actively chose to do it advances the illusion that one has a choice. One may know very well that no choice exists; but to save face by play-acting at choosing also avoids overt defeat that has to be seen and accepted as shameful. To say, and to act out, "It is my nature to become a victim, to give in to the will of another, and to glory in it" at least permits the speaker to lay claim to a nature of her own, a centered identity. This is the kind of behavior that underlies the analytic theories which hold that women are masochistic by nature and are echoed in the popular belief that women really enjoy rape and, given a choice, will opt for domination by a male.

To choose to be what one has to be! Theologians and philosophers have upheld the wisdom of such conduct for eons. But when the weak accept that view they often accept along with it an alien definition of what really is necessary, without questioning it. The human environment in which John had lived for five and a half years told him insistently that he had to be a victim; but, as it turned out, this was not true. And in spite of his apparent acceptance of the role, something went on struggling against it. John vomited the food he was forced to eat. He got sick. He injured his mouth yet again. "He seemed lost in day dreams all the time. If spoken to, he quickly went through the pretense of doing what he thought was expected of him, and put on a great though purposeless show of being busy. After a minute or two, during which nothing was accomplished, he again relapsed into day dreaming."[13] And, finally, he made so much trouble by his compliance in helplessness that his parents supplied another, a different, necessity: the therapeutic milieu of the Orthogenic School. There, very slowly, John began to learn that victimization was not the only possible life.

That was lucky for John, who found help in his new surroundings. In general, the weak have to help themselves. We shall explore the ways that have been used effectively to change the imperatives that seem to demand compliance, but while we are looking at disorders of power, it is well to make sure we realize how binding they can be. We have been looking at children who could not see themselves as capable of action or, often, feared the action that they believed they might take. And there are many more: Harry, who began to run away when he was four years old, because he feared his own violence. The picture of self he saw mirrored back from those around was an inhuman monster; not so much a changeling, like George, but a small ogre charged with acting out misdeeds his parents dreamed of but dared not do. There was Joey, who had decided to become a machine, and did it so successfully that "often it took a conscious act of will to make ourselves perceive him as a child."[14] A machine can avoid being swept by rage and fear. It does not have feelings. Mary believed that, at three and a half, she had killed her mother and naturally, therefore, dared not get close to anyone else. Such children have accepted images of themselves and definitions of life that are not true, and that isolate them from others. Without support that they can trust, they are afraid to connect with reality *even to try out alternatives.* In fact, for them, it is impossible to believe that alternatives exist.

These are reactions so crippling that they are lethal. They wildly exaggerate common experience, but they are not distinct from it. If they are marginal because they are extreme, they still indicate common problem areas in human relations. For women, the Second Sex, defined as "others" by norms and definitions that are not their own, these images from a flawed mirror are painful and instructive. How many women still settle for the illusion of "choosing" a life because they are persuaded that there really is only one choice? Many do it who would deny it, and many who do not do it discover that "choosing" once isn't the end, for one has to choose again and again, with steady persistence, and thus remake and reinforce the image of she-who-chooses at the same time. How can we, how can any of the weak, gain the courage to do that when the old image has taught us that we don't know enough to choose, that we cannot sustain a long-term purpose, that our urges are selfish and the selves who seek to fulfill them are too trivial to matter? All of that instruction tends to produce the kind of flattened emotional landscape that we observed in George or Paul. Some of us act out momentary impulses, and find them terribly unsatisfying. Others retreat into passivity and "adjustment." It is better, after all, to be depressed than desperate, better to be merely unhappy than suicidal. Of course it would be better still to be happy, but that would take so much effort, and for what? Only our selfish selves. If one undervalues oneself, one naturally undervalues one's emotions: "Be happy? You mean me? That's impossible. Anyway, how can it matter, if it's only to do with me?" Like George, we draw a picture of possible happiness, and call it "a nothing." Like Paul, we name ourselves Mr. or Mrs. Nobody.

We don't have to go on doing that. But to change the pictures we draw and the names we give ourselves in reality and not just in fantasy—in order not to trap ourselves in the interior world where being "King of the Universe" can be achieved by saying so—isn't easy. We need time and persistence, and help from each other, and most of all we need the firm belief that what we want to do is both possible and important. Blindingly true of women, that is also true for all those who live in the category of the weak.

CHAPTER 5

Messages from the Interior

Man shares with a few others of the higher mammals the curious privilege of citizenship in two worlds. He enjoys in daily alternation two distinct kinds of experience . . . each of which has its own logic and its own limitations; and he has no obvious reason for thinking one of them more significant than the other. If the waking world has certain advantages of solidity and continuity, its social opportunities are terribly restricted. In it we meet, as a rule, only the neighbors, whereas the dream world offers the chance of intercourse, however fugitive, with our distant friends, our dead, and our gods. For normal men it is the sole experience in which they escape the offensive and incomprehensible bondage of time and space. Hence it is not surprising that man was slow to confine the attribute of reality to one of his two worlds, and dismiss the other as pure illusion.

                              E. R. Dodds, The Greeks and the Irrational[1]

This is my wolf. He sits
at the foot of bed
in the dark all night

breathing so evenly
I am almost deceived.

Maxine Kumin, "The Appointment"[2]

The study of psychological breakdowns in children offers valuable information about patterns of growth, and about common reactions to threatening situations. But there are other roads into the inner world where the developing self wrestles with the demands made on it by external reality and so begins to develop the ability to use power in orderly ways, ways that produce inner control and permit creative interaction with the human environment. Of these paths to the interior, the study of dreams is the most famous and familiar. In many cultures, including the Greek, dream figures have been credited with a kind of objectivity even though the messages they bring may not predict events in the real world accurately, may (that is) have crossed transitional space and entered the dreamer's mind via the Gate of Ivory, through which liars pass, instead of the Gate of Horn. By the rational, fiercely scientific spirit of the eighteenth and nineteenth centuries, all dreams were held to be false and their messages simply nonsense. It was Freud who managed to return meaning to dreams and to begin analyzing their images in new ways, as reports from the unconscious mind, real though not objective.

Seeing them this way, we realize that they are creations of the dreamer, built on experience and emotional need, and that they have something to communicate. They are the products of human creativity, the same capacity which, in art, opens the truth of the interior world to others. The dream, of course, speaks in a language known only to the dreamer, but the process of organization works the same way. In fact, if we didn't dream, it is hard to see how we could understand the language of art or even the shared and sharable emotions that it conveys, for the creativity of the listener or reader is called on to interpret the artist's message, and it is in dream-making that we practice such creation. Makers of art are not conveying information about factual events; they turn these events into symbols. Symbols and structure together, then, present a framework of inner emotional reality that is far too complex to be sorted out by cognitive logic. Tentative, ambiguous, potential, half-showing, half-warning, and always questioning, a work of art offers itself as a way of saying and a way of knowing that lies somewhere between mystery and revelation. Understanding art demands an act of creation that is not too different from the artist's own labor of making; and both acts may well have been foreshadowed in the child's first creation of an inner psychic structure that matches and interprets the world outside.

Dream-making is the everyday functioning of the capacity to interpret by making, five-finger exercises in creating a symbolic replica of emotional experience that is puzzling or frightening or challenging and that has not been satisfied by events in the outer world. Dreams give us happy endings to desires when the world won't; and sometimes they also hint slyly why it is that the world refuses to grant our wishes. Thus they provide practice for ordering and reordering the inner images of reality. Always, frightening or happy, they clothe their messages in drama enacted by other beings. We may order these images about, we may flee from them, we may greet them with joy, but whatever of reality's rules we escape, we don't escape companionship. Alone in the interior space of the self, we still clothe our private emotions in the images of "our distant friends, our gods, our dead," those whose presence has weight for us. And if we dare to set up as kings of infinite space, the wolf may stir at the foot of the bed, or some ghost, some long-dead lover, may enter the drama to trouble our sleep. As relatedness is part of life in the real world, so it is part of dreaming.

One sort of dream is particularly useful as a means of exploring the roots of our conceptions of power. These are the bad dreams that plagued Hamlet as they plague us all. Like mental disturbances, they present clues to the way human beings react to stress and anxiety, and of course they are far more frequent. We all have them, though often we prefer to forget them and what they may want to tell us about menace and disaster and guilt. Surely these are messages that we could do without! But though the interior experience of which they speak is unpleasant, it is one that each of us shares with the rest of humanity: it is the experience of being powerless. Specifically, it appears to be a re-creation of the helplessness of infancy. At least this is where we can identify an archetypical source, for dreaming begins very early in life, and little children under the age of five pass a greater proportion of their sleep in a dreaming state than do adults. Apparently this child-adult ratio is even higher for bad dreams than for pleasant ones. Moreover, studies of sleep and the dream process report that children are not only more subject to the anxiety dreams we all experience, but also to the overwhelming kind of nightmare, pavor nocturnus, which is relatively rare among adults. These are traumatic terror-dreams that disorganize the sleeper's grip on reality and produce images that sometimes persist into the waking state.

Figures on the frequency of nightmare depend, of course, on how one defines it; but if we merely want to consider dream-response to strain and anxiety, we can accept those given by two investigators, Foster and Anderson, who reported in *Child Development* on the incidence of "unpleasant dreams." They asked parents to keep a record of dreams that were so disturbing that children waked at night and asked for comfort, or that lingered on long enough to be reported in the morning, dreams sufficiently upsetting for the children to need reassurance. During the period of the study, more than 90 percent of the children who were under four had such dreams. The figures fell as the children grew: 71 percent of the five-to-eights, and only 39 percent of the nine-to-twelves.[3] As the children got older it would appear that their growing competence to deal with the world around them supplied a balance to feelings of vulnerability. They certainly became increasingly able to sort out dream from reality, and they also had had more actual experience of controlling themselves, or the environment, so that on awakening they could contrast the capabilities they knew they possessed with the helplessness of nightmare.

This helplessness is sometimes felt as a paralyzed inability to move out of the reach of danger; and some students of the dream process have argued that there is a physiological basis for this sense of paralysis, for it appears that, in the phase of sleep during which most dreams occur, motor impulses from the brain to the nerve centers are blocked. An observer has described the onset of this REM (rapid eye movement) sleep as follows:

As one spends a night in the dream laboratory one cannot help being impressed as one watches the various polygraphic instruments just before a REM period that there are instinctual forces impelling the subject toward action. Everything seems to be activated. Then at the last moment it is as if a switch is thrown, and instead of waking and acting the subject goes into a different phase of sleep and plays out the action on a screen in the mind.[4]

The trouble with this explanation of the paralysis felt in nightmares is that the same motor block occurs when dreamers appear to themselves to be quite active. If "the switch is thrown" and this produces a feeling of paralysis in nightmare, why not in other dreams? Moreover, there's evidence that some of the most traumatic nightmares occur during a quite different stage of sleep where mobility is less reduced: where, in fact, sleep-walking episodes are triggered off. So the physiological explanation for paralyzed helplessness seems insufficient.

Psychological studies of dreaming offer another explanation of the powerlessness felt in nightmares: that of regression to a childish, or even infantile, phase of development. According to psychoanalytic theory, the complex and competent self, developed through the growing-up years to cope with outer reality, is laid by in sleep; and with the controls of ego and superego inactive, primitive urges and instinctual drives take over. Dreams are *triggered* by contemporary events and problems that have impinged on the dreamer during the day, but they are *powered* by anxieties (or desires) which derive from unresolved difficulties that lie far back in the past. The trigger may be trivial in itself, but it links to troubling earlier emotions that still exist in tension. In sleep, they sweep the adult back to the period in which vulnerability and helplessness were real—the period, that is, when the emotions were first felt: to helpless infancy, when paralyzed immobility was real.

Dreams, one might say, offer access to a memory bank holding experiences that are not just recalled, as in the waking state, but *relived,* at least on the emotional plane. They are a gate to the feeling-content of our past lives, much of it repressed and forgotten as far as consciousness goes, but reachable if the right stimulus is applied. The stimulus itself can be physiological as well as psychological. Neurological surgeons have been stunned to find that an electrical probe, touching a particular area of the brain, can produce in a patient the effect of reliving a past episode with a vividness that is far beyond that of ordinary memory. A mass of "relivable" experience is apparently held somewhere in the memory-store of the brain. In dreams, fragments of such experiences may well combine with others that carry a similar emotional significance, and one may surmise that this doubling of experience will seem to deepen its meanings and importance.

In this way dreams allow us to review, and sometimes to understand better, the dynamic processes by which each of us has become the person that she or he is. A recurrent part of this process is presented by the anxiety dream, or nightmare, in which we find ourselves confronting a situation that threatens to overwhelm our capacity for dealing with it, in which we are menaced by wild animals, by monsters, by fiendish strangers who may not —and this is even more unsettling—be entirely strange. The reason that nightmares resemble each other much more than do ordinary dreams is primarily the experience of vulnerability and powerlessness in the face of threat, threat to one's very life, that is typical of them. It seems to me that when we consider the way we arrive at our most profound conceptions of power and weakness, we cannot leave out this universal and not too infrequent experience of impotence and menace. Nightmares do not simply recall childhood experiences of fright in the face of danger (which may well have been totally misconstrued), they return us to these experiences; and by repetition and commonality, they tell our unconscious minds that these things happen.

Why human beings have nightmares at all is a large question and one that has been widely and inconclusively debated. For present purposes, a modest look at individual bad dreams as they take place in individual lives can tell us a good deal about the manner in which humans deal with stress; in this case, how they react to conditions of threat and anxiety. From the time of Freud on (and *The Interpretation of Dreams* was his first major work, published in 1899), it has been clear that nightmares are a special case of dreaming and present a special problem. Freud's assumption that dreams in general supply a fantasy fulfillment of wishes that cannot be satisfied in reality has always been difficult to stretch over terrifying anxiety dreams. What wish can they be fulfilling? The question was one of the factors that prodded Freud toward formulating the idea of a death instinct to oppose the pleasure principle. Logically, of course, one doesn't explain anything by positing the existence of an instinct, whatever the instinct may be. "Instinctive" causes are removed from investigation just because they are instinctive, simply there. If we say that nightmares indicate an urge in human beings to experience un-pleasure, we may be enlarging our view of human character, but we aren't explaining the occurrence of these dreams.

However, the significance of nightmares to individual human creatures and the emotional residue that they leave with us are susceptible to study, and an interesting examination of the question has been made by Dr. John Mack, head of the Department of Psychiatry at the Harvard Medical School. The material Dr. Mack discusses in *Nightmares and Human Conflict* is drawn both from cases he has observed in practice and from a wide range of published data. As we have noted, the essential features of nightmare include intense anxiety, a sense of helplessness in the face of danger, and the threat of violent attack. Mack points to another common factor, which is more easily observable in the rather simple situations that induce nightmare in children than in the more elaborate structures and more complicated lives of adults. Nightmares arise in situations of strain, fear, and anger, but they do not express the hostility of the dreamer to those who are causing these unpleasant emotions. Hostile the dreamer may be to others in the real-life circumstances, but in the dream, *hostility is projected the other way, onto the self.*

Let us look at Sam, aged two, and normally "a lively, happy child" at the moment when he had his first documented nightmare. Sam was being toilet-trained and he resented it. For several days before his dream he had been wantonly destructive, knocking over lamps and tearing up plants until his mother, at the end of her patience, punished him by shutting him into his room. A couple of hours after he was put to bed, Sam waked in fear, crying for his mother. All he could tell about his dream was "De thing. De thing gone." He was comforted, cried a little when he was put back to bed, but went off to sleep fairly quickly. When "de thing" appeared again two weeks later, Sam was able to communicate a little more: "It hurt me dere on de back and on de tummy." During this time Sam tried to "play out" his problems with his parents and his older brothers while he was awake, in alternating surges of destruction and affection. He was worried about a wolf that might "whack" him; and promptly added, "I whack you, Daddy," which he did. He was not happy about this behavior, however, and went on, "Dere's a wolf out dere. He kill me down," and made as if to whack himself.

Poor Sam was caught in a painful turmoil of emotions: aggression against those who were training him to comply with the standards of cleanly behavior that civilization insists on, and his own anxiety over yielding to the aggressive impulses that these demands on him awakened. When "de thing" manifested itself for the third time, he waked so frightened that he was taken into his parents' bed, but even there he could not fully throw off his terror. At breakfast "he seemed still to be under the influence of frightening hallucinations, cried loudly, and demanded to be held by his mother." Finally he was able to confide that "a lion" had come into his bed to bite him, but had "died" or "been broken." His sensible parents at once started a game of saying good-bye to the lion, which pleased Sam and helped him to get over his distress.[5]

We have here a perfectly "normal" nightmare in a normal child at a time of strain that is normal in our society. In a few months Sam had gotten over this "life-crisis" in his development in various perfectly normal ways. That is why his nightmare is of interest, because it can be taken as utterly typical and, due to Sam's age, as elementary. As Mack says, "The most striking thing about these dreams is that Sam, though aggressive in waking life, *was always the victim and never the aggressor in the dreams.*"[6] Now why should this be? Sam awake was certainly not terrified of his parents. Though often affectionate, he readily broke the rules they laid down and struggled rebelliously against their requirements. Why then in his dreams did he subject himself to panic terror?

One possible answer, Mack suggests, is that if you attack those you love, you are attacking those on whom you are dependent; in the case of a small child, those on whom you are dependent for your very life. What will happen to you then? Either they will punish you (and if you are furious, you will assume that the punishment will match the rage you feel), or your attack will succeed. But if it succeeds, you will, at the best, harm the relationship on which you depend and at the worst you will destroy the person who tends and protects you. It is very dangerous, Sam felt, for a child to hate his parents. And yet the hate was there. At night when he was alone in the dark it fell upon him, a terrible thing that hurt him "dere on de back and on de tummy." Later, no doubt, he would have called it wrong to hate his parents. Now he knew it was perilous. The danger of his own aggressive impulses overwhelmed him and, faced with it, he called for help. Three times "de thing" came and he was powerless before it. The third time he was not able to send it away before morning, and then he needed the help of the people whose demands had awakened this rage within him in order to conquer the rage by agreeing that the lion had existed but was now "broken" or "dead," and making a game of saying good-bye to it. Writes Mack in concluding his report on Sam's nightmares, "Although the dreams express murderous attack against himself, it is possible that they protect the dreamer from something worse, namely experiencing, or taking responsibility for, murderous impulses toward those he loves and upon whom he is so dependent physically and emotionally."[7]

What we are looking at is a lesson in the ordered use of power at the stage of growth where children begin to gain control over the violent impulses and overweening desires that, if given rein, would bring them into disastrous conflict with the external world and the Powers-That-Be who reign there. Sam's troubles show that it can be a hard lesson under the best conditions; but the penalty for not learning is worse, as the case histories discussed in the previous chapter make clear. Sam was learning to deal with relationships which asked him to say "No" not to the human environment, but to himself. His dreams were a way of testing, in the inner world, what might happen to him if he refused the requirements of outer reality, where the impulse to live as *he* wanted had run into other people and what *they* wanted. At this simple level, the problem of using power can be defined as accommodating what an individual wants to the demands of others, without giving in and giving up too much. A multitude of elaborate political constructions have been built around the uses of power, but this simple statement underlies them all. It is primary, in the sense that it presents itself first in such terms whenever we run into it, and also in appearing at a very early stage of life; and it is ultimate, for there is no getting around the existence of other people in the world where we live, or of the dependence each of us feels on others.

This dependence gives our ideas of power a built-in ambiguity. If we push too hard to dominate others and subject them to our individual will— if we try to behave as king of the universe, or of infinite space—then we in effect destroy these others as companions and peers to whom we can look for help in difficulty. The first difficulty we face at the start of life is making order out of the chaos of immediate perceptions so that the world around starts to make sense, to become predictable, to respond to our intentional acts. In order to do that, we need the validating presence and agreement of others, and so we don't dare devalue them to a point where their judgments and assurances mean nothing. We want to be able to trust both their wisdom and the affectionate support they give us in our struggle to grow toward our own wisdom and generosity. Angry as Sam was at the human environment and its discipline, he needed it desperately when his anger got beyond his control and frightened him with the dangers it might let loose. With that help and support he conquered his lion, and sent it away. He couldn't have done so by himself, for he had tried and failed; and for others to do it for him, in the paternalistic style that denied his own abilities, would have left him frustrated (like George), because he was denied any chance to take part in his own rescue. In fairy-tale terms, he had slain the dragon—but he had done it (as so often happens in fairy-tales) with the weapons and the words supplied by others: a kind of white magic that is a part of childhood. Getting rid of his lion was a step in learning to handle emotion, in learning self-control, in accommodation; but it had to be learned within a relationship that was valuable enough to make the accommodation seem worthwhile. Sam gave up something, a bit of autonomous willfulness, because he got back something valuable from people he valued.

In the social universe, the Parable of Sam reminds us that we all, weak and powerful alike, need to have our experiences explained and agreed upon as part of an agreed-on world. But who lays down the definitions that we accept as explanations and agree to abide by? In the first instance it is the powerful who lay claim to this right; and of course it's a right that can be misused. It can result in trivializing or distorting the needs and desires and the very self-images of the rest of humanity. But, as the powerful go about naming and structuring the world, they ask as well for the concurrence of the rest of humanity. Even the haughty assertion of their own correct interpretations, the wisdom of their own directives, does not seem really to satisfy them. They also want to persuade the rest of us that they are right. For, we may guess, without this agreement, without our validation of experience as they perceive it, they too would be at the mercy of their own nightmare threats, their own lions or wolves in the dark at the foot of the bed, and the bad dreams that haunt the infinite space within the nutshell skull. When the powerful reduce the value and the importance of the governed rest of us, they also reduce the reassurance that they can gain from our agreement to their definitions. In the power-dependence relationship, what the weak bring to the bargain is the validation of the power of the powerful: its legitimacy. We shall consider this later in more detail.

There is another link between power and bad dreams that is illustrated by the case of Sam. Nightmares remind us of our vulnerability, they teach us to look for help from others in order to understand our situation and manage the problems we confront. They also force us to live through, ourselves, some extreme conditions of life: desperate and terrifying confrontations with a force that is overwhelming. Says Dr. Mack, "Nightmares are about life and death matters."

And so, of course, is power. What nightmares plunge us into are the ultimate limits of terror that the disturbed children Bettelheim cites feel all the time—the threat of imminent death against which there can be no appeal, and which Sam expressed as "de wolf out dere [who would] kill me down." The other side of this coin is the power made over by the dreamer to the symbol of menace: that is, the power to kill. But of course that power doesn't exist only in dreams; it is the final dominion which the powerful or their institutions can exert over the weak. Dreams and psychosis do not reflect a fantasy force that doesn't exist when they show us the absolute zero of power in which one's life depends on the decision of someone else. Society claims that right in the real world as its ultimate sanction. We can't talk of ordered uses of power without holding its extremes in mind, or we shall be retreating into fantasy where what we want controls what happens and what we don't like isn't there.

Now, human beings, living in society, all know that these sanctions do exist; that the state claims, or has claimed, or may claim again the right to inflict the death penalty for behavior that flouts its regulations. And they know that the state can and does make war, and that killing and being killed are sanctioned in wartime. Indeed these powers are not just embodied in official legal codes. They are reinvented whenever a new power structure takes form. The Mafia establishes and reinforces its dominion by exemplary killings. Internal hierarchies in prisons and concentration camps assert their domination in the same way. Terrorists declare that assassinations are executions sanctioned by an alternative structure of government which they are setting up in the name of revolution-to-be, or of the people's will.

All of us, as I say, are aware of this in normal waking life, but we put it aside, usually because we have accepted the social rules and have no intention of breaking them. But why do we accept them? What has domesticated us so thoroughly? Of course it is the process of socialization that has done this; and in that process nightmares that force us to live through vivid experiences of danger and menace and attack have played a role, and possibly a substantial one. Bad dreams may have many functions, but I think we have to allow that one of them is that of a warning system in which we really—in emotional reality—go through by night what we fear to look at by day. We tell ourselves to be careful, not to go too far, or we will suffer; and what we suffer may be a penalty that has been played out in dreams.

How seriously individuals are affected by this kind of teaching, of course, depends on more than the thrust of dream-warning. It depends on the external circumstances of life. In conditions of rigid domination, children learn too well the lessons of caution and docility, because the interior experience of night terrors is reinforced by the actual course of events. In any society that is operating moderately well, however, it's unlikely that the threat of one kind of disordered use of power will force the bulk of humanity into overcompliance. Instead, the distress that nightmares bring us may work to set us looking about for ways of getting on together that are less threatening, and thus direct us toward the everyday virtues of self-control, negotiated compromise, and shared activity.

There is another public reason, beyond immediate personal reactions, why it is well for the governed to stay aware that "matters of life and death" are part of the power-dependence relationship: the powerful know it, and know it well. It is part of governance both in practice and in principle. The limiting case of the right to kill comes up again and again in the analyses of power that are written for, or by, those who occupy the seats of power. It may be presented as a problem of ethics or morality, but it often appears for discussion simply as a technique of rule: under what circumstances is it advisable for the ruler to invoke the death penalty? Machiavelli, shying away from idealistic and "imaginary" views on the uses of authority, declared it "necessary for a prince, wishing to maintain himself, to know how not to be good, and to use this—or not use this—according to necessity."[8] As for matters of life and death, "Men must either be caressed or else annihilated; they will revenge themselves for small injuries, but cannot do so for great ones; the injury therefore that we do to a man must be such that we need not fear his vengeance."[9] Two centuries later as the French Revolution entered its Stage of Terror, Bertrand Barère repeated Machiavelli's recommendation of annihilation to a meeting of the Committee on Public Safety, for "Only the dead never come back." If one fears their return, one had better make sure that they are truly incapacitated. Barère proved the truth of his own statement, incidentally, by coming back not just once but twice: under Napoleon, and again in the time of Louis Philippe.

But the question of rights and duties of rulers over the lives of their subjects attracts the attention of more soberly considerate monarchs. Very few have refused to use the instrument of sanctioned killing, for it offers itself insistently as the final testing point of authority. One such thoughtful ruler, K'ang-hsi, emperor of China at a time midway between Machiavelli and Barère, gives his conclusions with a calm stoicism that is no less realistic than Machiavelli's urgent counsel. "Giving life to people and killing people— those are the powers that the emperor has," he writes. Using them is not a pleasure, but duty demands it, for "sometimes people have to be persuaded into morality by the example of an execution. . . . The ruler needs both clarity and care in punishing: his intent must be to punish in order to avoid the need for further punishing."[10]

K'ang-hsi had reason to think hard about the uses of power, for he was of Manchurian, not Chinese, descent and only the second of his line to come to the throne. He inherited a large, ancient bureaucracy that he had to make work for him, and to complicate things, he faced, early on, a revolt by the allies who had helped his father. What techniques of governance would establish him as legitimate ruler over an enormous territory in which dwelt an astonishing congeries of primitive and sophisticated subjects, from horse-nomads to elegant Mandarins? "I have been merciful where possible," he wrote, thinking back over his long reign, "for the ruler must check carefully before executions, and leave room for the hope that men will get better if they are given the time."[11] But "in times of war there must be executions for cowardice and disobedience," and "the final penalty of lingering death must be given in cases of treason."[12]

There are elements in K'ang-hsi's thought that are absent in the approach to the matter of Machiavelli and Barère. The emperor is thinking in terms of a stable and balanced system of governance, where authority has the responsibility to consider more than its own convenience. He is aware of the realm that lies inside the limits of power, where governors and governed meet in some kind of relationship, and clearly he would prefer for matters to remain in that realm, and for governance to proceed without disruptive dissent, which would force him to extremes. And the governed cannot, in fact, ask for much more than that from the Powers-That-Be: the recognition of relationship, the restraint on their own whims exercised by rulers, the effort to communicate by example, and the hope for progress and improvement. Anything above that they had better not expect from even the best of governors but think about achieving for themselves, by their own decisions and actions.

As they do so, however, they will do well to remember that the ultimate sanction still lies in the hands of the ruler: "Giving life to people and killing people." The experience of vulnerability in the hands of overwhelming domination, felt in dreams, can be a reminder of the true edges of power and of the significance of the compact between rulers and ruled. The threat of death, the relief of survival, these may well have been daily events at some time in the long human past. Now they come to us in the dark, but the dreams allude to a real sanction that does exist at the edge of waking reality. The life-and-death matters of which nightmares speak are not figments of fantasy, but boundaries of the power-dependence relationship. If we think about power without bearing in mind those recurrent episodes in which we succumb helplessly and hopelessly to threat, we are omitting an underlying ground base of knowledge and emotion; of common knowledge and shared emotion which surely colors our experience of weakness in the waking world and indicates where disordered and extreme use of power leads.

There is another feature of nightmares that is familiar to many dreamers, and which, though it seems alien to waking life, may yet influence our unconscious images of power and do so strongly. This is the frequent appearance of *nonhuman* figures of menace. Sam dreamed up a couple or, better, gave animal names to the menace he felt, and Maxine Kumin's wolf is a real presence. Others, adults and children both, have had their heels nipped by lobsters: Jean-Paul Sartre writes of being troubled by these hallucinatory crustaceans well along into mature life. Some, like Captain Hook, have been pursued by crocodiles. A gorilla (from the Rue Morgue, I suppose) used to follow me down the hall to bed, but worse still was that creature from outer space, the Horla of Maupassant's story, who was, horribly, invisible, so that putting on the light did not banish him. He was by way of being a monster, and these too inhabit dreams: ogres, incubi and succubi, famous for squeezing the breath from devout monks, and nameless things that fumble at the shutters with printless fingers. One of Winnicott's patients was host to "a thing with one big foot and one little foot and one eye." Another was acquainted with "a man witch, with a wand that could make you disappear."[13]

Where these creatures take us is straight into the realm of magic; and there is good reason to think that *all power carries with it a tinge of the supernatural.* Heroic sculpture was shaped to a larger-than-life stature even among the humanistic Greeks, while Pharaoh towers above his tiny wife and antlike courtiers. Kings are consecrated, not simply crowned. Their rule has been sanctified by a divinity to which even Hamlet's murderous uncle could appeal. In our own time and our own country, which most of us would declare to be a secular democracy, every president between Harry Truman and Gerry Ford has been accorded an aura of glamour; sinister glamour in Nixon's case, but still there. Indeed, a sort of superhuman ordinariness has recently begun to attach itself to the memory of Truman.

Ford, intractable material for glamorizing in any case, succeeded to the presidency without benefit of an election campaign depicting heroic pretensions. He profited briefly from being anyone else but Nixon; but the pardon of his predecessor not only left him open to attack on moral grounds. More important to his possible claim on magic capability, the pardon displayed a sort of political tin ear—that is, any sense of politics as persuasive presentation—for it cut off the developing drama of Nixon's downfall like a curtain clattering down just as the last, climactic act opened. Until this clumsy performance, however, one almost had to be old enough to recall Herbert Hoover to envisage a thoroughly and incompetently human President. Carter's incumbency seems so far to be an accelerated run-through of the process in which an unexplained capacity to change things for the better is promised, to be followed by hangover morning, when the ruled awaken from dreams of glory to find the same old physical laws still operating. Even today, it seems, the governed are ready to accept the idea that the powerful are different from you and me, and not simply because they have more power. We grant them *a different kind of power* that contains some element of the supernatural.

Little children—and dreams, especially menacing ones, return us to the emotional conditions of early childhood—have difficulty in distinguishing between external reality and fantasy. They also are often puzzled about the true nature of living creatures. Children's stories feature animal heroes and animal villains, and I recall, myself, a small boy who regularly performed a rite of worship to a large, placid Persian cat who did indeed present a rather majestic presence. The cat took it in good part and the child presumably felt that if the creature did possess supernatural power, it had been safely appeased. Indeed, any object that appears to move by itself can "come alive" for a child: Piaget reports as typical a six-year-old who assumed that a marble rolled itself purposively down a slope because it wanted to meet someone at the bottom.

It is not surprising, then, that animal figures enter our dreaming, or that they often represent danger. They *are* dangerous, because we project onto them emotions that we are afraid to feel consciously. We don't want to admit that we harbor these feelings, and we direct them away and clothe them in alien images; but, of course, the emotional charge they carry gives them extraordinary life. They are apart, and yet they connect with us, seem to know our moods and even our hidden desires; which is natural, since they represent our desires and our dreads. They are both intimate and alien, the latter because they seem to be uncontrollable. Interestingly enough, it's been suggested that the first onset of nightmare-dreaming in children may occur at just about the time that they begin to show fright at the appearance of strangers, which is around eight months old. This carry-over of external fears into the world of dreaming is then echoed and iterated lifelong. The animals and monsters of nightmare, thus, reflect very early experiences of menace; their recurrence recalls that archaic vision and surely reinforces our readiness to attribute something of the quality of fantasy and uncontrollable magic power to those who claim authority over us.

Another unsettling characteristic of the denizens of nightmare is their ability to change shape. Children and adults both experience this ambiguity when a familiar figure turns, in middream, into someone else. I think we see here, again, the efforts all children must make to set up a world permanent enough to be trusted, where beloved persons can be counted on to return, and where real objects demonstrate their real continuity. So much of this learning is preverbal that the fears which accompany it resist neat summing up and spill over easily into threatening situations. Shape-changing monsters inhabit many mythologies, and though myth is not merely public dreaming, it does contain many of the same elements, projected out from the interior world. Even gods and heroes must contend with these possessors of secret power, as Thor did with the cat who was really a dragon, and Hercules with the Old Man of the Sea.

What the dreams and myths remember and recreate are memories of early, but real, feelings. Powerful parents and other inhabitants of the child's world are indeed experienced as changeable, and in vulnerable infancy, the change can seem overwhelming. When Sam's mother lost patience with him, her image altered. She ceased to be the source of comfort and love, and *turned into* an angry and menacing stranger. That happens to all children, of course, for human parents have never managed to raise their children without disciplining them and, short of Utopia, they never will; besides, being human, their emotions get away from them from time to time. In every child's life, therefore, there are moments when some loved and trusted person is transformed into a figure of menace and strangeness; witches, ogres, stepmothers, giants—the fairy-tales are full of them.

Such a shift is recreated in dreams as shape-changing, as a vision in which another presence looks out from the face one thought one knew, or a monster is somehow, inescapably, close and shockingly familiar. Permanence wavers and meaning grows ambiguous. Something is there, something very important; but we can't be sure just what. In the vivid intensity of nightmare, such a lurch in identity is terrifying. Probably it is the emotion that most easily persists into the waking state. Mack mentions a girl of twelve who dreamed of vampires and, from time to time, was haunted by doubts about her friends. Were they really who they seemed to be, or were they creatures from an alien world who wore these familiar faces and bodies as masks? Many of us, I suspect, can recall some such sensation of uncertainty about the realness of reality, and our inability to resolve our doubts. Might there not be some unknown, awful power abroad that could, in the light of day, change rules and transform identities as easily as dreams are transformed? I believe that these doubts from the night-world color our perceptions of power and the powerful and exaggerate the strength we attribute to them, by lending them an aura of magic.

Actually, magic is not exclusively the property of dream figures. It can be used by the dreamer as a defense. Some dreamers can call up a sense of external reality and belittle their nightmares as they wake. Others invoke their own defensive magic. Among the children whose dreams John Mack reports on was Laura, who was pursued by a skeleton and a "yellow monster" that followed her down the street, devouring children along the way. Laura fought back. A large stuffed animal that she took to bed would protect her, she told the doctor, by "blowing away" her bad dreams. Andy fended off the attacks of pointed objects by means of his own personal "superpowers," and Carol simply declared that she had something special about her and so would not get hurt.

In our civilization today we don't acknowledge the idea that the representation of an animal can protect us from danger, or that anyone possesses attributes which can ward off the blows of knives or razors by unseen means. But many other cultures have done so and some still do. Animal images, totems or gods, have indeed offered protection against the attacks of malevolent beings. Shamans and magicians have been credited with the ability to make weapons drop harmless at their feet. In other times and places other social mythologies, well established and coherent, have drawn the line between magical fantasy and events in a solid, real world in a different place from that which is current with us.

Now, culture-bound as I am, it seems to me that we are right, and that magic is part of an interior world of dream and fantasy, and does not operate in the external universe where I assume that cause and effect are governed by general laws that are scientifically explainable, whether or not science has yet got around to explaining them. But I also know that belief in logic and reason is not explainable by logic and reason, and that those who draw, or have drawn, the line in other places seem to themselves to be justified by evidence and logic in doing so. The point here is not agreement or disagreement about the power of magic, but what such ideas tell us about the magic of power: that human minds connect the first with the second, and that even the most furiously rational of creatures actually experiences such a connection in dreams, bad dreams most particularly. And in addition, some of those who are menaced in this fashion call on magical defenses.

Awake, normal and logical, we call these ideas childish, or perhaps psychotic, but that doesn't diminish the reality of the linkage between magic and power, either for menace or for defense, that they illustrate. Other societies have given this linkage a place in the world of external reality. Officially, we define it as being merely emotional; but, nonetheless, each of us civilized beings has to expect to spend some hours of every day in a world where emotional linkage operates with vivid actuality. When lurking menace threatens us there, it appears total and uncontrollable by logical means, and the shocks and perils we experience then may seem more intense than those of everyday. It's not surprising to imagine that we carry some effects of these inner events with us when we cross transitional space to waking life.

CHAPTER 6

Definitions and Misdefinitions

*Basically, there appear to be two views of the nature of power. One can see
people as dependent upon the good will, the decisions and support of their
government or of any other hierarchical system to which they belong. Or,
conversely, one can see that government or system dependent on the people's
good will, decisions and support. One can see the power of a government as
emitted from the few who stand at the pinnacle of command. Or one can see
that power, in all governments, as continually arising from many parts of the
society. One can also see power as self-perpetuating, durable, not easily or
quickly controlled or destroyed. Or political power can be viewed as fragile,
always dependent for its strength and existence upon a replenishment of its
sources by the cooperation of a multitude of institutions and people—cooperation
which may or may not continue.*

Gene Sharp,
The Politics of Nonviolent Action[1]

Growing up human, from a state of total dependency to reasonable
autonomy as a member of society, takes a long time. The processes of power
that we learn as we do so come a good deal closer to the second of Gene
Sharp's alternative definitions of its nature. Not only does Sharp see power
(in this description) as taking its rise in "a multitude of institutions and
people" and replenished only through their cooperation, he sees it as essentially dynamic, not static. In order that this replenishment can take place,
power is "continually arising." It seems, that is, to call on the native
creativity that can be found not just "at the pinnacle of command" but in
"many parts of society" because, as students of human development declare,
it is one of the necessary ingredients of growth and learning. Sharp's second
definition, and it is indeed the one he subscribes to, takes power to be the
product of a process of cooperation and interaction, and his suggestion that
this cooperation *may be cut off* points to the control over the process being
lodged not just in the hands of the mighty, but as being available also to the
multitudes. As I have been saying, the very ability to establish an independent identity that can trust the world and act purposively within it develops
only by means of the mediation and cooperation of others, beginning in the
first days of life. Whether we humans are consciously aware of it or not, our
human capacity to function independently—to judge our chances of success
in the surrounding context of life and to undertake prolonged, determined

enterprises that we frame and monitor ourselves—that is, our use of power —is based on the whole complicated structure of social relations in which, and by which, we live. Sharp's second definition, then, seems reinforced by the circumstances of existence and by our assumptions about the nature of power as indicated by the way we behave.

But the formal definitions of power current today don't run this way. They resemble, instead, the meaning Sharp offers first, as being a quality of command and decision emitted by those who stand at the pinnacle of authority. Certainly the treatises on power written for the powerful assume this to be the case. Plato's ideal guardians, philosopher-kings, were sharply separated from the unruly mass of folk by education, special breeding, and conditions of life. In order to function properly as masters they were to be distanced as completely as possible from ordinary humanity and its failings, living an ordered and communal life which would ensure that their judgments on proper action would be unanimous—that is, monolithic. "The relations of body and soul, of sovereign and subjects, or master and slave Plato subsumed under a single theory of authority and obedience. Moreover, in his cosmology he perceived a similar dualism of primary cause, which was intelligent and divine, and mechanical or slave cause, which was irrational, disorderly, and lacking in both freedom and conscious purpose." The administration of political power, then, was rationalized "within a vast cosmic scheme in which irrational nature was ordered and controlled by a divine, intelligent authority." So David Brion Davis sums up Plato's views on dominance and obedience in *The Problem of Slavery in Western Culture.*[2] And from the Greeks on, philosophers concerned with questions of power have directed their counsels to the great—to the agents of "divine intelligent authority"—whether they talked of ethics or pragmatic techniques of governance. Aging monarchs have themselves composed memoirs which will, they hope, prevent their heirs from falling into more than normally disastrous blunders, and ambitious revolutionaries, viewing a distant throne, have cudgeled their brains to work out the most moral, practical, beneficial, realistic, and/or all of these ways to wield the power waiting for them at the top once they get there. The alternative hypothesis—that ruling is a process which involves an active, two-way relationship with another term included, namely the ruled—is hardly examined.

It is true that the *existence* of those over whom the powerful are to rule well if they follow expert advice is acknowledged in these classic studies. The populace must be there as fodder for ruling, but they are perceived as mere material to be processed. Whether the results are good or bad is presumed to depend entirely on the ability and good fortune of the processors, who are in command, and whose purposes supply the leaven in the otherwise sodden lump of humanity. Under good government, as these works understand it, initiative can flow only one way, from the top down, and cooperation consists in cheerful and willing obedience. We can see these views reflected in a lot of traditional historical writing, where the powerful alone act, and alone possess individuality. In the past, there was indeed a degree of identification of ruler and people, when the king stood symbolically for his subjects and nation, subsuming their existence into his own. Remnants of this attitude are still preserved in the customs by which bishops sign their letters with the names of their sees and lords with the names of their domains, just as they addressed each other in Shakespeare's plays. And true to their role as symbols of the condition of the weak, women still customarily take their husbands' names when they marry.

Certainly, these analysts hold, the ruled fodder cannot be left to itself indefinitely. It must be watched, and readings of its mood taken from time to time, since from time to time it is known to break out into rebellion and disorder. But such breakouts are traditionally treated as problems of the powerful, difficulties to be dealt with objectively in the way that one copes with natural disasters, as the family of poor delinquent George came to deal with him. The reigning elite doesn't see these disturbances as an instructive expression of human emotions—natural anger at frustration, natural demonstrations of hope not quite abandoned, natural efforts to intervene politically by public protests against policies which are creating more problems than they solve. There are no lessons here for the powerful, for how can the governed have anything relevant to say about high politics? Like Plato's mechanical, or slave, cause, disobedience among the governed is simply "irrational, disorderly and lacking in both freedom and conscious purpose." Paying attention to their demands would be a waste of time.

I suspect that one reason why the great have trouble in granting relevant human significance to the behavior of the weak is that the weak are so numerous. A single individual, even the neediest charity case, can evoke sympathy and become an object of interest as well as benevolence; but the ruled are plural *per se,* bulked together, indistinguishable, interchangeable. They merge into a masked chorus whose numbers are more important than their identity, and when the numbers grow large enough, their sheer size becomes menacing. Even charity fails when it's asked to think of them in the mass. "If we were to give one of you such-and-such, this benefit you're asking for," say the powerful to the weak, "we should have to give it to everyone else." Now, the sensible answer may very well be, "What's wrong with that?" But as long as power is defined as an attribute which belongs to the powerful, the powerful can't make such gifts without feeling them as seriously impoverishing, unacceptable inroads on their hoarded strength.

So they react defensively. Whatever demands are being made run into a bland stone wall of inattention, a tactic based on the conviction that the fickle weak will soon get tired of making a fuss about what they can't use and really don't want. Power, say the powerful, belongs to us because we do know how to use it. Our own definitions assure us that this is so, and as soon as we can once again persuade the weak to accept these obvious facts of life, they will see that power is not for them. They are very well off as they are and they will soon realize it and accept their limitations, their diminished humanity. If in the end the weak get tired of accepting any such thing and rebel against a code which assures them that inferiority is their proper lot, the powerful take this as evidence of the exasperating intransigence of the fodder for rule, not as a message about the human condition.

If we choose the other of Gene Sharp's definitions, and begin with the hypothesis that power is not an emanation given off by those who stand at the pinnacle of command but one aspect of ongoing interactions among human beings of all stations, we have to take heed of what the governed say —not just their existence, but what they have learned from it. Now in practice many political systems do of course allot certain rights to the ruled, just as the daily intercourse of society brings us all, willy-nilly, into common activities and bespeaks continuing interdependence. But orthodox political thought doesn't pay much attention to the ordinary background noise of existence. The body of the governed forms a *crowd,* and crowds are held to work and to act by different rules from those which direct single individuals

No doubt that's true. There are emotions and ways of behaving that sweep through assembled groups and massed throngs of people and move them in special dramatic ways. In *Crowds and Power* Elias Canetti speaks of such crowd-emotions as allowing men to "free themselves from their burdens of distance" from each other and thus to transcend the limits of individuality, so long as the intense burst of feeling endures. Boundaries of self start to break down and emotions gain strength from physical closeness, and can then erupt into action of great intensity, though usually of short duration. Very possibly such experiences of coming together to resist immediate challenge, or to rush toward some passionately desired goal, cast back to prehuman and prelingual strategies employed in the face of danger or of the need for concerted attack. Religious ritual sometimes tries to create this deep bonding purposely.

But though a deeply moved crowd is indeed a special phenomenon, it is still a body made up from grains of humanity who are each and every one single and individual, each possessed of a personal will and purpose. After these crowd-seeds have come together, they fall apart again, and it's quite misleading to think of them as existing only in such a phase of indistinguishable closeness. It's easy to conceive of the weak this way, as a great faceless mass, but it's not very wise politically, for it invites the powerful to sum up the governed as different and as distanced from the lucky folk who hold the reins of power. But rules for crowd behavior don't always predict what the ruled are going to do.

Thinking of the weak as an undifferentiated mass, greedy but uncertain, childish and fickle in their purposes, creatures incapable of doing things sensibly themselves and therefore as needing to have things done for them, leads the powerful into another error. They tend to see the rights of the ruled as gifts granted to them by their rulers, not because they deserve such rights, but because morality demands it—or perhaps just to save time. The rights of the ruled are thus transformed into the duties of the powerful: ethical and responsible rulers are obligated to respect the rights of the rest of us, but the decision of how to lay out these rights, and how to administer them and guard them against irresponsible overuse—this is the perquisite of the powerful. The central, important question thus moves from the rights of the governed to the moral characters of their governors, and we find ourselves worrying about the ethics of rulers and not the practical prerequisites for living together in a world full of people.

Much of the time, it's true, treatises on the proper exercise of governance suggest that it's wise for the powerful to respect the rights of the ruled, but "wise" in this context seems to mean "advantageous for the powerful." If Machiavelli's Prince is in a position to "caress" his subjects, he is spared the trouble of "annihilating" them. "Wise" rulers will take care to exhibit a decent respect for the opinion of mankind whenever it's convenient. And alien as pashas and potentates may find the interchangeable parts of the populace, it's shrewd for them to make some show of being "like" their constituents: some folksiness or devotion to religion or vital interest in football or chariot-racing will blur any impression of arrogance. But when we declare that wise rulers are better than those who exhibit self-absorbed insolence, do we mean better for their subjects and for the process of governance, or better for themselves?

Indeed, what can it mean to say that the weak have rights within a system dominated and administered by the powerful, if power emanates from those magnates alone? By definition, the powerful will not only always have more power than the weak; any power that the weak appear to hold will have been handed to them by their rulers and can, presumably, be taken back. So there will be no limit on what the powerful can do except their own morality; no external deterrent can be found to prevent them from exercising power to its extreme limits. Rights are temporary gifts, granted if the powerful think it desirable but withdrawn at pleasure. Then, every minor matter of administration can be escalated into a matter of life or death, as rights go by the board; and in extreme conditions, they do go by the board. We shall examine some situations of this kind later on.

But perhaps the most pervasive problem which derives from setting up divisions of kind between ruled and rulers is that the concept of governance, as it becomes a special duty of the powerful, loses its connection with the community as a whole. The idea that government is simply management of common interests is acted out in smallish communities—at town meetings, any voter can demand the floor and remind officers that there are needs which are being overlooked. Some needs, of course, are always going to be ignored, or given a low priority in the interest of others; that has to be expected, and the more so as systems of government grow and become complex. That, however, is not my point; which is that when rulers and ruled get to be seen as separate entities, *the whole idea of common interest fades away.* This has an unforeseen effect on techniques of management. If decision-making doesn't take the possibility of common interest into account, then *all* decisions come to be made on the basis of confrontation, and joint action, instead of resulting from shared purposes, becomes compelled action. Consensus, town meetings, the full expression of public opinion, including those of long-winded bores—yes, of course these extremes are often impractical; but when shoot-outs at high noon become the standard model for settling disagreements, impracticality turns up at the other extreme. We are severely limiting the variety of methods available for coping with the inevitable ups and downs of life in either case, and arguing every detail out can be just as disastrously time-consuming as free expression. Most of the time, practically speaking, some sort of known and previously agreed-on procedure will serve as a frame for political action; and such procedures are often modified as they operate, in order to fit particular circumstances. These modifications are the contributions of the ordinary folk, down the line; they are inventive adjustments, in which political dictates are fitted to everyday existence. To use Gene Sharp's words, political power is thus replenished by the cooperation of a multitude of institutions and people.

Change and process are factored into the application of power, as it works in practice most of the time; but that isn't the view that our dictionaries take. They exemplify the contrary habit of mind, which takes power as an attribute of the powerful and sees it in static form, defining it as an intangible but somehow measurable quantity of force. A sample of their approach is enlightening. I quote here from the texts of two of the most famous. *The Oxford English Dictionary* (I use the Shorter OED for the sake of brevity, but it accurately reflects the original) divides its definitions into three parts. Part I deals with power "as a quality or property" and begins with the "ability to do something," which coincides with the creative power to act purposively toward a chosen end. Halfway through, however, this section mutates into definitions of power as "possession of control or command over others; dominion; government; sway; authority . . . political ascendancy." Part II considers power not as possession but as possessor, with the personal use of "ruler, governor," antedating the institutionalized "state or nation." "Spiritual being . . . ; a divinity" follow and next comes "a force of armed men." Part III deals with technical uses in mathematics, mechanics, and so on.

Webster's Third New International Dictionary has been taken to task for being representative of current popular use rather than prescriptive of proper usage, but if this is true, its value for our purposes is only increased. Webster's does not start with the idea of ability but opts at once for the aspect of dominion and control. "A position of ascendancy," it begins, and the first ability it mentions is "ability to compel obedience." Before we reach "capability of acting," in fact, we must note "a military force or its equipment," and the "ability to wage war." The aggressive qualities of power are much on Webster's mind, for "capability . . . faculty, talent" soon give way to "influence," "prerogative," and "legal authority," and "physical might" checks in before we arrive at "vigor, intensity." "A supernatural being or occult force" is coupled with "the ability to control them"; "strength, solidity" are nodded to with the first illustrative example implying menacing strength; and then we tail off to the technical usages.

If this is our true view of power, it is certainly an ambiguous one. No doubt it should be. These "good, bad, good, bad" aspects of power are all properly part of the central concept. It can be understood as capability, potentiality, the capacity to act. We saw how the nascent surge of being that thrusts itself into existence as children creatively process their perceptions of the world calls forth descriptions that are related to the use of power: power that must not be utterly frustrated if life is to survive on this planet. But equally "power" can frustrate, dominate, and compel living creatures to obey and so stop the process of creative imagination, setting up in its place what Winnicott called "the negative of civilization."

Our dictionaries have not intentionally put forward these philosophic ambiguities. They merely reflect our ways of seeing; and if contradictions exist in our contemporary estimate of power, then they exist outside the dictionaries, in the social mythology that structures our view of the universe and directs our logic and our conduct. It is up to us, not the dictionaries, to try to put this confusing list of good and bad qualities together and come to some general conclusion. Is it possible to resolve the contradiction between a limiting power to compel and a liberating power to act? This is not an abstract question. The need to use power safely and effectively is something all human beings face continuously, whether it involves a momentary mundane decision or a matter of life and death. It is tied in to our plans and hopes and actions. If we can't separate liberating power from limiting power, are we condemned to act in eternal ignorance of safety and effectiveness?

What does such a menace do to our willingness to imagine goals and to move toward achieving them? How dare we trust our own aspirations if we assume, as these definitions instruct us to assume, that ambition for oneself can be transmuted in the space of a breath into domination over others?

On the face of it, the dictionaries say that power is amoral; and no one would deny that. Our own experience tells us that it can be used for good or bad ends, and an essential part of early learning (both awake and asleep) is the discovery of how to tell one use from another, how not to go too far. But these definitions imply that there is no way to tell the use of power from its abuse, and that both elements are hopelessly intertwined. If that's so, however, there's no way to tell when we are acting acceptably, and we are forced to conclude that power is not just amoral, it's *immoral,* pitch that can't be touched without dirtying one's hands. If we can never distinguish ordered uses from the disorders of power, it becomes impossible to act without falling, unknowingly, into *guilty* action. Our current devotion to Lord Acton's famous dictum on power, "Power tends to corrupt, and absolute power corrupts absolutely," indicates that we do feel this way; in fact, the quotation is so often misquoted—by dropping the qualification "tends to," so that it becomes simply "Power corrupts"—that it seems as if we are even more convinced of evil consequences than Acton himself was. Unconsciously we extend the wisdom of the dictionaries by inferring that, if power can be either good or bad, *it can never not be bad,* and that any liberating use of power conceals a covert thrust to dominate and limit the capacities of others.

And after all, there is plenty of historical evidence to show that a liberating movement which begins with the use of creative capability for righteous ends may well run a course during which it is transformed into an exercise in dominating compulsion. How often, in our time, have we not watched the dedicated efforts of some group of the governed, struggling to free themselves from oppression and to achieve their own desired goals, and then witnessed the quondam rebels grow obsessed by the need to hang on to the power they used for their own liberation by setting up institutions that enforce their rule over others! We have come to expect that revolutions will eat their children and that liberating action will come round in a vicious circle to where it began, with the newly powerful callously putting down the eternal, universal majority of the ruled.

Are there episodes where this pattern has not taken place, where freedom has endured, and change has eased life for all, in the end? Yes, though all political changes will be tested in practice. But successes tend to get taken for granted and to disappear into the background noise of dailiness. We forget that what works was not always there, and notice what frightens or irritates us.

Suspicions of power among the governed, then, begin with doubts about one's ability to tell acceptable uses from those that go too far and may arouse troublesome repercussions. But these suspicions also extend to doubts about what other people may be doing: aren't they likely to go too far, too? If we can't trust ourselves, how are we to trust them? Here is a group, let us say, that is crying out for greater opportunities, for justice and freedom; and let's allow that it's clear that, in the past, these people have been deprived of such blessings. The changes they want are just. Still and all (we ask ourselves), will *they* know where to stop, once they lay hands on the power to change things? If there are no built-in limits to power, how can we be sure? Isn't it better to stay away from the whole struggle, forswear power ourselves, and equally forswear approving the use of it by any other group of the governed? If it has this mysterious life of its own, striving always toward extremes, corrupting its users in the intimate recesses of their minds, hadn't we better forget the whole thing?

Besides, change itself is upsetting. Let it start and we are continually finding strange faces in strange places, cumbersome new words and demands for unexpected behavior. In a society as complex as ours, and one that shifts so fast, both socially and in material life and technology, we are constantly being told to adjust to novelty. Old rules and old roles are questioned every day, and for those who were comfortable enough as they were, such questioning is unsettling: it challenges customs, beliefs, and even the old identity of anyone who sees no need for change.

We feel these demands as a misuse of power. When we are forced to reconsider our attitudes and our actions at someone else's behest, change becomes associated with the power of others to affect us against our will. At first, these adjustments may be mere annoyances—but how do we know where they will end, as "those people" go too far? And this malaise is another deterrent to our own willingness to reach for power, lest we awaken it in others when we try to change things ourselves. Besides, a good deal of contemporary popular psychology works to increase the doubts we feel about our impulses and purposes. Freud and his followers have told us that a lot of our reasoning isn't reasoning at all, but simply a form of rationalizing our unconscious desires; infantile desires too, which can't be very nice at best, and at worst must be selfish or obscene. So we begin to wonder whether the difference between liberating power (good) and limiting power (bad) may not be purely subjective. The good names—capability, potentiality, creativity— aren't these just cover-ups for unpleasant instinctual drives which we use when power belongs to *us?* And what we describe as compulsion, domination, and oppression—aren't these pejoratives attached to power when we don't own it, when it's *your* power or *their* power?

If that's the case, there's no way out of the dilemma. My creativity is fated to impinge on yours, my ambitious aims will always lead me to violate the boundaries of your territory. Confrontation becomes the inevitable, universal means of decision, not just the limiting case. Descendants of naked, killer apes, we are locked into conflict, defending our domains until one of us gives way. Or (the only possible alternative), you are Tarzan and I am Jane —that is, *old* confrontations have settled forever my place in your world or yours in mine, and we are and ever shall be ranked in a hierarchy, man above woman, white above black, lord above peasant. Then I can cross the border of your territory only as long as I can persuade you, by proper gestures of humility, that I am subordinate and you are master.

Our dictionary definitions of power, in short, operate to maintain the status quo; which is not surprising, since they are expressions of the social mythology that explains existing circumstances of life and offers counsel on behavior fitted to our functions and our place. The idea that power is an attribute that somehow pertains to certain individuals or groups inhibits other individuals and groups from challenging the ones that are designated as powerful. It does so in various ways, of which we can here discern two. First, if power is immoral and not just amoral, we can never justify our resort to it on ethical grounds. No matter how good our intentions, we may at any moment go too far and deviate into selfish purposes, so that we intrude on others and on their purposes. Second, since we can't appeal to morality, we assume that disagreements between human beings who are following their individual courses toward their selfish goals will inevitably be settled in only one way: by confrontation, in which a contest of hostile bluff can easily escalate into combat. Afterwards, when one has beaten the other, the loser will stand to the winner in an established status of submission and dominance. Winning can never achieve an equal balance of power, even if that is what the weak think they want. If they win, they will find themselves transformed into agents of domination. And if might makes right in practice, it makes wrong in moral principle; and nightmares will remind us of that.

What we are looking at is something both simple and subtle. The weak are being deterred from challenging the powerful by advance persuasion— persuasion which plays on the natural doubts of the governed in order to convince them that they can't trust their own motives when they try to improve their lot. Is it right and justice that they seek—or simply naked power? Those who doubt the justice of their cause go forth to battle with weakened will; and if battle is necessary whenever one wants to act, battle against those whose claim to the property of power is greater than yours, then the prospect is not hopeful to start with. No matter that ordinary existence suggests that our goals are often not entirely selfish but shared with others, that a good deal of leeway for action can be found before encountering opposition, and that arguments are not always won by blows while untenable positions can be abandoned without total loss—our formal views of power and its uses ignore these empiric realities. Rather like John, the child who preferred to give in before he was made a victim, we shy away from testing the strength and validity of our own purposes. By our conduct we indicate that the game of power isn't worth the candle.

Of course a queasy view of power is not peculiar to our age. Warnings that its use can turn into abuse abound and always have done so, while verses in praise of the simple life are a notable feature of corrupt and courtly civilizations. The joys of pastoral existence and the dangers that cluster round the throne have inspired poets for at least two thousand years. But a society, or a culture, picks its own touchstones, and ours has grown increasingly pessimistic. Even in the booming, optimistic nineteenth century, Lord Acton was not alone in his doubts on the course of power. Henry Adams said simply, "Power is poison," and added, "Its effect on Presidents has always been tragic." These are not warnings about abuses, they are judgments about the essential evil of power, no matter how it is used. They are views that have influenced our contemporary attitudes to power profoundly.

Now why should this be? Is it because the complexity of our huge and rapidly changing society undermines our confidence in the possibility of administering it competently and fairly? There's something to that, for it's certainly hard to foretell the consequences of our actions today, nor are most of the consequences that we hear about cheerful ones. Global communication networks are always ready to report bad news, which is so much newsier than good news. From uncertainty to doubt to distrust to fearful hesitation is a quick trip that brings its voyagers to the terminus of inaction. But can this be the whole story? Do we shrink away from power only because we doubt our motives and are uncertain of the consequences if we intervene in the political process? After all, the results of our own actions need not be any less predictable than the results of the actions of others, and at least we know our own desires and needs. If we let others act for us, we have no guarantees that they can do any better than we might, and we ought to be aware that the consequences, whatever they are, are apt to be less satisfying because they don't incorporate our personal goals. Complexity threatens the inactive as much as it does those who try to manage their own lives.

Well then, is our passivity due to the conviction that Acton and Adams are right, that power is poison and sets us on the road to corruption? We say it often enough, but it's nonetheless remarkably out of character for this civilization: in almost every other context of existence we seem quite happy to be corrupted. In few other areas do we evidence any distaste for amorality, or immorality either. From morn to night, from the *Today* show to the *Tomorrow* show, in *Playboy* and *Penthouse* and *Cosmo* and *Vogue,* in puffs and commercials ad infinitum, we are blandished and seduced toward indulgence and immediate gratification of all the showy vices that the vulgarest Lucifer could dream up to tempt our whims or snobbery or one-up-man-or-woman-ship. Fear of corruption appears as likely to motivate us as it did the Gadarene swine.

It seems to me that we must conclude that Acton's famous tag acts as a face-saver for us, as a rationale and not a reason. It supplies a convenient explanation for inaction and passivity, an explanation so widely subscribed to that we don't have to justify it. It really is odd to refrain from taking a hand in events and activities that affect one's own life. Someone, sometime, may well ask, "But why don't you want to use power?" If we can answer, "Because it is corrupting," we are let off the hook, and fast. We don't need to search about for more revealing replies when we have at hand this pleasantly sanctimonious response, which absolves us from any possible accusation of irresponsibility by demonstrating our moral sensitivity. In short, we have a screen to retreat behind. Acton's words suggest that further discussion is unnecessary, rather banal, in fact. So we do not just refuse to use power, we refuse to discuss it. Apparently we don't want to consider the possible consequences of passivity any more than we want to face the possible guilt of action.

Now, a retreat from involvement in the world of action is central to many religious movements and, at a personal level, the urge to find or to create an interior life that is enriching and that provides a pattern of meaning to illuminate the external world is a deep and fundamental human need. In our own troubled time, efforts to seek out new interpretations and to refresh old ones are natural; and if the practices of some popular cults seem naïve or bizarre—well, the reactions of those outside can't devalue the felt need for deeper meaning. Quack remedies don't lessen the actuality of disease, and some remedies prove themselves. But except for those few who are true mystics, interior journeys end with a return to the here and now, to the body social where we live. We do inhabit two worlds, and one of them is the boring old material universe. If we leave that in the hands of others, we leave our physical breathing selves in their hands as well. Long before Acton or Adams, Aesop had his say on the perils of political passivity: "Those who voluntarily put power in the hands of a tyrant or an enemy must not wonder if it be at last turned against themselves."

So what is it about power that puts us off, if it's not a desire to shun corruption or a high-minded urge to cultivate our interior gardens? If we don't like power, don't want to use it, don't want to think about or talk about our reasons—Why? I think it's fear. *Power is dangerous:* or so we believe.

And why do we think so? Because our minds have dropped the sense of relationship and community which can license the use of power, and which operates to control its use. Once we start to see power as an attribute of the powerful, one which can be used willfully and whimsically, we are forgetting the limits that the existence of a surrounding community provides. All of us have experienced, one way or another, what it feels like to be vulnerable and helpless, and we can't unlive those moments; but, like children waking from nightmares, we can ask for help from each other. We can set up a boundary between ordered and disordered uses of power and hang on to our ability to discriminate between them; and we can do it by trusting ourselves and our fellows to take part in the power process, trusting them and ourselves for acting on our common, similar, experience of being human together.

We need a boundary, both to the abuse of power and to our own fear of it. If power always corrupts, then we are always at the mercy of personal guilt, and of fear of just retribution, if we undertake any action at all. Blame can descend from on high, and we won't know what it is that we have done to deserve it. This fear has deep roots. From our earliest days, we've yearned to do right partly because we value rewards of love and approval, but equally because the opposite of reward is punishment and humiliation. Not to do right will provoke retribution within a relationship, and our very sense of identity and presence derives from relationships. Consciously we may not see the connection; unconsciously, we can never erase the awareness of the connections that shaped our lives, and that go on shaping them. Let our rational minds, and the reflections from them housed in the dictionaries, declare that power can increase indefinitely and compel the world to obey us, if we just have enough of it. Our unconscious minds know better; or at least they know something different. Push power past its proper bounds, they mutter, and *something will happen;* something unpredictable but thorough, something frightening and unforgettable, something that changes the tone and atmosphere of the world we live in. Our definitions may overlook, or deny, the ordered, relational processes of power, but the aura of danger that surrounds its misuse remains in memory. And if we think of power as merely a property to be seized and wielded by individual whim, then any use of it may be illicit and perilous.

Such ideas work to keep the governed in their place. If we avoid power because we think it's dangerous, a progression of withdrawal begins, so that fear of power increases our distaste, and our distaste assures that we remain ignorant and withdrawn, and our ignorance makes power appear ever more dangerous. This is a process of corruption by weakness, no new thought but a continuing possibility. When it happens, it tends to reduce the power relationship to one of settled dominance and submission, through the passivity of the weak.

As for the powerful, they suffer too by being set off from the rest of us and declared to be somehow inherently different. Let the governed agree that their own experience of life will not be useful for governance, then the powerful have to grapple with the inevitable problems of ruling—that is, of coping with events in the world of action—only in terms of their own moral and mental judgments, without being able to turn to others for agreement and reassurance. This distancing elevates them out of the human world and out of touch with their fellows, but it does not cure them of bad dreams. The loss of communion between rulers and ruled opens the door to fantasy and unreal expectations for both. It falsifies the nature of the relationship between weak and powerful and lessens the capacity of society to deal with the eternal matters of getting on together and managing the physical world.

CHAPTER 7

The Political Process

I will not dispute now whether Princes are exempt from the Laws of their Country; but this I am sure, they owe subjection to the Laws of God and Nature. Grants, Promises and Oaths are Bonds that hold the Almighty, Whatever some Flatterers say to the Princes of the World.

John Locke,
Two Treatises on Government[1]

If power does operate in the real world of activity as involving a relationship between governors and governed that is more than merely domination and subordination, what is the true nature of this connection? Our earliest memories, I have been saying, retain the traces of our first interactions with the powerful adults who controlled our world. Can this be taken as a guide to power relations in general? Are they analogous to the relation that exists between parents and children? Certainly the idea that the powerful stand in the position of parents, with the weak as their children, has been around for a long time and is deservedly popular with the powerful. It's true that *maternal* power is thought to contain elements of danger and, under the label of "Momism," is regarded as embodying a greedy and crippling clutch on the young. Demanding mothers, orthodox thinking has held, turn their daughters into "old maids" and their sons into homosexuals, both of them conditions which orthodoxy deplores. Paternalism, on the other hand, has often been put forward as a model which includes not only control over, but also affectionate regard for, their subjects among "wise rulers." At the same time, it reserves to the rulers the right to know what's best for the ruled, as parents (at least, male parents) are assumed to do within the family. If the weak rebel against such benevolent authority, this model casts them in the role of willful children who have not yet acquired the knowledge of the world that brings wisdom.

It is helpful to refer once more to the experience of women as an ancient and central category of the weak in order to evaluate the idea that proper uses of power can shape themselves on the parent-child model. Many societies have classified women and children together when defining their public rights and responsibilities. In classical Rome, where the paterfamilias had the right of life and death over the children, sons were released from his dominion at a certain age, but daughters only on marriage, at which point they were handed over to the authority of another male. Husbands were not legally permitted to kill a wife, as a father was permitted to kill a child, but a wife's "improper behavior" was accepted as grounds to condone the deed (as of course it has continued to be till very recently). The correct approach to the problem of an adulterous wife was to return her to the authority of father or brother, retaining some portion of her dowry. In matters of law no woman could act for herself no matter what her wealth or position, and had to be represented not simply by an agent, but by a "guardian." Many women in Arab countries, particularly in rural regions, still live much this kind of life, under the control of male authority and cut off from any independent participation in the activities of the community. Acquaintance is restricted to close kin, and even looking at passing strangers is an offense that draws criticism.

Indeed, it was not so long ago that our own Western civilization cherished the idea of childish dependence and ignorance of the world as being the height of feminine charm. At the same time, such ignorance was felt to be both cause and result of feminine frivolity (read, triviality): women were frivolous because they knew nothing about the way the significant operations of society took place, and, reading backwards, their frivolity naturally prevented them from being allowed to take part in activities which might give them some insight into these important matters. This view has not entirely vanished. Voices can still be heard today declaring that young girls are most attractive when they appear least capable of dealing with events in the outside world. Politics, economics, the processes of technology and science —these are very generally thought of as being masculine areas. Women who enter them are still conscious that they are going to run into reactions that question not just their capabilities, but their female normality. To be a woman and an engineer, a woman and a physicist, a woman and a research scholar is still thought of as implying deviance; and even women who do both jobs superbly find it necessary to emphasize their continuing commitment to female norms. "Of course I'm not a woman's libber—I guess I should say feminist," said a brilliant pioneer woman doctor to me a couple of years ago, in total contradiction of all she had been recounting of her own career. ("Yes, you are," I said.) At the level of everyday life, capable women abound everywhere; but the ability of our culture to see them is still not great, for the definitions which hold that they are anomalies still get in the way.

Now why should it be charming for women to be inefficient—incapable of balancing checkbooks, changing tires, reading a map? The clue lies in our disposition to sanction the power of the powerful by likening it to the power of parents. Father knows best. Children need to be looked after; and if women behave like children, then they demonstrate that they have to be looked after too; and that, in turn, puts the reins of power in father's hands. We may recall the public astonishment, a few years ago, over such minor details of courtesy as those of opening doors, holding a coat, or standing up when a woman came into the room: Why, asked the media, should women refuse these polite gestures? Feminists were held to be demonstrating their abnormality by a preference for rudeness. But of course, the demonstration was simply a rejection of the idea that adult women needed looking after; i.e., that courtesy can only run one way, from male to female, because males are strong and women need help, even to open doors.

What should interest us here is not only the idea that women ought to be looked after (and grateful for it), but also the idea that men should not expect or desire it. On occasion, one would suppose, everybody feels the need to be looked after, as we used to be in those golden days of love and care that nostalgia associates with happy childhood; we all pine for them now and then, and we all, equally, tend to forget how infuriating we used to find the limitations on freedom that went with tender loving care. Dependence can be very pleasant at times; but eternal dependence, assigned as part of an inescapable sex-related picture of the self, washes away one's sense of adequacy. Not only women suffer from that; in a recent study, *Decision Making,* Irving Janis and Leon Mann record a very high incidence of what they call "defensive avoidance" among male executives faced with the need to choose one plan over another. "Man, the Reluctant Decision Maker" is the title of their first chapter, and it's clear as one reads that Reluctant Man would often be happy to have someone open the door to action for him, and bow him through. One case of reluctance is cited from an earlier work by E. Chinoy; after numerous interviews with automobile workers, Chinoy "found that almost 80 percent thought of getting out of the shop, most to go into a business of their own. But despite their frustrations, feelings of alienation, and uncertainties within the plant, very few could bring themselves to leave. Most of the men, besides having doubts about their abilities, were unwilling to give up the security of familiar routines and established relationships with coworkers for the uncertainties of a new job."[2]

None of us, that is, wants to be adult all the time. But accepting a permanent status of "child" means losing the right to be adult at any time, it means living with limits on one's activities set by Someone Else according to Someone Else's opinions. That's necessary when we are infants, sensible when we are children, but humiliating in maturity. The resentment that black men felt when they were called "boy" is well remembered. The courteous acting out of women's diminished responsibility may seem pleasanter, but the message is the same. Adult white males are assuming the mantle of "father." We are to abide by his decisions (even reluctant ones), because he is looking after us. But that isn't true. The powerful are not the parents of the weak, nor are men of women, nor whites of blacks. Their opinions about our needs and purposes are not even well informed.

So, even though our knowledge of power was learned and authenticated by the presence of parental figures who acted with and through us in our early lives and guided us to our own ability to act, this relationship is not what we want to recreate as a model for ordered rule in the adult world of action. If we do that we are sentencing most of humanity to lifelong childhood.

We had better remember that our parents were not born to power. They had to learn it just as we learned it, from their parents or other intimate figures of infancy. For all human beings the first sensation of control and controlling, the first sanction to use these capacities in an ordered way so that they evoke a response from others, comes to us in our first months of life, by way of our guardians. *This is as true for the powerful as it is for the weak.* K'ang-hsi, the emperor of China whose thoughts on the proper use of power I quoted earlier, was proud of his skill as a hunter, but he remembered that he had not acquired it independently. "Everything I know about hunting," he wrote, "was taught to me when I was a child by my guards officer A-shu-mo-erh-ken: He always fearlessly corrected my shortcomings, holding back nothing, and I will never forget him."[3] Across the world in Paris, some few decades earlier, a record of the childhood of Louis XIII was set down by a certain M. Heroard, the court doctor. Louis was a bouncy little boy who enjoyed beating his tambourine and dancing to a violin, but neither his gaiety nor his royal birth saved him from discipline. "Naughty, whipped for refusing to eat," Heroard noted. "Calming down, he asked for his dinner and dined"; or, "Went off to his room screaming at the top of his voice and was soundly whipped."[4]

When we speak of the great being born to power, then, we are using inaccurate shorthand. We are leaving out what we really know: that they were born into dependent human relationships, like all the rest of us. The figures from the past who sanctioned power when it was properly used and punished its excesses must have left memory traces in their brains too. Even the great are subject to bad dreams, which can darken the feelings they have about their own might with an edge of danger. Their advisors may assure them that the power they hold is theirs by right, that they not only may but must use it—to uphold the office of the presidency, to maintain the status of the organization they head whether it's a great nation or a far-flung empire or a sound and profitable business enterprise—but advisors, after all, are themselves removed by one step from the wielding of power. It is the ruler they counsel who must grasp the thunderbolt and risk the danger.

In earlier, more static societies, rituals evolved over the years to make this risk seem more bearable. In certain periods a king or emperor was conceived of as actually divine, personally possessed of a handhold on the supernatural. Then any actions undertaken by this sacred being would partake of the essence of the sacred itself and be unassailable. It's interesting to note that this potentially enormous power was often severely limited: sacred kings were frequently restricted from acting in certain important political areas, or sentenced to die at the end of a term of years. Functionally, that is, their "omnipotence" was kept in bounds by one device or another.

In other societies, an established religion has supported the state but has stopped short of declaring the ruler to be divine. Though it was supposed to be otherworldly, this kind of support has been worth a great deal at the practical political level, as the father of Louis XIII acknowledged when he said that Paris was worth a mass. Henry of Navarre was a pragmatist, thinking in earthly and practical terms. For devout rulers, the support of a church can offer another kind of comfort, for it will be felt to stand in the place of the parents and represent higher authority. This authority then validates the actions of the powerful in their own minds, as parents do for children.

When the church sanctifies the coronation of a ruler, it certainly mingles the power of divinity with the secular power of the state and, from the point of view of the governed, it thus sets up a double measure of authority, both sacred and profane, to stand against possible rebellion. But this is not the whole story. The existence of a spiritual establishment engages another presence with that of the ruler in the business of ruling. We shall touch later on what access to divine power may mean to the weak. Here we need only note that though popes have been kidnapped by kings, kings have been humbled by popes. The memory of such encounters must have gone to reinforce recollections in the minds of the great that they themselves were born as human children, subject to whipping and to the fearless correction of their shortcomings. This kind of reminder of their humanity, shared with the rest of the world, helps keep the great in touch with reality.

Which is not to say that all rulers take much note of such incidents when they happen to others, or even see cautionary lessons in them when they occur to these rulers themselves. Some are and remain sensitive to the dangers of power, some seem to ride this great war-horse naturally, some arrive quickly at self-righteousness. Rulers who have been confirmed in their positions will assume that they can use their capabilities at will until they run into some limit. The trouble is that without some guidelines, who knows where limits lie? In the end they will finally be set, one way or other, by failure: in foreign dealings, in efficient administration at home, in surmounting the effects of natural disasters; but before that happens the powerful may well push compulsion and domination to excess. The human race has experienced such excess since time immemorial and remembered it in myths and legends. For the Greeks, the great god Saturn who ate his children stood symbolically for the disorder of excessive use of power, and when his son Zeus cunningly managed to survive and kill him, the action was seen as just and laudable.

Human fathers do not eat their children, but they have certainly beaten them, starved them, misused them for their own ends, and exposed them to die. Within the larger society, these family practices have been paralleled by efforts to deprive the weak of their claims on humanity. The old and valuable idea of a social contract, which establishes a rule of law among individuals, classes, estates, and castes, should not be taken to be self-enforcing, or it will offer only a shaky refuge. The more usual and accepted is the belief that power is an attribute belonging to a ruler or to a ruling class, the less solid will be any contract that this class will make with the rest of us. If we believe that power properly belongs to the powerful, we are giving them more than power: we are giving them the right to use it as they see fit, not just to direct events but to dominate the rest of us.

Here in the United States we have had some illuminating experience of the uses of political power in recent years. We have been living through a period of very rapid political change, and that always invites the testing of old rules for doing things and the invention of new expedients. Sometimes, when change is welcome, old methods are simply given new names, and continued in use. When change is widely disliked (and unless one sees or feels a need to change things, one will dislike it), old labels are employed to disguise new techniques. Any simple apparatus that proves handy can be developed, imitated, and used as a resort in new or problematic situations, until change in degree brings about change in quality. These things have been happening. Notably, the terms in office of Lyndon Johnson and Richard Nixon offer clear and still-familiar examples of presidential power used to excess. These two were very different men, but the actions of both ran beyond the accepted limit of power, and when they did, the human connections with those they governed became severely strained and the definitions and explanations of their deeds and policies came into doubt.

It's easy to attack Johnson and Nixon for succumbing to arrogance and insolence; and it's also easy to attack those they governed for sloth and complacence in the face of arrogance. That won't tell us much. I would rather consider, as objectively as possible, what it was that happened to our rulers not only in their political relations with the ruled but also, so far as we can tell from their words and actions, inside their own heads during the process in which they moved out of contact with the rest of us. The answer is instructive. Whether or not they suffered from bad dreams, the edge between fantasy and reality was blurred for them, as it is among children whose dream figures follow them into the waking state.

In the beginning Lyndon Johnson greatly enjoyed the exercise of presidential power. Of course he had been a master of personal political power in the Senate, but though his feats there were legendary, they were not played out on a wide stage. Now his mastery was visible to all. He had about a year's clear run from his accession to power after John Kennedy's assassination in November 1963 to the landslide election over Goldwater in 1964. During that time he seemed able to do nothing wrong. Certainly Kennedy's close advisors found Johnson unattractive, but even so, many of them stayed on to work for him, and their strictures were not much listened to until later, until *after* Johnson had already begun to get into trouble by continuing and amplifying Kennedy's more tentative but nonetheless evident policy of involvement in Vietnam. At the time of Kennedy's death, his domestic programs were stalled in Congress and it was Johnson's pride to get them moving again and see them through, which he did in short order and with no little fanfare. In the spring and summer of 1964 the irresistible energy with which he "jaw-boned" his opponents in Congress and in industry in order to complete the reforms of a generation of Democratic planning made him an object of admiring awe among his fellow citizens.

Things began to go wrong in the spring of 1965. The first notes of disaffection over Vietnam were heard. Programs of social change had gone far enough to exasperate those who didn't like them, but not far enough to satisfy those who supported them as opening moves toward "the Great Society." It was the period of the march on Selma, of the first student demonstrations and teach-ins opposing the use of American troops in Vietnam, and Arthur Schlesinger published a book on the Kennedy administration which became a ground-plan for the raising of a mythic Camelot. For Johnson, the glory days were passing.

He minded very much indeed, minded personally. His feelings were terribly hurt.

Now Johnson had run into opposition plenty of times before, both at home in Texas and in his old briar patch in the Senate. He had never liked it, but he had dealt with it cannily. This time something went wrong. He could not reach his opponents. He talked, but they didn't seem to hear him. There was a gap here—it came to be widely known as the credibility gap—and in some mysterious fashion this distancing of his hearers damped out his seductive, his almost hypnotic, powers of persuasion. It is frightening to find that methods which used to work don't work any more. It is frightening to feel that people are withdrawing from you and becoming inaccessible. So, that summer of 1965, Johnson tried something new, a gambit that had worked brilliantly in Kennedy's time. He planned a literary gala and invited those nonlistening intellectuals to the White House. At least he could thus get them within earshot and eyeshot and perhaps be able to talk to them as successfully as he had talked to so many recalcitrant politicians.

It was disastrous. Robert Lowell didn't come at all. Dwight Macdonald came and read a statement opposing Johnson's Vietnam operations.

The president was furious. The president's people denounced Macdonald's manners bitterly. The party that didn't come off symbolized and, indeed, intensified the rift that was developing between stubborn leader and doubtful followers; and Johnson formed an opinion, hardened during the remainder of his years in office, that there was an Intellectual Establishment, which existed as a monolithic structure and was unalterably his enemy. It lay, he was sure, beyond reach and reason, and it was working without rest for his downfall. He appeared to believe that its directives emanated from a center of illegitimate power located at Harvard University, and one sometimes had the feeling that he saw this Satanic Council and its minions in rather the way that devout Nazis envisaged the Elders of Zion and theirs. He hated them and, worse than that, he feared them.

He feared them because nothing he did produced an effect on them and their views. That, of course, is what happens when we create bogeymen for ourselves and attribute to them the reasons for our failures. Since they are not, in fact, the sources of failure, neither attacking them nor appeasing them wins back our success. All this kind of paranoid fear does is justify our hatred for our opponents. And Johnson did indeed have opponents. Some of them had quite sensible ideas about what might be done to prevent the disaster that Johnson was heading for. But since he hated them and, his fear told him, was justified in hating them, he did not listen to what they said. He cut himself off from those whose experience offered them information that might have been valuable to him, and trusted his own might and his own authority. As a result of this assumption that the presidency was a tool that he could use at will—an assumption that he had never made about the power he had wielded in the Senate—the reversal in his standing with the country was as dramatic as any in myth or legend. The image of "Big Daddy" became that of the ogre eating his young.

The story of Nixon's catastrophic last years in office is so recent that there is little need to recount the details. They indicate that a paranoia more devastating and further developed than Johnson's befogged his administration. From the recorded talk among themselves, it seems that Nixon and his advisors had lost any sense of a shared reality with those who had elected him, of a common ground of experience on which ruler and ruled could react as fellow human beings. Every communication from the White House was prepared as a "scenario," and in the preparation there was so little regard for the distinction between fact and fiction that one really comes to doubt that Nixon and his friends thought there *was* any difference. Not only were they busy creating fantasies, they committed themselves to maintaining them by acting as if they believed in them. That is a very difficult thing to do, especially under pressure, without starting in actuality to believe what one is acting out, to turn deception into self-deception. In spite of the multifarious testimony of the actors (or perhaps because of it), it is hard to guess how much Nixon and Company thought was true of the presentation they made to the country about the Watergate scandal and how much they consciously knew was false. Probably perceptions differed among them. What is certain is that they never tried to analyze the situation coldly—as hardheaded decision-makers are supposed to do in our culture—and judge when or whether to cut their losses. Fantastication continued to the end.

Nixon always found it necessary to support his use of power by some such scaffolding of rationalization, though it can never have gone so far before. One suspects that he needed it to justify his acts in his own mind and thereby protect himself against the dangers of using power, because he could not distinguish between ordered use and misuse. This points to the absence of a sense of connection with the people who elected him, as if they were too shadowy for their votes to satisfy his need for a feeling of legitimacy. In his last years in office his fears seemed to be growing to the point where he took little pleasure in power or in his once considerable abilities for manipulative politics. His actions became more and more defensive in spirit even as they became more aggressive in performance, as if he were moving to punish his enemies before they destroyed the presidency or undermined the security of the nation, as these institutions were understood in the Nixon administration.

We can follow this impulse most easily if we revert to the counsel of Machiavelli on effective governance. Machiavelli had learned his realism in the service of Florence as that sophisticated but small city-state tried to maintain its autonomy in dealings with nations of much greater size and power. His thoughts about power were certainly conditioned by the fact that in his negotiations with such monarchs as the king of France or the Holy Roman Emperor, he was always leading from weakness. It made him, so to speak, a functional immoralist. Only in very special circumstances, he felt, where corruption was absent from political life—and he had never encountered them—could a ruler govern well by the rules of ordinary morality, such as those that bound a private citizen. Under usual corrupt conditions a prince was justified in taking extraordinary measures to maintain his rule, if "necessity" demanded it (as it had unfortunately done ever since the fall of the Roman Republic).

I think what we see in Nixon's case is a frantic search for just such a necessity, one that would authorize extraordinary (that is, unconstitutional) actions. Looking at the results, it seems evident that the biggest believer in the "necessity (that) knows no law" was Nixon himself. But the existence of such a necessity has to be demonstrated plausibly enough to convince the public, that other member of the power relationship, and this Nixon could not manage to do. The "reasons of state" that forced him to violate accepted morality had a curiously cardboard air about them.

Johnson too had suffered from bogeymen who could not believe that his purposes were good and his actions justified, and therefore attacked his policies unwarrantedly. The bogeymen that Nixon set up as figures who were undermining national security were even less controllable than Johnson's. Where Johnson argued and wasn't heard, Nixon presented his scenarios of virtue necessarily breaking a few laws in the service of public morality, and the situation deteriorated still further. Necessity was getting out of hand. When the Washington *Post* printed reports on Watergate, Nixon and Company responded as if the newspaper commanded a body of armed men laying siege to the White House gates. When one lone citizen with a placard attacking the administration paraded himself in Lafayette Park, the president's men reacted as if he had been in possession of a laser beam directed at the Oval Office. Magic was edging into the picture, as it does in nightmare. Daniel Ellsberg and the Berrigan brothers were treated as if they were sorcerers working witchcraft. Clark Clifford, respected advisor to presidents for decades, had his telephone tapped because the White House learned that he was *writing an article* opposing Nixon's policies! What writer, what editor, would dare imagine that such terrifying power could be attributed to a few pages of prose?

Let us note how the idea of power as an attribute of persons contributes to this remarkable overreaction. Capabilities are being ascribed to Nixon's opponents that they simply could not have possessed: one can only say *magic* capabilities. Let us suppose, for the sake of argument, that the White House scenario was factual and that Daniel Ellsberg was really a Soviet agent. Suppose he had both intended to and succeeded in relaying the Pentagon Papers to the Russian Embassy. How could the Russians' knowledge of their contents have imperiled a duly elected American government, in the real world? Logically, rationally, it is very hard to believe that Nixon and his entourage could have taken the possibility seriously. The papers contained no sensitive current military information, and the Russians' political views of

Nixon's standing with the country were not likely to be affected by them either. This being so, why did the White House undertake the risky and possibly incriminating effort to discredit Ellsberg, using any means, legal or illegal? Why court danger? One ends by feeling that the inability to tell truth from fantasy, or to estimate what an opponent was likely to do because no shared reality was felt to exist with him, had combined to persuade the Nixon White House that *anything* was possible. If anything is possible, well then, Ellsberg might have supernatural powers; at least, behavior as practiced in the White House is explicable only on such grounds. Nixon had ended by believing in the supernatural force of the necessity that he had made up himself.

There is another bit of evidence that the Nixon team was losing its capacity to judge how life in the real world is carried on, what works and what doesn't, and within what limits. That is the interesting use of the word "inoperative" by Press Secretary Ron Ziegler. He seems to have meant by it that events followed each other in a particular causal pattern only as long as the explanation embodying these causes was stated by the White House to be in force; but that this pattern of causality could be ended whenever the White House decided to do so. Then another, quite different, logic of events would be substituted for it. It is rather as if reality were conceived of as a computer which could be programmed and reprogrammed at will.

And that idea, I think, did enter Nixon's mind, or those of his advisors. It is the other side of paranoia, the megalomaniac certainty that one can intervene in the workings of reality simply by what one says, and compel them to obedience without having to undertake the lengthy, difficult processes of action and negotiation, managing operations, following up on directives, bulldogging details—all the day-to-day actions, which may in the end produce results, and which of course may not. How much easier to wish, rub a ring or a lamp, mutter a spell! Freud called this fallacy "the omnipotence of thought." It is the way our minds operate in dreams, and children find it comforting, but have to grow out of it as they grow up.

Three years before Nixon's press secretary came up with the word "inoperative," George Reedy, who had been Johnson's press secretary, wrote about the tendency of the powerful to lose touch with ordinary reality in his book, *The Twilight of the Presidency*. Reedy is concerned here with both sides of the relationship, with the ruler enmeshed in fantasy, and also with those around him whose failure to oppose his fancies allows him to perceive them as realistically possible:

The concept of the overburdened president represents one of the invidious forces which serve to separate the chief executive from the real universe of living, breathing, troubled human beings. It is the basis for encouraging his most outrageous expressions, for pampering his most childish tantrums, for fostering his most arrogant actions. More than anything else, it serves to create an environment in which no man can live for any considerable length of time and retain his psychological balance.

I have some experience [he says later] with the reaction of human beings to irrational behavior, and it is clear to me that where presidents are concerned, the tolerance level for irrationality extends almost to the point of gibbering idiocy or delusions of identity. To put it more simply, no one is going to act to interfere with the presidential exercise of authority unless the president drools in public or announces on television that he is Alexander the Great. . . . This reluctance, of course, does not spring merely from awe of high office or fear of retaliation. At bottom, it is a reflection of the ultimate nature of the presidential office—an environment in which for all practical purposes the standards of normal conduct are set by the president himself. To those immediately around him, he is the one who determines what is rational and what is irrational, and the public reaction to whatever he does is not immediate unless it brings on catastrophe.[5]

The failure of the president's advisors to advise the president that his actions are beginning to carry him off the map of normality is the issue here. Reedy's analysis touches a vital point when he remarks that it is neither fear nor awe that motivates the advisors' hesitance, though both may indeed be felt. The real reason for the default is that the standard of proper behavior is left up to the president, that the ruler is held to be, *sui generis,* an actor whose actions can only be judged by himself. The relationship between the president and his men is thus being abdicated at both ends. And the reason is, to return to our definitions once more, that power is not being seen as a relationship but as an attribute of the powerful. Allow to rulers that special superhuman quality, and you set in motion the "invidious forces" that Reedy describes, "which serve to separate the chief executive from the real universe of living, breathing, troubled human beings."

Yet Johnson and Nixon both fell from power in the end. How did that come about? Was it because a larger, less structured relationship than that between president and advisors was not abdicated? I think so. In both cases, the true relationship between rulers and ruled somehow took hold. Johnson's good political hearing warned him that running for another term would involve him in disastrous humiliation. Nixon, much more obtuse, waited until his impeachment was a foregone conclusion. But both removed themselves, more or less voluntarily if sullenly, from a field of action in which defeat was certain.

We should take heart from this—though not too much. Plenty of far madder rulers have held on to power, both in our time and in the past, and used it more outrageously. From chronicles of the tsars and their successors in the Kremlin, of Roman emperors, Spanish Hapsburgs, Bavarian Wittelsbachs, Sicilian Bourbons, Baltic barons, and South American dictators, to name just a few, we know that fantastication is an occupational disease of autarchy. But we do have two examples here, from American history of the immediate past, in which power that was becoming illegitimate was removed, without bloodshed or revolution, from the grip of those who wielded it. It is worth looking at the background of these events as examples of what can happen to the powerful when those who are governed withdraw their sanction—consciously or unconsciously—from the governments that claim authority over them.

CHAPTER 8

The View from Below

A cynic will say that the land law of the Middle Ages came down to something very simple. In effect, a lord said to his men: If you do not render me rents and services, I shall punish you with force of arms to the utmost extent of my power. But men did not in fact speak of the distribution of wealth in this way, and there is no sense in saying that they were hypocrites. History and anthropology show that men describe their social institutions not in realistic terms but in mythologies, and what is more, the mythologies of a stable and successful society are not those which set men against one another but those which help them work together with good will.

George C. Homans,
English Villagers of the Thirteenth Century[1]

T he effect on the political process of the actions and misapprehensions of the powerful is easy enough to follow, because that is the familiar approach. Let us now try to assess the dynamics of the process from the other side. One thing is obvious: the reality of domination and the experience of subordination. In the bargain between rulers and ruled, the threat of punishment is overtly recognized by both members, and this awareness is reinforced regularly by examples. Now as in the thirteenth century, one member of the power-dependence relationship can indeed compel the weaker partner to obey: force of arms will be used against a sullen peasantry, bodies of armed men will contend with each other, battles will be won or lost, and some battles are true turning points in the course of history.

But whatever the overt mythology, other processes operate in our lives to maintain a stable and successful society, or even to let a shaky one cling to existence. It is not always necessary to proceed by confrontation. One party to a disagreement doesn't have to knock the other down before they can work together. Compromise keeps programs moving along by a sequence of giving and getting. Realistic decisions are not synonymous with the ukase of a single preeminent decision-maker but are based on the views and knowledge of many. Cooperation toward joint ends is not merely a mask for hidden rivalry; things get done that way.

Things get done that way in public as well as in private. Battles are won and lost, yes, but *wars* are settled by negotiations and treaties if they are really settled and not simply allowed to drag on from one adventure in confrontation to the next. Bodies of armed men can be kept in being as long as a feudal lord or an industrial state can afford to do so, and while they exist they can be charged to compel obedience from the inhabitants of the area they occupy. Even so, rulers discover after a while that the troops have begun to fraternize with the natives. Everyday habits undermine feudal or patriotic loyalties, and the line of confrontation blurs in dangerous fashion. Whether the troops simply listen to the girls they take to bed or have their throats cut by them or their kin, confusion sets in and blurs a once clear-cut adversary situation. No one knows exactly what's going on, pacified areas are suddenly blotched with blood, the conquered begin to add secret violence to public obedience, and confrontation ceases to be effective because no one knows quite whom to confront on what issue. Even history is puzzled. If, on the whole, the triumphant invaders come out on top, their clerks will write an account of a successful campaign to extend the boundaries of the empire. If, on the whole, they are first thrashed and then the remnants are absorbed, local historians will record a dastardly invasion of the motherland, and how it was repulsed. If disaster is general, overtaking both sides, we will have legends of heroes and celebrations of individual prowess which serve to comfort hurt pride; and all the time compromise and collaboration are at work to get the survivors through the business of daily life.

These common, unheroic processes form the greatest part of experience for every one of us including the powerful, who do not, after all, live in a state of eternal ceremony. Domination and subordination are facts of life, and when they are used "to the utmost extent of power," they form the limits of the social situation. Even well inside these limits, domestic tyrants exist, laying down the law to wives and progeny and venting in woman's place the frustration suffered in man's world, where bosses are hated and foremen cursed ineffectively. Groups of unhappy human beings clot together in fear and contempt for other human groups, scream slogans and throw bricks or bombs because of a difference in skin color or religion or language. Within institutions like jails and mental hospitals and the Marine Corps can be found swamps of everyday terrors. I do not mean to suggest, therefore, that a definition of power as the ability to compel others to obedience is inaccurate, or that in confrontation the dominant will not prevail if they behave sensibly and do not overlook the demands of reality; only that this definition is *insufficient*. There are other kinds of power that operate in other ways.

It was this kind of alternative power that worked to bring Johnson and Nixon down. Because it came from below, "arising from many parts of society," its effects are less easy to follow and its causes less easy to isolate. Nonetheless, rulers themselves can become uneasily aware of its presence, and both Johnson and Nixon (as we have seen) did indeed feel threatened by an opposition they could not clearly define. The bogeymen they set up represent their attempts to identify the source of the menace.

These efforts were not very convincing. How can we take seriously the idea that Macdonald and Lowell, a literary critic and a poet, could actually threaten the entrenched authority of the White House? Or that Nixon's landslide election could be abrogated by a rather disorganized propaganda campaign directed by Ellsberg and the Berrigans? Or by the reasoned opinions of Clark Clifford, an elder statesman long out of office, expressed in a magazine with a minuscule circulation compared to the audience open to a president via the mass media? It seems ridiculous, and certainly a disaffected intelligentsia has been ignored successfully by many a ruler. Yet the reactions of these two presidents leave no doubt that they were not just exasperated by such opposition, but felt it as a true menace. However inconsequent their attempts to name their opponents and analyze their motives, the endeavors themselves indicate that they sensed the existence of some kind of power abroad in the world that they could not control by the usual rules.

If we go by the dictionary definitions of power, this is very odd behavior. One feels rather like Dr. Freud contemplating the enigma of women: What do the powerful *want?* Theoretically they have everything on their side. If they can compel the governed to obedience, why don't they do so? Why do they hesitate? Above all, what are they afraid of? How do the weak threaten their masters?

There are two possible ways to answer. If we accept the world-model of power as being merely a matter of dominance and submission, the answer has to be that the powerful are crazy. They can have nothing real to fear from an external situation that they already control. The threats that disturb them must come from the interior world and represent emotions of doubt or guilt that are projected out onto lay figures which have no actual counterparts. Now, there is something to this. Those who make decisions for others can seldom be entirely sure that they are right in what they do, especially if the rules and guidelines on which their decisions have been based are losing accuracy or cogency. When decision-makers have grown distant from the real desires and needs of those they rule, it will be hard for them to find substitutes for the standard procedures, and their judgments may well become inappropriate, even irrelevant. Events will not follow predictions, self-doubt will increase with the possibility of losing control, and this the powerful are right to fear. But as long as they believe that ruling is their business and no one else's, they find it hard to see what's going wrong. A difference of opinion is taken to be deliberate opposition incited by cunning adversaries; and if they can't at once identify these enemies, they feel a need to invent some sort of hostile conspiracy.

This kind of paranoid reasoning certainly occurs; but it can't be the whole story. If the powerful fear the governed only because of their own emotional flaws, governance becomes a matter of psychology, lying outside the reach of social control or comprehension. In that case Lord Acton was too moderate. Power, it would seem, tends not only to corrupt, but to madden. Fortunately this doesn't appear to jibe with historical reality. Not all powerful rulers go off their heads. And even those who nourish neurotic fears and set up unconvincing bogeymen conspirators may do so because they have sensed a real threat that exists in the world of actuality, and then assigned it an erroneous cause. The second possible answer to the question "What do the powerful want?" allows that there was some justification for the worries that plagued Johnson and Nixon, that the governed really do possess the ability to intervene in the political process.

So let us ask again what the powerful want from the weak. It can't be the mere confirmation of their authority. They know they possess that, to begin with. This, then, is where the *legitimacy* of authority enters the picture as an insistent need. What the powerful want is assurance that their power is held rightfully, within a relationship which sanctions its use and validates the right of these rulers to rule. What the powerful need is the consent of the governed to their actions as proper, acceptable, free of blame; and this consent can be granted only *by the governed,* the other member of the power relationship. Force of arms and physical might cannot exact this grant. Though they can compel obedience, it is not willing, committed obedience. The assurance that any existing rule is ordered rule, any particular dominance proper dominance, can only be given freely as part of a common bargain, in exchange for something else. In personal situations, the weaker member will give up some initiative in return for reciprocal advantages— they may be emotional, or financial, or social (and they may of course be overvalued)—but they will be accepted as sufficient, and the acceptance will sustain the relationship. In politics, the governed consent to be ruled in return for an ordered, competent use of power that supplies them with a reasonably safe and stable environment, and this consent frees rulers to act. That is the purpose and function of the political process, the bargain between rulers and ruled by which society manages itself.

What we are looking at is something very different from confrontation: not its opposite so much as its consequence, the resolution of confrontation that conciliates conflicting purposes in the service of a larger community. Dictionaries may speak of armed force and compulsion, but when such things enter the political process they are not efficient. If the "utmost extent of power" must be used in everyday matters, it functions as overkill. When, on the other hand, rulers can assume that their actions will be seen as proper, as legitimate, their management of affairs is made easy. This is the simple, pragmatic reward they gain from the validation of their power.

At the same time the psychological burden of rule is eased. The consent of the governed assures the powerful that they have not overstepped the limits of the relationship in which their authority can be properly employed, that their programs and projects are justified, and that if bad dreams come, they can dismiss them with the positive statement, "Not guilty." The assurance of legitimacy shields the powerful from the erosive suspicion that they may be doing wrong without knowing it, undertaking action on the basis of individual judgment that is not supported by the human environment. Just as the bane of the weak is to sink into hopeless despair and passivity, so the bane of the powerful is to act with impulsive unreason and find themselves unable to stop. Both reactions weaken and hinder the political process. The hubris of rulers moves them inexorably past the limits where the validation of their power can protect them from its unpredictable and perilous consequences. *Something will happen*—unforeseeable, uncontrollable.

And it does. Something happened to Nixon and to Johnson, a confrontation with events that could not be resolved by the use of armed men, with antagonists who could not be compelled to obey. At first the problem appeared to be a disagreement over policy, but it went deeper than that. Arguments over policies can be fruitful—if there is still basic agreement on the meaning and the purpose of the policy; but the constituents of the men in power evinced a queer refusal to accept the definitions and explanations offered by their governors. Plans and projects began to go wrong, as if a loss of control over the external world were taking place. True, the opposition was fragmented and prone to self-contradiction. In ordinary times that should have made it easy to handle—or to ignore. Now it began to seem as if the model of reality which these presidents were offering the electorate was being rejected, their methods condemned out of hand. Something was happening: the bargain between rulers and ruled was dissolving.

This bargain (we can call it the social contract if we don't let the term persuade us that the arrangement is rigid and conscious) has various terms, and it functions at several levels. In its simplest form it provides that the governed undertake to leave the administration of the state in the hands of the great and to abide by the laws they establish. In return, the governors agree to see that the network of social interactions works in an orderly way, to ensure the public safety, and to deal with unexpected events at home and abroad in competent fashion. However, these obligations, vital as they are, make up only the conscious top layer of the relationship. They can be articulated clearly, written into the Constitution; but there are less accessible levels where the giving and the getting are harder to formulate. Thus, part of the obligation of the powerful is to be adequately efficient about their job, to see (let us say) that the trains run on time and the mail gets through and the banks don't close and the streets are reasonably safe. But they must be *efficient about the right things,* about matters that are important to the governed. That is, they require the consent of the governed not just to their rule, but to their definitions and priorities for action.

The student revolt of the sixties offers a prime example, with its demands for "relevance" in the curriculum. The academic establishment found this both painful and silly, and it responded inadequately because it did not take the demands seriously. In the seventies, it seems on the surface as if the Establishment had been right; but is higher education today any more relevant to adult life than it was ten or twelve years ago? Not much; and suffering institutions of learning are now facing declining enrollments and climbing costs. More important, a sense of fissure between education and adult life now reaches down into secondary education and is dropping to even younger pupils. Something is happening. An accepted relationship is ceasing to hold. As George Homans noted in the case of medieval land law, social institutions do not grow out of a shallow top layer of cognitive agreements for specific mutual benefits between powerful and weak. They are shaped and nourished by the mythology of a particular society and that mythology is the cultural and psychological expression of *community*—of the connection that binds rulers and ruled together. Social approval, the consent of the governed, is an affirmation of community.

Doubts about the value of the power relationship can arise at any level: over defined policy, over the competence of rulers to do their agreed-on work of governing adequately, over the commitment to the common relationship by those in command. In these doubts begins the exercise by the weak of the powers that are theirs, and consequently the trouble of the powerful begins there too. It is not easy to describe the workings of these powers, for the reactions of the governed are confused and diverse. They have had little experience in analyzing events and sorting out the causes of their distress: this is normally the job of those in charge. The grumblings of the weak are called forth by everyday experience, and they certainly begin by being incoherent, directed toward a number of apparently unrelated and superficial annoyances. To the powerful, these seem to have nothing to do with the matter at hand, or else to be so vague (the "relevance" of education to life) as to defy definition.

"What is your problem?" the powerful ask the weak once they decide that this dissatisfaction can no longer be ignored or laughed off. "Tell us what is wrong, and we will try to do something about it."

But for the weak the only honest answer may well be "Everything is wrong!" How can they evaluate the problems that bad times bring down on them? It will be bad times that set them grumbling as they strain the accepted bargained-out power relationship, but bad times put stress on established ways of doing things at many points. For some of the ruled, the problem may be prices—of food, or rent, or money to pay the mortgage or keep a business running; for some it will be unemployment; for those who begin to philosophize articulately it may be oppression and the need to rebel; for some, turning away from the good old ways of the past; for some, rampant materialism and the loss of spiritual purpose.

"Oh well," say the powerful to these confused and contradictory expressions of discomfort, "if you can't tell us what the trouble is, how can we do anything about it? Besides, if you can't state it clearly, it really can't be so bad."

Not being able to state things clearly is a double problem. What the weak don't have, in the first place, is information about the way the established structure operates. Presidents and generals and secretaries of state "see the cables," not private citizens; deans and professors formulate educational policy and vet the curriculum, not the students. In order to challenge the structure of power without making ridiculous blunders, the weak need information that they're not privy to. But they need more than that: they need the ability both to follow the reasoning of the powerful based on this information, and *then to disallow its force.* To develop these abilities without being coopted by the existing power structure is not easy; and in fact, many a power structure revives itself by absorbing and accepting the services of those who rise from the ranks of the governed and bring with them some unanswered questions and critical suggestions. Indeed, we can see this kind of interaction within the power relationship as a test case of its vitality. If the powerful are willing to listen to emissaries from the governed, the bargain between the partners is probably functioning adequately well. In the same way, if generalized grumbling can be heard and factored into governance, the legitimacy of rule is being demonstrated. It's when the old rules don't work that trouble begins.

What happens, as we've seen, is not just disagreement over policy, but the inability to resolve the conflict. The process of political interaction grinds to a halt as the governed reject the remedies offered them. The powerful can dismiss their grumblings and demonstrations for a while, but sooner or later a realization that things are out of hand will surface. If new methods can be devised and if they are effective, that's fine, but we are now positing a situation in which they aren't. Then the long association of the powerful with orthodox thinking leaves them facing a blank wall. They can neither act productively nor explain why they can't. It's baffling, it's exasperating, to know that one holds power, and yet to find that it doesn't produce the expected results. Some mysterious force seems to be intervening between one's intentions and one's goals.

Some mysterious force. What is this but another irruption of the supernatural into the calculations of rulers? But this time it is negative magic that
counters and undermines the positive assurance granted by the idea of a
divine right to rule. It offers an explanation for what has gone wrong, but
a very unsettling one. For if one knows that one possesses the attribute of
power and yet one cannot prevail, then clearly Something more powerful still
is taking a hand. What can it be? If one stands at the pinnacle of heaped-up
political authority, elected by a landslide vote to the highest office of the land
—and that is where Johnson and Nixon both stood—it is hard to believe that
the opposition forces, maintaining a totally unforeseen conflict in a state of
crisis, can be merely human. Somewhere in the back of the mind stirs a
suspicion that this antipower must be occult: it is bad luck, it is Destiny. Fate
and Fate alone—Machiavelli's Fortuna—can explain the queer bewitchment
that confounds action.

Of course it isn't the occult power of Destiny that is obstructing the
powerful in such a situation, it is the slow unconscious beginning of the social
process through which the weak withdraw their consent to the governance
of society by those whose actions are leading, through difficulties and defeats,
toward disaster. The weak can't initiate alternative action themselves, there
is no apparatus of rule to which they have access, but they can refuse to
participate in doomed action, or to add their imaginative supplement to the
ongoing process of coping with events. Where once they agreed enthusiasti-
cally, they can simply be silent. They may not be able to formulate realistic
goals and practical techniques for achieving them, but they can erode the
virtue of the goals and techniques set up by the powerful. They can withdraw
their attention, they can concentrate on other areas of interest and, finally,
they can start listening to other prophets who offer other analyses of world
order, new myths, and different rewards. In such fashion they indicate at
many levels how the sense of connection within a community has been
weakened. Then the powerful find themselves stranded in a world where the
old tried-and-true causality, linked to a now-vanished community, has
stopped functioning as a useful predictor. No one is listening; and as for what
people say, the powerful can't understand it. That is when they learn that
the old relationship between rulers and ruled has ended. Fate has veiled her
face.

Pause for a moment. Why do we say "her face"? Why in Western
mythology is Fate given feminine gender? This is not an irrelevant question,
for the mythic image of Fate, or Fortuna, symbolizes the uncontrollable,
unpredictable force of events in the external world against which even heroes
contend in vain. The Greeks saw her in triplicate, three spinster sisters,
Clotho, Lachesis, and Atropos, who spun the thread of life, twisted it together, and cut it off when its end was due. The Norns of Norse mythology

were female, and we should not forget the Sybils in whose prophetic books the future was written, or the Sphinx and her riddles, or the witches who greeted Macbeth with the deadly future title of king.

For our tradition (and the norms of tradition are formed on the basis of male experience) to allot to a female figure the ability to frustrate ambition and bring down reasoned plans reveals some unexpected psychic structures hidden behind our ordinary patterns of thought. They are formulations that can't be ignored in a study of the dynamics of the power-process, for they indicate deep unconscious assumptions in the minds of the powerful and, by extension, in the minds of the rest of us who accept our traditional social myths, as most of us do. In our myths it seems that the disturbing awareness of things going wrong, no one knows quite how or why, which develops as communal ties diminish, is ascribed not just to a supernatural figure, but to one of feminine gender. I wrote in an earlier book of "the myth of female power," which is the cause of a good deal of masculine concern about women's demands for equality, and which also operates to keep women in their traditional stance of submission because it presents them with an ascribed and mythic aura of authority, though there is little to support it in the real, nonmythic world. Here is an instance of how old and deep is the myth, and of the advantages that keep it alive. Disturbance, uncertainty, resentment that rise from external circumstances are "explained" by projecting them onto a causative image. The image is given the gender of "the other sex"—enigmatic and incomprehensible because she is "different."

Of course she is made different by social definition, the gender difference being so ancient and obvious that it comes to hand almost automatically. The power ascribed to her is made over as the reverse of the weakness felt by the powerful, which is unacceptable in their conscious thought, for how dare the powerful risk being weak? But what the image symbolizes is not just feminine opposition, but the underground, unconscious movement of withdrawal by the mass of the governed, the active consequence of growing alienation among the weak who can no longer feel a trustworthy sense of connection with their rulers.

As with so many symbols, the femaleness of Fate flows from more than one source. The myth of female power takes us back to the earliest stage of life when every child was indeed dependent on an infinitely more powerful adult who was almost certainly of female sex: mother, nurse, or other surrogate mother. It was she who sanctioned or disapproved the use of growing abilities and in her disapproval began frustration and conscious helplessness. Another element in the picture is the fickleness of Fate, which matches the fickleness that is held to be characteristic of women. But this is just another name for the unpredictability of those who are assumed to be different: women are not supposed to behave the way men do; minorities have their incomprehensible ways and their odd fashions of expressing themselves. Consequently, the way these people behave is inexplicable. In fact, fickleness is natural to those who are not in charge. If they cannot plan their own lives, as the great bulk of the governed can't, the only opportunity for some kind of control is to accept or reject the plans of others; but one does that for reasons quite different from the reasons for which the planners laid out their projects.

In the simplest terms, then, Fate represents the rejection of the plans of the powerful by the weak. To see the embodiment of this rejection as female points again to the central position among the weak which is held by women, who have been traditionally the creatures furthest removed from the ability to act effectively in the external world. There is another underlay of magic here too. If the power loose in the world that disrupts the regular order of things is *female,* then the old order of things has indeed been shaken. There is an eerie quality to the reversal of expected sex hierarchy that reinforces the occult nature of the frustrating opposition to one's desires.

This sense of disturbance in the world operates, in our time, below the level of conscious expression. But I think we can find, in the recent history that I've been reviewing, examples of behavioral response by the powerful that indicate its presence. Johnson, who possessed great intuitive judgment of the political process, was finally able to perceive that he was up against a "Fate" that could not be withstood. He withdrew from the presidential contest of 1968, not with much grace, it's true, but in time to save his face. Nixon fought. The question of why he made this choice will certainly be a battlefield for psycho-historians. My own view, for what it's worth, is that he was so sensitive to disapproval that he had learned to muffle his sensitivities entirely and this left him unable to assess the public judgment of his actions. However that may be, the reasons for his insistence on "fighting Fate" are not germane to my concern here, which is what he did and was constrained to do after the decision was made. I see it, in short, as a case history of the misuse of power arising from the inability to understand it as a relationship. It allows us to trace the way in which the loss of legitimacy can lead to the loss of actual power.

Nixon's reaction to his "fateful" loss of plausibility was a rigid refusal to admit what was happening. He denied that his repudiation had any significance by declaring that his critics were only a handful of irresponsible "radic-libs." Psychoanalysts call that kind of denial neurotic, but it can also be seen as a magic rejection of the world and an effort to create an alternate reality, if we want to use the language of dream. That is, he was matching his personal drive to power against the "wrongness" of the world around, interior reality against exterior. As the opposition became so large that it was realistically impossible to discredit all its members, he began to act out a denial of their existence, flying off to meet with other heads of state while Congress was already setting in motion the machinery for impeachment. He was acting *as if* the "bad dream" of his repudiation by the public could be ignored by this King of the Universe.

The fact that Nixon could not perceive or use or desire the support of the other member of the power relationship shows up most clearly in this climactic rejection of the value and even the existence of the governed. But we can trace it earlier in the reaction of his administration to the enormous election victory that returned him to office in 1972. One would suppose that a landslide triumph would be taken (to be tautologous) as a vote of confidence in the way things had been going. But Nixon greeted his reelection by soliciting the resignations of his cabinet and other high officials and let it be known that the executive branch of the government was to be reorganized into a much tighter and more hierarchical structure. Access to the president was to be even rarer than before and authority to be even more centralized: having stood off an attack by hostile Indians, the frontiersmen did not harness up their wagons and set their faces forward; they tightened the circle even more defensively.

In other words, the assurance of continued office and authority did not make this president more comfortable, nor did it suggest that if the public trusted him to govern, he might reciprocate by trusting them. On the contrary, the confirmation of his power triggered moves to seize still more, to weaken other arms of government, and to diminish the influence of popular opinion, both directly and by means of threats against the press and television. Now, it's clear from this evidence that Nixon suffered from some psychic flaw that produced these paranoid reactions. So, of course, did the disturbed children whose case histories I cited earlier on. But at the same time, in reality, there was a process of interaction going on that both tested and exacerbated his fears. This is a case history which illuminates the normal workings of the power relation by tracing what happens when it is mishandled. What we find is that ignoring the relationship limits the ability of those in power to act productively in the outside world; and that, in the interior sphere, magical responses surface which are very similar to those found in early life and outgrown in the main as individuals mature, because they don't produce results. Nixon resorted to rituals of office, magic assertions and repetitions of authority, as substitutes for adaptive, pragmatic, collaborative action with a body of the governed, even though this body had awarded him with a new term of office by a record vote. But Fate was not cajoled.

Nixon's commitment to confrontation as a means of rule was extreme, but that does not make it irrelevant to the use of authority. It matches our culture's conscious descriptions of government as an adversary situation in which the governed can't be trusted to act for themselves. They must be led; and if they grumble sullenly against the direction of policy they must be *forced* to follow. Nixon's particular style of ruling relied more on deception than force, though the mass arrests of peace demonstrators made clear that compulsion by bodies of armed men was perfectly acceptable to him. What we find in this example, then, is not just the unfortunate results of personal misrule, though this is part of it, but the effect of a misinterpretation of the nature of power that seems to be widespread. Viewing authority as a personal possession that must be defended invites this kind of mistake—and many others too. The tendency to reserve all decision-making for those few who stand at the pinnacle of power is another, and so is the assumption that an administration must never be seen to disagree, but always present a monolithic face to the public.

All these reactions can be observed in contemporary politics, and they all arise from a fundamental misjudgment of the political process. That misjudgment denies the relatedness of the use of power, and it both stems from and reinforces a basic lack of trust of the governed by their governors. This is in essence a denial of community; which is more than an emotional problem. To refuse to accept a communal connection with the body of the ruled guarantees bad government. It may lead to outright despotism (and we shall look at this extreme situation later). It may simply mean that policies fail because they have been instituted without regard to the views of the governed. It may result in frustrating friction that erupts into violence which becomes endemic, as it has in Northern Ireland. Most often it suggests to the governed that what happens in the world of events is no business of theirs. Then why bother with it? Assigning women to a place that is removed from the public sphere and instructing them to concentrate only on personal relationships is, as ever, the prime example of neglect and waste of human resources, but it is not unique. (It also illustrates our tendency to think of relatedness as being only personal and private.) The denial of community always limits the capacity of rulers to deal with the inevitable changes and shifts of events because it narrows and falsifies the basis of their authority.

This book is an attempt to analyze the powers that reside in the body of the governed, and I don't want to digress into recommendations to the powerful on the proper use of power. But since the governed have to survive, withstand, and sometimes correct misuse of authority by the powerful, it's useful from time to time to contrast proper and improper use. A simple example of how a ruler can listen responsibly comes from the memoirs of K'ang-hsi—no democrat, God knows, but a monarch who knew he should be aware of his lines of connection with his subjects and the advantages of keeping them open.

On tours [he writes] I learned about the common people's grievances by talking with them, or by accepting their petitions. In Northern China, I asked peasants about their officials, looked at their houses and discussed their crops. In the South I heard pleas from a woman whose husband had been wrongly enslaved, from a traveling trader complaining of high customs dues, from a monk whose temple was falling down, and from a man who was robbed on his way to town of 200 taels of someone else's money. But if someone was attacked in an anonymous message, then I refused to take action, for we should always confront a witness directly; and if someone exaggerated too stupidly, then too I would not listen. A man swam toward my boat in Hangchow with a petition tied around his neck, shouting out that he had a certain enemy who was the number-one in the world for committing evil acts—and I simply had my retainers ask him, "Who then is number two?"[2]

The White House plumbers, one feels, could have learned a great deal from the emperor of China, if only that the public demonstration of listening attracts the trust of the public.

The idea that the authority of rulers is strengthened by a climate of intimidation is counterproductive. It works to lessen the involvement of the governed in the political process and thus to make their willing and happy consent to the legitimacy of their rulers more difficult. For the powerful themselves, intimidation is a weapon that can turn in the hand and demonstrate not strength, but a lack of self-confidence. The hidden message of this behavior—and it is not hidden very securely—is that these rulers don't trust their own authority. And they should not trust it—if they are incapable of factoring into their analyses and their policies an awareness of the hopes and needs of the weak.

When they give their consent to the rule of the powerful, the governed do not ask that in return they be feared as messengers of Fate. They just want to be taken account of, to be reckoned as participants in the lengthy, complex business of managing affairs so that daily life in the world goes on without too much strain. They accept the power of the powerful; what they want is some assurance of common purpose that includes them as well as the elite. Enduring dynasties achieve this in various ways. Some recruit new members of the elite from a broader base by, for example, encouraging a church to train the talented young of the lower ranks. Some allow a less formal kind of upward mobility by admitting members of a striving middle-class as apprentice aristocrats. More generally, rulers take part in ritual demonstrations—not of their dominance!—but of their connection with the ruled in a community that all can join, as in state religious celebrations or patriotic ceremonies; or they go through rituals that require them to behave with a conspicuous show of humility, as the Pope does on Good Friday when he washes the feet of the poor.

By these gestures the powerful declare to the weak that they are all part of a bonded group, and that they as rulers can therefore be trusted to act for the group. If the weak agree, the powerful will be allowed a great deal of leeway. The weak will put up with a lot of discomfort as long as they believe that the powerful know what they're doing, and that what they do serves the weak better than what they could do for themselves. But when the ruled begin to doubt both the good intentions and the good sense of their rulers, the connection between the two members of the power relationship starts to fray. That is when the footsteps of Fate are heard.

CHAPTER 9

Magic and Power I

*Is the supernatural that "life behind" to which the Auvergnat Pascal referred
. . . where men seek refuge from the visible life before them? Or is it simply a
reflection of the conditions of that prosaic world . . . ? Lightning came to be
tamed, cattle healed, health improved; remedies were found for snakebite and
rabies; weather bulletins proved more reliable than astrological formulas or
ancient spells; and fields were fattened by chemicals; but old practices survived,
and especially where marriage, childbirth and death were concerned. . . . Those parts
of life that are most difficult to dominate, that are the most contingency-
prone, retained their magic aspects the longest.*

Eugen Weber, Peasants into Frenchmen[1]

I want to come now to the question that has been surfacing over and
over in this discussion: namely, the supernatural nimbus that is so readily
attached to our ideas of power, the "magic connection." Magic lingers,
Weber observes, in those parts of life "that are most contingency-prone"; and
this description applies to power even more aptly than it does to "marriage,
childbirth and death." But where does it come from? If magic beliefs merely
reflect the conditions of our prosaic world, how does the process come to
condition our reactions to status and authority? Why do we allow it to
influence our behavior, intensifying the readiness of the powerful to act and
inhibiting the weak from doing so? Theoretically, the supernatural is alien
to the philosophy of Western society today, where reason and science are
officially alleged to control and explain physical nature, where fields are
fattened by chemicals. Divine intervention is no longer acceptable as a cause
of the phenomena of our lives; the sacred is cut off from the profane and a
belief in magic is not intellectually respectable. Instead, it indicates deviance
from the normal.

And yet here is the magic aspect active still in the midst of our prosaic
world, and not just smuggled in but looming behind a relationship that is
central to the structure of both public and private life. Has this escalation
of "power" into "magic power" simply seeped out of the dreams where
figures we meet in daily life have been transformed into witches, giants, or
unnatural monsters? Or are these creatures the expression of a wider tendency for the human psyche to imagine that the true nature of power always
drives it toward a superhuman level? That may be what we fear, but cannot

this fear be offset? Why does our contemporary dedication to the secular fail here with such consistency?

"Absolute power," said Lord Acton, "corrupts absolutely," whereas he allows to power, freed from the adjective, no more than a *tendency* toward corruption. I think we can read here the suggestion that it may not be power itself that we should approach warily so much as its extreme limit, not power but absoluteness. After all, absoluteness is, by definition, unknowable and uncontrollable, not bound by ordinary rules. This, of course, is where the supernatural comes in—or seems to. We take it as signifying irresistible force. And yet in the past, human beings have tamed uncontrollable forces, domesticating (to name a few) fire, wild animals, and electricity. Once they were as uncontrollable as power seems, and magic was certainly associated with the first two, and invoked to dominate them at a time when its use was general. But now we can deal with them all sans magic. Why should we not domesticate power too, if we can demystify it and place it in a context of human interaction?

We won't do that magically, but step by step, through understanding; and part of what must be understood is the reason for linking magic to power and so increasing our fear of it. Since magic is per se superhuman and supernatural, it always threatens to become overwhelming. Indeed, when we say "magic" we may simply be using the word as a synonym for what we don't understand and can't control. Clearly, tying it to established power is useful for the powerful in any situation where the relationship between rulers and ruled has deteriorated to that of sheer dominance and submission. A recent traveler to Brazil writes of finding there "a tendency to think in terms of miracles," and quotes a former government deputy as remarking that "governmental decisions are presented as miracles, as if the country were administered by the Wizard of Oz." There, this account continues, "men who extract confessions by torturing enemies of the government acquire not only absolute power over the bodies of their victims, but magical control of the truth itself."[2]

The magical connection that Joan Weimer describes is, of course, a metaphor. The procedures she cites are to be feared—but not because they are magical. Torture is all too real; but the torturers do not control the truth, just its official version. That can be very effective, no doubt, but when magical control is ascribed to a Wizard-of-Oz government, the grip of the governed on reality and its operations is weakened; and the grip of the governors too, which can do them no good in the long run. Indeed, this is the thesis advanced by L. Frank Baum when his heroine unmasks the Wizard as a rather inefficient practitioner of legerdemain. What we have to consider in the short run is just the question that Baum's classic asks: Why do the weak accept the suggestion of a magical element in power? What's in it for them?

Something, certainly. Confronted with power, the weak, who are most of us, feel themselves not only inadequate but puzzled. That's uncomfortable. If we can just give a name to the forces that baffle us, we feel that we might understand them better. Even if we have to identify them as lying outside our own mundane system and operating according to other laws, it seems as if we'd get some sort of grip on them by placing them in relation to ourselves. If we know what to call them, they grow a bit familiar, a bit less scary. The impulse to accept special kinds of causality in order to fit unexplained data into any ongoing system is still alive today, in our "rational" society. We like explanations, we want to find patterns in events, because they appear to make existence more predictable and so to reduce our vulnerability to the unexpected. To take an obvious example, astrologers far outnumber astronomers and surely out-earn them too.

Rationally that's very distressing, but condemning a popular belief because it's irrational will not make it vanish; and unless reason takes account of the natural incidence of unreason it will betray its commitment to reality. Our emotions are mightily persuasive, and they declare that while in this case the predictions of astrologers may violate hypotheses of the science that we're supposed to respect, they are still very *interesting;* interesting just because they don't deal with the external reality that science goes on about, where stars and galaxies and quasars and pulsars behave in their extraordinary fashions (which after all we lay-people have to take on faith as blind as that which the astrologers require), these predictions are about *us.* Astronomers set us adrift in immensity; should one of them feel a momentary urge to relate news from space to everyday life, the impulse would be resisted as a temptation to popularize. But astrologers begin not with the universe, but with our fascinating selves. They make us feel ourselves importantly present in a nexus of meaning, and even if we suspect that it may be a falsely woven causality, we often find that it offers a feeling of power, supportive if illusory. We can discover a sort of rationale for it, too. The banalities of the horoscope put us on the alert for possible dangers or for opportunities that will be to our advantage. And how can we deny that dangers and opportunities lie about us? If false magic makes us look harder for them, isn't it helpful?

Beyond this, however, we accept the possible association of magic with power because (we believe) *we have experienced it;* and not only through the nightmare dreams where awesome figures inspire terror. We have all of us, as children, lived through positive, indeed exhilarating, moments where events seemed to undergo a magical enhancement. These moments have to do with learning—that is, with acquiring an ability to seize on just such potential opportunities as the astrologers promise to point out. Over and over again in our growing years we faced the need to do something *for the first time;* indeed, we face the need still. Some of the most vital "firsts" we do before we know it, as infants; but later we are aware of confronting a task that is done easily by others around us, and that we can't do at all. Nor can anyone tell us how to make that enormous first step. Try as we may, the marks on the page don't make sense, the strings on our shoes come undone, the buttons pop out of their holes, the ball flies in the wrong direction. We are surrounded by skillful people who manage these things without turning a hair, who urge us on and show us once more what to do—and we still fumble. Power to which one hasn't access seems incomprehensible. Then all of a sudden, between one day and the next, the child can bring off the impossible feat in which nerves connect and muscles tense to send the ball off to the right spot, or turn scribbles into words. *And that must seem like magic.* Certainly we've all watched delighted children show off their new skills, enchanted with their prowess but also—"Look at me! Look at me!" —asking the world to assure them that the magic is real and the ability there, and repeatable.

Even in later life this kind of experience has a tone of its own. Suddenly one's ears unblock to a conversation in a foreign language, one anticipates an opponent's tennis shot, or moves with a horse in shared action. Adults are able to remember how long and hard they had to work before they reached this point, and even so the change is indescribable, a click, "something else." We feel as if we had entered a new state where things happen in a different way. And that is how magic presents itself most convincingly; not simply as influencing the way things happen, but as an effective new causality that links events in a different fashion—the "Eureka!" effect. No magic, and we know it; and yet we have felt a breakthrough leap that disconnects one moment from the next. It is a real experience—but *internal.* Our mistake comes when we imagine that it applies to the outside world; and yet how tempting it is to do that. If once again we see people doing things we can't do, or think we can't do, out of our child-past rises unbidden the postulate that they somehow have access to mysterious, superhuman power.

And indeed the world is mysterious enough for supernatural power to have its attractions. Physicists themselves have given up the idea of complete predictability and incorporated uncertainty into their work as probability theory. Astronomers make and remake cosmologies as new features of distant space reveal themselves. When our understanding of the very structure of the universe is subject to radical change from decade to decade, one can see the emotional pull of star-charts that do not change, and horoscopes based on arcane traditions. Our need to know what lies ahead is so great that if reason can't tell us, we'll turn to the irrational, happy to have information on what to expect whether it comes from a shaman or a meteorologist. Superficially, we're right. If our expectations of the future allow us to cope with it better, that's all to the good. If they don't come true, no reality constrains us from shifting our interpretations of the words of the oracle, or positing some even-greater-than-expected unknowable force at work. Thus we can escape the onus of failure and the burden of guilt.

Both for the powerful and for the weak, then, the linkage between magic and power offers what psychoanalysts call "secondary gains," the defensive supports that are supplied by neurotic structures. Because these structures are both rigid and unrealistic, they entail a severe loss of free imagination and, indeed, of psychic energy; but the gains they provide impose some kind of order on emotional chaos, and they are hard to give up. For the powerful, the magic aura offers a validation of dominance over and above the consent of the governed; for the weak, a defensive shield against feelings of inferiority and ineffectiveness. Unfortunately, it produces greater losses, but they are less easily seen. Basically the loss is in a sense of shared humanity, which weakens the relationship between rulers and ruled by emphasizing differences between them. Then the weak attempt even less, and the great too much: Are they not justified by the magic connection? Of course if their projects go astray, they find themselves in a bind. How can the magic connection have allowed them to fail? It becomes increasingly hard to admit their mistakes and increasingly easy to deny them and annul their consequences by force. Might makes right, say the powerful; but might can never quite make reality, nor can the Wizard of Oz run a government. His miracles depend on his torturers, and on our fear of them.

In the end the touch of magic that persuades us of an exaggerated belief in the ability of human beings to control events also heightens our uneasy sense that there's something dangerous about power. For ruled and rulers alike, the exaggeration and the danger begin to attach themselves to the power-partner, who is subjected to a process of dehumanization. If rulers are sacred, their advisors are on notice that they differ from the rest of us in a fundamental fashion, and can't be judged by ordinary human standards. George Reedy points out how easily this can happen. On the other side, when the powerful come to believe that disaffection among the governed is due to the will of Fate, they misunderstand the cause of their problems and are unlikely to deal with them competently. Or they may see those they rule not as agents of Destiny, but as simply subhuman. They can then ignore their demands—"How can they know what they want? They can't think for themselves, they are children." But if the unrest goes on, fear will give the weak another shape. They become Alexander Hamilton's "great beast," or the mob that can't be reasoned with and must be put down by armed force. If absolute power corrupts, that may be because it can never deliver what it appears to promise, either to the weak or to the powerful.

And yet the tendency to believe that "authority, dominion, sway" can operate in a larger-than-life fashion is so common that we take it for granted. That is an additional reason why we should examine the idea. The things we take for granted are external outcroppings of the fundamental assumptions that shape our social mythology, the great structure of ideas that we have dreamed up without knowing it. We use it first to explain the universe and discover its laws—or at least to classify and name the events on which its laws are predicated, rather as Adam named the animals. We go on to extrapolate the rules for proper behavior so that we shall prosper within this universe by knowing and observing its laws. Our tacit beliefs, our "instinctive" reactions to events, are clues to the lines of force that formed and sustain this mythic structure. We never reason about these responses, and that indicates how deep their roots lie in our emotions, both of hope and fear. The things that we take for granted are part of the shared unconscious that any community holds in common out of our earliest experience of life.

Clearly the connection we make between power and magic, power and the supernatural, power on earth and the sacred power of the divine, is not due to some individual quirk. It has had a long history in which secular rule has been intimately intertwined with sacred authority. In the annals of our own civilization, anointed kings have governed by God's will and presumably, therefore, under God's guidance. The ruled believed this, and so did the rulers.

But that was a different world; and different specifically because belief in sacred authority was alive everywhere, not only in an uneasy and deviant bond with political power. Moreover, because supernatural power had to connect in practical ways with human life at an everyday level, it was continually restrained from moving toward an absolute goal by this or that mundane consideration. Besides, there were explicit limits to earthly power set by Church and by Scripture, which allowed absolute dominion to no mortal, only to God. In addition, it was not only the powerful who had access to divine guidance. Though a priesthood might claim the power to mediate between God and humankind, it was still assumed that help from on high was available, one way or another, to those who sought it, whatever their station. To believe in the active intervention of the sacred in ordinary life was not abnormal. At every level of seriousness, from the peasant who muttered spells against bad weather to the exercises of the mystics, efforts to deal with the universe included the invocation of the sacred. Reality, as perceived by our ancestors, demanded it.

If we want to understand why, we must try to think ourselves back into the circumstances of existence in a hierarchical, laborious, narrow world. Our lives have changed so completely, not just in obvious physical ways, but also in terms of what we can expect to control, that it's hard for us comfortable Westerners to do this. But we should not assume that a world ruled by agents of divine authority meant to its inhabitants what it would mean to us. Theirs was an existence of poverty, drudgery, and infinite repetition, day by day, season by season, year by year. The tasks that had to be undertaken in order to survive were accomplished by brute strength and physical skill based on the muscle power of men, women, and beasts, whose control was a particularly necessary skill, and whose presence was so vital and so ubiquitous that it served in a way to stretch the community beyond the limits of the human species. Every crèche, with its ox and ass, illustrated the extension of the miracle of Christ's birth to the animal world, while legends and fairy-tales abound in animal imagery, from the Frog Prince to the Hunt of the Unicorn. It's very likely, indeed, that this enlargement facilitated a further stretching of community to take in, at the other side, entities who were higher than human: angels, messengers of God, and plaguey demons, too.

For great and lowly alike, change was either imperceptible or catastrophic, occasioned by a flare-up of endemic war or by the incursion of violent strangers, by famine, plague, flood, or other natural disaster. It was an existence in which the external forces of nature made continual, inescapable demands on humanity and were met in the only way possible, by the unending iteration of series of actions passed on unchanged from one generation to the next, and acquiring thereby some aura of ritual in themselves. Men and women timed their activities to uncontrollable nonhuman powers: the cycle of the seasons, the migration of animals, the time to plant and the time to reap, the coming of children, the diminishment of energy through aging. They were faced every day by natural powers that were hugely greater than themselves, but which had to be managed somehow.

In that world with its few changes and fewer choices, it was both easy and necessary to imagine a still-larger universal power that controlled and directed the elements of nature and the pressures of society, and to whose assistance humankind could appeal.

Now, the analysts of childhood growth whose researches I have been using tell us again and again that it's essential for mental and spiritual health that human beings be able to feel that they can control some part of their lives, even if it's a small or very special part; can plan their actions and imagine a livable future. For our ancestors, who lived in a world of great and mysterious forces, the idea that they could themselves reach the most tremendous of these forces by prayer and through rituals of worship must have served just this purpose. The assurance that they had access to divine power allowed them to endure the chronic burden of life as well as its sudden acute terrors and to hope for a happier future, even if that future was to be deferred to another world. Without some hope for a larger, freer existence, survival would have been harder than it was; too hard, perhaps. In addition their creed declared that the powerful were also subject to God's will and would face a final judgment no different from that of the weak, when secular power would be overriden by divine. To dream of the mighty brought low might well appease present anger and envy felt by the weak. It also implied a shared humanity, in which all mortals were children in the eyes of God. Many a church offered the lowly a graphic image of this Day of Wrath for all.

Not only did the Church provide channels for the projection of anger, religious faith offered the devout psychological support in time of trouble. We can see well how this worked if we once again consider what happened when things went wrong, as we did in the case of disorders of childhood growth and in the vicissitudes of contemporary politics. To the Church of the Middle Ages, loss of faith was not just a cognitive error, an intellectual mistake. It was understood emotionally. Yielding to accidie, despair, distaste for life, was regarded as a sin—not just because it denied dogma, but because it constituted a rejection of God's love; a love He had proved by sending His Son to die on the cross as humanity's Redeemer. This inability to accept God's love and to trust in Him is the medieval equivalent of contemporary failure to surmount the first of the life-crises that Erik Erikson posits. In conquering that crisis, Erikson declares, the individual achieves "basic trust" in the world, the world that the medieval Church understood to be ordered by God's loving will. In an early work, *The Divided Self,* another analyst, R. D. Laing, comes close to merging the religious and psychiatric visions when he writes:

> The schizophrenic is desperate, is simply without hope. I have never known a schizophrenic who could say he was loved, by God the Father or by the Mother of God or by another man. He either is God, or the Devil, or in hell, or estranged from God.[3]

This excruciating despair is related to powerlessness, to the crushing belief that one is worthless, a creature whose feelings have no validity, whose actions produce no effects. The world is incomprehensible, its events are random elements of chaos. Or, even worse, one is convinced that one's actions may be effective, but never as they should be. To act is to hurt oneself

or those one loves, to frustrate one's ends, to guarantee a wrong result; there
are some searching explorations of this self-conviction of wrongness and
deviance in recent women's literature. It is a conviction that comes from the
basic human need to understand the way the world works, even if this
understanding condemns the self to doom or damnation. These selves have
reasoned from their inability to affect reality, and concluded that the cause
is their unworthiness. An alternative reaction is madness, that is, the construction of an alternate system of reality that sustains the self by interpreting
events in a different fashion from the norms. Both methods result in withdrawal, the first because any action is inevitably followed by new pain, the
second because the fantasy structure must be protected from contact with
intrusive, contradictory reality.

D. W. Winnicott, whose work with children did not preclude his thinking out from their treatment to a larger perspective, traces the onset of this
pervasive hopelessness to the loss of "a capacity for creative living." He saw
this capacity as an ability to bring imagination and will to bear on the
happenings in one's own life in order both to direct them and to understand
through them the way one's life connected realistically with the lives of other
purposive human beings. Losing this ability can occur for many immediate
reasons, but the result is the same: a permanent distancing is established
between the suffering individual and the accepted laws and rules of the
current social mythology. For such an individual, the rules don't work. One
is excluded from the arena of action by some stigma—by sex or race or an
unattractive handicap, or by a private experience of life that seems to set one
apart. Or one may have absorbed the idea that life offers rewards that are
not, in the end, delivered; or that the rewards that do come one's way will
produce more satisfaction than they actually turn out to bring. There are
many variations on the kind of divergence between oneself and accepted
normality, but the result is always some consciousness, never happy though
occasionally met with defiance, of being *abnormal.* At its worst this matches
the accidie, the death-in-life, that our ancestors feared and condemned as
mortal sin. Writes Winnicott:

> When one reads of individuals dominated at home, or spending their
> lives in concentration camps or under life-long persecution because
> of a cruel political regime, one first of all feels that it is only a few
> of the victims who remain creative. These, of course, are the ones
> who suffer. It appears at first as if all the others who exist (not live)
> in such pathological communities have so far given up hope that they

no longer suffer, and they must have lost the characteristic that makes them human, so that they no longer see the world creatively.[4]

But Winnicott was not one to welcome a view that denies humanity to any human, and he goes on:

> One has to allow for the possibility that there cannot be a complete destruction of a human individual's capacity for creative living and that, even in the most extreme cases of compliance and the establishment of a false personality, hidden away somewhere there exists a secret life that is satisfactory because of its being creative or original to that human being. Its unsatisfactoriness must be measured in terms of its being hidden, its lack of enrichment through living experience.[5]

Part of such enrichment would be the validation of experience by others, which would confirm the judgments of a secret life and testify to their significance because they were shared.

In a secular society, such validation would of course come only at a normal, secular level. But to our devout ancestors, the "real world" included the presence of divine grace, which could, in itself, confirm one's experience. Yet this grace was not a private, individual presence; or it was not only that, being offered by a religion that was shared with others, reinforced by common ritual, and based on ancient scripture. There was an authenticating public acceptance of private access to the sacred, that agreed-upon alternate reality. An interior life was allowed to exist which did not have to be entirely secret, and it could supply an emotional space (another sort of "transitional space") where hope could be nourished and a self that the outer world did not satisfy could receive enrichment and refreshment in ways other than material. Indeed, to the truly religious, this enrichment still comes as a source of inner strength.

Most of us, however, would probably have to say that we feel ourselves to be living nowadays in a world where religious tradition, including the imminent presence of the sacred, has faded and lost its dignity. It may become a kind of soothing syrup. It may serve as a sloganized structure through which a group, frightened by changes that seem out of hand, sets up a defensive-offensive bonding that allows its members to resist and deny alterations that they find distressing. In its trendy modern guise, it may provide an entertainment with overtones of not unpleasant terror. Whether or not this is true of what we conceive to be inside our heads, it is true of the way we behave. The secularization of our society has been severe enough to secularize and denature religion itself. Almost universally, churches and cults serve as political groupings with secular goals, not as links to an alternate reality that is felt to be profoundly set apart, truly sacred.

Older than Acton's dictum on the corrupting tendencies of power, and as much a part of our background thinking, is Marx's declaration that religion "is the opium of the people." Now in fact the full text of the sentence indicates that Marx appreciated the psychological comfort offered by what he deplored socially. "Religion," he wrote, "is the soul of soulless conditions, the heart of a heartless world, the opium of the people": but whatever the final interpretation, he was certainly pointing to the fact that what soothed the people also strengthened the mighty in the possession and use of their authority. By 1844, that is, when a shrewd observer looked at the politics of religion and saw it as a technique for maintaining dominance, he found an audience that understood and agreed.

Nonetheless, though access to the supernatural can seem to strengthen the powerful, faith can also serve the weak, and has in times and places other than ours, by keeping alive for them a sense of their personal significance and value and assuring them that they are seen and judged by a present God. This assurance can indeed keep the weak quiet and satisfied; but it doesn't always work this way. Access to the Godhead can also convince men and women to take issue with the powerful, to denounce the princes of this world as heretics, sinners, or oppressors. For such God-intoxicated prophets and saints, religion provides the sense of an alternate system of validation, which can stand in opposition to power-in-society. Moreover, if the mighty believe in their own creeds, they cannot also believe that religion is simply a tool for political aggrandizement: God judges the powerful as well as the weak. Obviously, not all the mighty could have been truly devout; but to the extent that faith strengthened their hand, it must also have whispered that another, greater power existed. At times, that may have restrained their excesses; at others, it may have given them the will to act decisively in moments of crisis. In short, if we now, as secularized outsiders, consider the idea of religion as an instrument of power, we can see that, like other instruments of power, it can work either well or badly in terms of social function.

It will certainly work *differently,* however, if it is placed within a believing society, rather than in one that has become thoroughly secularized. The difference has nothing to do with faith itself; it has to do with the acceptance of faith as normal and significant. "What everyone believes" has its own peculiar validity: it is central to the social mythology of the culture in which this "everyone" lives. But let everyone cease to believe, or enough "everyones" to tip the scale, and things change. A universal tenet—and it may concern religion, or the legality of slavery, or the proper place for women—can continue to receive lip-service or to linger in some cultural corner, but if it is no longer seen as applicable to activities in the real world, it will not move people to action. That, I think, is about our situation today vis-à-vis fervent faith in the capacity of the divine to intervene in mundane matters. This is an empirical assessment, not an ultimate value judgment on whether or not we suffer by our lack of religious faith; let me speak to that in a moment. Here I want merely to emphasize that *for us* the tinge of magic that we still feel to be part of power *does not mean what it meant to our ancestors,* because the supernatural and the sacred are not vital, central parts of our structure of belief. They have given up much of their authority, grown a bit shabby, and in their decline become political weapons or trade-goods for hucksters.

The influence of religious faith in the past, however, was complex and intertwined with many aspects of life. Before we leave that believing world, we might inquire briefly into the origins of faith; not as part of a theological discussion, but to consider socially, functionally, the central communal relationship that is felt to be an essential part of religious belief. The communal origin of religious faith was put forward by Emile Durkheim some two generations ago in *The Elementary Forms of the Religious Life.* Durkheim's diagnosis of the already-evident breakdown in contemporary social life did not go on to suggest that a reinvigorated religion would cure our ills; he was a social scientist, one of the first and greatest, not a prophet. But the loss of a sense of community offered the opportunity to study, by malfunction, what that sense had provided.

In Durkheim's theory, the larger-than-life Being that came to be called God is seen as a distillation of the emotions that the individual feels in relation to the group force of the community. "It is unquestionable," he wrote, "that a society has all that is necessary to arouse the sensation of the divine in minds, merely by the power it has over them; for to its members it is what a god is to his worshippers. . . . A god is first of all a being whom men think superior to themselves and on whom they depend. . . . Now society also gives us the feeling of a perpetual dependence."[6] The force of conjoint opinion—what everyone believes in—plus the intense emotions called forth by mass-ceremonials, Durkheim stated, combined to shape religious ritual and to raise the moral ascendancy of the community to a superhuman level. And he is surely right when he points out that the community *is* superhuman in its store of wisdom, its issuance of directives for proper behavior, and the authoritative force of its joint convictions.

For Durkheim, our sense of the sacred begins in a unique and necessary relationship, that of the individual to the social world, and it is felt as a reflection of the relative power of the group over the individual. But this emotion is not just one of external compulsion. It is internalized, not only by teaching and example, but by the participation of the individual in the rituals of religion, which the devout understand both to communicate with the sacred and to move the supernatural power to intervene in the affairs of this world. To some tiny but meaningful degree, therefore, believers stand in a personal relationship to the object of their belief, can reach out and grasp it through supplication and worship. Writes Durkheim:

> The believers, men who lead the religious life and have a direct sensation of what it really is . . . feel that the real function of religion is not to make us think, to enrich our knowledge, nor to add to the conceptions which we owe to science others of another origin and another character, but rather, it is to make us act, to aid us to live. The believer who has communicated with his god is not merely a man who sees new truths of which the unbeliever is ignorant; he is a man who is *stronger.* He feels within him more force, either to endure the trials of existence or to conquer them.[7]

Durkheim, however, would not want us to dismiss the power of the sacred when drawn on by believers as simply "psychological," if by that word we meant that its ground was either illusory or merely personal. Society is not supernatural in the usual sense, but it is superhuman. Indeed, he says, it has

> a creative power which no other observable being can equal. In fact, all creation, if not a mystical operation which escapes science and knowledge, is the product of a synthesis. [It is society, that] vast synthesis of complete consciousness [that is] the most powerful combination of physical and moral forces which nature offers as an example. Nowhere else is an equal richness of different materials carried to such a degree of concentration to be found. Then it is not surprising that a higher life disengages itself which, by reacting upon the elements of which it is the product [that is, upon us individual conscious human creatures], raises them to a higher plane of existence and transforms them.[8]

If we accept Durkheim's insights, we see how humankind has drawn its sense of its own multifarious collective presence into a symbol of omnipotence, and gone on to project this symbol out onto the screen of a joint, agreed-upon, "real world." Thus the power of religion, and of all our ideas of supernatural forces that connect with it, derives from the synthesis of relationships among human beings, which we call society. The projection outwards of our sense of a power greater than ourselves returns under the guise of the sacred, but it is rooted in the conjoint feelings of the living creatures from which it sprang. If this "higher life disengages itself," it cannot do so totally, floating off into space to exist by itself. It must continue to "react upon the elements of which it is the product"; when it ceases to do so, God is dead.

I have dwelt on this Durkheimian interpretation of religion because it extends the theory that I have been exploring—that power is fundamentally a relationship among human beings—to its furthest possible point. In religion is expressed the relationship of the lowest to the highest, or the tiniest and weakest to the greatest; and through it, the least can feel a connection to the might of the most powerful. In personal terms, we can see this theory of origins reflected in the course of our individual lives. The adults who teach us ordered uses of power when we are children, within relationships of trust and love, are transformed into supernatural figures in our dreams and nightmares and linger on there to reappear in our maturity, ready to caution us, or to sanction our desires. In Freudian language, the images that they assume both mask and present the superego. But they do not and cannot stand alone. Behind these gesturing images looms the whole of a culture, its language and art and folk-tales and morals, its accepted political processes, its ethical judgments, its science, its causality; and this structure, like the adults who taught it to us, can put forth an aura of transfiguring magic. It is at once the greatest of powers and the most intimate of relationships. It grows out of the community, and its ordered use authenticates a community among human creatures and instructs them to see each other as present and as significant.

Today, in our secular world, the "higher life" of which Durkheim spoke has disengaged itself so thoroughly from our ways of living and thinking that only archaic remnants are left to us. Can there be a renewal? If it is hard for us to imagine ourselves back into a world in which religion was as central to human experience and as intertwined with the structure of society as it was in the past, it is even harder to conceive of a new epiphany of higher life, truly expressive of our world (as Durkheim observed before me). The absence of faith is often mourned, but most such mourning is itself evidence of the absence of faith, even among its mourners, who seem to perceive it as cosy religiosity, middle-class morality, or complacent in-groupiness. If religion is indeed born from a sense of community, let us recall that it is the *power* of the community which is felt first and overwhelmingly. If faith delivers us from evil, it will not do so until we have felt that evil, felt it profoundly and in helpless terror, as children do in their nightmares. "Think not that I am come to send peace on earth," said Christ, at the advent of the faith that shaped our Western culture; "I am come not to send peace but a sword."

Any new faith that revives a sense of the sacred for our time will be as shocking in its emotional impact. Intellectually, it will not be a shabby revivification of disordered bits and pieces from the past, like the occultism of the present. Its social mythology will attempt to represent the totality of human experience in the modern world. It cannot (for example) see science and the technological instruments of life as its adversaries, though it may not make them a central theme. It will derive from a new and inclusive vision that explains our situation both to our minds and to our emotions, by illuminating this human situation with significance and value, and linking together, by hitherto unseen connections, all members of our society, weak and powerful both.

This Great Myth is as yet unborn and it cannot be created by conscious will. In this secular world, the supernatural elements that still fringe out from our ideas of power are relics of the past, less and less suited to the way we live now. If there are still sincere monarchists about, who believe in the divine right of kings, we would not condemn them for that; though we would be surprised to come on them. They are merely out of date, but they are consistent about it. What is actively harmful is the lingering charge of the old idea of sacred kingship when it attempts to persuade us unbelievers that, here and now, the powerful have a right to be where they are because they are there; that traditions should be honored because they are traditional. We contradict ourselves when we deny that they must be the result of divine intervention, and yet assume that because they were honored in the past, they should be honored in the present; even in a very different world of reality; even when their effects can be shown to be pernicious.

CHAPTER 10

Magic and Power II

*I do not think that all Zande magic is of great age. [It] has its current
tradition, its halo of rumor, mystery, and wonder, the birthplace in all societies
from which springs transmitted tradition, set legend and standardized myth,
stabilized by group ownership and handed over by . . . social machinery.
However, in saying that magic creates its own mythology, the problem has been
simplified. Does not belief create magic? Often a native will tell you, for
example, that a certain man has powerful magic to kill leopards. If you ask
your informant what magic is possessed by the hunter, he will say that he does
not know, but that he must own some magic or he would not be so successful in
killing leopards.*

 *Actual achievement is demanded of the man who wishes to sell his magic.
The fate of unsuccessful magicians, especially rainmakers in many parts of the
world, is evidence of this demand. . . . Primitive man is not a romantic, but a
hardheaded being, even in his magic, and there is no magic to attempt the
impossible.*

*E. E. Evans-Pritchard,
"The Morphology and Function of Magic"*[1]

A significant difference between contemporary Western societies,
which have been pretty well secularized, and those where magic and the
supernatural still play an accepted part is illustrated by the African people
whom Evans-Pritchard cites. In Azande society, where magic is a commod-
ity or service to be bought and sold, invented by new entrepreneurs or
imported from powerful neighbors as if it were an advanced weapons system
or a patented mechanical device, it is decidedly oriented to reality. That is
not the case with us. Azande magic is certainly linked with power, but the
linkage is open and official, whereas with us its existence is not acknowledged. The furthest we're likely to go would be to agree that some public
figure seems favored by remarkable luck. For the Azande, however, magic
is a matter of course, a part of the world of events. Public magic is more or
less controlled by a professional elite. One might compare it with the practice
of medicine, with banking, or with some particular area of government
activity, such as the foreign service. "Important magic," writes Evans-
Pritchard, "that is, magic which plays its role in large communal undertak-
ings or is practiced on behalf of the whole community or reinforces an
essential function of society such as war or government, is always to be found
in the hands of a few men."[2] Being public, being a normal part of life, it is

therefore subject to normal operating rules: that is, it has to prove its efficiency. The public will ask, "Is this sorcerer, or priestess, as effective as that
one?" Because magic is part of an accepted structure of beliefs operating in
the everyday world, it is susceptible to being tested by events for its relevance
and usefulness. Unsuccessful rainmakers or leopard hunters soon lose their
aura.

Here, then, is a link between power and magic that normalizes the
relationship by enlisting the supernatural in the pursuit of quite mundane
ends; and there are many examples from other societies in which we can find
clues to contemporary feelings. Far less prosaic is the connection of power
with the sacred to be seen in the concept of taboo. In it we find, strongly
expressed, the fear of power that our culture usually conceals behind a screen
of moral distaste. What we feel and dimly hesitate to look at directly is there
spelled out in action and recounted in myths. Here is another sort of case
history illuminating the effect of power-as-magic on the way human beings
approach its use; and especially on the fashion in which this supernatural
aura operates to emphasize the dangers of grasping authority. Reflected in
such notes from other cultures are examples of the ways in which the weak
may be persuaded that it's the better part of valor to leave the management
of power to others.

Taboo is a familiar enough idea involving the quality of being set apart
from the ordinary world and forbidden to approach by the body of ordinary
folk, most specifically and especially by women, whose essential characteristics are often seen as polluting. Taboo is a manifestation of the sacred in its
most highly charged form, operating socially to reinforce law or custom by
declaring that violation of a taboo is not just wrong—it is *dangerous,* dangerous in nightmare style. Step into a sacred enclosure, seek access to forbidden
knowledge or even stumble on it by accident, commit a disapproved act or
simply suffer exposure to pollution, and it isn't just human beings who will
assault you, it is a supernatural force that, once aroused, cannot be restrained. As with electricity in its early days, as with nuclear energy, only
the trained and adept—only the powerful—can approach the sacred; and
even they must do it with care.

In cultures where the linkage between power and magic is taken for
granted, those who break a taboo feel themselves assailed by overwhelming
forces, forces that are clearly connected with social obligations and the
upholding of custom, but which act by invading the interior world of the self.
Even in the course of prescribed ritual celebrations, the self feels itself in
danger from the mere presence of the sacred. The ceremonies inspire not just
awe, but terror too. Sometimes the fear that one will lose control over one's
identity and become a possessed and maddened instrument to be used by god
or demon is an expected part of the experience.

"Those undergoing a ritual who are 'brooded upon by the shades' are . . . unclean and *may not* cleanse themselves until the ritual enjoins it," writes Monica Wilson, describing ceremonies held at the death of a kinsman or on the equally perilous occasion of a difficult or abnormal birth within the kinship bond among the Nyakyusa, another African tribal society.[3] "Madness comes from the failure to purify oneself in the ritual, to separate from the shades [of the dead]. This sense of pollution, and the horror of madness with which it is linked among the Nyakyusa, is an expression of fear and comes very close to the sense of awe . . . and the 'Idea of the Holy.' " The chance misfortunes of existence—or that is what our own social mythology would call them—are seen by the Nyakyusa to portend larger dangers, against which public ceremonies must be invoked as protection. In some rituals, insane acts are specifically mimed, apparently as a prophylactic against the possibility that they will actually occur. It's as if the shades were a kind of supernatural Mafia, to whom protection money had to be paid lest they take over ordinary life, as well as the sacred.

Another maleficent supernatural force is that which can be invoked by sorcery or witchcraft. The Nyakyusa see it as "an innate power to harm others exercised by certain individuals"; but it too operates within a social framework. In "The Sorcerer and His Magic" Lévi-Strauss describes, in generalized form, the effect on an individual who becomes

aware that he is the object of sorcery [and so] is thoroughly convinced that he is doomed according to the most solemn traditions of his group. His friends and relatives share this certainty. From then on the community withdraws. Standing aloof from the accursed, it treats him not only as though he were already dead but as though he were a source of danger to the entire group. On every occasion and by every action, the social body suggests death to the unfortunate victim, who no longer hopes to escape what he considers to be his ineluctable fate. Shortly thereafter, sacred rites are held to dispatch him to the realm of the shadows. First brutally torn from all of his family and social ties and excluded from all functions and activities through which he experienced self-awareness, then banished by the same forces from the world of the living, the victim yields to the combined effects of intense terror, the sudden total withdrawal of the multiple reference systems provided by the support of the group, and, finally, to the group's decisive reversal in proclaiming him—once a living man, with rights and obligations— dead and an object of fear, ritual and taboo. Physical integrity cannot withstand the dissolution of the social personality.[4]

In such a case, the pollution, from which the Nyakyusa cleanse themselves in rituals designed to appease the shades of the dead, has become
ineradicable. No cleansing is possible. Taboo has *eaten the self,* for the
sorcerer's victim is not just a violator of taboo, but himself a tabooed object,
and therefore justly condemned by the healthy community, which must
protect itself by expelling him. This is a terrible punishment. We can see why
the Nyakyusa relate such a condition of self-accusation to madness, for it is
the situation of utter despair that Laing cites as occurring in schizophrenia.
Concurring, another analyst, Silvano Arieti, remarks in his massive work
Interpretation of Schizophrenia that in terminal cases "The patient seems
compelled to escape from perceptions," as if any state were better than life
in the world, and the best condition that which most closely approaches
death.[5]

These rituals and enchantments display obvious analogies to the nightmares that accompany childhood's inevitable brushes with social authority.
In the worst of bad dreams, the dreamer stands alone facing terror, separated
from allies in the supporting community. The sorcerer acts by deliberately
dissolving the connection between individual and community, declaring the
victim a "nonperson" who has been thrust into a state of "nonbeing." Indeed, rituals that aim at this effect are still in use among us, though they are
now marginal and their effects less overwhelming. Still, the cadets at West
Point, that citadel of power and its worship, use as strong a form of such
denial of existence as can be mounted today when they subject one of their
number to the ritual punishment of silence. No one speaks to such outcasts,
no one acknowledges their presence, and they can live for months caught in
a ghostly limbo, as unseen as air, expelled from the community as social
beings.

The Nyakyusa rituals meet the dangers and crises of life by reversing
the process and calling on the power inherent in the community to control
the incursions of the shades and thus protect its members from the loss of
a social personality. This seems to be done by the ceremonial declaration of
inclusion and connection between the living and dead—by the demonstration of an extended community that can temper the hostility of the shades
by asserting their relatedness to the living. Writes Wilson, "Mutual dependence of kin, living and dead, is expressed again and again. . . . Men tremble
at death—they are expected to—and in the ritual they receive comfort and
reassurance. . . . The ritual enhances fear, but it also overcomes it."[6] The
Nyakyusa do not deny death; instead, they manage it by placing it within
the process of social existence, and within a widened community.

Comfort and reassurance would seem to be the conscious purpose of
these ceremonies, but there is another social function that is linked to power
in a different way. The fear that is invoked is assuaged; but, before that

happens, the fear and the need for public support that it arouses (Wilson notes) "help to maintain order in Nyakyusa society" and to impress "on individuals their changing obligations within the kinship group."[7] *These rites operate as social controls.* They warn individuals that they must abide by communal custom if they are to avoid the terrible danger of finding themselves polluted, open to the revenge of the shades, with no one at all to turn to for help. I think we can see here a close resemblance to the condition of two-year-old Sam, pursued by a terrifying "thing," part wolf and part lion, that appeared in nightmare but could not be banished from the real world without the help of Sam's parents.

It appears, then, that the use of terror by a community against itself as a way of enforcing social controls is close to the process by which bad dreams teach children self-control. Taboo and ritual could well be described as the working of a communal superego. The remedy for pollution, by taboo or the death of relatives or some other catastrophe, is not denial, for the emotional consequences are as real as Sam's "thing." Rather, the polluted victim must tremble before the danger, and then be helped to move away from it. But this withdrawal can be effected only through established ritual contained within the framework of a familiar culture.

So behind the supportive features of this system, which enable individuals to survive the pain and grief that all must face, lies another function: the maintenance of the status quo. The frightened Nyakyusa can't cleanse themselves without these rituals, and at one time or another, everyone will need to be cleansed. Moreover small tribal communities often feel themselves in a very precarious situation, and rightly so. They are frequently under pressure to find adequate food supplies and sometimes under attack, threatened with collapse and chaos in the physical or human environment. It was not very many generations ago that our own ancestors were in much the same case. A grasp on the supernatural, a knowledge of the rituals that can invoke greater-than-human strength, must be highly valued for the protection it is thought to provide. Part of the power of the powerful is their knowledge of the means to invoke such protection and avert such threats: they are acquainted with the sacred. In every ceremony they intervene and direct the terrifying aspects of power to act beneficiently and depart without doing damage. So the community is shielded by those who can bargain with ghosts and demons. The weak need such mediators to do what is seen as necessary and highly skilled work, rather as we need brain surgeons. This felt need strongly reinforces the authority of the powerful.

These examples of the way in which authority can call on the sacred for aid against supernatural perils put us in touch with an aspect of power that is very much present in the here-and-now: the element of *risk-taking.* When sorcerers, priests, magicians, or shamans dare to approach a world of occult terrors, they legitimize their own authority by their daring. We, products of a secularized culture, may jump to the conclusion that Zande magicians and Nyakyusa sorcerers are no more afraid of the occult power of the sacred that they manipulate than we would be. That is a mistake. The terrors that these rituals enhance, control, and dismiss are not felt as false by the officiants any more than they are by their congregations. I suspect that the situation is closer to that of the children John Mack cited who were able to dismiss nightmare threats by declaring, and believing, that they themselves possessed magic powers. These professionals of the supernatural surely feel much the same way. Believing in the power of the sacred and being sensitive to its manifestations, they also risk believing in their own ability to handle relations with it. That belief is regularly tested in these encounters. The testing, I think, is analogous psychologically to the moments of danger offered, in ordinary life, by high-risk sports, when the self can ask itself "How do I stand up to danger?" Success in confrontation with peril provides a flush of ego strength: risk-takers enjoy risks which measure their capacities and push them to limits.

They are certainly supported in these trials by a particular kind of internal psychological structure, they are strengthened by training and long tradition, and these no doubt are the advantages that grant them a conscious sense of special ability. But that cannot be the whole secret. Some trust in access to a force beyond themselves armors them; and of this there is only one possible origin. If we allow that Durkheim is right to see in society the roots of the sacred, we should conclude that priests and celebrants, sorcerers and practicing witches, count on the strength of the group to supply the force that keeps them safe. Each individual is able to reach a reservoir of power larger than that of any individual because the role of mediator with the sacred makes each a symbol and representative of the group, acting in the interest of the group. These encounters both confirm the existence of the community and test the right of the chosen intermediators to speak for the community. Consciously, of course, success validates a belief that the powerful are touched with the magic they dare to address and manipulate.

Let us look at one widespread example in which the risk-taking aspect of power comes especially clear. In many mythologies we find tales of a strange figure whose central act is to *violate* taboo, and to survive unscathed —indeed, to be rewarded for this forbidden act. The "trickster-hero" is a familiar character in myth and folklore. Rationalized by the Greeks, he turns up in Homer as "the wily Odysseus." Even there he is ambiguous, and in myths from preliterate societies he is often downright puzzling. Not only is it unsettling to find that a player of tricks is held to be worthy of honor, what is even more remarkable is that he is honored *because* he breaks the sacred law. At first glance this appears to be a queer contradiction, but it will not do to dismiss it as merely an example of the incoherent workings of primitive minds. It has, in fact, a good deal to tell us about our own unconscious approaches to the danger of power.

Laura Makarius, who has considered this question in depth, offers a brief but profound analysis based on American Indian tales in "The Crime of Manabozo." It is not any characteristic of primitive thought that gives rise to the riddles in these stories of a magic violator of taboo, she declares; it is the repression of deep and contradictory desires within the societies that create them. When we discover what is being repressed and put it back into context, we find the tales easier to understand. "The deliberate violation of taboo," she writes, "constitutes one of the deepest contradictions of primitive life. *Its purpose is the obtainment of magical power.*"[8] In the trickster myths, we find, power is not being sought just for the aggrandizement of the hero, but also (in the end) for a purpose related to the whole community. That is, it's political power that's in question, which is to be gained, paradoxically, by flouting the laws and customs of the community.

In trickster-hero Manabozo's case, the overt crime he commits is blasphemy. Says he to his younger brother one day, "Everything is frozen over. There are no gods. There is no one more powerful than you and I. You don't know it; so I told you. We alone exist on this earth."[9]

What a hubristic claim of power! Unfortunately for Manabozo, he is wrong. Gods do indeed exist, and the Monster Snakes, gods of the underworld, forthwith take their revenge. They kill—not Manabozo, but his brother! Manabozo mourns. It is, however, grief which is as contradictory as the punishment that fell on the wrong victim, for when his brother's spirit returns, Manabozo drives it away to the land of the dead. This is not the end of the puzzles, for Manabozo goes on weeping for his dead brother in spite of the rejection of his spirit. In the end he is rewarded. The gods bestow magical power on him; and this in spite of the fact that (says the myth) his rejection of his brother's spirit has "caused all men to be mortal."[10]

It's a queer story indeed, until we address ourselves to what has been repressed. "It is well known," writes Makarius, "that among American Indians and among other peoples sharing the same . . . system of beliefs, the murder of a near-kin . . . is regarded as a means to acquire magical powers, and that this is the traditional way to obtain initiation into magic."[11] In other words, Manabozo has murdered his brother, sacrificing him to supernatural powers, who in return grant him a magical command over the sacred. In order to retain this power, he must send his brother's ghost back to the land of the dead.

Sacrifice is indeed a traditional way to obtain power; and we might recall that in the Judaeo-Christian myths of our own culture, the first murder of brother by brother occurred following a competition for favor with the Lord. Cain slew Abel after the Lord rejected his vegetarian offering of "fruits of the ground," preferring Abel's sacrifice of "the firstlings of his flock"; perhaps Cain concluded that blood-sacrifice was needed. However, fratricide is not the only road to power. In another version of Manabozo's story, he commits incest with his sister. A still different Ojibwa tale relates how a hunter enters the forbidden enclosure where a woman is secluded during menstruation, spends the night there, and marries her. Far from suffering for the pollution usually brought on by violation of this important taboo, he gains great luck in hunting.

Makarius sees these tricksters who gain power by violating the strongest laws of their society as reflecting and acting out a fundamental ambivalence present in the feeling of any community, certainly including our own. Law, or custom, is necessary; but it is repressive. Breaking taboo is an antisocial act, but from time to time everyone harbors antisocial impulses. *The trickster commits them for us.* He offers to adults the same sly pleasure that children get from the clever animals of fairy-tales and fables. Thus he relieves the pressure of antisocial desires within the community; and the communities we call primitive, we might remember, are more closely knit and intimate than ours. By relieving these repressions *he becomes a representative of the community,* and it is very likely that he survives because communal emotion is invested in him and, along with it, the communal power which is felt as sacred. There is also a ceremonial aspect to his acts. He does not perform them in secret and deny them (as Cain did). They are known and ritualized. "He assumes full responsibility for his actions by taking on himself the common guilt of his people."[12]

But the trickster's violations of custom and taboo are not simply symbolic. Neither his mourning nor his danger is seen as unreal. When Manabozo weeps for his brother, he really suffers grief; and by his action he truly enters the zone of danger and pollution. And in fact, is not the greatest sacrifice that could be asked the destruction of something, or someone, close and dear? Come back again to our own background of sacred myth: Why else did the Lord test Abraham's devotion by ordering him to sacrifice his son Isaac? It was Abraham's willingness to obey even this terrible command which won him the favor of Jehovah. And if Isaac was spared it was through no act of his father: it was the Lord who pointed out the ram caught in the thicket and declared that it would be an acceptable substitute for the child. Nor do the myths suggest that the violator of taboo does not stand at risk, hero or not: *it is the acceptance of risk that wins him his power.*

For his survival is itself the sort of magic feat that can be brought off only by a sorceror or hero; it is "the essential *trick* of magic, the violation of taboo."[13] It is proof of power: who but a hero could survive? Thus, while the taboo-breaker acts out community desires, he teaches the rest of the community to try not to do that themselves. Those who tangle with sacred law had better be sacred beings. Their survival establishes their magical character, rather in the way that the magic of the successful leopard hunter is established by his success.

Thus the system of taboo not only operates as an enforcer of law and custom by assuring miscreants that more-than-human retaliation will fall on them. In addition it establishes a demarcation line between the elite and ordinary folk, a line that ordinary folk find it easy and wise to agree to. The danger of calling down the wrath of the sacred is a deterrent to lawbreaking, while the demonstrated ability to endure such wrath confers elite status on the survivor. As long as the fear of taboo is strong—that is, as long as customary law is felt to be effective—the weak will stand in awe of the powerful and may even pity them because there is laid on them the obligation to confront divinity. Ceremonies in which priests and rulers deliberately violate taboos provide a continuing process of legitimation, confirming them in power. Such rituals are *feats;* wonder-working rabbis and monks performed them for our own ancestors. In them, the celebrant touches the hem of sacred force, and lives. Psychologically, the dares that children set each other are analogous, in that they work to create a hierarchy of rank.

There is an emotional logic to this that is persuasive: if you dare to do what I fear, I must allow you to be "greater" than myself in some fashion. But the ordinary logic of accepted cause and effect can't be entirely banished, and in societies where the taboo system reigns, some concession is made to the fact that these trickster-heroes are also lawbreakers. They do not get off scot-free. One form of payment is the sacrifice required for gaining power, a loss that is painful whether because a kinsman is slain or because, as with the sacred kings who know their term will end with their own murder, the sacrifice is one's own life. Another price is foolishness. These heroes often fall into their own traps. They fail, they are laughed at, and their stupidity operates as a further warning to the weak that violating taboos can be dangerous, and that even the powerful may one day go too far and receive a full blast of supernatural revenge for their daring. Their power is gained as part of a bargaining process that is never quite final.

There is something infantile about the trickster; in Freudian terms, he is a representative of the id. His natural sphere is lawlessness. He is, writes, Makarius,

> accredited with unlimited sexuality, pronounced phallic characteristics, gluttony and insatiable hunger. All the manifestations of pollution and uncleanness—blood, menstruation, childbirth, sexual and

excrementary organs, fecal substances, corpses—are his domain. No
wonder his comportment is foul, obscene, vulgar.[14]

And yet he is a hero: powerful though surrounded, as Lord Acton
would have been interested to see, by corruption. What he expresses is the
profound contradiction alive within each of us, and thus within society, of
the need for law and the urge to challenge it. But in proper Hegelian manner,
beyond thesis and antithesis lies a higher synthesis:

> The antisocial character of the violation of taboo shows how the
> trickster, represented as a friend of humanity, challenging the gods
> to improve the lot of man, is also represented as an asocial being
> destined to be banned by society. Because he is responsible for the
> most heinous of crimes—violating the basic laws of society—*he is
> potentially the expiatory figure who will take on himself the sins of
> mankind.*[15]

For us it may be easiest to see this strange being, scapegoat and challenger of the gods, as a revolutionary hero, reaching for power for others as
well as himself, and putting himself in danger of punishment and mockery
for his foolishness; as all breakers of stereotypes must do. Shelley, a poet-
revolutionary himself, discerned such a figure in Prometheus, the hero-thief
who stole fire from the gods, brought it to the world of humanity, and was
condemned to eternal torture for his gift. Is he made the sacrificial victim,
the "expiatory figure," we may wonder, because he failed to offer a kinsman
in his place as did Manabozo? Or are we witnessing in him a change at a
deep cultural level in which morally there comes to be no acceptable victim
other than oneself? Such a change would point, among other things, to the
greater singleness of the individual within a community whose bonds were
loosening.

Makarius makes clear that these trickster-heroes, in spite of their sacred
nature, fall far short of divinity. Manabozo introduces death to men, but he
cannot confer life or immortality. His magical power is "the dangerous
power of blood, inseparable from death." The myths underline this distinction:

> The hero is asked to give men the power to conquer women, good
> fortune in hunting and gambling, or the capacity to cure the sick.
> Such wishes are fulfilled, for they are obtained through the magical
> power of blood he wields. But those who come to him seeking
> immortality are brutally dismissed and turned to stone.[16]

We must be careful, it seems, not to confuse this kind of power, which is accessible to humans willing to risk challenging the gods, with the power that the gods "actually" hold in these mythologies. Potentially the trickster may be the linking expiatory figure who takes on himself the sins of the world and offers his life for their salvation, but the linkage of human and divine in the Christ-figure has not yet been made. And so the legends that describe ways of laying hands on power also declare that such power is limited, not absolute.

Tales of the trickster-hero not only embody illegitimate desires of the governed, they also test the strength of these urges and the courage of those who feel them. They ask the weak if they would risk copying the exploits of this singular figure in order to win power. Would they challenge custom and belief and traditional role-behavior and pay the price that is exacted? If you dare to aspire to this goal, these legends confide, then these are the ordeals you must undergo: the sacrifice of near kin (which in our time is not of course a blood sacrifice but the rejection of their teachings), the mockery of your fellows and, above all, a constant struggle with some authority greater than yourself in which you are the challenger, the rule-and-role-breaker. Are you strong enough? Brave enough? Steadfast enough in your purpose? In that case you may win through, you may gain the power you seek. But think carefully—is the reward worth the struggle? Such cautionary plots are not unknown in our own literature. They don't tell the weak that they must necessarily remain weak, but the invitation to power that they present is not one to accept lightly.

To the extent that this kind of thinking still affects our own understanding of the world and the behavior we believe to be proper, we are bound by our continuing acceptance of the dangerous connection that our ancestors perceived as existing between magic and power. To them magic was as real as electricity and automated machinery is to us. But it cannot be present to us in the same "normal" way, and when we act as if it were, we are allowing superannuated dogma to hamper our efforts to deal with contemporary reality. The logic of mythic thinking always contains motive; it is never simply analytic. Myth, legend, and ritual, we have seen, function to maintain a status quo. That makes them singularly bad in coping with change, indeed counterproductive, for change is the enemy of myth.

The old tag that I have used as a clue to mythic thinking, "Women's place is in the home," illustrates how myth misdirects action in the face of major shifts in our ways of living. Women today are in fact a bit more out of the home than in it, for statistics tell us that slightly more than half the women of working age in our society now hold paid jobs, outside the home.

But the doctrine that properly they have a special place with special duties involving the family responsibilities with which they are charged works to make these facts of life appear to be some huge mistake. If half the women in America have paid jobs, well, that's just too bad. They *shouldn't* have them. They are out of place, and anything done for them that encourages them to stay where they are is wrong.

This kind of thinking encourages social mismanagement because it obscures the real sources of the many problems that are consequences of social shifts, and substitutes the assumption that these deviant women are to blame for the strains that social shifts always create. If they have trouble fulfilling the demands of two jobs (for most of them are housewives too), they are told that the solution is to drop paid work and stay home: a prescription that, in most cases, is economically impossible and that would, moreover, guarantee that the community would have to get on without the contribution of talent and energy it could get from this group of people. These considerations do nothing to absolve women from blame. They remain scapegoats for an assortment of difficulties. Sexual promiscuity, masculine impotence, drug use, ineffective education, violence in the streets—if you can relate a social disorder to working women via broken homes and a rise in the divorce rate (or any other disapproved contemporary phenomenon), you have found yourself an answer. But because it is a false and inadequate answer, it results in inaction, so that no effort is made to discover and root out the real provenance of these problems. In this case, we are using magic just as much as the Azande do, but we don't know it; and we are using it less well because we are using it in a vacuum, ignoring the penalties that we bring down on women, families, and the community itself by our confusion. We are thus, unlike the Azande, using magic to "attempt the impossible."

On the political scene, the same kind of obscurantist impulse lies at the root of our belief that government office can bestow on officials an immunity to ordinary standards of judgment. Those who quote Acton on power, fearing it for themselves, might read on a sentence or two in the letter where his remark occurs: "There is no worse heresy," he writes, "than that the office sanctifies the holder of it. That is the point at which the negation of Catholicism and the negation of Liberalism meet and keep high festival, and the end learns to justify the means." The tendency for power to corrupt, that is, is not confined to the powerful, and the weak are not exempted from it by refusing authority themselves. When, within the power relationship, they sanction illegitimacy, says Acton, they too are corrupted. In the past the religious establishment might advance the doctrine of sacred kingship or divine right to rule, but it went on to declare that when ordinary standards of morality did not apply, extraordinary ones did: the purposes of God operated through the sanctified ruler and, since God was a loving father, He was mindful of His children even when He chastened them. It was never suggested that *no* standards existed. Today direct influence of the religious establishment has diminished sharply and therefore so has the value of the standards that it set, which at least assured society that its rulers would have to answer for their actions to a higher power.

It's true that remnants of these old assumptions about the existence of a divine overview of the process of ruling survive in the ceremonies in which public officials take an oath of office, affirm their obligation to serve the public in the public interest, and call on God to witness their words. The general feeling, however, does not take this as being a real contract with the sacred so much as a theatrical device which heightens the impact of an accession to power, but is not to be taken literally. If we glance again at our recent history, we note that during the process that forced Nixon out of office very little was made of any violation of his oath. Formal impeachment procedures would certainly have performed a ceremonial bow in that direction, but no one seemed to think it had much substantive importance.

Actually Nixon found very useful the public tendency to see his incumbency as giving him special rights. Over and over he presented himself not as a president elected by a political process that drew its legitimacy from the governed, even though the mandate he received in 1972 was enormous. It was instead the authority of the inherited role and title that he appealed to, an authority grander (he implied) than any that could be granted by an election. In his view, the voters were not the source of his power but rather the instrument through which it reached him. He did not act as their representative but as that of "the Presidency," and in the interest of the office (he claimed) he was bound, if need be, to act counter to public desires and even in contravention of the laws; the laws that bind the governed. It is very strictly a Machiavellian argument, which appeals to the mythic Necessity that the Prince is advised to invoke as the justification for deeds forbidden to his subjects (and to legitimize by the archaic equivalent of prayer breakfasts). There was considerable acceptance of this view, both in and out of the administration. In the summer of 1974 members of the Judiciary Committee of the House of Representatives moved as slowly as the regicides of Cromwellian England to confront Legitimate Authority, even when it was abundantly clear that Authority had not only violated its oath of office but broken a few good laws for its own advantage.

If the abuse of power is so long endured by the bulk of the governed, if consent continues to be formally granted even after some of the ruled majority have started to protest the policies of their rulers, there would appear to be reasons for this behavior that aren't strictly reasonable. It is possible that Nixon gained some support as an epiphany of the trickster-hero, even if he himself, yearning for respectability, would have been horrified at the thought. There is always some residue in the mass of the governed who enjoy watching the Establishment invaded and manipulated by the classic Outsider, and Nixon's behavior certainly presented this image, which was further strengthened by his early link with Joe McCarthy. But what protected Nixon most effectively was not the personality he projected, it was the general willingness of the public to assume that those who hold power somehow have a right to it, or they wouldn't be there. In this view, the action of the electorate is perceived as a ratification rather than a choice, and Nixon's insistence on the significance of his office as the source of his legitimacy was shrewd.

In short, the nimbus of magic surrounding power is still a force to be reckoned with. Take two axioms from that mythic emotional logic which can move us so much more immediately than can the logic of cognitive analysis: the powerful can control events (catch leopards, say the Azande; drive away the shades, say the Nyakyusa), so they must have some grip on the supernatural; the powerless can't, and don't. Then extend them causally: the powerful are rightly powerful because they can control, and don't seem to fear, the supernatural. The weak are necessarily weak because they can't and do. If most of us were asked about our capacity to command the course of events, we would have to admit that we are both dubious of success and a bit afraid to try. But we assume that this is just what the powerful *can* do, for they assure us that they are doing it. Therefore, *they must be different from us,* they must have an inborn ability we lack, they must be intended and specially fitted by nature, or by some divinity, to do what we can't—that is, to wield power unhesitatingly and with competence, unafraid of the flickering edge of the uncanny that surrounds it. Thus in our own minds do we validate their authority by creating a separation between them and us.

I think we will best understand the steps by which such a separation is created if we turn again to the separation between men and women as it exists in our society. The significance that is attached to the physical difference between the sexes operates very much like a magic legitimization of male ascendancy. The kind of power that our dictionaries define as an attribute of the powerful is one that is fitted for masculine exploitation, according to our sexual stereotypes, but alien to our image of femininity. Now all of us, at least to some extent, have incorporated the gender role assigned to us into our own personal identities, even if this incorporation takes the final form of resistance. Still it is there; even with those who see themselves as transsexuals, it is there to be protested against. And if you can persuade anyone (in this case, any woman) that something which she feels to be inescapably a part of her, that is, her sex, disqualifies her from using power, then you have gone a long way toward persuading her not to *try* to use it. Because she expects to use it incompetently and therefore to fail, she will elect not to try at all; and that decision sentences her to impotence, and removes her from competition with those who expect to use power well, because they are male.

Even evidence to the contrary will be ignored. A woman who accepts the idea that her sex is inept, by nature, at using power will disapprove of attempts by other women to do so. Female creatures who assume they are the equals of men will appear frightening, and the fear she feels will lead her to dislike and avoid them. True, their actions may speak subconsciously to deeply repressed impulses, but these impulses have been repressed because they are too dangerous to admit to oneself. For such a woman, the challengers of male dominance will be seen as troublemakers; and they *do* make trouble for her. If they succeed in their aims (she tells herself), she will be expected to copy their exploits and she "knows" she can't. If they fail (and that is what she expects, for how can women cope with the magic of power?), she'll still be worse off because their defeat will lower even further the status of women. Whatever happens, their mere existence arouses hostility in men (who by these definitions are powerful per se—at any rate, more powerful than women!), hostility which will be turned against women in general, even the humble, even the charming, even the feminine who despise and deny their sisters. So forget power and live by the rules; thus speaks the wisdom of the weak who are afraid to imagine themselves as being strong.

This attitude is not the result of any conscious conspiracy to keep women in their place as a second sex, a cheap pool of labor, ignorant, easily influenced consumers of goods and services—in short, an inexhaustible resource of manipulable semihumans, trainable animals. Certainly women have functioned in these ways over the centuries even more than have other groups of the weak. It's tempting, emotionally, to see such a situation as the result of a deliberate plot by those who benefit from it. Conspiracy theory not only "explains" human difficulties neatly, it absolves the victims from the charge of conniving at their own subjugation. But that kind of reasoning is both unrealistic and counterproductive: another sort of mythic thinking. When we imagine that our lives are ruled by cunning conspiracies against us, undertaken by the powerful, we are giving them more credit than they deserve. We are imagining that they possess more power than they really can mount, and by so doing, we weaken our own ability to resist. It isn't well-planned conspiracy that keeps us down but our own agreement to our unimportance, the acceptance of insignificance, the conviction that we deserve what we're getting.

This conviction grows out of the common acceptance, deep below the level of consciousness, of our own social mythology and the values that its definitions lay out for its believers, values that are part of the status quo. It's natural that we do this. If we go back for a moment to the early experience of the growing child, we see that each of us learns the world that is certified to us, the existing world as perceived by the elders of a particular time and culture. And we learn intensely, with fear, excitement, and hope. We adapt ourselves to this knowledge and create within our minds a reflection of the outer structure as it stands. We do not doubt, as we learn, that "whatever is, is right"—even if we sometimes find it uncomfortable to accommodate ourselves to these "whatevers."

It is only later in life, as the individual self comes together and trusts itself to judge differently from its elders, that we begin to admit, and express, our doubts. Even then we won't include the whole framework of our lives in the questioned area. We can't—this framework is both *what* we know and *how* we know. In Durkheim's terms, these selves of ours are the product of the impact of society on the individual. Individuals differ widely, but the shaping force is consistently there with its rules of logic, its directives as to status and hierarchy, its implicit judgments on such things as the presence of the sacred and the importance of common ritual or personal endeavor.

Any of us may be determined to see that some aspects of our society are changed for others that we are certain will be better; but there will also be much that we quite like and more that we are willing to put up with. Probably all of us accept a good deal more than we reject, though we'll be most aware of what irritates us into rejecting it. Nevertheless even the most revolutionary of us believes that quite a lot of what is, is right. Political rebels have found it easy to go along with sex inequity; economic reformers set up production systems that parallel the ones they attack; religious reformers create their own Inquisitions in the name of freedom of worship; and so on. We have absorbed the language we were taught, with all the logical or illogical connections among ideas that it carries within it, and have absorbed too the great body of useful information about practical techniques for getting on with other members of our world order. We love our own landscape, our own climate. And we have all invested a great deal of effort and ingenuity in adjusting ourselves to what we take to be inescapable, continuing, circumstances in the life around us. To a greater extent than we can know, these circumstances have shaped the roles we play, we have shaped ourselves to fit the roles and they, in turn, have influenced the image we see of ourselves.

It's obvious to any rebel, reformer, or revolutionary that challenging the way the world works requires a challenge to the power structure. That is not easy. But even harder is challenging our own acceptance of the world as it is, for that acceptance can trip us up from behind at any moment. Yet a real attack on the external set of a society demands an accompanying reform of the interior image of that society: consciousness-raising, to use a familiar term. To do that, we must drag the beliefs that we have learned and taken for granted up into consciousness where they can be examined, reshaped, or abandoned. Whatever is, *isn't* right, at least not all of it, and that's true inside our heads as well as outside. We have to tell ourselves so repeatedly, attentively; and if we are then to do anything about this change of heart, if we are going to reinforce it by action, we shall have to say to others that we have cherished wrong beliefs.

A conversion experience that overturns one's own long-standing pattern of values and thoughts isn't easy to maintain, even when it's supported by strong bonds with others who have been through the same crisis. At best some old friends will point out that one is disputing the wisdom of centuries as well as making a fool of oneself to fall for (to stay with our example) "Women's Lib." Some of us will plunge ahead, but some won't. It takes more than a spasm of insight to persevere in acting out a changed role. It takes repeated acts of determination, it takes the self-confidence of the trickster-hero who is willing to pay the price of mockery and pain for disputing the taboos of the gods. How many of the weak have ever had a chance to develop such committed courage and self-direction? Can one be certain that one is even judging reality accurately when others are so ready to laugh at one's new beliefs and appeal to the old ones? If fighting for "a man's job" is not only ridiculous but also the stamp of an aggressive and therefore unattractive woman who must expect to live at odds with the approved norms, then not everyone will go on fighting.

Those who do fight may find that they are not alone, and that their actions are indeed effective, and therefore reinforcing to their new beliefs; but to get that far, one must first act. Hangers-back and droppers-out will profit from no such reinforcement; nothing will tell them that they're really more capable than they imagine themselves to be. Stuck in the old pattern, they will naturally want to justify their acceptance of the way things are and will welcome arguments that declare "whatever is, is right." Those who turn away from the possibility of change can easily come to deny, even to themselves, that they can imagine better lives than those they lead. Let us again recall Bruno Bettelheim's patient John, who chose to become a victim because he could see no other alternative to being made a victim by force.

When the weak make this sort of choice, a choice that lets the powerful control the world by default, they are deciding to live, in Winnicott's word, "uncreatively." They don't just throttle down conscious ambitions, they shut off their imaginations. They—we—choose to live in "a world we never made" and to fit ourselves into personality patterns prescribed by others, sanctioned by tradition, but—and this is the crippling feature—not to be adjusted to the living, inner reality of this particular human creature; and not to be tested against outer reality, either, for this choice denies the right to judge outer reality on the basis of lived experience instead of social norms.

That would seem to guarantee safety to those who accept the peace of conformity. It doesn't. To give up one's individual, imaginative life does not put one in a state of satisfying beehive intimacy with others. On the contrary, it has the paradoxical effect of isolating human beings from one another. Those who are alienated from their own interior emotions and who have denied their ability to form independent judgments find it impossible to conceive the inner reality of others. Without trust in a true, steady, reasonably reliable self that reflects and responds to the world around, there's no way to recognize the selves of others and to form the connections that create community. The isolated self stands apart from these others, cannot trust them since it cannot trust itself, and therefore fears them. And it must assume that they are hostile as it projects this fear out upon them.

This deep sense of isolation from others is one of the existential conditions that strengthens the powerful without their having any need to conspire against the weak. Another is the trivialization of life, which convinces the weak that nothing they do or feel can be very important, so why insist on having one's way in the face of opposition? It isn't worth it. Third is the self-doubt and lack of confidence that persuade the weak that they can't prevail in any action against an established elite, whose ability to wield power seems magically to authenticate their legitimate possession of it. These unhappy convictions feed on each other: if you are sure that you can't achieve your ends, you will try very hard not to want them passionately. Unsatisfied desire hurts. Isolation also feeds into self-doubt. How can one person, alone, stand out against the order of things as they are, take on the role of taboo-breaker and hero? For how can one be sure that one's single, unsubstantiated opinion might, improbably, be true? We are looking at the social analogy to the primary life-crisis that Erikson distinguishes as testing the basic trust of one's self, and of the world around. These three disorders of vision form the psychological barrier that keeps the weak "in their place."

And yet the rituals and ceremonies and mythic tales which helped our ancestors to survive, as today they help other communities, have something else to say about power. These case histories illustrate the use of magic to set the powerful off from the weak; but they also declare that there are proper limits to power within which it can be used in orderly fashion for the good of the community, in order to counter the misfortunes and risks inherent in life. Moreover, they indicate that though it is difficult and painful to challenge the gods and break taboos, those who are brave enough may be able to do it. Old myths and rituals, strange to us because they incorporate other structures of belief, still convey a message we can understand: power is necessary but power is limited even when it has access to the sacred. In its proper use, it serves the community, not just the powerful, and therefore those who rule are obligated to those who don't. And this is not a meaningless moral maxim. Just as our nightmares have taught us, power is *dangerous* if it is used wrongly. Step over the limits, wherever they may be drawn within the community, and you will suffer. Those who ask too much, for immortality, for omnipotence, will be turned to stone. Because myths are not just descriptions of the world and explanations of its laws, but also prescriptions and injunctions, because they speak in the imperative mood, they teach those who believe in them to abide by the limits of power, powerful and weak alike.

Today, of course, the myths have faded and the clear meaning of these injunctions has been forgotten. All that remains is a magic edge still flickering round our perception of power. The awesome peril of supernatural punishment for its misuse is no longer centrally stated and affirmed by ritual in this secular century. If the sense of community is no longer embodied in the sacred, if fear of the supernatural no longer serves to keep the powerful within bounds, if its subliminal presence in our minds merely frightens the weak into continued submission—then this ancient guideline for the use of power seems to have turned into its opposite, and to encourage, now, any misuse that rulers may choose to employ in their own interest.

What then can constrain them from the abuse of authority, if there is nothing in this secular world to confront them with retribution and no other, sacred, world where divine sanctions will call them to judgment? Why should they not exploit power and magic to the utmost? Why acknowledge any obligation beyond lip-service to the good of the community as a whole? Is there any practical, realistic reason to suppose that the trend to the ultimate corruption of absolute power can ever be stayed, or existing tyrannies brought down?

Well, yes, I think there is. Why else does the idea of the limits of power exist at all, why is it repeated in myth and legend as being part of the structure of society in which we live? The techniques of use and control that the myths put forward may vanish with the world that created them; nonetheless, we feel on our own nerve-ends the danger of uncontrolled might, and poets, psychoanalysts, and sleepers continue to testify that those who imagine themselves kings of infinite space are haunted by bad dreams. Have we ourselves not witnessed how, in the historical scene, Fate on her chosen occasions has brought down the mighty from their seats? Though we have lost our sense of the sacred as an immediate part of life, the community from which it springs lives on. The governed can, and do, withdraw their consent to the acts of their governor, and the governors fall. Even though the remnants of magic work to uphold the status quo, the weak have powers by which they can challenge the great and limit the thrust to omnipotence and the corrupting perils of absolute power.

CHAPTER 11

Powers of the Weak I: Disbelief

*Power is a property of the social relation; it is not an attribute of the actor. . . .
Social relations commonly entail ties of mutual dependence between the parties.
. . . These ties . . . imply that each party is in a position, to some degree, to
grant or deny, facilitate or hinder, the other's gratification. Thus, it would
appear that the power to control or influence the other resides in control over the
things he values, which may range all the way from oil-resources to ego-support.*

Richard Emerson,
"Power-Dependence Relations"[1]

The thesis of this book—that powers of the weak exist and function
at many levels—naturally assumes that these powers differ from those of the
powerful, will often not be perceived as powers at all, and seldom be considered positive. To the powerful (we have seen) they appear as stumbling
blocks, limitations, and misfunctions in the ordained and expected conditions of life. For a balanced view we must move to the other side, trying as
we do to let go of our preconceptions. Powers of the weak are not negative,
but neither are they inherently moral or just; the voice of the people is simply
the voice of the people, not of God. Dr. Emerson's cool description of the
power-process counters a tendency to sentimentalize the weak that is as
common as our propensity to glamorize the authority of the powerful. Speakers of English seem to suffer from pervasive underdoggism, but the idea that
the weak are kinder and nicer than the mighty is tosh. True, the powers of
the weak are more limited and thus somewhat less likely to carry the groups
that practice them beyond the bounds of common benefit, but they are quite
as amoral, in themselves, as those of the powerful. Bonding together in
mutuality can also be felt as crippling peer pressure, while the refusal to
accept governance as legitimate authority can produce outbursts of violence
and looting, stubborn endemic crime, and gestures of terrorism.

Overall the weak are no more generally warmhearted, Dickensian dears
than women are by nature loving, nurturing, supportive adjuncts to husbands and bosses. Projecting such virtues onto those who do not hold power
falsifies their real position. Of course, it's easy to do; all of us would like to

find, sometime, a world in which the good and the bad folk were clearly set off from each other, and no doubt, as Bruno Bettelheim maintains in his study of fairy-tales, *The Uses of Enchantment,* children need to believe in the possibility of "happy endings" if they are to develop their capacity to hope and to act in a world that is, for them, dominated by knowing, powerful, adult-sized giants, masters of crafty magic.

But when our mythology instructs any class of adults that it is their role to be gentler and more virtuous or humbler than the powerful, it operates as a form of social control. The injunction, directed to women, that they should behave like "ladies" in public still carries enough weight for judges to acquit rapists who are taken to have "reacted" to "unladylike" behavior such as hitchhiking or wearing unconventional dress. Just as "nice girls" stay home and dress modestly, the weak are instructed to keep a low profile and practice the virtues of patience and humility. But if any of these human characteristics are virtues, they are pertinent for all to use: Why are men exempted from modesty or the powerful from patience and humility? Effective governance can use them all, when circumstances require.

There is nothing inherently "better" about the weak or "worse" about the powerful, as human beings. What is "better" is, first, that a relative balance should exist between the members of a power relationship, simply because one-sided relations are either unstable or else deeply oppressive and wasteful of human abilities. In addition, the limitations placed on the powers of the weak by the very condition of weakness do inculcate certain virtues and common responses that arise when these powers are used consciously and purposively. Thus, if the governed are going to withstand unwarranted demands from their rulers, they have to learn the value of loyalty to each other, how to hang together so as not to hang separately. Some of them, at any rate, had better temper wishful optimism with realistic drive. They ought to be reasonably truthful to themselves and their companions so as not to mislead each other. These are valuable human qualities over and above their practical usefulness, but the weak aren't blessed with them automatically. On the contrary, development of these attributes is a function of efforts by the weak to overcome their condition. Needless to say, they don't always succeed in becoming either more powerful or more virtuous.

A balanced power relationship, then, does not so much derive from "better" qualities in either partner as it tends to produce them through effective interaction. When interaction is effective, Richard Emerson tells us, it offers opportunities for reciprocal gratification; both members get something (enough) out of it, each has some control over the other by dint of controlling things the other values, and this reciprocity limits the extent to which one partner can dominate the other. Emerson's findings, he notes, are "anchored most intimately in small group research," though the theory formed on his observations is "meant to apply to more complex community relations as well." We are working back, then, from large political and social analyses of power to a level of personal experience.

In fact, a reminder that dependent individuals can influence others is salutary. In our time we are too apt to accept unquestioningly the contention that a single person is helpless to accomplish much alone; an opinion which, in itself, promotes the abdication of power by the weak. Emerson is considering groups of ordinary citizens down to children at play, and his observations are rooted in daily life, where we can easily see how mutual giving-and-getting sets boundaries to power. Here we find the ordinary, usual action of the powers of the weak within relationships that are rarely excessive. When we examine disorders of power, we have to turn to extremes: disturbed children, nightmares, the temptation among the great to reach out for constantly increasing authority. But when we come to explore its ordered uses, we find them operating in orderly fashion, in the lives we know and live out.

Even so, Emerson wants us to begin with a somewhat unbalanced relation, since what has gone wrong can point us to remedies. Let B be dependent on A, then, he says, in a situation that does not offer adequate reciprocity. B is giving more than she is getting for she is, in this pre–Woman's Movement paper, that classic example of inferiority, "a rather 'unpopular' girl with a puritanical upbringing, who wants desperately to date." A is "a young man who occasionally takes her out, while dating other girls as well." We need not consider Emerson's formulas to agree that A possesses a "power advantage" in this familiar parable; if we have not been there ourselves, we've watched from the sidelines. Now, A takes advantage of B's dependence by making "sexual advances" (which are assumed to be unwelcome because yielding would violate B's commitment to her own moral standards). What can B do to remedy this unstable and demanding situation? How is she to lessen the tensions within it?

One possibility is obviously to say "Yes" to A's advances or, as Dr. Emerson puts it, "to reduce the psychic costs involved in continuing the relationship by redefining her moral values." But, as so many Advisors to the Lovelorn have had occasion to point out, there is no guarantee that this will work: "The weaker member has sidestepped one painful demand, but she is still vulnerable to new demands"—probably more vulnerable, indeed, since A's ascendancy has been increased and B will, in all likelihood, be suffering pangs of guilt. So let B consider another alternative. If, instead, she renounces "the value of dating [and] develops career aspirations," she will effectively reduce A's advantage because she will be altering the relation between them in her own favor by withdrawing some of her "motivational investment" in the unbalanced relationship with A.[2]

Let us examine more closely what seems at first to be simply a change of mind on the part of B. In fact she is getting ready to set in motion a process that is not confined to the existing relationship with A, but can alter her status in the external world. She does not trivialize her own values (we may not agree with them, but they are hers) by substituting A's values for them without really accepting them; a concession that would tend to unbalance the situation even more. Rather, she is beginning to look for greater positive control over her own life by considering seriously the possibility of a career. Of course she can't stop with simply considering it; her "aspirations" must lead to some kind of action designed to bring about an advance in employment level, train her for a profession, or gain her a new skill. Fantasies don't buttress self-worth in any dependable way unless they are acted on. But if Dr. Emerson's Miss B (her adventures antedate the use of Ms. by some years) pursues the second strategy to its logical conclusion, she will not only have lessened her dependence for gratification on dating A; she will have laid the ground for other diverse relationships and "alternative sources of gratification." Beyond the operation of the pleasure principle, new skills and greater control over one's existence increase one's self-esteem.

Sociologists, we hear over and over, tend to labor the obvious, and perhaps these snippets from Emerson's theories seem to be doing just that. But what we have here, I think, is another of those examinations of the obvious that can lead to the nodes of meaning that tie our structure of beliefs together. In his designedly banal example of the workings of power and dependence, Emerson is illustrating the significance of alternatives: alternative paths to action, alternative views of potentiality. In many ways, the need for *creativity* in personal life and in larger social relations, which the analysts I have been using stress so strongly, can be described as a capacity to imagine alternatives to accepted roles and behavior. That is not the whole of the creative process, but it is certainly a vital part.

But when we place the ability to imagine other courses of action within the bounds of a relationship, we are looking once more at the effect of the *power to define.* If B were to accept A's valuation of sexual relations, she would give up her own power to define the phenomenon. Now, note that Emerson is not recommending that B enter into a debate with A on the topic and insist that her own views must prevail. Such a confrontation would not be likely to get her far or sweeten the feelings between them. Instead he suggests that she put up with the existence of a difference of opinion, and broaden the context of her life so that her dependence on A decreases overall. That allows her to continue to reject his definitions.

Confrontation can't always be avoided by the weak, nor should it be. But before it begins there will be a stage in which the weak look consciously at the world-definitions of the powerful and find them questionable. Politically (we observed) it became evident to ordinary Americans that Presidents

Johnson and Nixon were not defining the world situation accurately and that consequently their attempts to deal with it were becoming frighteningly inappropriate. It is here that an ordered use of the powers of the weak takes its start. The ruled begin to ask themselves whether such and such an event follows exactly from the cause assigned to it by the powerful; whether it is sensible to embark on a particular course of behavior just because they have been assured that it's inevitable for people in their position to act this way. Until this happens, the governed will be unable to think away from standard definitions, toward alternative explanations of events which point to alternative actions.

This attitude on the part of the ruled is usually given a rather unpleasant name; naturally enough, since it is being defined by the powerful. It is seen as *mistrust,* which can run on through *cynicism* to *alienation,* or *disaffection,* which leads on to *disloyalty*—and fetches up at *treason.* We can do best if we ignore the negative thrust of this sequence and return to the single emotion of "disbelief"; let us doubt, let us not take for granted, what the powerful say about events, their causality, their meaning and their importance. This isn't cynicism, which is as extreme as total trust. Trust assumes that maxims and media all speak the truth, cynicism that none does and that the truth can never be discovered. We must certainly trust our own purposes and our judgments of the world, and trust each other on the basis of our experience; but trust is worthless if it is indiscriminate. To say that children must learn trust, as Erikson properly does, is to say that they must *be able* to trust themselves and the world, not that they should do so always and automatically; and that they learn to do so on the basis of early experiences (which will certainly be diverse) if, on the whole, their experience is adequately supportive. Adults, with a wider experience, can test reality in the same way but with a longer life-history to judge by. One need be neither a cynic nor a sage to consider what the powerful tell us and what our social mythology offers as explanations of reality and inquire, Is all this true? Is it even plausible?

Oddly enough, it is by no means easy to ask these questions, even just of oneself. Why should this be? After all, mere disbelief in the orthodox, received view of life and in the power of positive thinking isn't subversive. One can disagree with majority opinions, surely, without making a fuss—without mounting protests, demonstrations, and marches, without joining picket lines, and equally without hooting and throwing missiles at such expressions of opinion by others, without writing letters to the papers, addressing meetings, inviting arrest, and going on hunger strikes. Simply, inside one's head, one says "No." Why should that be difficult? Is it, perhaps, because we know subliminally that once we do so we are going to take another step? Is there a human tendency to push on from thought to action?

Do we hang back because we sense that once a process gets under way it will press toward completion?

The reactions of the Establishment (any Establishment) seem to point to this conclusion. Negative thinking is held to be subversive in itself even if it gives rise to no action; a case, perhaps, in which the power to define turns against itself. The weak are often surprised to discover that a quiet group which has done no more than express disagreement with some official statement is suddenly assailed by caricaturists and preachers. Surely this is curious behavior. One can see that dissident activists might well come to a point where their common experience validates an alternative explanation of some political condition, at which time they begin to make propaganda for heterodox views; but why do the priests of the status quo require propagandists and censors when their own definitions already prevail?

Once again we find ourselves wondering about paranoid impulses among the powerful. If power is what they say it is—might, authority, the command of armies—what are they scared of? If, however, their logic is wrong but their grip on sanity is still strong, we must look at their emotions, not their verbalizations, and conclude that the weak do possess a power of considerable weight in the apparently private ability to disagree with the mighty. We considered, in Chapter 8, what it is that the powerful want from the weak, and it was suggested that *legitimacy,* not power itself, as the powerful define it, but rather the *right* to power, is the answer. In Emerson's terms, we can see this as "control by the weak over things the powerful value." Disbelief, then, signals something that the powerful fear, and slight as it may appear, we should not underestimate its force. It is, in fact, the first sign of the withdrawal of consent by the governed to the sanctioned authority of their governors, the first challenge to legitimacy.

In Chapter 8 we examined the value of legitimacy to the powerful by looking at the effects of its loss. To understand it fully, we should also explore the positive rewards of legitimacy: the full and eager granting of consent, in contrast to its withdrawal. It's interesting that our culture, with its usual predilection for thinking of power as an attribute of the powerful, describes this relation as devotion to a charismatic leader; it is the leader eliciting dedication that we see, not the long-suffering governed, moved for once to bestow their trust without stint. And it's true that this meeting of ardent minds in a springtime of belief is the highest award that the powerful can receive. The leader embodies in herself or himself the emotions of others, no compulsive force need be exerted, and the group seems to feel and to move as one, in an almost holy unity. In some fashion the community has come together and found an instrument-agent-commander to express its own "sacred" strength. In such participant action-governance there need be no compromises, no awkward bargaining, no losses, no friction. "We are not divided, / All one body we," thumps the hymn carried by the plebeian chorus. "Bliss was it in that dawn to be alive," sings the poet.

For the leader, such ease of action, such flowing response, must provide the acme of pleasure in power. It cannot last; it brings a fragmentary fleeting experience of an ideal situation that is close to omnipotence in which an "I" controls capacities that range far beyond the limits that human children learn as the normal human repertory available to normal human beings; a bit of magic or dream actualizing itself unexpectedly in everyday life. We should not marvel that the powerful value so highly moments when disbelief and dissent have vanished in a tide of mutuality that acts through them and conveys a sense of superhuman strength. No wonder the memory of such expanded potential nudges our rulers toward the propagation of agreement and the discouragement of dissent.

But the etymology of *charisma*—it comes from the Greek and means "divine gift"—itself implies relationship. Who gives this gift of power that can enchant the governed into joyful consent? We need only reach back to Durkheim's hypothesis that divinity takes its source in the group's impact on the individual: charismatic power derives from the community. The connection is implicit in Max Weber's famous analysis of charisma. Weber perceives leaders who possess this aura as representatives of the sacred. But he carefully distinguishes them from those whose divinity has been institutionalized and distanced from the governed within a formal structure. Like the magicians who validate their magic by its effectiveness in ordinary life, charismatic leaders are tested according to the immediate value of their power to their followers.

> The charismatic hero [writes Weber] does not derive his authority from ordinances and statutes, as if it were an official "competence," nor from customary usage or feudal fealty as with patrimonial power; rather he acquires it and retains it only by proving his powers in real life. He must perform miracles if he wants to be a prophet, acts of heroism if he wants to be a leader in war. Above all, however, his divine mission must "prove" itself in that those who entrust themselves to him must prosper. This very serious conception of genuine charisma obviously stands in stark contrast with the comfortable pretensions of the modern theory of the "divine right of kings," with its references to the "inscrutable" decrees of God, "to whom alone the monarch is answerable": the genuinely charismatic leader, by contrast, is answerable rather to his subjects.[3]

Not only is he answerable, says Weber, the power he uses "must be constantly reconfirmed." Charisma, that is, does not permit a leader to act alone, on impulse and without sanction from her or his supporters. This sanction may be unspoken, but the hero's freedom to act is dependent on the response of the ruled; and their response, in this case especially, takes place within the bounds of a felt relationship that runs from group to hero, an emotional bond connecting each with each. The hero's exploits, the miracles and acts of heroism that test and validate his or her power, may be celebrated and remembered as individual feats, but they are experienced as exemplifying and actualizing the needs and desires, hopes and dreams, of a participating community. The power to act daringly, successfully, is drawn from group strength and sanctioned by group authority; let us recall how the unconscious involvement of the tribe's emotions sanctioned the formally disapproved acts of the trickster. In fact, the hero becomes something more than an individual, even one of heroic scale; becomes, rather, the instrument, representative, agent of others. We are witnessing the exercise of a power borrowed from society and shared with society in a continuous back-and-forth flow. Such power is used with great ease because the bond between hero and constituents is immediate. For once, there is no need to compel the governed to an obedience that is now offered with joy. Indeed, it goes beyond consent and is felt to involve the ruled directly in the act of ruling.

This is the power permitted to the powerful by full trust, unconstrained and free-flowing. It is the joyful authorization of action in which the hero is hardly even an "I," simply the moving point of a "We." We can't expect to find it often, but where we do, it is marked by a special quality of humanness and wholeness and by the lack of formal, institutionalized structures of rule; though those cannot be absent for long. It appears to be open-ended, with communication and trust flowing two ways.

Of course the powerful desire this situation. *So do the governed.* We want to believe that things are going well, that princes can be trusted to act wisely and sages to foresee the future correctly. We would like to be looked after, to believe in fairy godmothers, wise old men, and the rest of the nurturing archetypes. But once past childhood it's dangerous to do so. These creatures are interior figures, symbols projected by our desires onto the outside world. If we imagine that they can be effective there, can make sure that you're OK and I'm OK and that all manner of things will be well without our doing anything about it, we are living in Camelot or Cloud Cuckooland. In a charismatic relationship, our motives merge with those of the hero, but only for the duration of the situation that has evoked and sustained the relation. If we don't hang on to a sense of our own, separate, motives and standards, we may well find ourselves in the condition of Dr.

Emerson's Miss B, with mutuality lost, values tangled, and alternative strategies hard to imagine.

The trouble with charisma comes when it ends. Then it's easy to plunge into a cynicism that refuses any trust, and our fall will be hardest if we have failed to see the temporary mutuality of charismatic trust as a strong form of interaction, and have instead granted the powerful a unique right to rule. By giving them total responsibility, we are arranging to see them as betraying us if anything goes wrong. Of course things go wrong. The ability of governors to govern reasonably well most of the time, enough at any rate to earn the support of their fellow citizens, is the most we can ask of them. Only in myths of a Golden Age do rulers exhibit an ability to govern well all the time, all by themselves, unaided by grumbling questions and angry shouts from the rest of us. The charismatic situation is as rare as it is long-remembered.

When, forty-odd years ago, E. M. Forster offered only two cheers for democracy, reserving the third for "Love, the beloved republic," he was warning his readers of the limits that reality puts on solitary virtues. Trust can go too far, become too absolute. A charismatic leader invites complete commitment, not merely consent; and such unstructured governance can tip over into tyranny because it finds no checks and balances to hinder excesses. We can suspect that this is happening when we observe that the group is not just expressing some skepticism, but that it is splitting, with some of the faithful becoming a palace guard that mounts a campaign against other erstwhile loyalists. Disagreements are natural in any community, but the bitterness of those who are feeling the loss of charismatic connection suggests that it was not the goals of government that sustained them so much as the emotion of bonded togetherness. But, as Forster says, government is not really the place to look for that emotion. There are many roads to tyranny, but overcommitment to charismatic interrelation is a short one. Even when mutuality is strong, ceding all power to the powerful is perilous.

For the ordered uses of power depend on their being two members to the power-dependence relationship, each able to control the things the other values, at least to some extent. The power relation is not conjoint and undifferentiated, not an overwhelming oceanic unity. Being human demands that each of us be an autonomous creature centered in an independent self. We form societies, but not those total colonies to be found among ants, bees, and termites, which can really be thought of as organisms. Human groups are flexible and fluid because human beings do each of us carry that separate, single brain within its nutshell skull, which records separate experiences and provides us with separate purposes; often similar, always in need of connection for validation and for action; but never the same. The brevity of any charismatic relationship may be all to the good. Its impermanence throws us back on ourselves and delivers us once more to uncomfortable, problematic actuality, where flexibility is an asset and static unanimity is maladaptive.

The urge to unanimity is an aspect of the power to define; or at least of its unthinking, taken-for-granted use. When in an earlier book I was examining the nature of myth, I had to conclude that a desire for universal agreement dwells in the social mythology of any community. The power to define, that is, is not simply descriptive, but also prescriptive. A description of the way the world works is a directive toward proper behavior in such a world: understanding and action are expected to connect, and every creed is also a code of moral behavior and, often, manners. Mythologies are dynamic; and indeed, learning something, in any connection, implies learning to do something with the knowledge one has gained.

But mythologies are compulsive as well. The behavior they direct is not just possible, but necessary: the "one right way" to react and respond to events. Failure to do so—disbelief in a definition, deviation from expected conduct—doesn't imperil just the misbehaving individual, but everyone else as well. It somehow—superrationally if not supernaturally—threatens the order of the universe. Challenge the code and you challenge the creed and strike at the heart of society. When we recall the decade of the nineteen-sixties (and for those who can remember, that of the nineteen-twenties as well), we come on repeated examples of orthodox outrage at mischievous manners, uppity ways, unexpected dress, which in themselves were utterly insignificant. But they were gestures expressive of dissent and disbelief. The Counterculture was cocking a snook at the Establishment. It upset the Establishment horribly; so horribly that it abandoned its own rational assumptions. Whether or not those who gathered to chant spells as a means of levitating the Pentagon thought their methods would work is moot. But why should the Establishment behave as if *its* members thought so? It is a remarkable, if unwitting, tribute to the effectiveness of disbelief, and to the value the powerful attach to legitimacy.

In Richard Emerson's terms, then, the need felt by our governors for general agreement on the rightness of their judgments and their actions is a handle on power for the weak: control over something the governors value. Dissent in any form, whether it touches on practical governance or not, can appear to herald the withdrawal of consent to legitimate authority; which makes legitimate authority very nervous. Sometimes this unease appears as a fear of change so great that it suggests the idea that any change at all will be total: revolutionary. Early reactions to the Women's Movement offer examples: a demand for equal wages was taken to imply a feminist takeover of the power structure that would reduce men to the status of slaves and sex-objects.

If one took the powerful seriously, they were granting more power to the weak than the weak desired; in fact, they were exercising the power to define in a state of panic. Unfortunately, that power was and is still sufficiently effective for many of the weak to be moved by it, and to put some stock in these definitions. The need of rulers for validation of their authority can operate as a bargaining counter for the ruled, but if they are to use it, they must hold tight to their willingness to disbelieve in what the powerful tell them they are doing. They must, that is, dissent enough, for a very useful part of the power to define is the ability to define the stance and the aims of one's opponents, and so continue to control the view they have of the world.

Ordered use of the power to disbelieve, the first power of the weak, begins here, with the refusal to accept the definition of oneself that is put forward by the powerful.

It is true that one may not have a coherent self-definition to set against the status assigned by the established social mythology, but that is not necessary for dissent. By disbelieving, one will be led toward doubting prescribed codes of behavior, and as one begins to act in ways that deviate from the norm in any degree, it becomes clear that in fact there is *not* just one right way to handle or understand events. Actually, we gormless fools of the weak are often much closer to practical getting-things-done than are our betters, when we begin to wonder about the unique ways to accomplish things that are known only to those who have a direct line to Olympus or access to the occult wisdom of the CIA or advance data on the progress of the Five-Year Plan. The deeper we get into the human, related world of governance and the farther from measurable physical laws and replicable scientific experiment, the more diverse become possible techniques for reaching acceptable goals. History and anthropology tell us that human beings have managed to set up social groupings of remarkable variety which are not only adapted to a wide range of physical environments but which also incorporate very diverse world views. Certainly there are similarities among these groups—one such is the universal existence of an elite which would like its authority to be considered legitimate—but there are enormous differences too. There may be models there that could be recreated, but even if there are not, the flexibility of humankind should both relieve us of fears that we are bound to go wrong if we change our institutions, and confirm our faith in our capacity to invent new ones.

Of course, disbelief is so easy and common that we may tend to disbelieve in the power of disbelieving. But if we are to come on real powers of the weak, we have to expect that they will be widespread, natural, and familiar. The question is not whether they exist, but how to use them in dealing with our rulers. I don't think we need disbelieve in the value they place on the ability of the governed to validate ruling authority and sanction its power by our consent to it; or else, to refuse.

CHAPTER 12

Powers of the Weak II:
Coming Together

There is one common safeguard in the nature of prudent man, which is a good security for all, but especially for democracies against despots. What do I mean? Mistrust. Keep this, hold to this; preserve this only, and you can never be injured.

Demosthenes,
Second Philippic

Demosthenes's testimonial to the value of mistrust is vivid and telling, as some who have trusted tyrants too long can bear witness; but, in the manner of orators, he goes too far when he declares that disbelief in itself is sufficient to protect democracies against despots. Unfortunately it's not true that if you "preserve this only, you can never be injured." Mistrust must be acted on, and effective action by the ruled is not solitary and singular, but joint and repeated. Of course Demosthenes's rhetoric was uttered in context: it was a *common* safeguard he urged, in a *public* address. It was not directed to isolated individuals, nor was he asking his listeners to indulge in philosophic contemplation of the dangers of despotism. He wanted to move them toward organized resistance against the threat to Greece posed by Philip of Macedon, a threat of invasion and conquest that was fulfilled all too soon. Mistrust was put forward as a necessary first step.

When mistrust is solitary, it can react against the doubter whether it questions political promises or orthodox wisdom about personal relations. Mistrust needs validation, and that comes from assurances that one's doubts are realistic and shared by others. For women, the frightening experience of doubting society's directives and then doubting one's right to doubt them is still very recent. The immediacy of female experience of change, in fact, is one reason for its usefulness. These things happened yesterday, or a few years ago; they are still happening. Many of the books that signaled the rise of the second wave of feminism bear witness to remembered anxiety of this kind among those who could not settle comfortably into the female role as it was presented to them in the fifties and sixties. Over and over they report how they came to mistrust themselves instead of the role. Wasn't their uneasiness neurotic, weren't they abnormal? The feminine mystique, as Betty Friedan made forcefully clear, does not just devalue the lives and purposes of women, it separates women from each other. Those who did not find a satisfactory identity in the Happy-Housewife-and-Nurturing-Mother image that was held up to them in the fifties and sixties were apt to regard their dissent as a sign, a stigma, of abnormality. The first taste of liberation came with the discovery that other women felt as they did: it was liberation from the doubts about their own health and sanity.

Indeed, it's too soon to talk of isolation and doubt in the past tense. Half a generation after Friedan's book appeared, *The New York Times* was reporting on a program conducted by a Long Island hospital to help victims of agoraphobia, "the fear of open and public places that results in an inability to leave home." At its worst, agoraphobia prevents its victims from crossing the street or entering a shop. Panic stops them in their tracks. It can feel, says one sufferer, like a heart attack. "I just couldn't function," said another. "I'd stay in the house and stand at the stove and stare at a pot."

As her words suggest, this is a sex-related complaint. Dr. Charlotte Zitrin, head of the phobia clinic at Long Island Jewish–Hillside Medical Center, estimates that 80 percent of agoraphobes are women, and in England the problem is called "the homebound housewife's neurosis." The seven women interviewed by Judy Klemesrud of the *Times* all said that their husbands were eager to have them find a cure for their condition, but Dr. Zitrin believes that this is not always the case. "Some husbands foster it," she said, "and are very uncooperative, and impede their wives' improvement. They like to keep their wives at home and dependent." She added that cured patients often set about changing the patterns of their marriages, "even to the point of separating from or divorcing their husbands."

This finding suggests that the disease is a kind of retreat into paralysis for those whose mistrust of life is pervasive but who can find no support that will settle the question of what to mistrust—oneself, or the surrounding circumstances. Without such an answer it's impossible to act, impossible to try to change the status quo, for that means that one is criticizing one's life as it is; but to do that, one has to be willing to trust one's own judgment, trust it very possibly in the face of disagreement from an "uncooperative" husband who finds criticism unacceptable. This is not just an emotional bind. It results from a perfectly logical cognitive uncertainty that can surface in any mind: Am I right, or are the rules right when they tell me I'm wrong?

Therapy for agoraphobia may not intentionally answer that question, but it does so in practice. Its victims meet each other and find out that they are not lonely sufferers, but patients with a common complaint. The powerful may find it odd that a shared experience of weakness can strengthen the weak; but out of the sharing comes an ability to trust those who have been caught in the same bind as oneself. Treatment is diverse: individual work with a therapist, antidepressant drugs for some, and active conditioning to overcome anxiety and panic. But the first ventures that these patients make to hitherto unreachable terrain, such as a shopping center or a restaurant, are taken together as a group, and the support of the group is a potent factor in persuading its members that they can trust the ordinary human creatures that they are to deal with the ordinary ups and downs of existence. Like Dr. Emerson's Miss B, though at a different level of decisive activity, these people change and enlarge the context of their lives through new relationships; and in the same way, they diminish the overpowering value of the relationship that has somehow hurt them and held them back from intervention and interaction with reality. Fiction (and some of it by improbable authors) has dealt well with the strength that the weak can give each other: a late story of Kipling's, *In the Same Boat,* describes the quite asexual relationship that allows a man and a woman to save themselves and each other from neurotic terror and return to their normal lives.

So the powers of the weak are dependent, like those of the strong, on validation through shared experience within relationships; more dependent, in fact, since the strong are more likely to trust their independent judgment because they have acted effectively on their own initiative at some time or other. The weak, by definition, are weak. Which is not to say that they cannot change, or that the individuals who make up the governed masses are all alike, sunk in an undistinguishable plurality. They will always include heroes and rebels who can, and do, undertake solitary deeds of daring. But how are these deeds to be understood by the rest of the governed, what can they mean? Here is another example of the bewilderment the troubled weak can feel about the significance of events and emotions: Should I trust what the rules seem to say, or my own judgment? What are these people doing? ask their fellows. Are they crazy, to challenge authority, deny the rules of behavior, disrupt ongoing activities with their shouts and slogans? The martyrs of early Christendom are remembered as martyrs (remembered at all) only because their acts were comprehensible to other Christian believers who registered and preserved the significance of what the martyrs were doing. To the rest of the Roman populace, they must have seemed simply mad; and if Christianity had not survived, the courage with which they affirmed their dissent from Roman orthodoxy would be forgotten.

Martyrs, heroes of the weak, angry voluble rebels—they need an *audience.* A true constituency would be better, but at the very least, an audience must hear their words. And in fact, if an audience can hear and understand the message their actions spell out, a group will already be forming which shares disbelief and mistrust of the system and can act as a network of observers and informants that will create a coherent public opinion. As this happens, negative doubts begin to form positive links between mistrustful individuals. They are becoming a sisterhood, a brotherhood, a community. They may be quite unaware of it, but they are already building a new framework of belief, not simply differing from the old. The agoraphobes who dare to cross the street are able to resist old messages of fear by substituting new affirmations. In the fabric of everyday life, we know how mundane, purposeful groups like Alcoholics Anonymous and Weight Watchers provide the support and communication systems which help their members to believe that their own intentions are important enough to work for, and to go on working for.

Like the first power of the weak, dissent and mistrust, this second one, *coming together,* doesn't sound like much. Aren't the weak always doing this, cohering briefly into some artless cluster for some ill-defined, or some simply personal, end? And of course they are. It's as natural a human activity as questioning and disbelief. Once again, its naturalness is not a reason to devalue it. Devaluing the everyday, the personal, the ordinary, is one way that the judgments of the powerful trivialize the lives of the governed, and so promote the indecision and lack of ambition for which the governed are then criticized. If the weak agree, they will go on distrusting themselves, assuming that the committees or sodalities or clubs they found can never really accomplish anything, merely add a pinch of spice to their drab existence. They will also go on agreeing that their lives are deservedly dull and drab and that trying to change them is all but hopeless; except, perhaps, for those clever few who manage to learn how to act as if they were powerful and so merit a chance to rise. In fact, the advice of the powerful on how to stop being weak by aping the manners of the powerful is of very little use to the weak, as we shall see. The natural impulses of the governed to distrust their rulers, to set up their own like-minded companies, and to seek change through group action are much more effective. If the powerful don't know that, it's because they accept their own judgment about the governed, and it's not a good one.

For the governed, therefore, the second step toward achievement—forming their own groups for their own ends—has got to be firmly rooted in the first power of the weak, mistrust of the powerful and their opinions, since the opinions of the powerful on the subject of the weak are both ignorant and self-serving. Disbelief and mistrust shared with others act as a protective shield beneath which a new trust can grow, trust of oneself and one's fellows. Coming together sets up a bridge that stretches from dissent to positive action.

Without such support and connection, solitary dissenters can lose their way in a gulf of anomie and apathy, drop-out and cop-out, the Slough of

Despond where John Bunyan's pilgrim found himself mired in his progress. The power to define, possessed by the powerful, will piously continue to declare that the weak belong there, because they are weak. But a tautology is not a definition, let alone an explanation; in this case, it's a manipulation. To say the weak are weak is of course true, but if the statement is held to mean that none of the weak can hope to change their condition, it functions as an effort to impose a static rationalization on the ever-shifting data of reality: that is, it's an attempt at social control by fiat. Political action is not in your nature, say the powerful to the weak. Cop-out and drop-out, that's all you're good for.

Now, cop-out and drop-out are, in fact, political acts. They are not very effective ones, far less effective than bonding into groups, but political nonetheless, and not totally without felt results. They are a kind of silent withdrawal of consent which, at the very least, denies the powerful access to the capacities of their fellow creatures, who have turned their backs on the endeavors of the powerful to rule, and refused to participate. In extreme conditions, as under slavery, there is often little option for the weak. Eugene Genovese in *Roll, Jordan, Roll* reassesses the "shiftlessness" that southern slaveholders attributed to their slaves and suggests that it is better understood as purposive "disguised disobedience."[1] We can go on to see that though it might be disguised from the masters, it could not be hidden from other slaves, and consequently that even this minimal resistance must have had an element of mutuality and common action. Such "disguised disobedience" refuses the cooperation and the creative consent that the masters want, and demonstrates that these aspects of interaction are under the control of the slaves, who can choose not to give them.

Under slavery bonding was a necessity for survival and it was therefore largely defensive. The very idea was feared by the powerful, however, who fought it in every way that did not hinder the economic purpose of slavery —that is, work, and often work in gangs. Social and cultural means were employed to offset the danger of putting slaves to work together, and these restrictions were tightest on the large plantations that produced cash crops, where huge numbers of slaves labored concurrently. Enforced illiteracy was a conscious way to prevent slaves from keeping in touch over time and distance, and the repeated stories about "the grapevine" through which news spread by word of mouth tell us that the phenomenon was of great concern to the powerful. Social continuity was also discouraged. The breakup of families could not be condoned in a Christian society, but it was certainly ignored; and as long as the slave trade was lively, the owners of huge Caribbean plantations were quite willing to "turn over" their labor force by working its components to death. Undoubtedly the unconscious set of mind that saw the slaves as less than human—sometimes brutes, sometimes children—was designed to reduce the self-valuation of the slaves and their will to serve themselves before their masters. Rumors of slave revolt kept alive a nightmare sense of the need for such measures. Now, these are extreme conditions, margins of the normal power process, and in these circumstances covert coming together can do little more than nourish shared feelings of distrust and can seldom support any action more challenging than disguised disobedience.

But outside of the extremes where defensive action is all that can express shared experience, drop-out and cop-out don't promote any degree of mutuality at all. They are prebonding, and indeed they prevent it. The weak who withdraw from participation in active life weaken the powerful by diminishing the number of active followers, but they weaken themselves even more, and thus they increase overall the distance between the two members of the power-dependence relationship. At worst the symptoms of agoraphobia are reproduced mentally, as distrust turns inward against the self, and the only common experience appears to be a sense of solitary impotence. In less acute conditions we take political apathy for granted as natural to a time when nations, states, and cities are simply too big for any individual effort to influence their governance. And that's true for individual efforts; but not for group action.

Even in the past, when political units were smaller, cop-out and drop-out were dubious weapons for the weak. A recent study of justice in late medieval England concentrates on the crime of murder and methods of punishment or deterrence in an age at least as disturbed as ours and certainly as lacking in popular political activity: "a brutal reality of trying to administer laws without public cooperation." Not surprisingly, people had ceased to credit a legal system that could bring hardly more than a third of homicide cases into court and could convict only 17 percent of the accused, with the result that better than nine out of ten murderers went unpunished. But withdrawing support for this inefficient system of law did not benefit the weak. Instead, there was substituted reliance on "the time honored custom [of settling arguments] by fighting until one disputant either died or gave up." Whoever profits from a breakdown in law and order, it will not be those least able to stand up to unprovoked confrontation, especially if they stand alone.[2]

Our contemporary view of political apathy is very much influenced by this apathy itself; that is, it's smugly and naïvely unpolitical. A consensus exists that a decline in the popular vote in elections indicates a feeling of no confidence in the political system, and no doubt it does. But neither of the usual reactions to the situation does more than try to assign blame. Conventional wisdom condemns the nonvoters as irresponsible, much as the slaveholders labeled their slaves shiftless. In both cases, the cause for the phenomenon is held to rise in the nature of the weaker member. Equally conventional liberal thinking regards failure to vote as a judgment on the system. It is, but it's a very ineffective one. "It doesn't make any difference," say the nonvoters. "My vote won't end corruption, or outweigh special interests." True again, but *not* voting gives a positive advantage to the interest of others.

It is wrong, however, to define this withdrawal as "irresponsible," for surely to vote without conviction is less responsible still. What we are looking at, I think, is another instance of insufficient dissent. The governed are rejecting the value of a political system they don't believe in; that is, they are refusing to accept the rules and the definitions of governance put forward by the powerful. But they still accept the definitions that apply to themselves and their interests, they still see themselves as unimportant and incapable of changing things, they still regard *their* special interests as too trivial for them to advance by political means. They have got far enough to doubt the maxims for good citizenship put forward by our social mythology, they are aware of its growing shabbiness and its fading grip on reality, and many still feel that "something should be done."

But not by them. If that's irresponsible, it's due to a learned irresponsibility of exactly the same kind as the learned properties of the feminine role: having been barred from the world of action, women are blamed for their ignorance and incompetence in relating to this world when they do try to enter it. The weak have been told that politics is a matter for leaders and that they are by nature followers; and how can followers undertake autonomous action? So dissent and distrust must grow strong enough to question the role assigned, the image of weakness and incapacity. The real basis for change comes with a new self-image, validated by others in the same boat. Those who demonstrated against the war in Vietnam had got this far. They disproved doubts (including their own doubts) about their personal ability to act effectively by acting together, for an interest they shared. When individuals blend into a movement, individual goals become a joint purpose that won't be trivialized by self-doubt, while individual confidence increases because action is demonstrated to be effective. There's nothing new about this, and of course that's just the point. This power of the weak is also natural, familiar, and not too hard to use; not easy, but available. And each step points to the next: separate distrust is found to have realistic grounds when others feel it too. These others then come to be seen as possible allies for common action. And action leads on to suggest some degree of planning and organization for a sustained effort to do the "something" that has to be done.

It has happened time and again. We can find a good example in our own Western civilization when, some two hundred years ago, a new class of urban, industrial labor began to take form and find a coherent identity. The process is well documented. It took place long enough ago for us to examine its course with some objectivity, but not so long ago that the sentiments and reactions of those involved are too alien for us to comprehend them easily. How the weak found an inner defensive strength in the face of social upheaval produced by undreamed-of technological and economic change, with few if any guidelines to direct them, is an instructive story. Indeed, it's a story that isn't finished yet.

The story begins with pressure from outside, pressure that was destroying the old patterns of living and working that had kept 90 percent of the world's population occupied at static, repeated tasks in rural surroundings. Our ancestors were peasants. There were variations by region in the degree to which medieval forms of subsistence persisted, but even where towns were large and craft industry well established, urban folk were dependent on the health of the countryside. Two years of bad harvest brought famine everywhere, and the towns themselves would have died out except for continuing immigration, bringing in new blood.

Of course there were technological inventions, improvements in agricultural methods, and changes in the volume and range of trade, during the thousand years or so from Charlemagne's crowning to the onset of the Industrial Revolution, but these shifts took place at a pace we would call slow; and, overall, production of goods and food and the provision of services continued to demand muscle power and human skill. Artisans usually worked in family settings, where apprentices were part of the household. The greatest accumulations of labor occurred in agriculture, on the huge estates of Eastern Europe, or the *latifundia* scattered here and there along the Mediterranean, from Portugal through Sicily to the Balkans. This was no Golden Age. Peasants and yeomen farmers scratched out a hard living, and the enclosures of common land favored the well-to-do—as, indeed, did new methods of farming, which required both large holdings and money investment to make them profitable. Serfdom did not ease in the East during the eighteenth century, and in the West, the number of rootless farm laborers rose. Even so, the pace of work was still controlled, in the main, by custom and the weather. A great lord might own thousands of acres and control hundreds of workers, but the work was done farm by farm or village by village. There were few machines and those that existed responded to muscle power, or—like gristmills—to wind or water.

Consequently, when the Industrial Revolution came to birth in England in the late eighteenth century, it administered a twofold shock to the workers it gathered in. Almost as alien as the gearing of work to steam-powered machinery was the initiation into a large, concentrated workforce, living away from the land. Cities there had been—London in 1800 already held a population of nearly a million—but they were not substantial seats of industry. Of the urban pre–Industrial Revolution population, George Rudé writes, "At the top of the pyramid was the small minority of aristocrats, gentry, patricians, rich merchants, officials and upper clergy; in the middle a larger group of petty merchants, manufacturers, professional people and what the English called 'people of the middling sort'; and at its base, there was the large and mixed population of small tradesmen, master craftsmen, journeymen, apprentices, labourers, domestic servants and city poor." The components and percentages varied somewhat from state to state and city to city but, writes Rudé, "In no city at this time—not even in Manchester—can one speak of a distinctive working-class population, in the nineteenth century sense, with its own distinctive manner of living, dress, entertainments, speech, culture, lodgings or residential districts." Stronger than any sense of common destiny among city workers was a feeling of fellow-craftsmanship: "Though the issue of wages might divide them there were still overriding issues that bound the small master and journeyman together. . . . Even in London we find master weavers and their journeymen marching together to Parliament on a number of occasions in the 1760s and 1770s."[3] These artisans, whether they owned a business or not, regarded the craft, or "mystery," in which they had invested their learning years as the equivalent of property. To find it replaced by a mechanical process seemed to them expropriation.

Moreover, it was an expropriation that disrupted living styles and family relationships. Before the advent of the factory system, "Weaving had offered an employment to the whole family. . . . The young children winding bobbins, older children watching for faults, picking over the cloth or helping to throw the shuttle in the broad-loom; adolescents working a second or third loom; the wife taking a turn at weaving in and among her domestic employments. The family was together, and however poor meals were, at least they could sit down at chosen times. . . . Work did not prevent conversation or singing."[4]

To our minds, these laboring children may seem distressing; but in those days all children began to contribute something to family earnings, or survival, when they reached the age of seven or eight. The advent of the textile mills that destroyed the family weavers described here by E. P. Thompson didn't stop child labor. On the contrary, the mills sucked in children at the expense of adults. *They were cheaper.* The same consideration brought women to the factories in place of their husbands. By 1834 an estimate shows the number of adult females employed in the mills at about 103,000 with adult males at 89,000; and the working day could run to fourteen hours.

E. P. Thompson's classic work, *The Making of the English Working Class,* can't be compressed into a page or two. By theme and by illustrations it shows us the process by which a hitherto unrelated group of the governed, thrown willy-nilly into a situation that compacted them together, managed, out of their weakness, to arrive at a sense of common identity and of defensive strength. They were subjected to inhuman conditions, totally unforeseen, taking effect at a rate of speed that defied the ability to adjust, knocking out earlier connections and social agreements, and subjecting workers to the requirements of an unknown force, the machine. Life had not been Utopian in earlier days, far from it; but it had been comprehensible. Now, old rules ceased to work, and where people had experienced some control over their lives and their labor, had known periods of seasonal slack, had at least been able to choose which task to undertake first, all this was lost when the machine entered. Sunrise, sunset, rain, sun, and wind had structured the working day, and the nearest time came was the sound of churchbells. Now there was a factory whistle that dominated the hours and the people alike.

If power were indeed nothing but an attribute of the powerful, the ordinary people of England who were thrust into an intolerable and irresistible situation would surely have ended in a condition of slavery. In fact, they made no revolution in these years when the peasants of France rose, across the Channel. But they did respond to the disruption of their lives, disruption of meaning and purpose and the simple dailiness of living from morning to night, by an inner integration. Where, earlier, they had identified themselves by the region where they lived, or by the craft they practiced, or by the religion they professed, now they began to see themselves as joined into a new element, a class with common interests. "The working class," writes Thompson, "made itself as much as it was made."

They had little enough to help them, save relentless pressure. The old rural community life was breaking up behind them, as they clustered and coagulated in the growing industrial towns and cities. Those artisans who attempted to live by their craft, in competition with the machines, found their incomes forced down to starvation levels. The new "Poor Laws" thrust those who could not maintain themselves into workhouses, which abandoned a policy of systematic starvation only to institute one of determined psychological deterrence, where families were deliberately separated from each other and any private possessions remaining to inmates were confiscated. "Our intention," said one assistant commissioner, "is to make the workhouses as much like prisons as possible."

This inchoate, accidental group of the weak was up against a highly structured society too, and one that had been frightened by the revolution in France that was demonstrating the fundamental humanity of the privileged classes by cutting off their heads. The English Establishment didn't intend to soften the lot of those it saw as adversaries, and it saw them everywhere. Even those who still managed to work as individual craftsmen could be controlled by an explicit use of the power to define. Let a cotton-spinner, who took his raw material from a master, worked it at home, and returned the finished product, disagree with the master-spinner on the grade of what he delivered, which of course determined what he was paid for it. He had no recourse but to summon this master before a magistrate. And who would that dignitary be? "The whole of the acting magistrates," wrote a disgruntled spinner, describing his own district, "with the exception of two worthy clergymen, [are] gentlemen who have sprung from the same source with the master cotton spinners." If, as was usual, the workman lost, "he dare not appeal to the [higher court] on account of the expense."

Certainly apathy and alienation were features of this time of travail. Fantastic sects flourished, drink and drugs offered a retreat to those who could pay for them; but something else was happening too. Despite the highly diverse origins of the newly recruited industrial workers, and despite the desperate conditions of their lives, they were coming together:

> When every caution has been made, the outstanding fact of the period between 1790 and 1830 is the formation of "the working class." This is revealed, first, in the growth of class-consciousness: the consciousness of an identity of interests as between all those diverse groups of working people and as against the interest of other classes. And, second, in the growth of corresponding forms of political and industrial organization. By 1832 there were strongly-based and self-conscious working-class institutions—trade unions, friendly societies, educational and religious movements, political organizations, periodicals—working-class intellectual traditions, working-class community patterns, and a working-class structure of feeling.

Later in his study Thompson sums up the social effects of this integration:

> By the early years of the 19th century it is possible to say that collectivist values are dominant in many industrial communities; there is a definite moral code, with sanctions against the blackleg [Americans would say "scab"], the "tools" of the employer or the unneighbourly, and with an intolerance toward the eccentric or the individualist. Collectivist values are consciously held and are propagated in political theory, trade union ceremonial, moral rhetoric. It is, indeed, this collective self-consciousness, with its corresponding theory, institutions, discipline, and community values which distinguishes the 19th-century *working class* from the 18th-century *mob*. [5]

What emerges from these observations is that the process by which the weak reach a position of negotiation with the powerful involves, first, "the consciousness of identity of interests" and then "the growth of corresponding forms of . . . organization." These are the steps beyond distrust and dissent. They implement a new ability to define the world and to direct proper behavior by the governed themselves, counter to the directives of the Establishment. The consent withdrawn by the ruled from their rulers seeks a new center offered by the emotion of mutuality and supported by the beginning of a separate structure.

Mutuality of feeling and organization for action are not the same thing; but when Thompson mentions them together, he is suggesting that the common vision of them as opposites is wrong and that their virtues can enhance each other. Mutuality alone is emotionally rewarding but impermanent. Many of us have felt the glow of well-being that sometimes descends, like a special grace, on this gathering or that joint effort. We've worked in a political campaign, we've been at a conference where strangers turned into friends, we've gone on pilgrimage (Victor Turner has written insightfully of the euphoric bonding that occurs as a cross-cultural phenomenon among pilgrims to Mecca or to Catholic shrines in France, Ireland, or Mexico), we've discovered sisterhood or experienced some other form of "communitas," Turner's word for the feeling. Memories of such occasions remind us that mutual trust is very much part of human life, but they will remain memories unless they give rise to some sort of organization.

Equally, organization without mutuality rapidly degenerates into bureaucracy. Without mutuality the machinery is just that, and because it is, it can be used for purposes very different from the original goal for which it was created. Such a diversion of purpose need not be intentional; it may be the product of self-deception, for a natural law of organizations seems to lead those in charge to imagine that they, and only they, know what ought to be done and how to do it. Without a real effort to maintain communication, operators tend to split off from the rest of the group and set up as a new elite. The remainder will be seen by the operators as audience, or followers, or dependents for whom good things must and will be arranged —but not as participants who know their own interests best. And so structure turns into power structure. It need not happen, but it can best be prevented if those who are setting up organizations are aware of the danger.

The intolerance toward eccentricity—or, to put it bluntly, peer pressure —of which Thompson speaks, often appears first as a reaction to this kind of stratification and separation within the group. Unattractive as it is, it has its uses. If a group of the governed is to act as a group—and only by doing so can the weak get some purchase on the powerful and exert some control over events—it will have to discourage individual reactions that appear erratic and confusing, in the interest of delivering one strong, clear message. Besides, such faults are considered typical of the weak: they are indecisive folk, they don't know their own minds, and so on. Division of opinion therefore discredits the strength of the group. Of course differences will occur within any new structure, and sometimes they are both valuable and necessary; but new groups have to expect that their opponents will attempt to reduce them once more to a congeries of unconnected individuals: "Divide and rule." Peer pressure, like any other pressure, can go too far, but it is one method for achieving unified action in support of common goals. It can also work as a counterbalance against the tendency of an organization to develop an enlightened top layer which assumes that it is the repository of legitimate authority and that the rest of the group, down below somewhere, require looking after by those who really know what ought to be done.

Part of the task of creating an effective center for action, then, is to keep mutuality and structure in touch with each other. The structure exists to serve and implement the common purpose that shaped it out of common experience and shared need for change. If it works well—or rather, if it is worked well—it sustains the relationships that framed it because it builds an ongoing process of action and interaction out of what would otherwise be a static emotional experience, and it forms new links as it does so. All of this has been said before many times, but it's easy for the governed to forget what their ancestors knew and to have to invent solutions to problems all over again. That is one of the debits stemming from our lack of a history of the governed, or even a body of traditional legend that could root a group or a class in the past.

Such history differs by point of view as well as by content from traditional studies. The extent of life that is looked at now is much greater than it used to be, but even today when historians are increasingly concerned with the data of ordinary social and economic life (so much so that some voices are already raised to question this approach), the actual existence of common people is hard to grasp in anything like its full emotional quality. The sheer physical difference in conditions contributes to this difficulty. Demographic horrors of infant and maternal deaths, epidemics and plagues, hunger and accident and toil, can be established quantitatively, but they present such a dark and stark contrast to the everyday facts of existence in the industrialized West that we either turn away in fear and distress or assume that the people who could endure these lives must have been different—hardened brutes to match the brutish events they suffered, oafs and clowns, blockish and dully patient, but not like us.

That defensive reaction is understandable, but it cuts us off from our own past and allows us little depth of memory in which to understand ourselves, the circumstances that shaped the present in which we live, and even our possible future. This impoverishment is most inhibiting for those whose lives and backgrounds lie outside the familiar mainstream, though much of mainstream recollection too is now lost to general memory, preserved only as a rather intimidating academic subject for study from outside. We don't want to repeat the lives of our ancestors, we cannot now follow the traditional patterns that fitted their circumstances. But when we cease to feel the reality of their presence as human creatures like us and related to us, we lose part of our own sense of identity, of dignity, of value. Like the dead invoked in the rites of the Nyakyusa, our forebears too can add strength to a group that is finding its identity. It's our need for the actuality of a peopled background that gives its importance to new work in black history and women's history, not simply the data of oppression that justifies present rebellion. Even more than the spur of anger, we need to be able to understand the weight and meaning of the lives that lie behind us.

Thompson, deep in working-class history, is supplying such a base for revaluation of the whole past and of the dynamics of power relations as well. The fact that some of his expressions are unexpected emphasizes his nontraditional approach. When, for example, he speaks of "trade union ceremonial" as an aspect of collectivist values and links it to "political theory" and "moral rhetoric," we may be puzzled by the importance he attaches to it. Isn't this kind of ceremonial just nonsensical pomposity, a blurred and uncouth version of the ritual of king and court, or of religion, slapped together in order to inflate banal occasions with bogus significance? But that's an elitist question, which implies that the only good ceremony is traditional ceremony. Ceremony and ritual are ways to call up and renew mutuality. They demonstrate in action the compact among members of an organization whatever it may be, and though words can wear out, repeated ritual acts reinforce each other and communicate a kind of jointness that words cannot convey, a jointness that reaches back toward early prehuman, prelanguage empathy. Sacred ritual carries a larger message than that of dogma and doctrine. By involving the body as well as the mind, it speaks of shared human circumstances. Ritual and ceremony move joint belief *outside of time* by turning passing days into a repetitive cycle of doings and declare to true believers by their regular return that the creed these acts celebrate is eternal. Even to the ordinary observer they speak of something that endures beyond the immediate chance and will not be undone by one defeat. For how many centuries did Jews say, on Passover night, "Next year in Jerusalem?" If they had not, would that year ever have come?

Then, too, ritual declares the significance of the event it celebrates and of the group that meets to carry out the ceremony. It is an affirmation of dignity and worth in the face of flattened and trivialized life, and so it counters the definitions of the governed that the powerful put forward.

The process that transformed the eighteenth-century mob into the nineteenth-century working class was a response to disruption of accepted and workable, if far from ideal, patterns of life; but it was not simply a reactive, defensive adjustment to pressure. As they responded, human beings found ways to survive as human beings by means of the new patterns that they created. The governed are not, and were not, raw material to be "manufactured" into a new order of being by obedience-training and behavior-modification. They were active participants in the creation of a new group entity. Dissent and distrust of the powerful; a regrouping of folk who had not felt themselves connected but who discovered their commonality under pressure; and finally, the setting-up of organizations that allowed emotions and impulses to gear into continuing activities so that purposes would not go astray or goals be forgotten: these three powers of the weak contained the excesses of change by insisting on the presence and enforcing the demands of the second member of the power-dependence relationship.

These are all ordinary human responses that lie within reach of ordinary people. Skepticism isn't hard: if we merely listen to what the powerful say one season and remember it the next, we can't help knowing that grandiose programs don't often come off, at least not as planned, and that elegant theories can turn out to be rubbish. On the everyday level we enjoy being with friends who share our interests, and we have most of us taken part in some kind of organized activity toward a given end. Suppose we find ourselves in a situation where it's imperative to move beyond everyday living and take on some vital, large-scale effort. Why panic? Why imagine that we must act differently, in some arcane fashion known only to the powerful? The approach to effective action need not change with the scale of the endeavor. We do the same kind of things, use the same instruments of relationship and interaction, we discuss our doubts, share our experience, and discover our common sense of what must be done, and we organize ourselves to do it. Some people will always be more useful at practical operations than others, but dividing humanity into a handful of natural leaders and a mass of followers sets up a false polarity. Why should we be frightened of doing, in matters of significance, what we do all the time quite naturally for ordinary ends?

The source of our hesitation is that deadly triad of definitions that the governed accept and use against themselves. It lies in lack of self-confidence, in trivialization of one's own values and goals, and in the isolation that invites a vision of oneself as a solitary individual, impotent in the face of the mighty. But when the governed do that, they are throwing away powers that are quite real, for in fact they are not set apart from each other, and their aims are worth as much as those of others. Once the ruled set about it, they can affect reality by using natural human capacities; and why should they not set about it, when things go wrong? If orthodoxy were working well, if the powerful were in control of events—why should things be going so wrong? Why should the governed not lend a hand?

This is the kind of thinking, say the powerful, that undermines authority. So it does, and a good thing, too. Authority that can be undermined with ease must already be pretty shaky. Now, at any time, even good times, some measure of mistrust in authority will always exist somewhere; but it will be outweighed and dismissed if the powerful are really serving the community adequately. Corrosive, contagious mistrust doesn't balloon up without cause. It's the product of a power-process that is ceasing to deliver effective governance and efficient public management, and the governed know it. That kind of governance doesn't deserve the trust that would legitimize its authority. The powerful may declare that public mistrust is a leading indicator of cynical immorality and breakdown, but withdrawing consent is not a moral act, but a political one: the first step toward public action in a different direction.

Schematically, we can match the three powers of the weak to the three definitions by which the powerful inhibit the autonomous purposes of the ruled. Mistrust of the powerful begins to narrow the gulf that seems to separate the weak from their princes. If princes can go wrong, the lowly can at least infer that they themselves don't have a monopoly on going wrong, while the great always do the right thing. Such distrust must go far enough to reject the belittling images that the weak are offered by the great, or the magic connection will enter to "explain" the situation by implying that even when they seem wrong, the great have some secret and mysterious hold on power that is unknown to the weak. But when the ruled begin to join hands and to speak their minds to each other, mutuality puts an end to isolation and increases confidence. A new, growing sense of community with others who share one's views of the world makes these views, and the judgments based on them, seem more important. Views and judgments won't be abandoned so easily. Shared goals are worth more, may even be worth fighting for, especially now that allies in the fight have been found. A group that is knit together begins to believe that it's looking at a realizable future, at changes that can actually come about in the world out there.

How are the governed to put this program into effect? What means can preserve the naturalness of mistrust, coming together, and planning some more-or-less permanent structure for action, and also strengthen the conscious impulse to do this in the face of the opposition and ridicule for doing it that has to be expected? How, at the same time, can the threatened defects of overstructure on the one hand and on the other the birth of internal dissension be avoided, or at least minimized? The technology of organization is something that the weak need to learn, and to learn not by rote, but inventively enough to elude the traps that plague the process by dividing rulers from ruled and diminishing community. I want to come to these questions soon for not only are they of great importance tactically, they also supply critical insight into our contemporary problems of governance. The trouble with Utopias is usually that they are full of brilliant ideas for desirable ends, but overlook the means of getting there.

There is still, however, an area of danger and darkness that must be taken account of. If we want to understand the uses of power, we must explore the misuses. The positive values of powers of the weak are real, but these powers throw shadows too, and they are very evident today. The proliferation of violent, millennial cults assails us in headlines and full-color television newsclips, time after time. Bonding (it seems) is ever ready to get out of hand, and matters of life and death are demonstrated as being within the control of these groups both by murder and mass suicide. Coming together (such stories suggest) may be as dangerous as power is corrupting.

At the same time, popular literature outlines techniques for getting ahead on one's own, so that members of the weak can better themselves individually by learning little lessons in success through putting a foot on the ladder that leads to status in the Establishment world. The "Me Generation," as it's condescendingly called by those who are already sure of their place and identity, is being sent a message; and it's a powerful one because in many ways the data of reality, as they are presented, appear to give it credibility.

The message runs something like this: if you join with others in bands that reject the established and orthodox social structure and the mythology that sustains it, you are venturing into a howling wilderness of sects and cults where no maps exist. By rejecting the familiar power structure, you are taking the risk of becoming a pawn in the hands of some charismatic madman. (We don't at the moment seem to have produced any madwomen, but of course that too may come.) Better, far better, to restrain your feelings and modify your desires and ambitions; better to take as a guide some practical manual on how to make it "the company way" and satisfy your aspirations by finding a comfortable niche in the here and now.

This is of course the sort of message which any Establishment is always beaming out to its audience. We can hardly expect anything else, for those in charge of business are not in the business of thinking up alternative ways to manage what they're in charge of; and if enough comfortable niches exist at not too inaccessible a range, well and good. But these estimates fall on the lowly as directives for action or nonaction, as answers to the tactical question of how they can influence the world of reality so that it better fits their hopes and better uses their talents and energies. To mistake the directives of their rulers for practical answers to their own needs for greater autonomy is evidence of a good-hearted belief in community on the part of the governed —but it is naïve. Here is where distrust should begin, with a good dose applied to the instructions which tell the timid and solitary, that if they ape some eccentric tricks of powerful behavior, they will be taken as members of the ruling group. Alternatively, there are the horrible examples at hand of what can happen to the sects and the cults of the bonded: they may (who knows how?) be transformed magically into the Manson family or the People's Temple.

Mistrust. Keep this, hold to this, preserve this only. It is not enough for salvation, but it asks us to consider whether the judgments that are built on the data of reality are valid. We cannot deny the existence of terrifying gangs capable of outlandish actions; but how should we understand the significance of their existence and their actions? Evidence in themselves of how deep alienation runs in today's society, they do indeed cry out in warning. But the warning is to pay attention to what they show, not to turn away from reality and paper over the fissures in community and the despairs of the weak. Our general, public need is to recreate a sense of common purpose, of joint humanity that includes the desperate, not to read them out of our world in terror and disgust. This is a time when society as a whole needs the knowledge of life that the desperate can convey because they are buried alive in trouble. It is a time when denying their humanity and the meaning of their experience will only falsify everything the rest of us think and do, not just morally but pragmatically. When things are stable, the world can run on the basis of limited input; not when the skies are falling.

A working society endures as a more or less institutionalized process of interaction between rulers and ruled, well within the margins of tyranny and terrorism. But these margins are not irrelevant. They are part of the dynamics of power and governance. They do not deny the need for interaction, communication, joint effort; they simply follow the fault lines where breakdown becomes increasingly likely. Like the case histories of psychic failure, they show us what goes wrong. Let us look now at some examples of breakdown.

CHAPTER 13

Extreme Conditions I: Political Despotism

Foreign visitors sometimes ask: Why, if you really have so many shortcomings, don't the people take steps to correct them? There is no simple answer. . . . One of the reasons for the stability of the regime is the fact that living standards are rising, however slowly. . . . But there is a still more important fact: the immanent strength of the totalitarian regime—the inertia of fear and passivity. . . . Although the radio daily informs the ordinary Soviet citizen that he is the master of his country he realizes very well that the real masters are those who . . . speed through the deserted, closed-off streets in their armored limousines. He has not forgotten how his grandfather was dispossessed as a kulak. And he knows that even today his personal fate depends wholly upon the state: upon his immediate or remote superiors; upon the chairman of the housing committee; upon the chairman of the trade union committee, who may or may not decide to get his child into kindergarten; add possibly the KGB informer working next to him. . . . He is subjected to the same kind of training as a horse; and he submits to the training in order to survive. He deceives himself.

Andrei Sakharov, My Country and the World[1]

The extreme political conditions of despotism, slavery, tyranny, and repressive dictatorship pose a challenge to a theory of power in which the weak are held to interact with the powerful within a human relationship of community and thus to influence the events of their lives, at least to some extent. How, under tyranny, can the weak exert any control over affairs? How can we consider a situation of totalitarian dominance as being any sort of relationship at all? Aren't such conditions exactly those posited by Acton's dictum that absolute power corrupts absolutely? Doesn't this limiting case, in fact, invalidate any optimistic faith in the efficiency of intervention by the governed in their own governance?

A short answer to these questions is that if there were no protection against absolute totalitarian domination we would all be living in such a condition—1984 as eternity. But the problem is too interesting and important for a short answer to suffice. These questions raise others that are more functional: How is it that we do avoid tyranny quite a lot of the time? What happens when it does triumph and why is it able to do so? Can we discover remedies to prevent its success and to destroy it when it exists? What human strengths and drives—what natural defenses—exist which counter the obvious tendency of a dominant partner to reduce the relationship to total, static, irreversible dominance? Are ordinary powers of the weak enough, and if they must be adjusted to circumstances, what changes are needed and how can this be done?

We had better begin by examining the character of absolute rule, which will not be hard since we've had a good deal of experience of it in this century. Let us look at one well-documented example of the dynamics of despotism, namely the Stalinist terror that descended on the Soviet Union in the nineteen-thirties. My choice of example is based on convenience, not politics; there are plenty of analogies between Stalinism and right-wing systems of terror. We can, for instance, match a statement by Aleksandr Solzhenitsyn that the essence of the Gulag system is its "arbitrariness" with Bruno Bettelheim's recollection, from Hitler's camps, that one method of destroying personal autonomy was to remove "all ability to predict the future and thus to prepare for it."[2] Silencing of opposition, banishment, show trials, torture, forced confessions, fill the files of Amnesty International from sources round the world. The advantage of using the Soviet example lies in the wealth of its literature, including testimony from the victims, analysis by historians and political scientists, and observable contemporary effects. The documentation is extensive and it's been discussed and debated for forty years by articulate witnesses and theorists.

As with a good deal of history, it's not easy to start at the beginning, for that involves deciding on what the beginning is. Certainly the seizure of power by the Bolsheviks in October 1919 is related to earlier Russian history, to which we will want to cast back from time to time in any case: resistance to tsarist autocracy by highly verbal nineteenth-century revolutionaries offers its own instructive examples of efforts at change by the governed under an absolute regime. One point relevant to Bolshevik success is the value of a coherent and structured ideology as a basis for opposition to a totalitarian system. It would appear that opposition to extreme conditions must itself be extreme in at least one sense: it must challenge absolutism absolutely. Rebels against a tight ideological system can't reject one phase of it and go along with another, as if they were opposing a moderate, pluralistic form of government. They need an integrated alternative structure of belief to set up against the one in place: a creed, a symbolic system of their own that offers a new explanation of reality. Without such a structure of belief, a rebellion can be encapsulated, controlled, and coopted, because it will accept part of the existing system—but no part of an absolute system can be detached from the whole. Here is an eloquent illustration of the effect of tyranny on the use by the ruled of their powers: bonding must be tight and its rationale must be both conscious and structured.

The price paid for a tight, coherent system is, of course, *inflexibility;* and in fact, the tsarist regime itself suffered from being caught in the same bind, unable to adjust to the social and governmental modernization it tried to inaugurate. Thus, freeing the serfs in 1861 did no more to help autocracy deal with its problems than assassinating the tsar twenty years later did to set off a revolution. Neither the Russian economy nor the Russian political system was flexible enough to make space for a new class created by fiat, a class with an unexamined relationship to the rest of society, now asked to continue its old occupation on new terms. Where the English working class participated in its own birth and the creation of its own identity and autonomous values, the serfs were handed "freedom"—an undefined and uncertain gift. In his study of the yeasty forces at work within nineteenth-century Russia, *The Shadow of the Winter Palace,* Edward Crankshaw writes that the

> whole complex of traditional existence could not be changed over-night simply by changing the status of the peasants, who had to go on living in the same huts in the same villages, in the same rigid social groups or communes, cohering around the same elders; in the shadow of the same masters; at the mercy of the same tax-collectors, bureaucrats, police. The same numbers were living off less than the same amount of land, cultivating it by the same primitive methods: the only difference lay in a partial redistribution of the land and the severing of traditional bonds of mutual responsibility between gentry and peasantry. The sense of disorientation was acute, and it showed itself as often as not in the refusal of the liberated serfs to pay the redemption dues on the land they regarded as their own.
>
> And this was only one side of the picture. The other showed hundreds and thousands of landowners, great and small, required to surrender their slaves with no compensation at all and at least a third of their land with compensation that was inadequate. . . .[3]

As for the tsar himself, the active agent of change, he seemed to ignore, if not deny, the whole event:

> [It did not] even occur to him to address the people as a whole, explaining his intentions, indicating the difficulties, proclaiming a happier future, but appealing for cooperation in a mighty task. He spoke only to his nobles.[4]

Here we see an armored and absolute system, which could not adjust to moderate change even when the initiative was its own. Change occurred, of course, but it was always late and grudging, always made under duress, and always succeeded by attempts to return to the previous status quo. No wonder, since piecemeal pragmatic adjustment was so unsuccessful, that the overthrow of autarchy finally came at the hands of the adherents of another integrated symbolic system, a universal creed calling for worldwide revolution.

Even at the time, the ideology of Marxism was seen as quite inappropriate to a sprawling, undeveloped peasant nation—or congeries of nations; but the challenge it offered was as absolute as tsarism itself. Never mind that its programs and theories had been extrapolated, by Germans living in England, from the experience of a working class forming itself under the social and economic pressures of industrialization, and that almost everything about the setting and characters of this drama differed from the Russian situation. Marxism offered a complete and coherent alternative system of belief and directives for action, and therein lay its appeal. Therein also lay a latent and long-acting danger, for the divergence between theory and reality imported an element of falseness into the Soviet system at the very beginning. But the Marxist myth, more complete by far than any program of liberal reform, structured and definitive where anarchism was not, presented itself persuasively as an alternative to the myth of tsarist autarchy. Its persuasion did not reach or convince the masses of Russia in 1917. The October Revolution was made by a grim and determined handful. But Marxist theory supplied a base for action and argument in every imaginable circumstance while, for its followers, it served as the very symbol of their bond.

Obviously the tsarist past helped to shape the regime that overthrew it. Democracy, representative government, the constraints of a constitution enforced by judicial action were as unattractive to the one as to the other, and centralized state power could hardly surprise and provoke a governed body that was habituated to autocracy. But the Stalinist purges, trials, and repression of the nineteen-thirties were not an anticipated outgrowth of 1917, and a long and technical argument has centered on the question of their cause. As put by political scientists, the question runs something like this: Did Stalinist terror develop naturally out of Marxist theory, by way of Lenin's practice, or was it an aberration produced by a paranoid personality? We would do better, I think, to ask it another way: How did it happen that neither Marxist theory nor Lenin's practice provided any kind of safeguards against exploitation by a paranoid personality? Changing the thrust of the question, however, in no way diminishes the value of the massive amount of documentation and comment on the course of events and the connections between them.

To cram a hundred judgments into one drastically brief opinion, then, let me say that Marx's contribution to the potential appearance of Stalinism seems to me to lie less in what he said than in what he didn't say; namely, in the lack of consideration given to the transition period between successful revolution and the final happy achievement of Communism as an operating system, when the state and the need for it would wither away together. To the extent that Marx was writing a *Utopia,* he shared the tendency of Utopians to concentrate chiefly on goals. The transition to Communism was to take place under the dictatorship of the proletariat, with a political party functioning as its agent, and Marx's hypothesis was that the proletariat would grow by absorbing the rest of society and incorporating it within its own purposeful community so that the Party would inevitably represent a consensus. The state would be necessary only as long as it was needed to put down the resistance of the capitalist exploiting class; and since the political system was just a superstructure thrown up by the underlying machinery of production, to say that the state was unnecessary was to anticipate its disappearance.

However, the definition of politics as secondary to economics worked together with the expectation of the disappearance of the state to downgrade the importance of the institutions of governance that would operate during this transition period, and of the political methods used by the operating functionaries. Because it was assumed that their rule would be short, that they would hold and use authority only as the arm of an ever-growing majority consensus, and that the disappearance of the state was both the ultimate desideratum *and* the inevitable result of the end of the class struggle, these temporary rulers were left without much in the way of guidelines. Which could be interpreted to mean that they could do anything they liked as long as they felt it to be in the interest of Party and proletariat, whose purposes, again, were supposed to be unalterably linked together. No doubt Marx saw these factors as directing those who actually exerted the function of rule, but—

But in historical fact the Bolsheviks came to power in Russia without much of a class base to support, much less to monitor, them. In a brief but valuable analysis, "The Social Background of Stalinism," Moshe Lewin recalls the very shaky acceptance their regime enjoyed within Russia at the end of the Civil War in 1921. The Bolsheviks had survived, but only just. Moreover in the first political trials, under "War Communism," they had already liquidated their left-wing rivals, the Mensheviks and the peasant-oriented Social Revolutionaries. If that assured their grip on official power, it also lessened the likelihood of any wide support outside their own ranks. In addition the siege mentality, which has been a feature of Russian governmental thinking for centuries, had been roused by the failure of revolutions in Western Europe and, of course, by the military intervention of the West in support of the White armies. Writes Lewin:

> Lenin, in a number of pronouncements, showed that he was perfectly aware of the isolation of the Bolsheviks in the country they had conquered. The working class had almost vanished; the ex-tsarist officials who populated the offices [of government] were alien; the peasants were deeply dissatisfied . . . the party membership needed purging; the top layers and the old guard were exhausted. . . .
>
> The self-perception among the leaders of "isolation," of the lack of an appropriate social base was crucial. With it went an acutely neurotic fear of dangers for the movement, of its being either swept aside or, more perniciously, losing its identity [that is, being coopted]. . . . In a situation in which the commitment to their basic ideals was not shared by the masses and was confined to a relatively small layer, this layer found itself under inexorable pressures . . . [which increased] their vulnerability to dangers inherent in the transformation of dedicated revolutionaries into rulers. They had always known that they might be in power one day—but they had not anticipated that this would occur in social isolation. They hoped and were accustomed to see themselves as leaders, not rulers.[5]

So instead of the sort of social base Marx had envisaged, a growing working class whose dictatorship by means of the Party would simply implement the desires and intentions of the great majority, Lenin found himself with only a government apparatus as his instrument—a state. Moreover, as Lewin points out, the exigencies of war had created not just a functioning and controllable state, but to go with it, a "fully fledged practice and ideology of statism [with] direct and wide-ranging state intervention, mass coercion, [and] a centralized administrative machine as the main lever of action."[6] By default, then, in the absence of a working class, a new social base replaced the proletariat as the bearer of revolutionary impulse and process: the bureaucracy.

There could hardly have been a more unlikely substitution. The instinct of a bureaucracy is to sit still and formulate procedures. It can erode policies but not invent them. But in a nation where disaffection was almost as widespread as social turmoil, the state offered a means of control and enforcement. Consequently the revolution that was to be made in Russia came through the instruments of governance, from above, not from below as an expression of the will of a working class. Discussion and debate within the core-group of the Communist Party was certainly freer under Lenin than under Stalin, but the consent of the masses was not sought and the peasant majority was particularly distrusted. Not only were they stubbornly devoted to their religion, but also to the private ownership of the land that had so recently become theirs.

Nonetheless Lenin, a realist, was ready to supplement the initiative of the state by private capabilities, under the New Economic Policy of the twenties. Politically, in Moshe Lewin's view, "the strategy was to maintain a strong state but not to indulge in 'statism.' It was a strategy that kept the powder dry but looked seriously for a maximum of social support, not only for the purpose of staying in power but also for the purposes of peaceful transformation and development." Concomitantly, however, as Hannah Arendt has noted, Lenin was extending the use of the state beyond the traditional Marxist purpose of crushing the resistance of the exploiters. In addition, he maintained, it had the function "of guiding the great mass of the population—the peasantry, the petty bourgeoisie, the semi-proletarians —in the work of organising Socialist economy."[7] Prior to the seizure of power, this had been the job of the *Party,* whose coercive ability was limited. Now it was handed to the *state;* and the state, in Marxist doctrine, is always an engine of coercion. Thus coercion was now allowed to have a *positive* value while, at the same time, desired positive goals were to be achieved through the coercive state. Even before Lenin died, then, the disappearance of the state had ceased to seem absolutely desirable.

At his death, the struggle for control of the whole revolutionary movement became a struggle for the state apparatus. It's not surprising that Stalin, whose efforts had been concentrated on using the apparatus, should win out over, say, a political theoretician and publicist like Bukharin. The very isolation of the Party cut it off from outside influence. As Lewin says, the "constant narrowing of the apex where the decisions were taken [made the Party] vulnerable to a significant element of chance in the outcome of political struggles." Chance did not produce Stalin, but it favored him.

His accession to power brought another shift in practice. Stalin not only developed the bureaucratic state as an instrument of rule and revolution from above, he also elevated the security services, the secret police, to a position independent of the rest of the state apparatus. It became answerable only to him, and he was quite ready to use it *against* the rest of the bureaucratic power structure. Lewin seems to believe that this was a reflection of his desire for complete personal power, and no doubt this drive played a part; but it's possible to surmise that another motive moved him too: a desire to keep the bureaucracy in its place and off balance, deinstitutionalized, so that complacent orthodoxy should not take over entirely. At any rate some similar impulse can be found in Mao's "Cultural Revolution," which attacked the very structure he had helped build.

Stalin used the coercive power of the state cleverly, moving first toward the "positive" goal of collectivization of the land. It was impossible for Party members to disagree with the principle, and therefore hard for them to object to the techniques that were employed. Later, when they faced their own liquidation, they reaped the harvest they had watched being sown, or sowed themselves. Roy Medvedev in his account of the origins and consequences of Stalinism, *Let History Judge,* lists a few of those who found themselves on the wrong side of policies they had praised. Krylenko, for instance, who had been Commissar of Justice, and who had assured "bourgeois Europe" that "class conscious workers and peasants" agreed with the Soviet regime that "wreckers" need not expect to be dealt with by legal trials, "probably realized his mistake in 1938, when he was condemned and shot without any legal procedure."[8] Medvedev quotes the memoirs of another old Bolshevik, Dobrinskii, to show the connection made explicitly:

> Poison was accumulating back when . . . they forced a peasant to turn in flax though they knew very well that it had not grown [i.e., ripened], when directives were issued to crack down on sabotage, to bring saboteurs to trial, though they knew . . . there was no sabotage. . . . When they brought such "saboteurs" to trial . . . the procurator knew there was no sabotage at all, but still he sanctioned the arrest. The judges . . . knew that the muzhik was honest, but they tried him. And now the same procurator has sanctioned your arrest and the same judges are trying you. The principle hasn't changed. It is simply being given wider application.[9]

The show trials of the nineteen-thirties wiped out the middle and upper echelons of the Party, which formed the only group whose dissent to Stalin's autocratic rule might have been immediately influential: to use a sociologist's phrase, the "significant others." Very few connections existed with the mass of the governed; their protests were unheard, for opposition was now defined as counterrevolution, and communications were thus cut. In addition the alternative ideology that had existed among the peasants—their traditional religious beliefs—had been annulled by the collectivization which destroyed them as a class. Meanwhile, in the trials, official ideology was turned against the accused. Had you voiced the orthodox Marxist doctrine that the state was destined to wither away? Then were you not attacking the very bulwark of Communism, the Soviet power, and thus identifying yourself as an agent of foreign imperialism?

Mental and physical violence were used to extract confessions from the accused whenever necessary but weren't always necessary. The military particularly signed rather quickly. Even when it was used, it was only one element in the process. For many of the prisoners, twisting the ideology of

Marxism-Leninism produced a kind of despairing confusion that left them with no coherent defense other than an assertion of their innocence. But "innocence" was subject to redefinition. This tactic struck at the heart of their intellectual commitment to their beliefs. It introduced an element of absurdity, irrationality. And this was increased by the absurdity of the crimes of which they were accused. How could anyone take seriously the idea that (for example) Bukharin had plotted to murder Lenin, his friend and comrade? This charge was, indeed, too much for Bukharin to swallow and he denied it to the end, although he declared himself guilty of much. Officials in charge of agricultural production were accused of deliberately contaminating butter and destroying eggs. The purpose was to set them up as counterrevolutionary scapegoats for the failures of the regime.

But a further effect was to turn justice into a farce. Discrediting the prisoners also discredited the process until judges and prosecutors were wallowing in lunatic triviality along with their victims. Unmasking the heroes of the revolution as spies and agents for the enemies of Communism devalued heroism and revolution too. Yet no one could fight free. There are those who believe that Bukharin was endeavoring in his extended political-cum-philosophical statements to Vishinsky, the prosecutor, to put forward an alternative formulation of Marxist doctrine or even to reverse the accusations and direct them against Stalin. If so, the technique was too delicate, too hard to follow. And always Bukharin declared that the Party was preeminent: it could not be opposed without the rebel setting foot on a path that could lead to treachery. *He* had not done that, and therefore he was innocent; but by maintaining his innocence on these grounds, he was equating opposition with guilt. Bukharin left a testamentary letter with his wife, which she committed to memory for safekeeping, as Nadezhda Mandelshtam did with her husband's poems. Years later, when Khrushchev had succeeded, Bukharin's letter was published. In it, he declared his innocence once again (and movingly) and appealed for vindication. But the vindication he sought was not at the hands of the people, but by the Party. It would come when the Party restored him, posthumously, to membership!

In the end what Stalin brought about by the trials and purges was not just the annihilation of his rivals but also the destruction of Marxist ideology as a creed possessing autonomous value. He made it into nonsense, into what he, through the Party, said it was, so that no one could use it against him. In fact, no one could use it at all.

Contemporary observers speak of the very widespread mood of cynicism that seems to grip Soviet Russia today. The great myth of revolutionary brotherhood, of an egalitarian future, died in the thirties, and nothing has replaced it. War and the defense of Russian soil aroused patriotism and nationalism, and military success validated these emotions; but chauvinism offers no impetus toward creativity. Intellectually it is deeply defensive. There is still only one operative creed in Russia, and it lies across the country like King Log. Courageous dissidents do defy it, but there is no organized alternative system of beliefs to support their opposition. We can see in Pasternak and in Solzhenitsyn an awareness of the potential value to be found in a reborn religious ideology, but a new creed lies in the future. The old orthodox structure of Christian doctrine, which could appeal to a wide population, vanished with the independent peasantry that was its social base. Moshe Lewin believes that the Stalin "cult of personality" was created deliberately in order to supply the populace with lay icons and ceremonies, processions and pilgrimages, which reproduced in shabby fashion the rituals of religion. It devalued the earlier creed without offering an emotionally satisfying substitute. Religious remnants exist today and they strengthen their adherents, but they don't come out of the old Russian tradition. The Jews have gained a valuable sense of patriotic identity from the rise of Israel and the current emigration there: when, for instance, a Ukrainian doctor was brought to trial recently (supposedly for accepting bribes but actually as a result of his denunciations of anti-Semitism) and was asked his nationality, Dr. Mikhail Stern replied: "So long as there is one anti-Semite left, I am a Jew." From another group comes the Lithuanian *Catholic Chronicle,* a useful *samizdat* report on repression and defiance. But Judaism and Roman Catholicism are both peripheral faiths within Russian culture and neither, therefore, provides an accessible center outside the group to which it is native. The antireligion of Marxism *and* contemporary Russian nationalism join to immunize ordinary people to their doctrines.

Scientists like the Medvedev brothers, Andrei Sakharov, and Yuri Orlov have put forward versions of rational liberalism, but the tension and emotional heightening that such beliefs produce seem insufficient to rouse a wide response in opposition to tyranny. Besides, in Russian minds "liberalism" is tainted by old associations with the compromises of ineffective Menshevik-style social democracy (defined thus by Communist history) and tied too closely to the materialism of the West. Our material goods are welcome in Russia, but they don't supply ground for building an ideology. For that one needs more than disillusion with the present. One needs hope for the future embodied in some vision of a good that is larger and more significant than individual comfort. Hedrick Smith, in *The Russians,* quotes another dissident scientist, Valentin Turchin, on the current climate of opinion:

> There is an unbelievable cynicism among people. The honest man makes the silent ones feel guilt for not having spoken out. They

cannot understand how he had the courage to do what they could not bring themselves to do. So they feel impelled to speak out against him to protect their own consciences. [In addition] they feel that everyone everywhere is deceiving everyone else, based on their own experience. . . . Soviet man believes that the whole world is divided into parties . . . and that there is no real honesty. No one stands for the truth. . . . This cynicism greatly helps the authorities keep the intelligentsia in line. . . . People can travel to the West . . . and it makes no difference, so long as there is this pervasive cynicism that it is just the other side speaking. This cynicism provides the stability of the totalitarian state today. . . .[10]

Add to this mood the economic pressure on the individual of a system that controls the right to work and to earn, and of a censorship that prevents easy communication and circulation of news about events and ideas. As Sakharov writes sadly, "The Soviet citizen is a result of a totalitarian society and, for the time being, its chief support."

If human beings functioned entirely by logical self-interest, this acquiescence would be unshakable. If you're dependent for job, for advancement, for any sort of favor—your child's admittance to kindergarten, for instance, which Sakharov cites—on the regime and its functionaries, how can you not choose safety? Doesn't sheer realism demand that you ignore doubts, discard your questions before they trouble you too much? Well, it seems that human beings can't manage to do that completely, even for safety's sake. The Soviet citizen, as Sakharov also says, is *mistaken;* acquiescence does not buy safety for the individual or stability for the regime. Absolute force demonstrates that *anyone* can be destroyed—Bukharin, the Party theoretician, Yagoda, the ex-head of the secret police; Tukhachevsky, the brilliant Army commander—and if that is the case, if there is no safety anywhere for anyone, why acquiesce? Fear is the answer, naturally; but fear *by itself,* without the offsetting balance of some sort of hope, appears to be psychologically deficient for effective governance. Cop-out and drop-out do not, in the long run, supply a motivating force for members of a functioning society.

Sakharov gives an example of the deterrent effect of the regime on individual innovation:

A man by the name of Khudenko, who headed up a socio-economic experiment under Khrushchev, died in prison about a year ago. As the head of a big state farm, he was given complete autonomy in all financial, economic and personnel matters. He succeeded in reducing fivefold the number of workers . . . while . . . increasing output and raising wages. . . . It was plain that these changes were advantageous

. . . but they ran counter to the conservatism, cowardice and selfish interests of the [bureaucracy]. So they decided to get rid of Khudenko. When the state farm was closed down by order of a . . . ministry, Khudenko filed a petition in court demanding that the workers be paid the money they had earned. He was charged with attempting to damage the state. . . . The punishment for this kind of crime ranges up to the death penalty. But he was accorded "clemency" in view of his past services . . . and was sentenced to eight years . . . which . . . turned out to be a death sentence for him.[11]

The totalitarian state, in short, has got into a state of semicannibalism. It can't use its efficient managers. It can't mobilize its innovative talent. Sakharov is very clear about this:

Writers, artists, teachers, and scholars are under such monstrous ideological pressure that one wonders why art and the humanities have not altogether vanished in our country. The influence of those same anti-intellectual factors on the . . . sciences is more indirect but no less destructive. A comparison of scientific, technological and economic achievements in the USSR and abroad makes this perfectly plain. It is no accident that for many years . . . new and promising scientific trends in biology and cybernetics could not develop normally [or] that all the great scientific and technological discoveries of recent times—quantum mechanics, new elementary particles, uranium fission, antibiotics, electronic computers, the development of highly productive strains in agriculture . . . and the creation of new technologies in agriculture, industry and construction—all of them happened outside our country.[12]

One is reminded irresistibly of the scientific vacuum that the Nazi purification of the academies brought about in the nineteen-thirties. "And how is mathematics in Göttingen now that it has been freed of Jewish influence?" the *Reichsminister* of education asked one of the remaining professors, an Aryan and uncompromising in his devotion to truth. "Mathematics in Göttingen?" replied Dr. Hilbert. "There is really none anymore."[13]

What then is to be done?—a familiar question in Russia, having been asked both by Lenin and by Chernyshevski before him. Can the weak use their powers against a state that can jail them, starve them, exile them, or arrange their disappearance—a state that has made the natural processes of dissent, coming together, and organizing for public action so unnatural as to be all but out of reach? In these conditions the question Sakharov cites, "Why, if you really have so many shortcomings, don't the people take steps to correct them?" can never have an answer, for it ignores the problem of how the weak are to confront the state.

We have to rethink the query in the context of reality. Years of terror have had the effect of immobilizing articulate opposition and halting the process of political interaction, even (it would appear) at the top, within the core-group; certainly it did so under Stalin, and one suspects that political maneuvers at the Politburo are still conspiratorial. Opposition was redefined as treason, and the definition was accepted even by those it victimized. In a kind of universal ghettoization, the whole body of the governed has been distanced from membership in the political process. Because the rulers cannot trust the ruled as participants in a power relationship, they retreat into a defensive stance. They discourage the rise of any bonded group, they cultivate suspicion, and find it profitable to spread unpredictability from the detention camps to ordinary existence.

In these circumstances the immediate responses of the governed range from acceptance through cop-out and drop-out to disguised disobedience. We are indeed witnessing the appearance of a few articulate dissidents, and this is a hopeful sign of vitality; but, as they tell us themselves, their survival still depends on support from an international audience. They offer themselves as present, as reminders that the choice of rebellion exists at an intellectual level, and with great courage they establish the first of the powers of the weak by acting out their mistrust. But until a responsive group gathers round such prophets to signal the appearance of the second power of the weak, asking why people don't act is not politically sensible. The best question is probably *how long* such a state of affairs is likely to continue, and how to prepare for the time when it ends. These are limiting, extreme conditions; they are inimical to the use of creative imagination—which is not a luxury, but a necessity for dealing realistically with changing circumstances. In this atmosphere, neither human beings nor their activities can thrive. *Something will happen.* How can the weak use their powers then to exploit it?

Some Soviet thinkers have been wondering about this. Historian Andrei Amalrik, writing in 1969, hypothesized that the precipitating "something" might be war between Russia and China. He recalled how the "militantly ambitious foreign policy" of the last tsar led to the Russo-Japanese war, how defeat and social strains provoked the first effective modern rebellion in 1905, and how the inability of the regime to alter its policies and its structure laid the groundwork for its involvement in the First World War and, inevitably, for its defeat followed finally by the cataclysm of 1917. The economic pressures that a Sino-Russian war would produce, he thought, would disrupt the home front beyond the control of a bureaucratic government in need of arms and material, and of transport from the industrial cities to a distant front. Disruption, he felt, would be seen as an opportunity for the assertion of nationalist ambitions by the various peoples who make up the federated state of the USSR, and the Great Russian chauvinism evoked by World War II lends plausibility to his view.[14] Confrontation on nationalist grounds could then lead to civil war . . . What might come later he did not attempt to predict; but if we accept the analogy with the dissolution of the tsarist state, it brings us to the Bolshevik takeover of the revolutionary situation of 1917. The advantage they exploited then was neither size, nor experience, nor wide support: it was the bonded structure of the group and the blueprint for action supplied by Marxist ideology.

But whether the Soviet state can avoid the disruption Amalrik suggests as a possible future does not depend on the ideology of some still-to-be-established group of dissenters; it depends on its own pragmatic ability to abjure the rigidities of ideology in favor of an increasingly flexible relationship with its own citizens. The dissidents that we know about speak to the world on issues of tolerance and human rights, political questions that liberals and democrats find understandable; but one suspects that other causes for mistrust exist in other areas, and could become magnets for dissenting groups too. Even now there must be, within the Soviet system, professional people who find the government's apparent dedication to irrationality extremely irritating on the simple grounds of its inefficiency. The scientists and technicians, of whom Sakharov speaks, have to think rationally in their work. They have to make contact with reality in order to get anything done. Half a century ago, in the days of forced collectivization, minions from Moscow could declare that the peasants were saboteurs if a crop wasn't ripe at the moment when Moscow declared that it should be. But you can't run an agricultural system that way, even if you can still dispose of too-efficient managers who show up the shortcomings of others. You may have to get on without innovation, but you can't ignore the reality principle and set the time of harvest as your own sweet will desires. Practically speaking, technicians have an obvious ground for bonding in the everyday reality that they have to deal with in order to do their jobs. Questioning of procedures on professional grounds may also seem less threatening to the regime than political dissent.

Nonetheless (to draw another analogy with the Nazi system), it was just such a group acting for such a reason that plotted the assassination of Hitler in the only attempt that came close to success: the army officers who decided they were looking at military defeat, in June of 1944, if they didn't get rid of the omnipotent lunatic who was in command of the German war machine.

Centers for disagreement on whatever grounds need some means of communication. It is hard for any outsider to know how extensive and how effective are the *samizdat* networks of private publication within Russia, but their existence at least means that total control of communication by the government has been circumvented to some extent. And they are, of course, supplemented by rumor, by word of mouth—the grapevine, that oldest form of news dissemination. In a nice paradox, Solzhenitsyn and Medvedev tell us, transit camps for political prisoners serve as centers for exchange of information and news: what has happened to so and so, what is going on here or there.

The very lethargy of the general mass of the governed may encourage a growth of minor adjustments and general give-and-take; not only because the people seem uninterested in political issues, but because the government itself is indifferent. After all, the discrediting of Marxist ideology, begun by the state itself, is now two generations old. Marxism today, as understood within Russia, offers no exciting or illuminating vision of the world, it appeals to no idealistic instinct. One joins the Party as a way of getting on. The degradation of Communism from creed to convenience may well have downgraded the value of all creeds; and thus, the reaction felt by the state to the menace of disagreement. This would not in itself increase the appetite of the regime for debate, but it might slowly diminish the area where disagreement was thought of as treachery. Then the need for pragmatic questioning about technical procedures might be more easily met, and professional discussions, in turn, could make general discussion easier. All this is a time-consuming process, but it would, over time, decrease the gap between rulers and ruled.

In such an atmosphere one can imagine successful managers and technicians beginning to share an anonymous system of beliefs that wouldn't be thought of as dissidence, but would in effect reestablish a dialogue on how to get things done. It might function as a sort of Avis-Marxism, using the "We try harder" approach to challenge inflexible orders as inefficient without any intention of attacking them as dogma. The repetition of unexpected failures in prediction by accepted myth will, sooner or later, discredit that myth. Then new explanations of the way things work have a chance to be heard.

Could an effective political opposition to tyranny grow out of such bits and pieces of mistrust and such limited groupings? Not in the face of a determined despotism able to retain a firm grasp on the world of events. But one of the inescapable characteristics of a despotic state is that it invites the intervention of outside circumstances against which it cannot react flexibly. A bonded group is necessary to oppose tyranny, but a bonded group mistrusting all others does not administer well the power it may seize. It is too small, it depends on precepts that have hardened into dogma, and on a blueprint for action that necessarily gets out of date as conditions change.

All of this can increase the vulnerability of a regime by building incompetence, ill-considered judgments, and great difficulty in retrieving them, with
the result that money and human skill are invested in mistaken projects.
Thus, Russian agriculture, badly weakened by forced collectivization in
1930–32, was then subjected to mismanagement according to the notional
theories of Lysenko. It hasn't recovered yet; and one of the causes for such
popular outbreaks as have actually occurred in the Soviet Union has been
food shortages and high prices. Something happened, and its consequences
have not been overcome.

In extreme conditions when the power-dependence relationship approaches a limit where the bulk of the citizenry has been reduced to subjugation, customary thinking will logically declare that nothing can be done:
traditional forms of power are beyond the reach of any rival to the absolute
ruler of the state. Orthodox thinking, in that case, can only counsel acceptance of the situation—continued hopeless subjugation.

So what opposition to tyranny seems to require is unorthodox thinking:
a sense of the value of nontraditional uses of power, those that "are often
assigned in hierarchic and stratified societies to females, the poor, autochthons, and outcasts." If there is no one to oppose despotic rulers except the
ruled and the weak, it is the natural—the autochthonous—powers of the
weak to which society must turn.

CHAPTER 14

Extreme Conditions II: Survival and Resistance

Men can live without justice, and generally must, but they cannot live without hope.

Eric Hobsbawm, Bandits[1]

Powers of the weak may be more fitted for use by those caught in situations where open opposition and confrontation are out of the question, but they must still be grasped. How can human courage and determination be mobilized to do so in an atmosphere of dread? Everything conspires against so much as an expression of mistrust, while the stance of the powerful appears to deny any common bond or possible channel of communication from ruled to rulers. It would seem that the great are declaring that physical might is sufficient support for their authority, that they do not need the consent of the governed in order to establish legitimacy. Instead they have chosen to depend on armed force and intimate, ubiquitous supervision: the housing committee at home, the KGB man in factory or office, the shadow of state terror, and terror itself; or on division, isolation, and imposition of stigma on some group that is labeled "inferior" because of race or color or sex. The behavior of tyrants repudiates the idea of a social contract, or degrades it to enforced agreement in a static pecking order of command and submission.

Let us exercise the first power of the weak and mistrust these appearances enough to subject them to analysis. We can see at once that they carry a double message, both intellectual and emotional, and that the emotional element is there in order to deter the weak from using reason to question or doubt what the powerful say when they define the world. But are tyrants actually able to disown and abandon all relations other than subjugation between themselves and their subjects? Once the ruled ask this basic question, it directs them to look at the external world with their own eyes and form their own judgments. When they do, they discover that the powerful are lying, whether they know it or not. What happens under tyranny, old-fashioned or new, does not obliterate the need of the powerful for the consent of the governed. True, tyranny uses the ancient rule, "Divide and conquer," to limit the number of the governed who must consciously consent to their commands, but the agreement of the rest of the ruled is needed too. It is sought *in disguise,* under cover. This is certainly not a good bargain for the governed, but it is a bargain nonetheless: some offer has been made, though accompanied by threats (the emotional factor), and agreed to by both sides. What is agreed on is a *symbol* of legitimacy, which the ruled allow to stand for their active, conscious consent to a relationship that is actually unbalanced. The balance is made up by the weight of the legitimizing symbol.

This disguised social contract, of course, shrouds the ruler's obligations in protective layers of myth that deaden the force of protests from the ruled. Sanctification of a monarch by the religious establishment is a familiar symbol of legitimacy, which ensures that the governed can withdraw consent to the crowned king only when distrust is broad enough to doubt the sacred sanction as well as the political capacity of the monarch. In another symbolic dress, a reputation for patriotic heroism may mark the hero as uniquely worthy of political office: witness Charles de Gaulle, who commanded consent to policies and acts that no mere politico could have inaugurated. Or a special sort of capacity to rule can be claimed and bestowed by inheritance, royal or Rooseveltian or Rockerfellerish; or power within a hierarchy can be acquired by means of mandarin training in one ideology or another, which is taken to guarantee effective management of events in a way not possible to the uninitiated. As these qualities become accepted symbols of authority, they themselves confirm authority as legitimate and grow into mythic representations of the right to rule. The consent of the governed is then reduced to agreeing that these forms properly represent their communal connection to the ruler. The ruled cannot deny their subjugation to the tyrant unless and until they are willing to deny the whole body of social mythology in which his legitimacy is embodied. Making such a denial requires both courage and intellectual force. It is possible, as we shall see, but hard and rare. The alternative is the dark valley of apathy, alienation.

In this bundle of messages and reactions magic is clearly at work to widen the gap between the powerful and the weak and to persuade the governed that they lack some essential quality for managing affairs: decisive-masculine-deediness, for instance. And since affairs have to be managed somehow, by someone, management will be left to the powerful if there are no volunteers from the weak. Then the weak will have to put up with the methods the powerful use, up to and including tyranny; or at least, the weak will think so. And they do put up with a great deal. Unfortunately their forbearance goes far to persuade the powerful that they will put up with anything and, as a corollary, that these too-patient creatures are unable to manage things for themselves. Meanwhile the simmering resentment of the governed, which can't challenge the authority they have legitimized and still accept the magic symbols of legitimacy, becomes displaced. In part it turns inward and becomes self-doubt. In part it is directed against inappropriate objects.

Innumerable examples exist. Here is one from nineteenth-century Russia, a region where extreme conditions appear to be endemic. Many unhappy peasants and overburdened workers, on whom the oppression of landowners, nascent industrialists, and bureaucrats fell heavily, believed that the tsar was really *on their side* against these magnates: just so did English peasants led by Wat Tyler appeal to King Richard II to free them from the feudal service exacted by their lords. A young Russian revolutionary, Elizaveta Kovalskaya, noted the reaction of a group of Kharkov metalworkers to news of an attempt on the life of Tsar Alexander II: "They came up to me and declared indignantly, 'It's all the work of the nobility, they did it because the Tsar freed the peasants.' And although I argued with them for a long time, I couldn't fully dispel their suspicions."[2]

In such situations the dissent of the governed is deflected away from its proper target. Not only does this protect the target, it decreases the efficiency of dissent by making it seem clownish. The powerful can laugh at these fools, and the weak themselves have to admit that their clumsy efforts at influencing events don't work well. That increases self-doubt. Kovalskaya put it clearly: "The peasants and workers of Russia were dissatisfied with their situation, but they lacked faith in their own ability to overthrow the established order, and this prevented them from rebelling. The people had to be instilled with the necessary confidence."[3] Kovalskaya was right about that, although the methods that she and her fellow terrorists used did nothing to bolster the confidence of the governed. Blowing up the tsar (and another revolutionary group managed to do it two years later) horrified the peasants and workers of Russia, who had generally got no further toward opposition than individual questions. As yet, they felt no bond with the revolutionaries; indeed, did not understand what the rebels were trying to do. The old sacred symbol still held firm in their minds, they still accepted the mythic relationship binding them to the Autocrat. It's worth remembering how often aspirants to power in peasant societies have claimed to be lost heirs to the throne. They claimed possession of the symbol of power in order to lay hands on the reality.

Let us not forget the existence of the cognitive element in the consent given by the governed to tyrants as we turn to the emotional side—dread, awe, sheer terror. For natural—inevitable—as fear must be when the weak face unbridled oppression from the state, this fear is *intended*. It has a political purpose—to interfere with the normal functioning of the human beings who make up the mass of the governed, separate them, and sink each one is isolation and paralysis. Function—normal prudence—is converted to dysfunction—panic. The effect is rather like those diseases in which the immune reaction of the body is turned against the cells of the body. Caution and forethought are so stimulated that instead of guiding future action they prevent it.

But however tyrants and dictators threaten the governed with brute force, they never, in the last analysis, command adequate physical strength to rule by force alone. They could not hold down rebellious subjects if these subjects were to join in wholehearted rebellion, and from time to time this is demonstrated, as it was in Iran in 1978 and 1979. State terror is a tool used to frighten people into policing themselves. It magnifies physical force by invading the mind, and awakening the nightmare figures who know every nuance of weakness because they are created there: figments of a mind that is turned against itself.

This is indeed an extreme condition. Part of its awful effectiveness lies in the fact that human creatures shy away from thinking about it at all. We lose our grip on objectivity, on analytic thinking, and terror succeeds because its impact is magnified by our own willingness to overestimate its power. Not only do the governed contribute to this end by reacting with fear, those who are threatened assume *in advance* that they will do so, that there's no way to prevent panic. This is another magical concession to a tyrant who (we're all ready to think) can not only brutalize bodies, but invade minds. "Newspeak" and "doublethink" will transform old, normal habits of thinking and feeling so that the inner self becomes a stranger.

Interestingly enough, once we steel ourselves to examine the psychological operation of extreme repression, an element of trickery appears, for this is not what seems to happen. The self is not tampered with so much as it is *immobilized; and it is immobilized by a forced confrontation with its own moral values.* Terror exploits the familiar prudent question of risk-taking: How much do we stand to lose by any action if we fail, against what success will gain for us? In this case, is it wiser to be safe when we look at the danger of being sorry? In extreme conditions, "Safe or sorry?" is elevated to a dilemma of excruciating significance. Charlotte Beradt, a journalist living in Germany in the nineteen-thirties, recorded the dreams of a number of ordinary people who felt themselves threatened in one way or another by the Nazi regime. What she found was a kind of mental lockjaw. Anxiety dreams were everywhere. In them the dreamer was invited again and again to take some action in the face of danger and could not manage to do so; did not dare to move a finger. Said a forty-five-year-old doctor, recounting a nightmare:

Storm Troopers were putting up barbed wire at all hospital windows. I had sworn I wouldn't stand for having them bring their barbed wire into my ward. But I did put up with it after all, and I stood by like a caricature of a doctor while they took out the window panes and turned a ward into a concentration camp—but I lost my job anyway.[4]

"My friend was being attacked and I didn't help him," a woman student remembered,[5] and a young girl said simply, "I dreamt I was no longer able to speak except in chorus with my group."[6] It was a group to which she was assigned, not one she had joined by her own positive choice.

What we see in these dreams is not a transformation of personality, but a struggle against transformation. Undoubtedly there are behavioral effects of this inner confrontation which mimic a psychic metamorphosis: external action is inhibited because energy is bound within the interior world, decisions are prevented or distorted. But there is nothing magic about these shifts. They result from observations of an exterior world on which the tyrant is able to act, but these alterations cannot subvert natural law or shift the boundary between physical and mental reality. If, in the face of repression, the governed can still hold to mistrust, they will not, of course, be *safe;* but they will preserve the inner citadel of the self and with it the capacity of judging the exterior world in terms of their own interests. It may be that they are reduced to minimal action, to "disguised disobedience" which will be renamed pejoratively by their masters, but testimony from those who have lived under terror tells us that resistance begins here and that survival does too, with this first and last power of the weak. Dissent is the intellectual steel which strengthens the self in the face of the tyrant's weapon of induced panic.

The weapon is used in many ways. Arbitrariness, Solzhenitsyn and Bettelheim agree, is one. It disguises, magically, the truth—that despots cannot punish everyone, that some will survive even forced labor and the death camps. But the very randomness of disaster threatens everyone symbolically because it threatens anyone. Magic is smuggled in again under the name of Fate. Random, unreasonable arrests give terror the quality of a force of nature, a storm so enormous that no one can withstand it. And yet, contradictorily, though it declares that no one can be safe and all will be sorry, it promotes the policing of the self and moves on to self-policing by groups of the governed. For it suggests that the beast of power that cannot be assuaged by rational acts may be satisfied in some irrational fashion. Men, says Hobsbawm, cannot live without hope; and the term is used here in its generic sense—women, Hobsbawm would allow, need hope as well (though they know a good deal about getting along on very little of it, a knowledge that could profit all the governed; we shall come to this). In general, however, it's true that those who despair of life are not long for it. Randomness, then, turns hope against the hopeful, *if they accept as true the world it posits.*

And that is the tyrants' world, in which the weak are worthless, cannot act, cannot find allies to join them in their dangerous dissent. Resistance is impossible, and that leaves only the alternative of utter obedience. Individual obedience wipes out dissent, bonded groups now become dangerous, and those members who oppose the state must be betrayed to the state: we are moving beyond analogy to the failure of the immune reaction; this is the transformation of a group into a cancerous growth. It has not just ceased to act in its own interest, it has entered into collusive action against itself and against the rest of the body politic too, for the example it gives asks others to act the same way.

Psychologists speak of an attitude of *learned helplessness.* That is exactly what tyranny endeavors to teach. Whether the subjects are laboratory animals used for experiment or potentially restless members of the ruled, pain and punishment are doled out randomly. Efforts at control thus come to nothing: and the creature, whatever it is, is educated into a belief in its own absolute impotence. This belief increases its vulnerability. By contrast, members of an experimental group which are allowed to control, or even simply to predict, the timing, length, and intensity of shock are able to endure a higher level of discomfort. Analogous tests of human volunteers have found that the ability to determine the extent of unpleasant physiological events not only reduces anxiety but actually raises the threshold of response to pain. Translated into political action, those who have not learned to be helpless in the face of threat—who are willing to risk the "dangerous" answer to the question "Safe or sorry?"—are more apt to be safe. They stand a better chance of survival because they retain an ability to judge the world for themselves.

What tyrants want, Orwell and others tell us, is to remake the minds of their subjects, and this indeed is what we fear: the invasion of the mind without the mind's knowledge or consent, the subversion of the will, secretly, silently, irresistibly. Big Brother wants exactly that, his purpose is to act on us magically and steal away our will without our knowing it. But in fact, there's no magic to it: Big Brother's real instrument is *terror.* Minds can be remade in only one way: by repeating the original process of socialization through which individuals learned the world and came to maturity. The jailers who served Stalin and Hitler (and serve their successors today) "reeducated" their victims by beatings, hunger, and deprivation, but physical force is not magic. The locus of change is in the external world, and tyrants are able to control a good deal of it, but not all. They can change the rules for interaction with the governing power and disrupt expected relationships between rulers and ruled, but they cannot become kings of infinite space who reduce events to conspiracies. On their side they have a part of universal human experience—the world that our nightmare dreams can still evoke, a world of terror and powerlessness. But in spite of our dreams, human beings have managed to learn something else from experience: the difference between nightmare and reality, the sure existence of a relatively predictable, partially controllable waking world where men and women interact reciprocally and groups or individuals affect each other in known ways. It is only when we lose a sense of the difference between internal and external reality that absolutism prevails absolutely. The basic trust of reality that we learned in our first creative conquest of the world is our defense against the magic image of a new system presented by the tyrants.

How to preserve this basic trust, the hope (Hobsbawm reminds us) that we must possess in order to survive? By means of *mistrust,* the cognitive element, which the ruled advance to counter the definitions of the powerful, in a determined willingness to disagree with the mythic system offered by their rulers; and of course, as ever, such disagreement needs others to validate it. But without it, tyranny wins and minds do change. Both the Stalinist and the Nazi terrors testify to that, as do other witnesses from the past. Let me be clear. What I am saying is that courage and strength, powers of the powerful, are admirable, but *by themselves they are not enough* to prevent capitulation. They must be matched with an intellectual commitment based on disbelief that is shared and supported by that of others. The choice of valiant resistance or servile obedience to terror is a false choice if it is merely emotional. The masculine ideal of valor and unbreakable strength will not save the hero caught in the tiger's claws any more than will a demonstration of utter subservience. Of course there may be no chance of survival, no "safe" at all; but if one does exist, it will not be found through individual emotions and expressions of them, whether of subjugation or defiance. To survive, to resist, to oppose, and to create a future in which opposition may succeed and life change—for this, we need the whole self, body and mind, intelligence and the courage to strengthen each other: and not only our own courage.

The value of fundamental intellectual mistrust is made clear in Solzhenitsyn's encyclopedia of the terror phenomenon. Here he cites the ineffective, usual reaction of a victim to random arrest. It is not anger, but astonishment.

> The darkened mind is incapable of embracing these displacements in our universe [that is, the shifting of rules in the external world], and both the most sophisticated and the veriest simpleton among us, drawing on all life's experience, can gasp out only: "Me? What for?" . . .

That's what arrest is: it's a blinding flash and a blow which shifts the present instantly into the past and the impossible into omnipotent actuality.

That's all. And neither for the first hour nor for the first day will you be able to grasp anything else.

Except that in your desperation the fake circus moon [that is, the screening image], will blink at you: "It's a mistake! They'll set things right!"[7]

The shock is often worse for the powerful than the weak and they are less able to deal with it. That shows up in the reactions of the defendants brought to judgment in the show trials of the thirties. Stalin's old comrades appealed directly to him again and again. "Just as though Stalin had been sitting right there in the hall [and some eye-witnesses think he had a secret window through which he watched the proceedings], Yagoda confidently and insistently begged him directly for mercy: 'I appeal to you! *For you* I built two great canals!'" (They had been built with slave labor.) While Bukharin, theoretician, intellectual, Party spokesman, was awaiting arrest, as he did for months, immobilized between safe and sorry, he wrote letter after letter to his old colleague Stalin, "Dear Koba," and got no reply. But he neither looked to the safety of himself and his family (his wife and small child were held hostage when he was finally taken), nor did he take any political action—except to write another letter. In spite of what was happening before his eyes, he was unable to mobilize mistrust and proceed. Solzhenitsyn sums it up:

Bukharin (like all the rest of them) did not have his own *individual point of view*. They didn't have their own genuine ideology of opposition, on the strength of which they could step aside and on which they could take their stand. Before they became an opposition, Stalin declared them to be one, and by this move he rendered them powerless. And all their efforts were directed toward staying in the Party. And towards not harming the Party at the same time.

These added up to too many different obligations for them to be independent.[8]

Still entangled in the symbology of authority that allowed Stalin to declare himself legitimate in his tyranny, the defendants were of divided mind. As if they were living in some perverse fairy-tale, the dragon's prey appealed to the dragon for mercy.

It isn't lack of courage that produces this effect, it's lack of clarity. "Why did they confess?" journalists, historians, novelists, and psychologists have asked for years. How could these revolutionaries, these heroes who had survived tsarist repression and the hazards of civil war, have been frightened into such humiliation? But this is to consider only the emotional factor in the situation. It was an *intellectual* error that confounded the victim of terror; they perceived the situation incorrectly. "You are an opposition," said Stalin, and treated them as such. They refused to understand what he meant. He declared that the community they had shared existed no longer, and they did not believe it. But if the other member of a relationship will not recognize that any common interest exists, appealing to common interest does no good. Instead, it increases the contempt the tyrant feels for the weak. And these heroes had become the weak without knowing how to survive in the role.

What women know about living on a minimum ration of hope becomes relevant here. One difficulty about using "men" as a generic term for "human" is that when it's applied to social circumstances it has the effect of making male experience appear to be the norm. Thus it blurs women's experience when it doesn't happen to match that of men. Circumstances have accustomed women, over a good long period of time, to live with a low ceiling on aspiration and to expect a considerable amount of unpredictability to come our way. We don't plan for the future much because we have not had much to say about it. Traditionally our outward identities are named and defined by others to a greater extent than are those of men, and open dissent is less welcome: rebellious boys are more admired than sullen girls. These conditions make for circumscribed lives, and often for wasted ones, but under their pressure women have had to evolve some defenses: secondary gains, which don't offset overall losses, but make survival possible at a lower level. And if one is eventually to oppose tyranny, one must first survive. The variety of lives that women have led at different times and in different sorts of society make up a dictionary of survival techniques. Many of them are so useful against the extreme conditions of despotism that they are reinvented by victims of tyranny.

Basic to survival is avoidance of shock, for shock precipitates panic, the "Me? What for?" reaction of which Solzhenitsyn speaks. If one is more or less habituated to unexplained oppression, one is spared the worst of the panic impulse; at least the prospect of being in someone else's power is familiar. The necessity of living with a low profile doesn't awaken an immediate shame response in those who have not aspired to anything else. Putting up with mediocrity and inferiority is a strategy that has been named "fear of success." It's better defined as fear of somebody else's idea of success, however, if it's not success that the world has frequently presented as a possible goal. Prudent hesitation to reach for such a goal produces the well-known pattern of females bunched in the middle of achievement tests, leaving the extremes of high and low to males, but where unobtrusive mediocrity conveys survival value, prudence is useful. If no success is possible, fearing success conserves energy. This is not the best way to live in normal circumstances; but shrinking the ego is preferable to entering into collaboration with tyrants, not only morally but practically. There's not much to gain, and a self to lose.

None of these means of survival necessarily suppresses internal dissent. The expression of formal agreement, women know very well, doesn't have to be the whole truth: cross your fingers behind your back and lie away if you have to, children learn, and as long as women are asked to think of ourselves as children, we don't forget how to do that. "You can't trust them," say men, and they're right, they can't. Women don't trust men either (though men prefer not to know it), but the need for distrust neither angers nor surprises us. Until we start to believe that another way of living might be feasible, we naturally hesitate to commit ourselves wholeheartedly to a world we can't control. When bad times come though, the very distance that has separated women from central action eases the pain of confronting the past. Or, to put it in the terms that Simone de Beauvoir made famous, those who have had a status of "other" assigned to them are automatically removed from the task (and the opportunity) of creating any accepted social mythology. "Others" do not participate in naming and defining the world, and underground disagreement with its rules does not, therefore, inflict the same kind of interior conflict that males experience. Over the centuries, the masculine establishment has noted and deplored such female willingness to break the rules of morality. It has been ascribed to innate weakness of some kind —of moral sense, or of reason, or of the superego—or simply to a more primitive and childlike nature. Well, it's hardly surprising that those who are refused the right to be responsible end by feeling the commandments of society less acutely than do those who composed them.

Another way to say it is that when women are asked to choose between being safe and being sorry, we find it a less agonizing choice than men do because, in our experience, there isn't a great deal of difference between the two. One is never wholly safe, one is never free from sorrow. One hopes for the best but not very intensely—what can "best" mean? One may at times negotiate prudently, wary of limits, but they are always limits that have been set by other people. For women, extreme conditions do not change the world as devastatingly as they do for men. We expect to negotiate and bargain at whatever level we occupy.

Of course the weak need something beyond survival techniques in order to do more than survive. But until it is possible to set in motion the slow process that can sustain opposition and begin to intervene in the power relationship, they must be able to preserve a kind of obdurate judgment of their own which refuses to accept the total vision of a totalitarian state. On these minimal foundations new groups will have to come together, new systems of belief base themselves. But survival, and survival with the ability to distrust and to disagree, as an autonomous individual, comes first. It's one of those necessary miracles that the human race has been able to produce because the techniques for doing it have been deposited in the underground treasury of knowledge confided to the weak, learned and taught and retaught by women over millennia.

When in the detention camps survival was hardest, the weapons used against the weak were shock and shame. Pain and physical abuse were supplemented by humiliation. It was intended to degrade prisoners in their own eyes and in the eyes of their fellows. Not only was the self-esteem of an individual attacked, but the possibility of validation from others who were worthy of respect was undermined by showing them as unworthy. Most lethal in the camps, the process was used everywhere as a means of reducing the governed to the status of bad children: immature beings who accepted dependence and irresponsibility as facts of their own natures. I hardly need to suggest the analogy with the definition of women in many societies including, till recently, our own. Under extreme conditions those who are unable to muster mistrust and dissent, and who consequently incorporate this self-image, become incapable of independent action; at the worst, zombiesque robots who are instruments of an alien will. Magic? No. But agreement to the terms of a debilitating myth, yes. We should note that not only the prisoners and victims of terror are affected. So are the functionaries who process human beings as if they were fodder, "under orders," like Eichmann. The enforced shift in self-image that produces this state is made easier by shock and panic.

Shaming is produced by presenting the familiar dilemma of "Safe or sorry?" as a matter of life or death, and a tormented death at that. The prisoner resolves the confrontation between moral values and a chance to live by choosing to live; but the decision to abandon values indicts the self. Accepting the will of Big Brother is presented as a matter of choice. One wills to give up one's own will. Then how can one trust the creature who makes such a choice? Shame becomes an integral part of survival, and in another turn of the screw, the equation between the two weakens the necessary human urge to live.

Solzhenitsyn describes the effect of compliance: the enormous difference between the needed decision to survive in the camps and "the awesome vow . . . to survive at any price." "Simply to 'survive' does not yet mean 'at any price,' " he writes. " 'At any price' means: at the price of someone else." [9] Losing the first power of the weak, mistrust, at once leads to betrayal of the second, bonded fellowship. Because in the camps the gain was so little and so transient—a bowl of soup, a handful of cigarettes, a slightly lighter work assignment—the triviality of the reward further cheapened the value of the self that survived. And the choice was presented again and again. Over and over the victims acknowledged how low was the price they put on themselves.

The emotional choice dictated by fear meant to lose one's inner self, and often the loss of a self that could hope meant that choosing survival was lethal. But individual bravery could be lethal too. From the Nazi camps, Bruno Bettelheim describes how the system used the emotional choice of courage *against* the brave. A prisoner who tried to protect others, and was merely seen by an ordinary guard, would usually be killed, but the central administration was cleverer than the reactive guards, and if such bravery "came to the attention of the camp administration, the whole group was always punished severely. In this way, the group came to resent its protector because he brought them suffering." [10] Once again, the second power of the weak has gone by the board in the absence of the first, though this time betrayal works the other way. Heroism by the old rules sprang from no basis of shared feeling and intellectual agreement to dissent, and it did not change the external reality, which the tyrant was able to control.

What survivors of the camps have to tell us is not how to survive so much as it is how not to. Survival, after all, was quite random. There was no price sufficient to buy it, no rule to guarantee it. Prisoners lived or died by accident. But what they can and do tell us is how to survive as an autonomous human being, if survival happened to be your fate; and the recipe begins with mistrust. Reject the definition of yourself put forward by the authorities: a subhuman creature, a flittering ghost in a nightmare world, incapable of thought or action, and always isolated from the peers you have betrayed. Hang on to the ability to observe and to judge. If dissent must be silent, dissent nonetheless. Here is Solzhenitsyn's advice:

> Stop as soon as possible being a *sucker*—that ridiculous greenhorn, that prey, that victim. . . . And keep as few things as possible, so that you don't have to fear for them. . . . Own only what you can always carry with you: Know languages, know countries, know people. Let your memory be your travel bag. Use your memory! Use your memory! It is those bitter seeds alone which might sprout and grow someday.

Look around you—there are people around you. Maybe you will remember one of them all your life and later eat your heart out because you didn't make use of the opportunity to ask him questions. And the less you talk, the more you'll hear. Thin strands of life stretch from island to island of the Archipelago. They intertwine, touch one another for one night only in just such a clickety-clacking half-dark [railway] car as this and then separate once and for all. Put your ear to their quiet humming and the steady clickety-clack beneath the car. After all, it is the spinning wheel of life that is clicking and clacking away there. What strange stories you can hear! What things you will laugh at.[11]

In Hitler's camps, Bettelheim found his way back to the basic trust of the individual self as a ground for mistrust and rejection of presented reality: he used his professional experience as a psychoanalyst, trained to observe behavior and assess emotional responses.

I can still remember . . . the moment when it occurred to me to study the other prisoners. Early one morning toward the end of my first month at Dachau I was deep in the middle of what was the favorite free time activity: exchanging tales of woe and swapping rumors about changes in camp conditions of possible liberation [that is, in Solzhenitsyn's words, "being a sucker . . . a prey, a victim"]. There were only minutes, but that did not rule out intense absorption in these conversations. As before on such occasions I went through many severe mood swings from fervent hope to deepest despair, with the result that I was emotionally drained before the day even began, a day of seventeen long hours that would take all my energy to survive it. . . . It suddenly flashed through my mind, "This is driving me crazy," and I felt that if I were to go on that way, I would in fact end up "crazy." That was when I decided that rather than be taken in by such rumors I would try to understand what was psychologically behind them. My interest in trying to understand what was going on psychologically is an example of a spontaneous defense against the impact of an extreme situation. . . . Although at first I was only dimly aware of this, it was meant to protect me from a disintegration of personality. . . . To forget for a time that I was in the camp, and to know that I was still interested in what had always held my interest before, seemed at first the greatest advantage of my efforts. . . . As time went on the renewed self-respect I felt because I was managing to occupy myself in ways that were meaningful to me, became even more valuable.[12]

Bettelheim had found the cognitive base for self-esteem that permitted the denial of life as defined by the tyrant in silent dissent tuned to a different belief structure. Because the philosophy of his profession could effectively predict the behavior he saw, it validated his bond with an alternative paradigm. Solzhenitsyn seized on life-in-the-present, enriched by the presence of others, not so much contrary to the structure of the camps as persisting outside, around, and through it, a culture of the weak as stubborn as weeds thrusting their way through cement, and somehow perpetuating the capacity of coming together; a capacity demonstrated, in time, by strikes and rebellions within the camps themselves.

Dissent, the first power of the weak, can preserve the mind though not the body; but an alert mind, able to judge for itself by its own stubbornly maintained precepts, stands a better chance of saving the body it inhabits than does a subservient robot. Solitary and secret dissent can't lead to effective action—coming together for joint resistance is the step needed for joint rebellion; but without it, resistance isn't possible because no community can take shape. Yet even at the depths of extremity the naturalness of coming together can assert itself in resistance. Nothing may happen further, no structure organize itself to strengthen the impacted group into a continuing community; but Solzhenitsyn and Bettelheim both recall the unheralded, unintended appearance of spontaneous merging.

The example Bettelheim gives is interesting just because it did not extend to active rebellion, and yet was strong enough to defeat the system for the moment. It occurred at Buchenwald, an extermination camp, where any attempt to escape was punished by mustering all the prisoners into the open, where they stood at attention for as long as the administration directed. They stood so on one winter night, unfed, without overcoats, after twelve hours of work. Twenty died of exposure. Then discipline broke down. That did not mean open, active resistance; there was no means for heroic single action. Rather,

> threats by the guards became ineffective. . . . Whereas before [the prisoners] had feared for themselves . . . they now became depersonalized. It was as if giving up individual existence and becoming part of a mass seemed to offer better chances of survival . . . at least for the group. . . .
>
> Unfortunate as the situation was, the prisoners felt free from fear as individuals and powerful as a mass because "not even the Gestapo can kill us all tonight." The guards no longer held authority, the spell of fear and death was broken. When this stage was reached,

a quasi-orgiastic happiness spread among the prisoners who by forming a mass had defeated the Gestapo's effort to break them. . . .

Before this change in attitude took place, before the prisoners
gave up their individualities, they had been shocked and weakened
by their inability to help their dying comrades. [Shame, that is,
contributed to the very immobilization which caused shame.] Once
they abandoned hope for their personal existence, it became easier
for them to act heroically and to help others. [They were refusing to
survive "at any price."] This helping and being helped raised the
spirits. Another factor was that because they had become free of fear,
the SS had actually lost its power, since the guards did seem reluctant
to shoot all prisoners.[13]

Here is a loss of self that is not a betrayal of self because it is not a
betrayal of community, but creation of a community, unpredictable, intense,
and profound, which defied despair for the time that it endured. And for the
time it endured, it altered the relationship between these weakest of the weak
and the all but omnipotent system. It was a confrontation that the nightmare
world could not defeat, only destroy. But because it changed the external
world in defiance of the powerful, it was not defeated, the prisoners were not
shot down but allowed to return to barracks, and so some lived. At the end
of the world, the damned somehow changed the rules of hell.

CHAPTER 15

Extreme Conditions III:
Opposition and Rebellion

[The French] revolution, broadly conceived, did not really begin in France at all. In 1789, the American Revolution was almost fifteen years in the past. The Irish Volunteers and the Dutch Patriots, from the late 1770s, rose in armed and organized defiance of their governments. At Geneva, a minuscule revolution ran its course for a generation after 1763. A Belgian revolution broke out in 1789 independently of events in France. In Poland the Four Years' Diet set about revolutionary reforms in 1788. But except for the American Revolution, none of these enterprises was successful. Seen in this light, the peculiarity of the Revolution of 1789 in France was simply that it was able to sustain itself. The leaders in Paris had a mass following throughout the country.

R. R. Palmer,
The World of the French Revolution[1]

The step beyond spontaneous defensive bonding in resisting extreme conditions is the creation of some sort of permanent structure that, in Palmer's words, can sustain itself. We've looked at the process of organization as it took place in eighteenth- and nineteenth-century England under hard, though not lethal, circumstances when displaced laborers, craftsmen, and migrants from the farms drew together into a coherent mass, capable of self-direction though not as yet for effective intervention in governance. The "French" Revolution (Palmer's thesis is that it was in fact a European revolution) of course offers the classic example of how a relatively disfranchised and diverse group of citizens came together to overthrow an old order and to set up a new system.

In extreme conditions a continuing, connected organization is as much needed, and harder to build; and study of the process is hindered by a lack of data on how this has been achieved in the past. For one thing, there are few records of subversive activity, since keeping them is so dangerous as to be lunatic—unless and until subversion succeeds, at which point official myth-making takes over. Moreover the process begins and takes shape as a series of improvised, reactive responses to events. Beyond this, the predilection of our culture to see initiative as embodied in leaders obscures the doings of the many. Even such recent successes of bonded, mass action as those of the satyagraha movement for self-rule in India and of civil rights in the

American South, which were undertaken with and effected by the persistent endurance of many, are interpreted as proceeding from the will of an individual leader. Gandhi and Martin Luther King are remembered—as they should be—but the anonymous mass of the governed who willed freedom with them grows dim.

Still, there are enough bits and pieces of the past that can be put together, once they are freed from the grip of myth, to give us an idea of how structures of rebellion take shape, and of their strengths and vulnerabilities. The emotional toughening that a dissenting individual gains from membership in a group is clearer, however, than is the cognitive element. Nonetheless, an articulate creed, or an ideology, is manifestly essential to enduring resistance and rebellion. Any loss of flexibility is less important under these conditions than is the hardening of intellectual commitment. Flexibility is, in any case, forced on the weak under tyranny by their separation from each other: resistance is always having to be invented over again and adapted to some immediate context. What these groups need is a sense of continuing community which can be carried *in memory*, as Solzhenitsyn would put it, from island to island of the archipelago of repression, forming unseen bridges between them. The immediate emotional experience of community, as in the massing together of the prisoners at Buchenwald or in any transcendent merging with others either in mourning, or defense, or celebration, can become a ground for positive action only if it is memorialized and so made recoverable and usable as a reference. Thus, in bad times when public organization is totally impossible, a shared system of beliefs becomes a symbolic representation of the group and its connectedness.

A coherent creed, in short, has its own positive strength over and above the negative power it possesses as a ground for disbelief in the existing system. The bond it creates among its members is to the creed itself as well as to each other, and the creed thus becomes a symbol that includes movement, members, and bonding. It is a mythic representation of a new social compact within the group and so it confirms that another community is taking shape, an alternative structure that will order a better future. And such a symbol is needed for the grave and consequential acts by which tyranny is brought under attack. One must have serious reasons for the effort, and one must be able to explain them to an audience, for the existing power structure will certainly use orthodox myth, with its already learned and familiar causality, to discredit the rebels: to denounce them as criminals, to declare them mad, to paint them as purveyors of evil and disorder.

In a creed, then, emotional support combines with mental commitment to an alternative and articulate set of concepts. Together they produce in the creed's adherents a powerful dedication of the whole self. It is this devotion of mind and heart that lies at the root of the courage that rebellion against despotism requires, for more is needed than personal bravado. In a way the tyrant ends by creating his own bane: if no one can oppose this hideous strength but martyrs, martyrs will somehow rise up.

The psychology of martyrdom doesn't command much attention today except as it is included in the proliferating studies of terrorism. The use of terror as a weapon by the weak will be considered shortly. Here let me say only that it should not be confused with martyrdom, though that, of course, may ensue upon terrorist action. Central to the development of cohesive and effective resistance of any kind, violent or nonviolent, is the ancient question of the ability of martyrs to hold to their faith in the face of torment and death. Courage is expected of the powerful—dash and daring, risky adventures, laughter in the face of doom—but how are the weak able to develop and hold to this odd obstinacy? A pseudo-Freudian explanation, to the effect that martyrs are masochists seeking punishment for some neurotic private guilt, is no explanation at all, simply an attempt to discredit and obscure an awkward human capability by defining it as deviance.

Some martyrs, it's true, do express guilt for earlier recantation of their faith, but far from being private or separate from the cause for which they suffer, it is bound up with it. They have wavered, compromised, or like Peter, denied their Lord. In so doing (they feel) they have broken the bond that sustained them in community and disrupted the devotion of the mind to its own committed beliefs. Martyrdom reaffirms both community and intellectual self-respect, and the affirmation is more vital than the punishment it entails. Even for those who die alone, dedication to the symbol of shared belief and shared emotional community has become so deeply integrated that they can act, alone, as if the support group were present. Just as little children learn that people and things have a continuing objective life of their own even when the child can't see them, so these believers come to trust the permanence of their connection and compact, contained in the creed they share.

No more than we think of them as masochists, however, should we think of such activists as automata, blindly carrying out the will of the group. It would appear from the notes and records we have that personal reaffirmation and recommitment are part of the continuing affinity of the group. For each, the whole position is thought out and questioned again and again as a way of coping with doubts. It is interesting to turn for the moment from history to art, which has its own ways of communicating the abstracted truth of experience, and watch Bernard Shaw, in his analysis of martyrdom, developing the factor of rational dissent in the character of St. Joan.

Joan is an unthinking, almost elemental, natural force when she comes on stage, but her final choice of martyrdom (and Shaw insists that she choose) follows the realization that her captors have tricked her. They have advanced reasonable arguments to persuade her to doubt her voices. She may not agree to their contention that it was the Devil who spoke to her, but there is no one she can turn to for validation of her assertion that her voices were those of saints: no one else heard them. Reasonably, then, she has to admit that she could be mistaken. Her capitulation is reinforced by fear of the rack, but it comes out of natural interior doubt.

Then she discovers that the bargain offered her by these logical men is false. *She* must be mistaken, they argue, but they cannot allow that *they* might be. The whole weight of myth, the power of church and of state, have been arrayed against her—in service of a lie! Her jailers have degraded themselves by cheating, but worse, they have degraded the entire concept of free choice and honest thought. It's impossible to strike a bargain with a system that conducts itself this way. To agree with her inquisitors is simply contemptible, one might as well "agree" that two and two make five. It is then that Joan chooses the stake. The rationality of her opponents has turned in their hands and shown up their own intellectual falseness.

This, of course, is Shaw's interpretation of the road to martyrdom, and though it's convincing, we can hardly take it as being Joan's own. But we have testimony from other true believers to the same point, illustrating the power of intellectual conviction. These people don't believe "because it's absurd," but because *anything else* has come to seem absurd. In his study of how shifts in language use and style reflect changed perceptions of reality, *Literary Language and Its Public,* Erich Auerbach records the story of another young woman who accepted martyrdom some twelve hundred years before Joan went to the stake. Vibia Perpetua, "a young woman of distinguished family, carefully educated, and married in keeping with her station," was living in third-century Carthage when she became a convert to Christianity. This greatly distressed her father, for among other things, he feared that his daughter would fall prey to the persecution of Christians that the Emperor had ordered, as indeed she did. To Perpetua, however, there seemed no other course possible. Here is her description of a sense of changed identity, inescapable, and deniable only by speaking untruth:

> While we were still under police surveillance [that is, before she and her friends had actually been arrested], and while my father was attempting to make me change my mind by his word and, because of his love for me, trying to undermine my decision, I said to him: "Father, do you see, let us say, that vessel standing over there, a small jug or something of the kind?" "Yes, I see it," he said. And I said to him: "Can you call it by any other name than that which indicates what it is?" And he said: "No."—"Nor can I call myself anything else but what I am, a Christian."[2]

What we see here is a renaming of the self, in the teeth of orthodox definitions. It was compelling. Infuriated though her father was by her words (he "hurled himself at me as if he wanted to tear my eyes out"), he was overcome and left off arguing. Perpetua, with her friends and her brother, suffered for the faith which they had made theirs (or which had made them its own), but the annals go on to assert that she went to her death not just with resignation but in triumphant affirmation of an altered self, stained with a new dye. In her own eyes she was not a stigmatized deviant, but a participant in a new and uniquely important relationship that extended to a connection with the sacred. It was not simply a culture counter to Roman orthodoxy that sustained her, formed on Roman thought and denying it, but an autonomous structure of belief, complete and authentic in itself; a structure that armored its adherents against circumstances. Their heroism was almost incidental to their purpose, though it confirmed it.

But if the making of martyrs can be traced to strong bonding and intellectual commitment, what of the results of their fate in the world of action? Perhaps their suffering, and their willingness to suffer, are not the results of simple delusion; but is it not delusive to imagine that martyrdom can, in itself, contribute to change—especially in the face of entrenched monolithic power? What do martyrs gain but death? How can this advance their cause? Is it not just another gestural act, producing no follow-on? Sometimes it certainly is—the story ends with the death of the protagonist and is forgotten, as we would expect. The dead are dead.

What's remarkable is that this does not always happen. Here we see once more how powers of the weak are bound up in plurality. When martyrdom is effective, it is because the memory of the dead is not excluded from community, but continues to resonate among fellow human beings to whom the martyr's sacrifice speaks and who keep its memory green. To the core-group, and beyond this to the general audience, once channels of communication have begun to form, an act of martyrdom becomes a message that affirms the creed for which the sufferer has died. Martyrs act out a reversal of the definition and the behavior assigned to the weak by their masters. They show the mean and the lowly how faith can strengthen them to confront the mighty with dignity, declare that their own beliefs are life-worthy, trust their own courage.

Martyrs celebrate the casting-out of fear, and that is a potent political act. "It is not sanctions themselves which produce obedience," writes Gene Sharp in his study of the use of nonviolent action by the governed, "but the fear of them." On the face of it, it seems as if martyrdom should increase fear of the sanctions of the powerful, and the Establishment certainly expects this to happen: it executes, exiles, and imprisons dissidents for this very purpose: to threaten the rest of the governed. But it is mistaken. The victims' willingness to face the stake or the firing squad has the opposite effect.

For martyrdom is not a passive death but an acting-out of dissent. As Shaw puts it, Joan *chose* her fate. Martyrs declare by their deeds that some position unacceptable to the Establishment is significant, and they hold to their declaration in the ultimate test. The powerful may call them deviant, crazy, criminal—but the message of the martyrs speaks louder. Everything they suffer for adhering to their position elevates the importance of the position, while their courage conveys to the weak the astonishing ability of this faith to endow the humble with heroism. Once more, this is not magic. The locus of change is in the outer world. But if, in external reality, the ultimate sanctions at a tyrant's command can't silence a martyr or produce recantation, the weak are led to doubt that sanctions are so much to be feared, and even to distrust the injunction against crossing the magic line that cuts them off from the powerful. The symbolic act of the martyr challenges the symbolic authority of the despot. Through it, a member of the weak touches the magic aura of power.

Clearly it is in the tyrant's interest to prevent this, most especially to blur and confuse the message that martyrdom carries. One method is the direct assault on the victim by threats, abuse, and torture, in the hope of producing recantation. Another, as with Joan, is mental confusion and self-doubt—recreate the moral confrontation within the self, suggest that one's creed is a collage of interior fantasies. These are personal attacks. Public methods rely on the credibility of the Establishment's statements as opposed to those of the dissidents: these are not martyrs but criminals, not martyrs but dangerous madmen. All of these means can succeed, the governed must not imagine that they cannot. But what the governed can and should remember is that *these are all political acts,* and political acts recognize implicitly the existence of another member of the power relationship. The elite are acknowledging the presence of some force with which they must reckon. Of course they prefer to prevail by threats rather than to negotiate; but if these threats are mounted against an opposition in being, which can itself distrust and dissent, which has already come together sufficiently to formulate a system of belief, and which has undertaken action that can be comprehended by others of the governed—then the powers of the powerful will be most firmly countered by the powers of the weak.

The Stalin trials have already told us something about what happens to victims who have not been able to form a resistant group with an interior loyalty or an interior rationale. Surprised and shaken, the heroes of the revolution could not save themselves. Not surprising; but they could not communicate their experience to the governed masses, nor even to their old comrades. Stalin labeled them traitors, criminals, and saboteurs, and they could not refute him, these articulate thinkers and speakers. One theory holds that they sacrificed themselves "for the good of the Party." If so, it did the Party no good at all.

Russian history, that treasury of emotional extremes and ultimate deeds, offers contrasting examples of coherent opposition to the repression of the tsars. The revolutionaries of the nineteenth century became rather reluctant terrorists whose campaign against the tsar ended in a morass of confusion and disillusion. But they differed from Stalin's victims, first by their chosen and considered stance of opposition and, second, by the existence of an inchoate public distrust of the way the system worked, if not of the tsar himself. In the early days of activism, Vera Zasulich shot and wounded a brutal police officer in his headquarters in Leningrad. The public understood what her act was intended to convey: it was retribution for the death by flogging of a young radical prisoner. So considerable was the sympathy felt for Zasulich that she was actually *acquitted,* and hurriedly smuggled out of the country to Geneva before a second trial could be held.

The decision by one wing of the dissidents to employ systematic terror weakened the public support that had saved Zasulich. The message of "Retribution" was blurred, and the regime was able to persuade the nascent class of bourgeois intellectuals, from which most of the radicals sprang, that an analogy could be drawn from these revolutionaries to the "Possessed," Dostoevski's "Demons." Even so, they were not entirely discredited, and some penumbral tinge of martyrdom survived. Sofia Perovskaya, coordinator of the final attack on Alexander II, came from an ancient and respected family, and when she threw in her lot with the assassins, her judgment could be questioned but not her sacrificial devotion to the cause. She and her co-conspirators were hanged (very clumsily) before a crowd of eighty thousand spectators, and the image of martyrdom, whether or not it was judged to be deluded, certainly prevailed over the attempts of the regime to present the victims as criminals. For one thing, the moral support of the ideology they shared preserved their dignity. Only one of them broke under interrogation, and he was just eighteen.

Human nature is not predictable, but it is sometimes repetitive. On the eve of her execution, Sofia Perovskaya wrote her mother about her fate and her convictions in very much the way that the Roman Perpetua had spoken to her father:

> I have no regrets about my fate. I shall meet it calmly, since I've long lived with the knowledge that it would come, sooner or later. And

really, Mamma dear, my fate isn't all that dismal. I have lived according to my convictions; I could not have acted otherwise; and so I await the future with a clear conscience.[3]

Perovskaya, who was as antireligious as she was antitsarist, was not supported by the sense of connection to the sacred that Perpetua felt; but the connection to a group of believers dedicated to enforcing the "people's will" by action was a firm enough footing for courage. Her mind was not torn by confusion, her way was clear, both before and after the act of assassination. Having chosen, she went forward, free of the trap of the dilemma that caught so many, "Safe or sorry?"

How destructive that trap can be is indicated by an assassination attempt that misfired: the officers' plot to kill Hitler in June of 1944. The English historian, John Wheeler-Bennett, recalls it thus:

> To be a successful tyrannicide requires a complete singleness of purpose, a recognition that the action meditated and planned is an end in itself. It demands a dedication which transcends the love of life and takes as a foregone conclusion the virtual certainty of death. It needs courage and self-sacrifice of a very special nature.
>
> If, for example, on that fatal summer morning in East Prussia ... Claus von Stauffenberg had been content to devote himself to the success of his primary project—the killing of Hitler—he would have remained in the conference room at Rastenburg and thus prevented ... the well-meaning but inept Colonel Heinz Brandt, from moving the briefcase containing the bomb from where Stauffenberg had left it within a few feet of the Führer to the other side of the baulk of timber supporting the table, thus protecting Hitler from the full blast of the explosion.[4]

Stauffenberg, Wheeler-Bennett notes, had his own personal reasons for falling into the trap of confusion: the conspirators were planning a provisional government to take over after Hitler's death, and Stauffenberg was scheduled to be State Secretary of War. How attractive, then, to be safe instead of going up himself, along with bomb and Führer! We must assume that a German officer, with all his professional training, who was already involved in a conspiracy against the head of state, did not fail his duty because of simple cowardice as defined by the elite to which he belonged. But unlike the young intellectuals, men and women, who passed the eighteen-seventies in attempting to rouse the workers and peasants of Russia by acts of revolution and defiance, his mind was befogged by the dilemma of "Safe or sorry?" The cognitive element worked against the emotional factor. The moral of the story is that his clutch at safety gained him a future only four hours long, for he was shot the same evening, after the failure of the officers' plot.

The intellectual value of an ideology for the dedicated is that it promotes the commitment necessary to combat repression. If one believes in these dogmas, one does not waver or act against one's intentions. But there is a second advantage as well: it encourages the oppressed to formulate coherent programs for action. It was the possession of such a program that allowed the Bolsheviks to take power from the more representative but indecisive provisional government then attempting to rule Russia. That may well turn out to be regrettable after the event and, equally, some programs are sure to be founded on fantasy instead of fact, hopelessly overambitious, obsessively rigid, or suffering from any number of other faults. Just the same, any group that aspires to the overthrow of a system must have some agenda in hand. One can cry over the annals of spontaneous rebellion against despotic governments—the courage, the hope, the creativity—and the collapse that planlessness makes almost inevitable. Solzhenitsyn's description of the revolt in the prison camp of Kengir says it all:

> Proclamations appeared in the mess hall: "Arm yourselves as best as you can and attack the soldiers first!" . . . "Bash the Chekists, boys!" "Death to the stoolies, the Cheka's stooges!" Here, there, everywhere you turned there were meetings and orators. Everybody had suggestions of his own. Come on, think—you're permitted to think now: Who gets your vote? What demands shall we put forward? What is it we want? Put [the security officer] on trial—that's understood! Put the murderers on trial!—goes without saying. What else? . . . No locking huts; take the numbers off! But beyond that? . . . Beyond that came the most frightening thing—the real reason why they had started it, what they really wanted. We want freedom, of course, just freedom—but who can give it to us? The judges who condemned us in Moscow. As long as our complaints are against [the structure of the prison system], they will go on talking to us. But if we start complaining against Moscow . . . we'll all be buried in the steppe.
>   Well then, what do we want? To break holes in the walls? To run off into the wilderness?[5]

Now, the revolt at Kengir was not ineffective. The prisoners developed an internal structure of governance, they negotiated terms for better conditions (reform, that is, not revolution), and they held out for forty days. In the end, they were overpowered by the military, special troops; but even so, some easement of conditions in the camps generally appears to have occurred. Nor, realistically, could one revolt overthrow an entrenched power. But we witness here the scramble for priorities and purposes which leaves any rebellion in danger of cooption by one organized force or another. The sheer fact of revolt, the bursting joy of coming together and acting meant much to the prisoners and should affirm to the outside world the inherent strength of human hope and resistance. But Clio, Muse of History, is not a cheerful giver. Something will happen—this time it was the death of Stalin and even more significant, the downfall of Beria—but how are the weak to profit by the event? The answer to that question will not come from Clio, but from the governed.

So opposition to the elaborate structures of despotism, which attempt to direct every aspect of existence, appears to require an ideological dissent capable of disputing them on intellectual grounds and of substituting another community for the state. The overthrow of the Shah of Iran at the turn of 1978–79 was orchestrated by a Moslem leader who could put forward a coherent religious system opposed to the Shah's rule not just emotionally but cognitively, at least to the satisfaction of his followers. The people of Iran were able to fall back on a creed where the collectivized peasants of Russia could not. This is not particularly good news for the governed: a creed lacks flexibility just because it is articulated, and like any other structure of beliefs, it may turn out to be totally inappropriate to the circumstances an incoming revolutionary government faces. Then the question becomes: How adjustable is this system? But at that point we are already dealing with the powers of the powerful, which is not the purpose of this book.

In a prerevolutionary situation, however, the existence of a known structure of ideological concepts, or dogmas, or mythology, internally coherent and presenting a comprehensible pattern of causality, is valuable to the governed not only as a symbol of bonding and a foundation for planning. It also improves communication both within the core-group and beyond. If the deeds of some movement can be interpreted meaningfully by the rest of the governed, they will be much more acceptable because they can be placed in a comprehensible context. We have already seen how the attack by Vera Zasulich on Trepov, the Petersburg chief of police, was taken by the general public to be an act of retributive justice rather than attempted murder. In the same way, Solzhenitsyn describes how a group of ex-guerrilla fighters from the Ukraine, shipped to a special prison camp for politicals, began a process of serial killing of informers and were able to count on total support from other prisoners because these acts were understood as just revenge for evil done. The good citizens of Petersburg would not have taken a shot at the chief of police themselves; the inmates of the camp at Ekibastuz did not command the daring or the technical skill to make knives and use them. But as expressive popular language puts it, they got the message. These were not murders, they were executions.

This brings us to the currently absorbing question of terrorism, which can be best approached, I think, as standing at the limit of the political process opposite to that enforced by tyranny. Terrorism is disruption of the power-dependence relationship from the side of the weak. It signals the abandonment of trust in ordered governance, and the retreat to a position of pure antagonism. No use talking any more; and so the weak turn to direct action—arson, kidnapping, assassination, bombing—in order to compel the powerful to change their ways or, at least, to demonstrate their inability to govern by law. This is a challenge by force to legitimacy, an armed withdrawal of consent. As with state terror, but this time from the other side, an attempt is being made to change the external world in order to change the inside of the heads of the other partner in the power-process.

Like state terror too, this is an undertaking that observers tend to approach on moral grounds: terrorist action is wrong. But morality as defined by the powerful is universal only as long as it is not challenged. Rebels and revolutionaries advance their own moral system (based on the creed or the ideology that sustains them) which counterdefines terrorism as revenge, justifiable as self-defense or characterized as the justice of a future system of governance: not murders, but executions. To them, Establishment morality is nothing but hypocritical social control exercised by the respectable managers of official violence—judges, police chiefs, the military, the coercive state—as a means of keeping power in their own hands. They see their deeds as reasoned opposition to a system of law and order that is mobilized against them and the class, or race, or nationality, or religion— or any other defined and organizable segment of society—that they feel they represent.

This contest of moralities tells us very little politically about the actual effectiveness of terrorist activity. Each side naturally appeals to principles, but the contest between principles is not going to be settled on ethical grounds; or not, on earth, *in vacuo*. Each side deploys its principles *as a way of appealing to a third force*—the bulk of the population, neither rulers nor terrorists, who can be influenced to give or withdraw consent to or from one contestant or the other. This is not a battle of force, it's not even a rational debate, it's a drama. Moral arguments, political demonstrations, symbolic gestures—all have a part in the presentation, but the rules of the game are not moral or political, they are esthetic. *Terrorism is theater.*

In the plot as it's played out, the terrorist group tries to compel the masters of official violence to modify their programs and policies through the use of counterviolence. By attacking individual members of the power structure, the Red Brigades (shall we say) declare to others of the ruling Establishment, "Watch out! You may be next!" In more indiscriminate acts —bombings, hijackings, machine-gun fire—terrorists demonstrate to the upholders of law and order that they can't enforce the order they praise, are weaker than they think, and had better compromise.

But of course the plot is not aimed solely or even chiefly at the opponents: it's also intended to impress the audience. Just as the purpose of state terror is to immobilize the governed, so the purpose of terrorism is to disrupt the structure of governance and show it up as a paper tiger. Another kind of fateful randomness is invoked as evidence of breakdown in the normal political process. In either sort of extreme condition, the loss of interaction between rulers and ruled is exploited to make a statement: nothing more can be negotiated.

The statement is not true, for all human events are negotiated one way or another. But negotiation is made difficult in these situations because a common relationship, a community, is being denied. Confrontation becomes the only way to negotiate, and that means that in every circumstance the limits of the power function are brought into day-to-day political arrangements. Every question becomes a matter of life or death (or so one side or the other maintains), and as a result the proceedings overheat until the whole system seizes up.

Nevertheless, what is going on is still a process of negotiation—by threat. The plot of the drama suggests that these threats are aimed at the other side: give in or die! And certainly, death is the final argument in matters of life and death, at the margins of power. But, to be blunt about it, once they are dead, the dead no longer care about the argument. Nor, speaking pragmatically, are they any further use to their executioners *in themselves.*

Their value lies in the perception and exploitation of their fate by others: Are they martyrs or criminals? The threat that execution (or murder) makes is not to the dead, but to the living; who else could it affect? Extreme conditions may seem to illustrate the collapse of all community, or any possibility of bargaining, and the appearance of total control or total disruption, but in fact these limits of power are useful only as threats. Outside the grip of nightmare, matters of life and death are the concern of the living only. As George Homans points out, a powerful feudal authority might menace his dependents with force of arms—but the last thing he really desired was to execute those who worked his land. He wanted his rents and the service owed him by a living tenantry. The gestures he made toward "utmost force" were intended to influence activities in the everyday world; and so is the

manifest content of the drama presented by terror from either side—ultimate, inflexible confrontation on principle, illustrated by violence. Its purpose is to persuade the audience that the existing-authority is legitimate—
or else that it is not.

No human situation is simple. The statements that terrorists make by
their deeds allude to a moral system: they ask to be judged as right or wrong.
Kill the Fascist murderers! Revenge the innocent! say the activists. Assassination is a *moral* action: this bully is not a victim but a criminal who deserves
execution. And the state, in its turn, cries, Punish these brutish hooligans!
Or, if (as in Stalin's time) a revolution is eating its young, the zealot dictator
orders: Expose the traitors and saboteurs! Purge and purify your government! The purpose of these declarations, however, is not moral but political,
to elicit the consent of the governed.

But the audience of the governed is swayed by still a different system
of psychological response. The moral statements of the extremists, made for
political ends, are judged as techniques of persuasion. What moves the
audience isn't moral right or political effectiveness but esthetic plausibility.
Which claim is convincing? Murder or execution? Saint or witch? Hero or
madman? Martyr or deluded fool? The answer will depend on the perception
of the audience. Does it still allow some degree of legitimacy to the government, still feel a common interest and connection? Or does it accept the
reasoning of the activists and find their arguments comprehensible and convincing? Can it, in short, follow the drama with sympathy, or is it confused
and put off by blood and violence? Here's a relevant case, described by a
historian, H. Edwards Price:

> Uruguay was already experiencing inflation, unemployment, popular
> unrest, repression and a deadlock between Congress and an unpopu-
> lar President when the Tupamoros opened their terrorist offensive in
> 1969. They . . . chose a "crisis of legitimacy" as the occasion to strike
> . . . and they proposed a strategy of mass mobilization and armed
> insurrection to overthrow the government. Their terrorist campaign
> was only a beginning. . . . [In it] the Tupamoros carried out armed
> robberies, kidnappings of government officials and foreign repre-
> sentatives, and spectacular jailbreaks to release captured comrades.
> The major function of these terrorist tactics was to develop the image
> of the Tupamoros as a parallel national authority, capable of defying
> the government, exposing public corruption, and enforcing "revolu-
> tionary justice" on specific enemies within the repressive apparatus.
>
> The latter tactic, however, led directly to their defeat in 1972,
> when a newly elected President with popular and Congressional
> support called on the military to crush the Tupamoros, in response

to their assassination of four officials. . . . The terrorists failed to maintain a situation in which their violence was seen as more legitimate than the violence of the government.[6]

Important in this brief run-through of the ascendancy of the Tupamoros is not only the emphasis on the central question of legitimacy; of equal significance is the strategy they proposed of mass mobilization and the transformation of individual terrorist acts into civil war. Terrorism *alone* implies a situation in which the weak have challenged the powerful to a contest of armed force and, by definition, the weak possess less force than do the powerful. In fact, terrorism has appeared fairly often at a time when the weak are being driven back from the hope of political advance by less violent means and is resorted to as a tactic of desperation: a means of being heard, because no one has seemed to be listening. This was the feeling, often expressed, of the idealistic revolutionaries of the eighteen-seventies in Russia. The English suffragettes instituted a campaign of violence against property after the governing party in Parliament had failed to carry out a commitment to support votes for women: normal political methods, they decided, had been betrayed. Historians Hobsbawm and Rudé, describing the rebellion and defeat of militant agricultural laborers in early nineteenth-century England report that the "silent, embittered, vengeful campaign of poaching, burning, and rural terror" was a late development when earlier hopes had given way to desperation and isolation.[7] At that stage, terror ceases to be a purposive effort to present a group of the weak as legitimate aspirants to power and becomes an uncontrolled emotional outburst. The cognitive element, the attempt to persuade, to communicate, and to validate one's goals for the audience has got lost. In losing the hope of legitimacy, terrorism loses the impulse to reach a larger group, to push its frontiers out, to mobilize the masses. And consequently the dramatic force of the statements it makes by its deeds declines. They are less convincing. In the end, they are not even comprehensible. Then heroes are madmen, sent off to psychiatric wards, saints are burned as witches, and martyrs are forgotten—criminal elements who deserved their fate.

The ultimate weakness of terrorism as terrorism is that it invites a dissenting opinion from the audience; and it will probably receive just that if it does not go on to become something else, a mass movement—which may or may not fail, in its own right, but represents the clear involvement in action of a much larger group. As the quotation from Palmer at the head of this chapter makes clear, we remember the revolution of the late eighteenth century as French because earlier attempts in other parts of Europe could not mobilize massive numbers of adherents. Unless that happens, any movement—and especially one using terrorism, which is by nature theatrical —is forced further and further away from the fabric of ordinary life and closer to fantasy. That happens, of course, because ordinary life is growing unbearable, but the distancing of reality leaves the process open to distortion and manipulation. Let us take one last look at the Russian revolutionary movement, which I've been using as a chief example of the power relationship in tense and extreme conditions.

The general sympathy that brought Vera Zasulich a verdict of acquittal in her trial gave way, during the next few years, to puzzlement over the aims of the radical groups that had launched a campaign of systematic terror; and after the assassination of Alexander II, puzzlement was succeeded by revulsion. Then came a sullen peace of repression in the eighteen-eighties, changing in the nineties to growing unrest, which was promoted, at least in part, by the same process of industrialization that had set off the protests of earlier years in Western Europe. It was unrest strong enough to sap the central emotional bond that had always bound the peasantry to the tsar. The old system was passing, if slowly, and nothing else seemed to be taking its place. This fraying of sympathy was accentuated by external circumstances—something happened. A bitter famine in 1891 was followed by a series of poor harvests and, in 1897, by another famine. But the administration of the peasants' tsar was committed to pushing industrialization, and it had no money to spare for famine relief. It did almost nothing to alleviate the misery in the countryside.

Desperation brought another outburst of terrorist activity, not surprisingly from the party that associated itself with the peasants—the Social Revolutionaries. But though it acted *for* the peasants, it did not try to act *with* them. The Combat Section of the Social Revolutionaries, which was the terrorist arm of the party, swore revenge—but it chose to inflict it *in secret*. Now, an effort to mobilize the masses for civil war was impossible under the circumstances; but the cloak of secrecy donned by the Combat Section not only prevented it from explaining itself, so that its dramatic gestures were unclear and unconvincing to its audience, it also opened the door to infiltration by the state police, the Okhrana.

This penetration reached baroque proportions. In one of the weirdest instances imaginable of the symbiosis of victim and violator, the head of the Combat Section was, for years, an agent of the Okhrana! "Yevno Azev managed to penetrate the S.R.s so deeply that he himself can hardly have known when he was acting as police agent, when as revolutionary," writes Edward Crankshaw in *The Shadow of the Winter Palace*. He planned assassinations, and whether or not he revealed them to the police became almost a matter of whim, or perhaps of personal political maneuvering. Incredible as it may seem, "he organized down to the last detail the killing of the Minister of the Interior Plehve [his own chief] and the Tsar's brother, the Grand Duke Sergei."[8]

And Azev was not the only double agent. The situation, that is, can't be understood as the result of the fantasies of power of one mazed megalomaniac. A network of spies and counterspies occupied the murky ground of confrontation, infiltrating radical groups and assisting in the making of revolutionary policy. The drama that the left wing was mounting was edited constantly by the Okhrana. No wonder its statements were blurred! Lenin himself, in exile, welcomed a dismissed police spy and refused to believe him guilty. The whole process of confusion and betrayal boiled up in the horror of Bloody Sunday, a climactic scene of disorder where purposes crisscrossed in a fog of misreading. On January 9, 1905, an unarmed throng of workers and their families assembled in St. Petersburg to petition the tsar for the redress of grievances. They marched toward the Winter Palace behind chanting priests carrying ikons and pictures of the tsar in the hope of receiving a promise of intervention—Wat Tyler and the peasants coming again to Richard II. No one has ever established the exact role of their leader, Father Gapon. He certainly began as a police agent, undertaking at the direction of the Okhrana his mission of building a workers' organization loyal to the tsar and opposed to the radical (and tiny) groups of the left-wing parties; but apparently he went on to sympathize with the workers he was charged with propagandizing. In a truly epic confusion of mind, he both led the march through the streets of St. Petersburg and informed the police of the route it would take.

The police, for their part, matched him in confusion. They did not forbid the march, nor did they hint to Gapon that it might be met with force. In fact, the local city police actually held up traffic for the marchers. But as they approached the square in front of the Winter Palace, they were met— not by Nicholas II, who had taken himself off to Tsarkoe Selo—but by fire from twenty thousand troops, fire directed into the crowd. No one knows to this day how many died in this horrific example of what can be achieved by the divided mind.

One hesitates to draw lessons from history; there are always too many unknown factors. But we know that the party of the active terrorists, the Social Revolutionaries, ended in pawn to the more controlled Marxist Bolshevists, who reserved their use of violence until it was time to lay hands on the official instruments of power. That can't be the whole story; but it illustrates the very general rule that what matters in a public situation is what is perceived to be going on by those in the audience observing it. If believers in terrorist action see it as sufficient in itself to bring about political change, they misunderstand its real nature—the dramatic gesture that communicates fury and the determination to overthrow orthodox social structures, beginning with orthodox definitions of morality. Unless they use it as no more than one element in a larger political process (and in all probability not the most important element), they are indulging in magical thinking, as if they could change the world without bringing into the struggle that great resonant mass of the rest of the governed and turning it from audience to participants. Terrorists may be totally sincere when they declare that they represent the weak, in whose name they act, but sincerity in politics is significant only as it contributes to persistence, endurance, and determined communication. One does not destroy the state by gestures; that is fantasy. Unless the slow process by which the governed declare their dissent and mistrust of their rulers has begun, unless groups are already forming for the second step in opposition, terrorist action speaks to the wind. The curtain can come down on the drama and the audience leave unmoved.

CHAPTER 16

Practical Politics I:
The Value of Doubt

Logic is the art of going wrong with confidence.
Anonymous[1]

The limits of power illustrated by tyranny and terrorism exist; that can't be denied. And at these limits the definition of legitimacy is reduced to a brutal and elementary level. As self-motivated interaction in some common interest is replaced by force, legitimacy becomes little more than the ability of the governing power to inflict death, declare it to be justice, and require the governed to accept this fiat as truth. But the active political process is more than its limits. Even under extreme conditions some hidden resilience remains to mark the human species: a stubborn, if covert, disagreement, a profound refusal of commitment by the individual self to a system that bans all choice. By contrast, when the political process is operating reasonably well, the need for force lessens as interaction maintains a course between the extremes by virtue of its own indwelling momentum. And the process is far more important in human existence than are its limits, just as health is more important than sickness. The uses of power are general, they affect everyone, potentially they are open to influence by everyone. There is no way not to be part of them.

But of course there are different ways to be part of them. Powers of the weak, power as used by the powerful, these are appropriate or inappropriate to the situation of this determined leader or that resistant group of the governed. And beyond the suitability of usage to circumstance is the question of practical judgment, as opposed to wishful fantasy mixed with neurotic fear, two emotions that open the door to magical thinking. Skeptical "Anonymous," who contributes the definition of logic that heads this chapter, reminds us that even the most close and rigid reasoning is no barrier to magic —unless the underlying premises from which logic takes off are continually checked against surrounding physical and social circumstances. It is such reality-testing that keeps us from going wrong with confidence.

The status of women, said Marx, measures social progress; and I have been extending his insight to argue that the *experience* of women supplies a prototype of the conditions which eternally shape the needs and the possible actions of all the weak. This is easier to see today than it ever has been. The enormous, varied throng of women is becoming ever more active in its doings. This muttering and movement started as a response to external pressures arising from economic and technological change, which now reach deep into the supposedly secluded sphere once called woman's place. Something has happened; happened, been seen to happen, and awakened an answer. But let no one imagine that women, shaken into activity by change, are responding to events with mere reflex action, nor that our foremothers slept dreamlessly through past centuries. We possess a history, even if some of its lessons had better be unlearned.

Nor is external pressure from change the only cause for women's current intervention in the power-process. Just as great is the positive attraction exerted by the new possibilities that change offers. In the past, women were bound to physical inevitabilities of childbearing and social inevitabilities of child-rearing. Out of these grew definitions of proper female behavior, definitions modified from time to time by more or less baroque whimsies of male anxieties. If this role was accepted, it was not because women thought it was right, but because there was no perceptible alternative.

What has happened is the end of such inevitability; and not only for women, of course. The journey on which we are embarking exemplifies the experience of all groups that are in the process of making, or finding, an identity and reaching out for greater self-direction. The very fact of change undermines the credibility of the status assigned by a society to any of its parts, for ideally, that status is held to be inevitable and therefore permanent. Slaves, said the Greek philosophers, were slaves because they had the souls of slaves: a kind of spiritual sociobiology.

So the enterprise of discovery that women are now undertaking is universally relevant. As it goes on, it's being monitored and discussed by those engaged in it and, to some extent, by those who aren't. If a celestial laboratory could set up an experiment in social transformation, it could devise nothing more illuminating. We are enjoying the richest opportunity any scholar could desire to observe the workings of human psychology as it endeavors to adjust to profound alterations in the context of life.

In the remainder of this book, therefore, I shall be concentrating more closely on this epic undertaking: on women's activities and the responses they call forth from the existing hierarchy. But other groups should have no difficulty at all in finding analogies to their own endeavors, even though their struggles begin in different places. Certainly there are differences in the past existence of, say, black men and white women, which condition the approaches each group will naturally employ as its members push toward greater participation in the world of action. But both groups find themselves facing the same situation: the power structure explains that participation requires the adoption of goals, ideals, and ways of thought and interaction as they are understood and ordained by the structure. Action in the male world, action in the white world (and to white males, from which group the contemporary elite is drawn, the world of events and political process is thus defined), follows white-male rules. Those who want a place in the game (we'll come to the implications of that term later) have to learn the rules and leave behind the unacceptable customs, traditions, and comportment of the "inferior" group from which they spring.

Just as victims of tyranny are told that survival depends on resocialization, so in more normal times ambitious individuals learn that the road to equality runs through the same territory. The process doesn't proceed by imprisonment and torture, but it demands the same abandonment of the past and denial of one's group identity in order that one may accept the goals and learn the behavior prescribed by the hierarchy. If the elite is made up of middle-class white males, then logic confidently requires that all initiates— black or female, female or black or both—must approximate the mind-set and the behavior of middle-class white males.

Let us defer the philosophic question, Is this a good idea and a worthy aim? and consider first whether such a metamorphosis is possible at all. Now, human nature is protean, and the capacity to learn doesn't vanish in the teens of life. But does the ability of women to learn how to act and think like men (and a number have demonstrated that the capacity is there) guarantee that those who do so will henceforth be accepted as if they *were* men? Will that satisfy the terms of the hypothesis? Does acting and thinking like a middle-class white male, that is, ensure that the accomplished individual is accorded the promised status, *treated* like a white male?

We've had the chance to watch a pretty full demonstration of this question asked and answered in the past few years in the efforts to factor Affirmative Action programs into the ordinary operations of life. On the face of it, programs to remedy discrimination in education, business opportunities, openings for specialist training, appointment to political office, and so on, are deserving of great praise. The Establishment has agreed with activists from the governed that inequities do exist and has attempted to set them right, so that natural ambitions for improved economic and social positions felt by the governed can be accommodated. From a broader social point of view we see a healthy effort to let talented and able people contribute to management and governance. Since these people bring a diversity of experience with them, the process looks like enriching the operations of government as well as opening the door to social progress.

However. Even though the political Establishment responded formally to demands from below for wider opportunities, it's been very difficult indeed to *implement* these programs efficiently. For all its confidence, logic does not explain why. Those in the upper ranks of the hierarchy can hardly deny that upward mobility is a good, old-fashioned, virtuous American aim, nor argue that ambition to rise "within the system" is likely to be characteristic of subversive elements; and yet the welcome offered these aspirants has been anything but warm. The academic community, for example, which guards the philosophy and the fundamental social and intellectual traditions of our culture, has mustered all the authority of its scholarship to question the entire principle of Affirmative Action: Does it not set itself in opposition to a quality identified, by academics, as "academic excellence"?

To some outside the academy it would seem as if bringing in a wider range of students, with a greater experience of life, might enhance the educational process and increase the breadth and depth of the talent pool that the process is charged with turning out; that "excellence" might actually be enlarged if the challenge of working with a new population of students were to meet a worthy response. Instead it appears that the masters of the academy assume that excellence has been defined once and for all. We cannot now ask the real-life question, "Excellent for what purpose? In what conditions?" It was answered long ago and the answer is forever embodied in standard academic procedures, the One Right Way to provide an expected student body with a proper fund of knowledge, along with the rules for thinking about it. Those who hold this conviction believe sincerely that any change —in the students recruited, in the aims of higher education, in methods of instruction—will necessarily *dilute* the established, discrete entity, academic excellence. The status quo must therefore be defended against all invaders, because any invader brings change, and change equals deterioration. Carried to a logical extreme, one supposes that the elders of the academy should still be teaching, in Latin, the Trivium and Quadrivium; and are not doing so only because fluent Latin speakers (as Hannah Arendt said of benevolent despots) are in such short supply.

Meanwhile, as this battle of principle goes on, the Establishment has given ground at the level of practice and admitted (rather grudgingly) some women and some members of minority groups to areas and ranks where they have seldom penetrated in the past. Though this is an advance that should not be belittled, it is almost universally accompanied by bestowing on these incomers a special role, that of "token." Like the Latin particle "num," which assumes a negative answer when it's used in a question, tokenism shadows the hard-enough role of apprentice with a glum expectancy that the apprentice is going to turn out incompetent. That's not very comfortable for the incomers, though they are now at least offered an opportunity to choose between comfort and ambition. The discomfort felt by the power structure, however, is really more significant for all of us, because it demonstrates that the senior member of the power relationship doesn't believe its own principles. Here are eager apprentices, trying to learn how to operate by standard procedures; and here are the powerful, who have upheld the universal value of these standard procedures, evidencing the strongest doubts that they are universal. "Behave like us and you will get on," say the powerful to the weak —until the weak try.

So we have yet another case history that shows up some of the flaws in our vision of power. If the role of "token" signifies successful admission to the hierarchy, it also signifies being out of place: a lone black among whites, a foreigner in a preserve of the native-born, a couple of women in niches once occupied only by men. When the Establishment indulges in positive, or wishful, thinking it emphasizes the apprentice role and speaks of the incomers as learners, the first avant-garde swallows of an approaching summer, which they can expect to enjoy once they have learned to "pass." To the elite, these lucky members of the upwardly mobile have arrived at a desirable status where, if they cooperate, education for management can begin. No doubt they will be a bit awkward at first, but the way to deal with them is to stuff them full of maxims, shibboleths, and conventional gestures, so that they are not obtrusive: resocialize them. Rules for dress, rules for behavior, are revealing. Imitate white middle-class males, but do it suitably. Women should carry briefcases instead of handbags and wear suits, but suits with skirts, not trousers; mimicry, not usurpation, is the key. Try to be similar but don't think you can be the same. These people, say the powerful benignly, may never master the inner essence of using power properly, but presumably they're bright (or they wouldn't have got as far as they have), so it ought to be possible to teach them how to comport themselves decently. Thus the positive thinkers. To the negative, tokens are an expedient forced on them by circumstances and must be ignored as far as possible; certainly on any matter of substance.

This attitude is not peculiar to our time. An illuminating example occurred during the First World War, when the British Army found itself hideously short of officer-candidates as the slaughter in the trenches wiped out available supplies at a furious rate. The army finally resorted to promotion from the ranks. These lieutenants, captains, and occasional majors (they seldom climbed higher) were known to their superiors as Temporary Gentlemen. One has a sense today that female or black executives, newly come to industry, figure in the minds of boards of directors or executive officers as holding the same transient rank, for the duration of Affirmative Action. Certainly the questions that tokens raise by "making it" always have to do with the fit between themselves and their new positions, not with any advantageous effect they might have on the structure. How good is their adjustment? How far have they come along the road to "normal" behavior?

What is implicit, sometimes even stated, is that they are never going to get far enough along that road. Let them think like middle-class white males to the last dot on the i, let them learn all the proper gestures and use them in the right context, tokens by definition are not integrated into the company to which they have moved. They always carry a label which identifies them as originating in a not-normal-to-the-Establishment group. Able black professors and professionals working in a white world, efficient women engineers and scientists, are not seen as simply able and efficient practitioners. Their race and/or their sex is built into their identity, just as class differences were with the Temporary Gentlemen of the British Expeditionary Force. Because their deviance from the norm can't be overlooked, "normal" behavior as prescribed for the rank they occupy will never be accepted as normal for them.

What does that mean? That social progress is impossible? Of course not; it just means that it's impossible by Establishment rules based on Establishment logic. Tokens can certainly become normal—but the way that they do it is by means of *a change in the situation,* a real shift in the external world that forces a shift inside the heads of the elite, *so that normality is redefined* by adjusting the premises of social thinking. What sort of change in the situation? The simplest is by quantity: increase the number of tokens sufficiently for their presence to be taken for granted, and they cease to be tokens. Then they are something else—a new element in the context where they are placed. Seen thus, they have already changed that context and are free to go on to change it more. We haven't got this far with the movement of women and minority members into the upper echelons of business, government, or the professions to which Affirmative Action is supposedly dedicated; but the breakdown of class structures in Western society (the external world) over the past fifty or sixty years has accomplished, analogously, the demise of the Temporary Gentlemen. Which is a sign that social change happens, but not that it's easy. Indeed, the replay of the procedure demonstrates how resistant a power structure is to accepting new members even when it makes the rules, even when it knows it needs them.

What are we to conclude from this example? It certainly emphasizes the usefulness of mistrust, in this case mistrust of standard procedures for getting on as outlined by the powerful; as Solzhenitsyn said, "Stop being a sucker." More than that, it also points toward the usefulness of the second power of the weak, strength as a member of a group. If men and women entering the power structure from backgrounds not usual there are inevitably tagged as tokens coming out of another group, it's realistic to accept the fact, even wiser to exploit it. When Marx referred to measuring progress by "the position of the fair sex (the ugly ones included)," his joky parenthesis was neither a bit of whimsy nor a canard. He meant that if women are to move forward to any measurable degree, they can only do so as a group, without regard to the fact that some of them will possess attractions that appeal to the gallantry, or the affections, of influential men. Women-as-a-sex can't rely on male preferences for the pretty and the witty to put them in positions of power or influence, or permit male contempt for "the ugly ones" to hinder their opportunities. Progress is not individual and it will not be brought about by favors from the powerful.

But if permanent progress is not individual, the converse is not true: individual advances turn into social change *when enough of them occur*—when we stop thinking of them as being made by tokens. Observations by women scholars are useful here. In a recent book on personal interactions within contemporary corporate settings, Rosabeth Moss Kanter analyzes the changes in the perceptions of tokens that occur as the number increases, even rather slightly, shifting from what she calls a "skewed group" to one that's merely "tilted." If the incomers number only one or two they find themselves in a skewed (that is, an extreme) situation where they face difficulties and pressures that go far beyond the ordinary testing that any apprentice runs into. The "dominants" in the group treat them like invaders whose absorption is unthinkable and whose differences must constantly be reaffirmed so that mere familiarity won't earn them even partial acceptance as normal, and thereby question the premises of prevailing logic. But let the group become tilted instead of skewed—and that may mean adding only three or four more tokens—and the situation alters. Now these dangerous intruders can be defined as simply a minority, and the presence of a minority is a fact of life that can be dealt with by known rules, not a menacing intrusion of incomprehensible strangers.

Kanter's comment on the adjustments that follow is interesting: "Minority members have potential allies among each other, can form coalitions, and can affect the culture of the group. They begin to become individuals differentiated from each other as well as a type differentiated from the majority."[2] What happens is that when enough "tokens" assemble, they start acting in familiar and predictable political ways; that is, some of their strangeness is dissipated, and it becomes possible for the dominants to think about them as human individuals instead of magical figures of pollution. For the tokens themselves, the second power of the weak becomes usable: a group comes into existence, and if you are part of a group, there are ways of acting that allude to the strength of a group. A minority group will certainly not be accepted as equal, but it falls within a known political spectrum, and political processes then become available for use.

In addition to an improvement in the situation for tokens who thus lose their extreme isolation and deviance, a further alteration can occur: "Minority members . . . can affect the culture of the group." Bring enough women into a male setting (or substitute any categories you wish), and the setting itself begins to adapt to their presence. Normality begins to redefine itself, for in fact, resocialization works both ways. Because the power-process is a process and not a permanent, static hierarchy of dominance and subordination, it is reciprocal. Each side influences the other.

Note that we are now on the track of a reply to the worrisome and important question of *cooption,* one that naturally concerns the political theorists of all radical groups, which take their origin in criticism of the status quo. Won't newcomers to the power structure find that they come to adopt the methods and doctrines prevalent there simply because they *are* there, built into the structure? ask the philosophers of dissidence. If women's past experience has been the factor which created the differences—social, cultural, psychological—that exist between men and women, differences that are valuable and potentially enriching, what will happen if the experience of both sexes becomes increasingly similar? Won't women take on male attributes that have been cited as flaws in masculine character, and grow aggressive, competitive, and unresponsive to the emotional needs of others? Might not these masculine traits be exaggerated by those who adopt them late and must therefore use them without having learned the inbuilt restraints that primary socialization provides by way of peers and parents? Don't pushy women push even harder than men, who learned as little boys to be good team players?

Even though there are plenty of competitive males who seem to have forgotten those useful lessons, fear of cooption is certainly legitimate; but we should beware of jumping to the conclusion that it's inevitable. Cooption happens; but it happens *inevitably* only to those who believe that the past experience that incomers bring to a new setting has no value or relevance of its own. We are back at the fundamental question of importance, of the long underestimation of the significance of women's lives and history. In this view —and at times it seems to have a half-life nearly as long as the two hundred and forty thousand years of plutonium—women entering a masculine field arrive like new-laid eggs. Past ways of interacting with the world will be abandoned, since they have no meaning; and the very fact that what is being abandoned is shared with other women devalues them as friends and allies, and so contributes to the egglike isolation of each incomer as she strives to model herself on the male character in order to deal with the masculine universe in the proper, the only, One Right Way.

Readers who have come this far with me will know that I am about to suggest that we at once mistrust this static view from the top. Kanter tells us something about the first step away from isolation as a token, and the immediate change that coalition and alliance among minority members produces in the way that the resulting political situation is understood by the powerful. Any account of the movement of immigrant ethnic groups out of the ghettoes first assigned to them, toward the mainstream of American life, carries the story forward. Assimilation is a two-way street. The powerful are, yes indeed, more powerful than the weak; but they are hampered in the use of their power by certain faults. They are, for instance, less flexible and less creative in coping with unexpected events because their creativity long ago went into devising the system as it stands (e.g., defining academic excellence) and they are committed to what they have devised. Incomers are the ones who bring refreshment with them. In the last hundred and fifty years, who can reckon the worth of the contributions made to America by, let us say, the Irish, the Jews, and the Italians, to name merely the most obvious of those who have changed our cultural image? So women's ways of approaching people, women's understanding of the psychology of growth and change that derives from raising children and mediating in personal relations of all kinds, women's awareness of the nitty-gritty demands of everyday implementation of grand programs with all the minor adjustments and repetitions required to do that, these—like black humor, music, and language nuance—are going to become first comprehensible and then accepted as part of normality. In a process of interaction, each partner is sooner or later affected by the behavior of the other.

Of course, adjustment by the dominant to the behavior of the minority may well come later rather than sooner. Newcomers can speed up the procedure if they don't just accept their perceived membership in an outgroup, but exploit it for their own ends. The advantages to be gained by mutual action within the power process are substantial and various. Mutuality broadens knowledge by sharing experience and current information. It provides support. It prevents the fantasy-thinking that isolation breeds. Above all, it matches the circumstances. The upwardly mobile from unorthodox groups are going to be thought of as agents of social change, whether they like it or not. It's part of the condition of their mobility.

In fact, they may not like it at all. Professional women in high posts, women writers and artists of the first rank, often say with profound conviction that they don't want to be judged as women, but as professionals—as writers, as artists, as effective lawyers or doctors or senators—and so on. Alas, the decision is not up to the individual. It's a decision that is arrived at by the Establishment of whichever profession she has entered, and Establishments don't change their guidelines quickly. Past the token stage, women in male contexts can be seen and judged as individuals; but the tag of "female" is still there. Women writers, for example, have been finding responsive readers for over two centuries and a few, a very few, have been allowed into the high critical canon and were taught in the academy B.W.S., or Before Women's Studies. But even for these, for Jane Austen and George Eliot and Emily Dickinson (as for Mary Cassatt and Georgia O'Keeffe), a consciousness that *this* creator is female is still part of the image that each presents. Normal is male. Women may write very well indeed about certain areas of life, but (says orthodox thinking) these areas lie outside the mainstream and cannot offer ground for profound moral insights or significant explorations of ethical dilemmas. At the operating level of making a living, it's happily true, women writers can do as well as their male colleagues; a fact that's explained traditionally as a tribute to the ancient (if not innate) female capacity to please and entertain, the Scheherazade effect. Recently the range of women's writing has widened and is seen to have widened, but few indeed are the serious writers or scholars who are judged without an attached gender-tag, simply as professionals.

If women still lag in literature, where we've been active for centuries, we can expect greater barriers elsewhere. Equally, the work of black artists and writers is almost never separated from their racial origin and judged in the serene realm of Pure Ideas. If they write about black life, white critics find it hard to separate content from the talent that shapes it. If they don't do so, the fact is apt to be noted as unusual. In the performing arts, or in sport, physical performance gets linked to racial or sexual stereotypes; black musicians are endowed with "rhythm," black athletes are granted "primitive" or even "animal" strength. Symphony orchestras find it suitable to hire women harpists before they hire women violinists, and violinists before trombonists or trumpeters or tympanists. Let us suppose that all new entrants into the public world aspire to climb the ladder to success on their own, disavowing their background; which is of course not true. *It makes no difference.* For anyone who happens to have been born female, or born black, to have Spanish as a first language, to have emigrated from East Asia to the American mainland, climbing the ladder to success is never done alone: it *is* social progress. Social progress, to come back once more to Marx, is defined by the ability of these abnormal folk to climb the ladder at all. They will not be able to get a foot on the first rung unless the system is being challenged and showing cracks. The pioneers who mount the first challenge do not expect to be judged as professionals. They know that they bring their origins with them. When incomers can even hope to be judged as professionals, a fair amount of progress has already taken place.

There's nothing particularly altruistic about recognizing the fact that if one is perceived as a member of a group one will get on better if one doesn't forget the fact that individual progress and social progress go together. Neither is it untowardly selfish to want to climb the ladder by oneself and to be judged as a professional. In an egalitarian society that's what individuals should be able to expect as a matter of course, in a taken-for-granted process that would reward brains and drive and creative initiative on an equal footing and widen the range of human potentiality as it did so. But we don't live in that world. And when the governed act as if we did, they are yielding to the sort of opiate-of-the-people fantasy that both misdirects and inhibits action.

The fantasy also invites misinterpretation by the powerful. In our nonegalitarian society, difference is assigned rank within the hierarchy. It may be far from the intention of the ambitious artist who says, "Don't judge my work as women's work, don't apply limited standards to me, judge me at the full stretch of work in my field," but unfortunately this demand can be heard by Establishment critics as meaning, "Femaleness is an attribute I do not wish to share." These hearers will go on to assume that the speaker secretly agrees with the definition of her group as inferior. If not, why should she disavow it? That may not be what she means to say, but her statement does not reject the doctrine that women are not equal to men, that feminine work is less important and feminine skills limited by some indefinable sexual attribute. Since it doesn't reject the dogma, it can be taken as agreement with it; that is, as an acceptance of *stigma.*

Stigma. The term is worth consideration, for it represents a permanent status that is very close, experientially, to the more temporary role of token, and thus it casts light on the relationship between "normal" people and others. In his study of the phenomenon, Erving Goffman defines the term as "spoiled identity."[3] The spoilage can be occasioned in many ways. Sometimes the flaw is physical: crippling, blindness, and deafness stigmatize those they afflict. A recent study done at the University of Southern California for the American Cancer Society reports that "many blue-collar workers stricken with cancer return to their jobs facing hostility from employers and co-workers."[4] Mental patients who have emerged from commitment confront an even more hostile and suspicious world.

It's true that the ethics of our society direct the normal to deal charitably with the disabled—but charity does not erase the difference in status. On the contrary, it often intensifies the consciousness of distance between the healthy and the physically handicapped. Stigma may also derive from some "blemish of character," Goffman continues, and that phrase covers a multitude of disapproved traits: dishonesty, mental disorder, alcoholism, radicalism, to name a few. Or stigma may be "tribal," based on race, nationality, or religion. In any case it presents itself to both normal and abnormal partners in the relationship as "an undesired difference." It evokes displeasure and embarrassment in the normal.

The stigmatized, that is, are rule-breakers, anomalies in the system. Obviously those who break away from traditional roles are candidates for treatment of this kind, and women who move into man's world expect to have to legitimize our presence there. A whole repertory of transitional behavior is being invented for this purpose; but what is interesting is that it differs from masculine behavior in the same situation. So what is required of women is not a demonstration of successfully learned masculinity, *but of remaining and residual feminity.* We are being asked to admit that we can't get rid of it; and that, as we shall see, is exactly the statement that society requires the stigmatized to make in their interaction with normals. The conclusion we have to draw, I think, is that *women are stigmatized anyway, whether in or out of our proper place.* As Elizabeth Hardwick remarks, "Biology is destiny only for girls,"[5] and it is a flawed destiny, a spoiled identity, whether the girl's fate takes her abroad or leaves her at home.

The experience of the stigmatized makes clear that women will not travel a short, sweet, and logical road to equality by means of proving that we possess, and can use, the same abilities that men can command; logic can mislead the fair sex just as thoroughly as it does the unfair. The process of resocialization goes by way of the world outside, and until we can see a redefinition of normality beginning, we shall live in a society in which feminine behavior is always characterized by traits that would be embarrassing if used by men, and females are taken to belong to an alien tribe whose rituals are sometimes comic, sometimes irritating, and occasionally and endearingly childish. Whether or not these opinions are openly stated, they are still acted out. And this, I think, is the real reason why cooption is less of a threat than it may appear in theory: if men cannot accept women as equal, normal, creatures within a masculine-structured and -oriented world, cooption into that world is impossible. We have no choice but to change it.

I raise this point not out of pessimism, nor in order to preach a need for patience either, but rather in order to evaluate the clear evidence that progress by women, and by other groups among the weak, is not straightforward. It will not be brought about simply by clear thinking, though that is needed. It will not be achieved through charitable and generous action by others, no matter how helpful that may be, particularly to the souls of the others. It is a product of intelligent political action in which the weak use their powers and take advantage of external opportunities. As I write, the fact that some progress has been made toward more freedom of action for women is calling forth the quite apparent reaction that things have gone far enough: perhaps as far as they can go, perhaps as far as they should go. I think we can estimate what this means best if we apply to the current situation some of Goffman's conclusions on the operative effect of stigmatization. When we do this we find that the powerful seem to feel that they have been behaving charitably toward women, and that women should be grateful for this kindness. Their charity has allowed us to appear in a wider arena, and to undertake innovative action, almost as if we were normal. But we are not, and our public appearance is neither cause nor cure for this deviance; it was laid on us to begin with. We were offered a private place because we were anomalous; we do not become so by leaving it.

That is exactly the position of the stigmatized: they break rules by being, not simply by doing. As with the halt, the deaf, and the blind, the stigma of femininity is not wiped out by the charity of the great. Nor can it be removed by the angry protests of the bearers of stigma: no use to declare that one is as normal as anyone else in one's work or feelings or ambitions. The physically stigmatized, Goffman reports, don't express the anger they feel because it usually makes matters worse: the normal resent having their charity rejected. And as long as the disabled, or the tribally distinguished, or the "cured" mental patients, cancer victims, or females are bound by the norms of a society that perceives them as deviant with a force that can't be challenged, then they must accept the spoiled identity in public no matter how they feel in private. It's another aspect of resocialization in which the self is adjusted to standards set by others for the convenience of others; or, as Simone de Beauvoir wrote a generation ago, of acceptance by women of "otherness." In every encounter with a normal person the embarrassing fact of abnormality has somehow to be "managed." A special, inventive twist is required simply to preserve the ordinary forms of social intercourse, some expression in behavior-language that both acknowledges the "flaw" and glosses it over, so that the encounter is not too uncomfortable. The stigmatized are expected to do the inventing, and most of the time they do: token women affirm that they have not forgotten their womanhood, and that the males with whom they work are still permitted to treat them with the usual male-female gestures and expressions that accord with the standard image of femininity. In public encounters one acts out otherness, presents the stigmatized "spoiled identity."

The process of learning how to do that begins early for those of the stigmatized who are born to such a condition, but Goffman provides an illuminating citation from a book by a man who was suddenly crippled, and so did his learning in fully conscious maturity:

I also learned that the cripple must be careful not to act differently from what people expect him to do. Above all they expect the cripple to be crippled; to be disabled and helpless; to be inferior to themselves, and they will become suspicious and insecure if the cripple falls short of these expectations. It is rather strange, but the cripple has to play the part of the cripple, just as many women have to be what men expect them to be, and the Negroes often have to act like clowns in front of the "superior" white race, so that the white man shall not be frightened by his black brother.[6]

It would seem, at first blush, that there could be no need to recommend the powers of the weak to the stigmatized—to urge them to mistrust the judgment of a society that regards them as spoiled. Surely they do that! Equally, they testify that coming together is a vital necessity for them, since only with those in the same boat can they feel, and act, like "normals." All that is true; and to some degree, groups of the stigmatized have begun to campaign for the right to be regarded as equal and ordinary. And yet, they are not so perceived; helping the handicapped is still charity. I believe that we must assume that there also exists, in the situation, an invitation for the stigmatized to mistrust the public label, *but not to mistrust it enough;* to agree that the group of the abnormal—useful as a refuge, and for the release of emotion—does not provide a ground for action secure enough to change the label and wash away the stain of spoilage. The power to define is still at work, and the definition of deviance has made its way into the self's own image of the self. If one is inescapably "other," what use is it to identify oneself with a group of "others," since this label is the very source of one's discredited status? Without deeper, active distrust, the stigmatized believe that nothing can change. They are powerless to redefine themselves, and dependent on the spoiled identity in order to have an identity at all.

Moreover, the charity and understanding of the situation with which the kindhearted powerful view these unhappy and angry people only contribute to the problem. Sympathy devalues the emotions of the stigmatized. "Naturally they are angry!" say normal folk. "Who wouldn't be resentful in their position?" So resentment is built into a continuing situation. It does not become a force for revaluation but simply a background noise. The powerful take it for granted and cease to register the shouts from below. As long as they can see the stigmatized as objects of charity, they won't see them as dangerous enemies. They won't see them as agents of change, either.

So those who have been labeled as abnormal, for whatever reasons, will stay where they are until profound dissent alters self-image, and coming together can be felt to be a source of strength. Then the next step is possible, organized action to adjust the external world. Of course, when they refuse to act any longer as objects of charity, these new advocates of progress must expect that upholders of orthodox relationships will "become suspicious and insecure" and no doubt, hostile. Those who want change will be seen as enemies, even though the goal they aspire to is the simple one of normal treatment by Establishment rules of logic. Just as the powerful define the status of the weak, so do they also define conditions of confrontation. Astounding as it may seem, aspiring to be normal can get people labeled as enemies by the normal.

CHAPTER 17

Practical Politics II:
The Burden of Orthodoxy

*Normal science . . . is predicated on the assumption that the scientific
community knows what the world is like. Much of the success of the enterprise
derives from the community's willingness to defend that assumption, if necessary
at considerable cost. Normal science . . . often suppresses fundamental novelties
because they are necessarily subversive of its basic commitments. Sometimes a
normal problem, one that ought to be solvable by known rules and procedures,
resists reiterated onslaught. On other occasions equipment designed for the
purpose of normal research fails revealing an anomaly. In these and other ways
besides, normal science repeatedly goes astray. And when it does—when, that is,
the profession can no longer evade anomalies that subvert the existing tradition
of scientific practice—then begin the extraordinary investigations that lead the
profession at last to a new set of commitments, a new basis for the practice of
science.*

Failure of existing rules is the prelude to a search for new ones.

Thomas Kuhn,
The Structure of Scientific Revolutions[1]

It's hardly news to say that the norms of our society are not formed
from universal experience but, rather, based on the customs, perceptions,
activities, and expectations of a limited upper group. And, after the upheav-
als of the sixties, which passionately challenged the legitimacy and the
relevance of our dominant mythology, we know from our own experience
that normal politics, like normal science, can find itself under attack, sus-
pected of suppressing fundamental (and much-needed) novelties. The field
in which the power-process operates, of course, is much wider and less
structured than is that of scientific research. Other cultures or subcultures
share an era with the one that sees itself as mainstream and definitive. When
the latter falters, the variant and anomalous cultural visions push themselves
forward.

They are not autonomous, needless to say, not independent structures
presenting themselves as substitutes for orthodoxy; but they do exist as bases
for questioning. Minorities, women, immigrants, the poor—all the stigmatized—know that the legends and parables of the powerful turn on issues that
are not germane to their own dailiness, crest in crises that are out of tempo
with their lives, and culminate either in mythical happy endings or tragic

results that are too grand for ordinary existence. Their own exemplary tales are different; folklore, not epic.

Naturally these alternative, half-shaped mythologies of power do not lead quickly to coherent political opposition. The awareness of their difference from the great impinges most strongly on the governed via the emotions, as a sense of distance from events and, in the beginning, as doubts of one's ability to acquire the magic skills needed for governance. The ruled may know well that things are going wrong, but the rulers are still allowed the power to define the occasions and causes of these maladjustments. As long as the governed feel themselves divided and isolated, they are not apt to think practically or politically about "the failure of existing rules." Consequently such analysis as is made of our discontent with civilization tends to fall away from the social or public arena toward personal psychology. Such analysis tells us that we have individual midlife crises to overcome; everyone must expect the trauma, but yours is yours and mine is mine. They may be similar, but we must face them alone. We tend to search for private explanations of public events in the childhood experiences of heroes and to castigate political alienation as resulting from narcissism and self-indulgence.

Such thinking is natural but maladaptive, especially for the governed whose individual efforts can have little effect on circumstances. It does not come to grips with the social factors that underlie and influence personal disappointment and distress and can be approached only publicly, in group array; indeed it disguises the existence of public factors. Russian children know, or used to know, a comic figure called Dr. A. I. Bolit, whose name, translated, means "Ouch! It hurts!" Some reactions to the malaise of our time appear to be confined in similar fashion to declaring that it's painful. So it is, but expression isn't action. We can't deal with personal problems until we trace their sources in the context of life that invites a particular kind of breakdown or ties some special, exasperating penalty to success; hitches tokenism to upward mobility or makes sure that double-career families learn a lot about double binds.

Much of our difficulty in living with the social change occasioned by our own scientific and economic advances (and by living with it I mean not only adjusting to it, but building on it for further advance) stems from the too-small base of experience out of which our norms grow. The maxims for success laid out by the powerful are never much good as guides for those who aren't powerful. They always include as much pious self-justification as useful advice. But at least in times of growth and progress they recommend inventiveness: the "new men" have got on by using new methods, and others may do so too. But in spite of the hopes of the sixties—and the real advances that took place then—the upsets of our own day are seldom welcomed as progress. If they bring hope for some, they bring disorienting confusion to others.

This goes back, I am convinced, to the fact that the powerful still retain the power to define what is happening, even when they too are confused and disoriented because their own interpretations of events are based on archaic social myth. Their guidelines for the successful use of power are discouragingly static. Political problems, like those of "normal science" when the basic paradigm is failing, "resist reiterated onslaught [according to] known rules and procedures." These rules were hammered out on the grounds of life as lived and known by a limited group of males, and they betray the women who try to use them in standard fashion without judging and testing them in terms of their own knowledge. To say this does not belittle or discredit the experience of these men. For them it is, or at least it was, valid. Over the centuries since Plato and Pythagoras reasoned, conjectured, and discussed their perceptions of reality with their friends and disciples, it has built and buttressed our own world view; and few of the changes in that view have originated anywhere else. But the rules formulated for intervention in the world that matched that view now point in wrong directions and, being rules, resist being shifted around to incorporate wider experience.

Beyond the damage that methods of using power as prescribed by the powerful do to the weak is the harm that they do to the powerful. I asked in the last chapter whether the governed could use power according to the procedures laid down by their governors, and concluded that they could not do so profitably. I want now to ask whether any group, or individual, of whatever rank, can use these prescriptions productively today.

Current thinking about power is deeply negative. In part that's due to the assumption that ours is the only way to think about it and that, if we fail, there is no alternative system that could be devised to take its place. We do not see that our thinking is influenced by the limitations of the group in which it takes shape: a group that has developed some of the rigid characteristics of caste and goes on to extend its own caste-rules illogically to other groups. It is, moreover, a caste which feels itself menaced and hemmed in by events that it can't predict and that seem too overwhelming for any creative invention to manage. Any human being suffers a loss of self-confidence in these circumstances. Most of us are all too familiar with such a plight. But the powerful have laid claim to the right, and therefore the responsibility, to manage events. Not being able to do so comes as a shock. Are they no better than the passive and womanly weak? Fear of inadequacy in situations like this invites action that can only be irresponsible, action that is not a realistic response to reality but a product of unfaced emotion. The urge to act somehow, anyhow, and show oneself a man and a leader overrides the unsettling knowledge that the consequences of action are obscure. That reaction lets down the bars to violence when anger stirs, and fear that Fate has gone out of control surely evokes anger.

We looked at examples of this sort of behavior in recent presidential history. Johnson and Nixon, aware that their control over governmental processes was wavering and that public response to their actions was not what they expected, both gave prompt evidence of official arrogance. But it is not only at the center of the executive branch that standard procedures are working sloppily. Loss of control shows up in other joints of the body politic: in policies that seem to work against each other and in a growing bureaucracy that isn't interested in policy at all. It shows up in prosperity that marches hand in hand with inflation as tokenism goes with advancement, and in the replacement of experienced judgment with statistical and econometric formulas that might be useful as data for judgment but can't take its place. Loss of control appears in the relation of our society to the physical world as unpredictability and the negative results of overcontrol: experimental drugs that were going to save us from plagues and famine in one generation leave the next a heritage of disease and despoilment.

One result of clinging to old rules is rigid and uncreative action. Another is panic reaction toward opposite and contradictory behavior. The uprush of belief in the occult, the mushrooming of new sects, and the search for religious experience outside the traditional churches testify to a widespread desire to channel and structure experience anew and, at the same time, to a devaluation of old structures. Violence and outrage make the headlines, but the growing uneasy awareness that things are not working is at least as disturbing, for it is coupled with a sense that they can't be made to work. A sequence of failure is generalized into an expectation of future failure, and this undermines any ability to use power, because it discredits the likelihood that it can be used well. Thus a vicious circular argument of self-fulfilling doom establishes itself, not just among the weak but, most debilitatingly, among the powerful.

I don't have the space, the time, the knowledge, or the wisdom to discuss adequately the clouded pessimism that haunts our world. Do I need to describe it? It is perceived in many shapes, which change and dissolve and shade into each other: apocalyptic war destroying civilization if not all of life; a famine-generating escalation of population; spreading pollution of the environment; corruption in politics at home and inhuman repression abroad; repetitious, unrewarding work that is no longer expected to offer satisfaction in itself; a rate of social change too fast for human nature to accept; the breakup of families; casual sex divorced from love; the creation of a ghetto population outcast within society and excluded from the economy; the demoralization of youth by vacuous and superficial education; the trivialization of high culture by commercial interests, or its increasing mystification by serious artists whose work grows more and more incomprehensible to the public at large; the disappearance of spiritual values; and—worst of all—the conviction that there is no way to cope with these ills (or all the others I have overlooked) that will not itself intensify them or bring worse in its train, so that the only choice seems to lie between isolation and impotence on the one hand, and dehumanizing rigidity on the other: a termite society of programmed survivors.

No one could address this whole Götterdämmerung of problems substantively and en masse. And whether or not this description expresses their essential existence, they do have to be addressed somehow, however partially and tentatively, for they will not blow away by themselves. In order to do that, however, the emotional aura that surrounds them must first be considered. It's an aura that, if taken seriously, foretells a future that can be met only with stoic despair, while if it's merely denied, it moves us into a fantasy world where we repeat old gestures that no longer carry conviction or affect the actuality in which we dwell. If we are to shake ourselves free from the paralysis that these emotions produce, we must find alternatives, beginning with alternative techniques for analyzing our difficulties, and dealing with them. Standard procedures function as positive deterrents to productive thinking and planning. We need to invent new ones, to set out on a search for new social hypotheses that may serve as a base for political paradigms, to use Kuhn's word, analogous to those that have regularly refreshed the systematic thought through which scientists have interpreted and influenced the physical world.

Both the sense of doom that shadows the future and the conviction that our ways of interacting with the power-process are inadequate and yet all that we have to use—these unhappy and inhibiting beliefs derive from the view of power that sees it as emanating from the few who stand at the pinnacle of authority. When the powerful assume that all creativity lies within this elite, and when they know that for this elite the salt has lost its savor, they can imagine no other resource to turn to. Then the governed accept their role as simply to be governed and directed and treated like children, folk too humble to see themselves as potential creators of new ways and worlds. But until the weak can seriously entertain that vision, we will have no instruments worthy of the challenges we face.

What can we say about the mood of clouded anxiety that haunts us today if we examine it critically, as we must if we are to move beyond it? As a beginning, let me submit that it seems to be strongly sex-linked: a male phenomenon; which is not surprising, since it is linked to the experience of the power elite. Women aren't immune to it but it doesn't originate in their

lives. It impinges on them through the traditional channels by which important male experience is made known in order to educe support from those
whose duty it is to support and share vicariously. Male leaders are the source,
those who feel themselves at once duty-bound to exercise power and act
effectively, and convinced that they don't know how, in present conditions.
They expect female sympathy for their dilemma, though not with really
hopeful concern, and in fact it doesn't do them much good; support from an
inferior, less capable group may strengthen the ego but it offers little in the
way of practical help for action in man's world, or so the myth tells them.
Some portion of men, indeed, have always found the traditional masculine
role unattractive. Now the possible rewards it offers seem diminished, and
the possibility of failure increased; and failure, of course, is itself a breech
of proper manhood. Those who risk it are exposing themselves to public
shame, to stigma, showing themselves as no more capable than women.

This is not an individual trauma but a public one. Unfortunately it is
seldom felt as such, just because the masculine ideal of leadership in the use
of power, of *mastery,* calls for individual might, heroic stature, lone suffering
that can win, perhaps, a solution born of the mind of a single genius who
has achieved a new vision. How marvelous it is, indeed, when a human being
of either sex attains such a triumph! But of course it is not the only way to
solve problems, and it may be particularly inappropriate at a time of multiple, rapid change. Then the shared experience of a purposeful group might
afford more insight. If these groups are going to be most effective, they need
to call on a diversity of background, including that gained from living out
a different gender role. And the members who provide diversity must be
taken seriously in their differences: it is these differences that matter, that
permit marginal, flexible, and original ideas to be put forward out of a
hitherto prohibited realm of thought.

One of these ideas, of course, though not the only one, is exactly the
value of women's existence and awareness. Let us look briefly at the feelings
and theories that hinder men from perceiving this value, for the view will
cast light on the flaws in current patterns of power-use. We have to begin
with the male conviction of male superiority, and add to it the present fact
that this superiority is not now felt to bring sufficient reward. Men's lives
don't come up to expectations, and many men feel personally deprived, not
just disillusioned in a general way.

Not all unhappy males blame women for their problems. Quite a few,
and these are usually the more thoughtful, believe their plight to grow out
of the circumstances of life as a whole; either unchangeable circumstances,
which will always tie discontent to civilization, or ones produced by current
change. These men think in terms of philosophic universals. The separation
of the sexes and the hierarchical rank assigned to each appear so inevitable

to them that they simply cannot regard women as a sufficiently important social factor to explain (for example) the decline of the west. *Men* are suffering, that is what's significant; *men* find themselves confused and torn by the external problems of meaning and the intrusive practical dilemmas of governing a politico-economic system unmatched in its complexity. The idea that these difficulties could somehow be related to the enforcement of dumbness and inessentiality on a majority of humans does not penetrate their patterns of thinking. Their awareness of women's presence in the public world is pretty well confined to irritation over the fuss these creatures are kicking up by selfish demands for "rights," and thus further complicating an already distressing situation. Even those who believe that Yes, in good times women should be introduced to the operations of the great world, that in principle they have a right to enter it, find that their timing is terrible. It will take so long for women to learn how to behave and think like men! Why must they pick this era of difficulty to boil up a tempest in a teapot?

Less thoughtful men are rather more angry at women. They are usually less thoughtful because their lives have not given them much opportunity to think productively, to think and plan and have something happen as a result. That is, after all, the experience of all the governed who stand in a situation where they are more accustomed to following directions than giving them. And to the extent that these men feel themselves not in control of their lives, the threat of women's demands is greater than for their powerful brothers because it seems to be immediately competitive with their own needs. In their view, then, women's restlessness and rebellion might in fact *be* the reason for the evils from which the age suffers. But they don't resent women just because they fear competition. Their hostility is the product of bitterly learned knowledge that they are limited in their own choices and dependent on what they have had to learn for themselves, with some pain, about the current hierarchy and its operations. And at the same time, a seductive fantasy of power—unlimited, uncontrolled, growing toward an explosion of fury—tempts those whose real lives are most unsatisfying. A feeling that women are changing the rules is hard on those men who doubt their ability to do any rule-changing themselves. If you have denied your own creativity as part of a bargain for survival in a structured society, how can you not resent—and desperately—those who belittle and attack the structure that you have had to commit yourself to as part of the bargain? (At least until some alternative can be imagined.)

Though the male mystique with its emphasis on individual responsibility makes this situation most painful for men, the feminine mystique is still strong enough to persuade many women to share it second-hand. Any strong male emotion—in this case, a doom-laden atmosphere, an irremediable absence of joy—is easily communicated to women; not just because their role has been passive, but because for generations females have been trained to survive by knowing and responding to male states of mind. It should not surprise us that many women share male views and male fears of change. What's truly surprising is the number who don't, who differ, question, dissent, say one thing and act differently—as if disagreement, long hidden, had had to feel only the slightest breath of a new spring to surface, stubborn, wily, smiling, flexible, and indomitable. But this disagreement has not yet extended itself (except for a relative few) to a point where it is ready to undertake a major challenge to masculine philosophy and social definitions. Cognitively, the male view of life as unpromising and deficient still holds sway; and in my opinion it operates as a social control on women's hopes and ambitions. The old sensitivity to male unhappiness, which has had survival value, now hinders women's readiness to hope and plan and work for happiness: it lowers one's ability to believe that happiness is possible, and so promotes the acceptance of half a loaf.

The disillusionment of the masculine power structure with its own rules is not hard to document, or to understand. Let us look at some of the recipes offered to the governed in current guides to gaining and using the powers of the powerful. They come in all forms and degrees of seriousness. If critical scholarly inquirers still assign only to leaders the right to lay out problems and formulate goals, then the mystique of leadership runs deep. By the same token, commercial advice on How to Get Ahead tells us about the popular incidence of the assumptions on which it is based, especially if the book achieves best-sellerdom. Our world has many mirrors, and those which seem distorting help to define the range of distortion our society is prepared to put up with. Social historians have found guides to etiquette and formal behavior for success illuminating as to past systems for interaction, and today's are just as useful.

An (apparently) uncomplicated program for climbing the ladder by means of canny tricks is always a popular approach. Michael Korda's bestselling *Power: How to Get It, How to Use It* will serve as an example of the genre.[2] Cheerfully brash about its ploys, instructive through what it takes for granted, it's as much addressed to ambitious members of the ruled as were the works of Horatio Alger. But Korda stands Alger on his head. The virtues of the Protestant Ethic, the value of hard work, and the usefulness of honesty as a policy are reversed in favor of Oneupmanship.

Korda's ploys need no more attention than Alger's plots; but his premises are highly informative, not just in themselves, but because the sales of his book indicate that they seemed plausible to a considerable audience of the governed. Central among these premises is the idea that, first, power is a game and, second, that it is a zero-sum game: "Your gain is inevitably someone else's loss," and vice versa. This gambit fits contemporary assumptions about power: it is not just amoral but immoral. So if you want it, you must accept that you will act immorally. Popular Machiavellianism might easily stop there, but Korda, like Machiavelli, proceeds to justify acting immorally. Reasons of State enforced by Necessity laid this duty on the Prince, but they can hardly apply to the worries of an ambitious junior executive. Korda offers in their place a first argument based on self-defense: If you don't get them, they'll get you. His second is a good deal more clever: Power is a game. You must indeed act immorally to get on, but your actions are unimportant, because you are simply playing a game.

Korda's book is superficial but his premises aren't; and since they seem to be rather widespread, they're worth considering for clues as to the logic of popular cynicism. The first, that human creatures don't share a community and survive only by ruthless competition, is a commonplace that reflects the age-old policy of "Divide and rule." Encouraging the governed to believe that they can't form alliances is a familiar weapon of the powerful. I don't mean to suggest that Korda advances it for any conscious purpose, simply that it's part of the atmosphere where his ideas take form. More novel is the presentation of power-struggle-as-game.

One sees the attraction of the formulation. If power is immoral, but also desirable, those who feel its tug can lessen the pangs of conscience while they do what they want by imagining that they aren't really doing these nasty things, they're merely playing. Now, anxiety over the use of power is a real drawback for the weak, and appealing to conscience as a means of enforcing the social rules that benefit the powerful is not just a nasty ploy but an effective, and dangerous, means of social control. When Shaw's Alfred Doolittle attacked "middle-class morality," he was rejecting just such an effort to turn the consciences of the poor against their own interests. However, if we ease our minds by devaluing our actions and calling them play, aren't we moving not just our actions, but our lives and ourselves out of the real world and into a realm of nonseriousness?

When action is conceived as having no consequences that matter—and that in effect is what reducing the power-process to a game brings about—something happens to the context of life in which our actions take place. It too loses all seriousness, all reality. We're heading back to the condition of those confused and desperate children, whose histories we quoted earlier. They were unable to establish a sense of their own existence and inner being because the world in which they lived was not affected by what they did. Let that happen often enough and meaning drains out of existence, value drains out of the self. To do something one feels is bad and *not to have to pay for it* reduces the significance of the self as well as the deed. If we glance back at Winnicott's case history of George, delinquent in the midst of a family that supported him by refusing to punish him, we see how the license he was given hindered the development of a centered, controlling self within the boy.

Now for Winnicott the concept of "play" is central, but it is defined in a way very different from the idea of life as a game that denies the consequences of one's actions in the external world. Play takes place within the transitional space where interior and external worlds meet and interact, and it permits a temporary suspension of the rules of full reaction to all action, but only a temporary one. The suspension is functional. It allows testing of what one does as a necessary part of learning and of creation. It's not a denial of the seriousness of action but a means to discover how the processes of action will work out, in order to use them properly in the serious and consequential outside world. Such experiments permit adjustments and these too are part of learning. Play allows children to explore new areas of existence and locate limits of action, so that they don't overrun them in ignorance. These limits are made clear, but the reactions are also playful and don't carry the full weight of serious response. Adults and children, teachers and learners, agree to remove what they do from reality and carry on the process in a special realm of "as if."

In much the same fashion, Bruno Bettelheim's theory of treatment within an institution designed to undo maleficent relationships with the human environment and nourish alternatives that enhance growth is based on interaction and response. Both are moderated, but they are accurate. Good therapists acknowledge, to themselves and to their patients, that they are indeed affected by what the patients do. They are really hurt, or angry, or delighted—and above all they are interested. They temper the consequences of these actions but they don't deny them, for unless patients can see that they move those around them they feel themselves invisible and impotent; indeed the emotions that patients call up in their caretakers are both part of the therapy provided and, in themselves, diagnostic tools that illuminate the troubled relationships that have damaged these children.

Used well, then, games and play are a vital component of human life and its creative emotionality. But they are misused if they replace reality instead of prefiguring its events and processes. A game theory of power offers only secondary gains that don't offset corresponding losses. As an effort to counter the debilitating pessimism of our time it works against itself, for it ends by diminishing the actor's grasp on reality.

Where popular cynicism tries to reduce the burden of guilt felt for grasping at immoral power by reducing the importance of all one's actions, another approach uses moral rules to isolate the immorality of power from the necessity to act. This hypothesis declares that what's immoral about power is the impulse to use it selfishly, and that one can avoid corruption and guilt by rejecting actions that are self-serving. In the view that Michael Korda's book expresses, every sensible soul who wants to get on must act immorally, and even those who don't want to will be forced to do so on pain of becoming a rung in someone else's ladder. David McClelland, professor of psychology at Harvard and long-time student of the need for achievement alive in human beings, argues the desirability of the altruistic alternative. McClelland, one might say, is soft where Korda is hard. His approach is different too, aimed not at a popular but at a more academic audience. His analysis grows out of lengthy studies on motivations for achievement; his data is not confined to Western culture or to the male sex, and since he is a member of the Society of Friends, we may guess that he is not committed to the One Right Way of enforcing authority through confrontation. In *Power: The Inner Experience* he is at pains to distinguish among perceptions of the nature of power and to examine the various kinds of behavior they give rise to.

McClelland sorts out these differing ways in which power is seen, and the need for it expressed, as stages in a progress toward maturity; and though this term is not specifically defined, it involves flexible judgment and the ability to select patterns of behavior that are appropriate to different circumstances. The mature are not lumbered with compulsions to act, or react, in stereotypical fashion but can choose realistically among several. In a discussion of leadership—that is, the use of power within a respondent group— McClelland describes as immature the employment of a personal style operating in a mode of dominance and compulsion. He prefers another way of leadership that he believes is typical of more gifted and successful managers. These leaders see themselves as altruists who use their power for others. They do not want to force their followers to concur on goals or methods, but instead to influence and educate them. The role of such a leader is "to make clear which are the goals the group should achieve, and then to create confidence in its members that they can achieve them."[3]

In a society in which, as he says, "the exercise of power is viewed negatively," McClelland is consciously seeking its "positive face. After all, people cannot help influencing one another; organizations cannot function without some kind of authority relationships. It is necessary and desirable for some people to concern themselves with management, with working out influence relationships that make it possible to achieve the goals of the group."[4] He is surely right to emphasize the element of sharing and of common interest that is part of what he calls social, as opposed to personal, ways of using power, and he notes the need for seeking out appropriate techniques for reaching desired goals so that methods and ends don't contradict each other. He values the confidence that a good leader creates in his followers and sees it as producing the "feeling of competence they need to work hard," which feeling of competence then fortifies growing self-confidence in one's own capacities, apart from those of the leader. He's well aware of the classic dilemma of the altruistic leader who must ask

> at what point his clear enthusiasm for certain goals becomes authoritarian insistence that those goals are the right ones whatever the members of the group may think . . . If he takes no initiative, he is no leader. If he takes too much, he becomes a dictator—particularly if he tries to curtail the process by which members of the group participate in shaping group goals. There is a particular danger for the man who has demonstrated his competence in shaping group goals and in inspiring group members to pursue them. In time both he and they may assume that he knows best, and he may almost imperceptibly change from a democratic to an authoritarian leader.[5]

And not only is McClelland sensitive to the threat to this style, altruistic leadership, in the possible assumption by both parties to the relationship that the leader knows best. He is also able to move beyond the ethical problem as stated here and perceive that the solution doesn't lie with the leader alone. If his followers

> are to be truly strong, he must continually consult them and be aware of their wishes. A firm faith in people prevents the development of the kind of cynicism that so often characterizes authoritarian leaders. A second safeguard is social: democracy provides a system whereby the group can expel the leader from office when it feels that he no longer properly represents its interests.[6]

What is wrong with this humane description of the positive face of social power? Its eagerness to see the leader employed in the service of the group, its awareness of his need to consult with his followers, and its declaration of their right to withdraw consent from an unrepresentative leader are all admirable. These approved leaders carry the stamp of moral responsibility and of a decent respect for the opinion of mankind. And yet—

They are not participants in the process on a level of common humanity. That is the essential problem, and it isn't moral at all, it's political. McClelland's leaders cannot *not* be leaders, they cannot move out of this role into one of marginality, beyond the structure, where for better or worse they know themselves no better or worse than their fellows, and find refreshment in "the sentiment of the wholeness of the total community [felt as] an undifferentiated whole whose units are total human beings."[7] Instead they keep their distance, in spite of their "concern for group goals, for finding those goals that will move men, for helping the group to formulate them, for taking initiative in providing means for achieving them, and for giving group members the feeling of competence they need to work hard."[8] They still possess—and they feel no need to yield—*the great and primary power to define*. They are all but unmoved-movers, who will set the group on its proper path toward goals that the leader discovers. The leader must take the initiative, and if he takes none, then "he is no leader"; and a leader, it appears, there must be, one who does not think of himself and is not thought of by others as coequivalent with the rest of the group.

Where does he come from, then? Does he arise out of the group? The question doesn't seem to occur to McClelland but it would appear not, for the examples he offers of this style of leadership tend to be of *teachers*. But as between teachers and pupils, there cannot by definition exist the unconscious fellow-feeling which helps to provide a leader with a sense of participatory involvement. Consultation with the rest of the group is in order for a good teacher; but when McClelland praises it, he does so from the point of view of the leader: it profits the teacher to understand the pupils' mentality and ambitions. Consultation may be undertaken ostensibly to strengthen the mood of the followers—but that is because the role of the leader is "to give strength to others and to make them feel like originators of ideas."[9] Well, I think we must ask, as this formulation invites us to, *Are* the followers strong, independent of their leader? *Do* they originate ideas? Or do they just feel *as if* they did?

It's clear, I hope, that I don't want to quarrel with the ideas of power that Dr. McClelland expresses, but with what he overlooks, and with the distortions that this oversight forces upon his moral perceptions. His definition of social power still centers on a leader. Indeed, he writes, "the ultimate paradox of social leadership and social power [is that] to be an effective leader, one must turn all of his so-called followers into leaders." But once this is done the new leaders do not remain in a reciprocal relation through which the group will influence events; they fly off to found new colonies of their own, where each will provide initiative to another group caught in outer darkness. One is somehow reminded of a high-minded imperial system where dedicated altruists take up and then pass on some more acceptable version of the White Man's Burden. In the most ethical way and with the best will in the world, McClelland's vision is still of a system in which power emanates from those at the pinnacle rather than "arising from many parts of society."

I am not overlooking McClelland's reference to democracy, and to the provision that it has the right to expel a leader; we have examined illustrations. But until this extreme is reached, McClelland seems to regard democratic society as dependent on its leaders for its goals and for the methods of achieving them. He quotes John Gardner with high approval for a description of the socialized leadership role, "when he said that leaders 'can conceive and articulate goals that lift people out of their petty preoccupations, carry them above the conflicts that tear a society apart, and unite them in the pursuit of objectives worthy of their best efforts.' " It is impossible, reading this, not to wish for reports from the pettily preoccupied on how *they* felt about pursuing objectives "conceived and articulated" for them as being "worthy of their best efforts" in the opinion of someone else. Did they agree on the desirability as well as the worthiness? Did they congratulate themselves on having, finally, made the acquaintance of someone capable of calling forth their best efforts? And best in what sense, to whose standards —their own or their leader's? What happened if they disagreed? Did they simply take their leave, or were some of them so bad-mannered as to retreat into disguised disobedience? Would their leaders have known it if they did?

The impulse to do good for others by helping them to achieve goals that you are sure will profit them is widespread. McClelland is wiser than most altruists in warning against the enthusiasm that can turn into authoritarian insistence. But even if it stops short of that, it has the effect—once we turn our gaze from the leader to the rest of the group—of undermining the independent perceptions of the led. A leader carries legitimate authority. His followers will always tend to give more weight to his views than to those of anyone else, often including their own. And so they come to cede to the leader the task of defining not just the Good as an ideal principle, but their own good in the circumstances of their own lives.

And at the same time it is indeed hard for leaders to quell their enthusiasm, cease to promote their beliefs and preach their credos. It's really an unnatural exercise. Here the screw makes another turn: just because it is unnatural, being undertaken for a good from which one dissociates oneself, it further distances leaders from participation with the group. In McClelland's view, leaders *must* be altruists: a purposive contra-Machiavellian stance is required of them. Followers, however, are naturally, selfishly, concerned with their own desires; and so they are stigmatized, stamped as less worthy. This is a vision in which the fact that there are two members of any power relationship is colored by ranking the two in a permanent moral hierarchy. Of course identity of interest is rare, but here it becomes impossible. Nor do we, in fact, require identical interests from both members, simply a wide enough overlap of common purpose, shared by rulers and ruled. This community will maintain a working relationship at the political level, and that is all we want or can hope for . . . Altruism condescends if it defines itself as acting *for* others; better that we should act *with* others in a process that will reward our own desires, as part of a "we."

David McClelland's concern for moral leadership posits a pleasanter world than that where Michael Korda lessens the burden of guilt for immorality by lessening the reality of one's aims and actions. But, though the presence of moral responsibility in public life may beneficially limit the range of unpleasant things that people do to each other, it is not a substitute for political process. By inviting leaders to concentrate on their own motives and standards, it hampers their awareness of what's actually going on as their policies are pursued. "Am I doing right?" they ask themselves, and if they ask themselves as insistently, "Are we achieving our purposes?" that's fine. But the second question is the crux of the affair, and if the first becomes more pressing, it invites our governors to see themselves as tutors (which is McClelland's stance) and/or parents. The dangers of that attitude we have considered in an earlier chapter, and noted the tendency of paternalism to reduce the recipients of "doing good" to a state of infantilism in which the significance of their own impulses is ignored.

When, in our thinking, we concentrate on the morality of leaders instead of on the political process of interaction we are tacitly accepting the thesis that the weak are not just weak, but powerless to be anything but followers. Even where, as with McClelland, the analyst of power explicitly recognizes that a relationship exists between rulers and ruled, interest focuses on the personal ethics of the powerful. What the governed think, what conscientious struggles they may experience—these things do not matter. If followers are loyal to their leader, that is a triumph for the leader, not the result of a choice made by the followers. If they fall into distrust and disaffection, the roots are sought in the clumsiness or lack of charisma of their guide. In a recent study, *Leadership,* James McGregor Burns begins by firmly defining power

> not as a property or entity or possession but as a *relationship* in which two or more persons tap motivational bases in one another and bring varying resources to bear in the process. . . . The arena of power is no longer the exclusive preserve of a power elite or an establishment or persons clothed with legitimacy. Power is ubiquitous; it permeates human relationships.[10]

Indeed it is and does. But in spite of this valuable perception, Burns finds it difficult to imagine any political action arising directly from the camp of followers, undirected and unmediated by a leader. If they become "activated" it is in response to "an activation effort" from above. And if by chance some follower initiates an independent step—well, then, a state of leadership at once descends upon, and redefines, this ex-follower. Leaders are advised to consult with their constituents and learn their needs, but the leaders interpret these aims and set the goals. Without leadership, groups are fated to stagnate in a condition of bureaucratic stupor.

Burns's difficulty, I think, arises from the common addiction of the academic elite to thinking in terms of static principles and universal definitions instead of process. In the realm of cognition it is much more comfortable if things stay put, leaders here, followers there. For the people thus defined, however, who harbor ambitions, are pursued by desires and nagged by obligations, staying put is unnatural as well as awkward. But the need to redefine those who move makes for another sort of discomfort. We have noted how incomers to high status find themselves tagged as tokens. Because their status is changed, the value of their past experience falls away, their lives are cut in two, and the lessons they hold in memory are disavowed. If leaders are so sharply distinguished from followers, those who move up a step will find themselves in just this situation; and it is a situation that denies the continuity of human existence and personal identity.

Within the power relationship, Burns is perfectly aware that the members interact, that this process moves from motivation toward goals, and that "followers who [seem] impotent [may] unexpectedly exert influence." And it is, after all, quite natural that in a book entitled *Leadership* he should focus on this quality. But while the *transactional* leadership, which is a matter of negotiation between "persons with certain motives and values" in order to "realize goals independently or mutually held by both leaders and followers" is valuable politically, he allows, it lacks high moral value. Its object "is not a joint effort for persons with common aims acting for the collective interests of followers but a bargain to aid the individual interest of persons or groups going their separate ways."[11]

Transforming leadership, on the other hand, is elevating. Through it, "leaders can also shape and alter and elevate the motives and values and goals of followers through the vital *teaching* role of leadership."[12] And so we find ourselves once more inquiring whether the reciprocity that Burns ascribes to the process of leadership can ask anything more from the weaker partner than the ability to hear and be motivated by leaders. The professorial impulse to equate leader with teacher and follower with pupil seems irresistible.

At any rate the works of these students of the morality of leadership help us to see that while leaders can distance themselves from the rest of their constituency by sheer selfish drive for personal gain or fame, they may do so quite as thoroughly by an unacknowledged conviction of their own moral superiority, greater insight, and more penetrating reason. It's the assumption of separation that invites irresponsibly immoral behavior because it permits leaders to see themselves as different; as set off from others and, eventually, above the law. If power tends to corrupt; if, as Lord Acton went on to say,

"Great men are almost always bad men," the corruption takes place through a failure in relationship, an attenuation in the process of interaction.

Lord Acton was, of course, a member of the male elite, as are the professors and the publishing executive I have quoted in this chapter. Pragmatically speaking, it is well for members of the elite to worry about the morality of those who stand in dominant positions. But it's a good deal less important for the rest of us to worry about it. What we want from the powerful is not just morality (though that is certainly a bonus) but sensitivity to the operations of the political process, which includes an awareness of our presence and of our demands. How, in fact, are the powerful to learn anything useful about morality unless they hear it from the governed? It's surely not the potential abusers of power, the great men who may be bad men, who can be trusted to see the line where abuse begins. It's the abused who know that. The eyes of the powerful can be blinded and their ears stuffed to deafness with self-righteous joy in their own high moral standards just as much as by suspicious resentment of the effort the governed make to change their status or ease their burdens. Progress of the fair sex does not depend on the generosity of the male elite. Generosity is always welcome, of course; but by definition it comes and goes at the will of the great. How then can it be depended on? And when was it ever offered freely to *all* the weak, the ugly ones included? Here as everywhere the governed make progress most surely by trusting their own strong, coherent, articulate, agreed-on purposes implemented by independent action. If the male elite would take Thomas Kuhn for a guide, they would be more ready to see a decline in the effectiveness of their rule as a sign of practical malfunction, of increasing misfit between their theoretical paradigms of governance and changing contemporary reality. That kind of breakdown, says Kuhn, calls for a creative search for alternative theories that not only explain current difficulties, but also point toward newly structured approaches to the future, new questions to be asked. It does not call for a retreat into guilt and traumatic anxiety, which is then projected outward as a vision of the Twilight of the Gods.

Men cannot live without hope, said Hobsbawm. A corollary of that dictum seems to be that if hope can't find grounds for existing in the actual circumstances of life, it will seize on fantasies and give way to wish-fulfillment daydreams that deny problems instead of trying to resolve them.

CHAPTER 18

Impractical Politics I: The Hidden Agenda of Community

> *The characteristics most highly developed in women and perhaps most essential to human beings are the very characteristics that are specifically dysfunctional for success in the world as it is. That is obviously no accident. They may, however, be the important ones for making the world different. The acquisition of real power is not antithetical to these valuable characteristics. It is a necessity for their full and undistorted unfolding.*
>
> Jean Baker Miller,
> Toward a New Psychology of Women[1]

The intellectual weakness of current thinking about power and its uses may seem relatively unimportant in the face of the violent underside of contemporary frustration and gloom. I dwell on it because those who desire to intervene in governance from below need to develop a thorough, whole-self distrust of the world-definitions derived from the current orthodox structure of beliefs. Our definitions are not just static, they are characterized by an insistence on polarities: of gender roles, of a power dichotomy between governors and governed, and, related to both, of thinking as differentiated from feeling. These divisions are embedded in our social mythology, taken for granted and glossed over, not because they can be proven, but because they can't. They're stubbornly problematic and the problems they raise seem insoluble. Consequently, calling attention to them gives rise to malaise and even anger, and efforts to analyze them make it worse.

Jean Baker Miller, like Dr. Richard Emerson's Miss B (in Chapter II), is enlarging the context of the question, and thus avoiding confrontation, by approaching it pragmatically. She is asking us to think about characteristics assigned to women not as inherently feminine, but in terms of their usefulness in a human world. Victor Turner, in his definition of social inferiority, which stands at the head of this book, speaks similarly of powers assigned to the weak, to women and others, which carry connotations that are quite apart from our usual definitions of the division between powerful and weak. These characteristics "foster continuity and create the sentiment of the wholeness of the total community"; that is, *they oppose polarization and dichotomy.* They too have importance for making the world different, for they extend the range of potential action and interpretation of action by affirming the value of connection and mutuality.

In working toward alternative systems of thought, agents of change will want to avoid falling into the traps that unresolved problems set today. Let us not polarize thought and feeling so sharply that the use of one mode prevents the use of the other. The orthodox view of power is dangerous, our feelings tell us so. But our thinking minds speak too; these theories of dominance and of its impact on human relationships are also wrong, not only wrong in a moral sense, but wrong intellectually and functionally, wrong as a means of effective governance, incorrect, unproductive, a failed paradigm.

We need both to think and to feel about the dangers of polarization. Its basic error lies in narrowing the range of creativity, which is our best hope for adjusting to and managing change, by denying a full grasp on experience to weak and powerful alike. The weak, we know, lose their chance to take a hand in managing the world because their lives and their experience are trivialized; what they know isn't important and their capacity to draw conclusions from it is small because they act on the basis of feelings, not reason. To the powerful, therefore, falls the duty of directing events. The right way to do that is by objective, impersonal reason. Private lives and private emotions must be separated from public judgment and responsibility. The scientific reasoning that has facilitated exploration of the physical universe is thus taken to be the proper instrument for regulating the world of human relationships and social operations.

This is a real error in judgment, an error induced as much by a failure to think clearly as to feel justly. In the human world, emotions (including one's own) are vastly influential. If the powerful don't take them into account, they are leaving out a large part of life, especially their ability to predict what people (again including themselves) are going to do. To a certain extent, this problem is perceived; but dealing with it is another matter, for though the emotions of the powerful are held to exist, they are in the main regarded as unfortunate flaws that detract from objective judgments and not as sources of either intuitive knowledge or purposive strength.

Irving Janis and Leo Mann, in their study, *Decision Making,* are convinced of the supreme value of cognitive approaches to judgment and aware of the problems raised by emotions. Good decisions, they maintain, are based on "vigilant information processing," and they summarize recent literature on the topic to arrive at seven criteria which will "determine whether decision-making procedures are of high quality." These are laid out as steps in a cognitive process, and the closest we get to emotion comes in the third, where the human creature who is facing the crux of choice "carefully weighs what he knows about the costs and risks of negative consequences."[2] If that arouses anxiety, however, it doesn't get into the procedure. Anxious or not, the decision-maker goes on thinking.

Of course a cool mind in a tough situation is highly valuable; but part of the situation is exactly the paradoxical need to think while feeling, to distance emotions from the crux of choice—and to judge, as one does so, whether these emotions may not also be part of the information that should be processed vigilantly. When we make a rule which says, "Think, don't feel," we are leaving a great deal out, not only the difficulty of following the rule, but also the context of the situation the rule tells us not to consider. Janis and Mann see the first problem, and sympathize with their reluctant decision-makers, "beset by conflict, doubts, and worry, struggling with incongruous longings, antipathies and loyalties, and seeking relief by procrastinating, rationalizing, or denying responsibility for [their] own choices."[3] What they don't consider is, first, the effect on human beings of telling them to ignore their emotions, and, second, the fact that not only is this inevitably impossible, it clouds and blurs the choice to be made, for unconsidered emotions do not disappear. The importance of alternative actions will always be affected by the emotional weight that these actions carry, both in prospect and in consummation. Janis and Mann know perfectly well that emotions get into the decision-making process, that (for example) commitment to a choice lowers objectivity, but they see such commitment only as a fault. Their advice is not to do it, and their work consists of breaking down "vigilant information processing" into small steps that can be followed by rote, while emotional reactions are held at bay.

There is an implicit judgment here that certainly doesn't originate with these authors and for which they can't be held responsible, a judgment that emotions are dangerous and ought to be excluded from decisions and from actions, which are properly based on collecting available information and thinking about it in practical terms. But feelings are horribly practical too, and when they are ignored, they can backfire. Here is a view of the world in which Janis and Mann's decision-makers function, from a retired business executive talking to Studs Terkel about his experience of top-level management. "As a kid living through the Depression," Terkel's subject took as a model "the tycoons, the men of power . . . the guys who have no feeling, aren't subject to emotions." But as he himself rose in the hierarchy, he found out that these supermen were not immune: "They all got the same fears." And what did they do about them? Confront them, deal with them, think through the implications of what they felt? No. They hid them.

When the individual reaches the vice presidency or he's general manager, you know he's an ambitious, dedicated guy who wants to get to the top. He isn't one of the gray people. He's one of the black-and-white vicious people—the leaders, the ones who stick out in a crowd.

As he struggles in this jungle, every position he's in, he's terribly lonely. He can't confide and talk to the man he's working for. To give vent to his feelings, his fears, and his insecurities, he'd expose himself. This goes all the way up the line until he gets to be president. The president *really* doesn't have anybody to talk to, because the vice presidents are waiting for him to die or make a mistake and get knocked off so they can get his job.

He can't talk to the board of directors, because to them he has to appear as a tower of strength, knowledge, and wisdom, and have the ability to walk on water. The board of directors, they're cold, they're hard. . . .[4]

This dog-eat-dog vision of life is certainly extreme and exaggerated; colored by emotions felt but not considered. Extreme though it is, it expresses a common enough view of what leaders and decision-makers must do, and what they must avoid. Management men in the large multinational company that Rosabeth Moss Kanter surveyed cultivated an impersonal style and avoided any expression of feelings, but that did not rid them of emotions. Kanter comments on one result of this repression that chimes with Victor Turner's thought: "It is ironic that in those most impersonal of institutions, the essential communal problem of trust remains."[5] Because it does and because it cannot be admitted and explored, those in charge find themselves in real difficulties when they come in contact with strangers. Can they trust them? They don't know; and without being able to trust their own emotions to tell them, they have no way of judging. The powerful must be discreet; but discretion extends beyond what one knows. It also covers how one feels, and therefore who one is. It raises, says Kanter,

not technical but human, social, and even communal questions; trust and its origins in loyalty, commitment, and mutual understanding based on the sharing of values. It is the uncertainty quotient in managerial work, as it has come to be defined in the large modern corporation, that causes management to become so socially restricting: to develop tight inner circles excluding social strangers; to keep control in the hands of socially homogeneous peers; to stress conformity and insist upon a diffuse, unbounded loyalty; and to prefer ease of communication and thus social certainty over the strains of dealing with people who are different.[6]

If Kanter's observations are right, it appears that emphasis on impersonality as the proper style of management must severely hinder the very process that Janis and Mann see as underlying decisions of high quality: the ability to gather and vigilantly process wide knowledge about alternative possibilities. One really needs the whole self, emotions and all, to learn and to evaluate possible courses of action. Cognitive analysis isn't enough. Invalidating emotional and intuitive responses to conditions narrows experience severely. Moreover, the unadmitted feelings of the analyst, projected out on the world, create a mirroring context of misapprehension and potential hostility.

Gender roles clearly intertwine with questions of proper status behavior in the attitudes that our social mythology attaches to emotionality. In his work on developmental transitions in the lives and careers of men, Daniel Levinson touches repeatedly on the barriers to self-integration which our current sex definitions create. "The masculine/feminine polarity was of great importance to all the men in our study," he writes, and adds that it "is often reflected in the distinction between *thinking* and *feeling*. It is often assumed that men are by nature more logical and 'reasonable' than women—more analytical and intellectual, cooler, more interested in how things work. Women in turn are supposed to be more emotional and intuitive, more likely to make decisions on the basis of feelings rather than careful analysis."[7] But, as Levinson shows, the denial of emotions in itself gives rise to emotions, and can delay and hamper decisions. It was very hard for these men to analyze their options either vigilantly or effectively. Fear of emotionality got in the way. "Paul Namson" spoke of the anxiety he suffered over giving up a career as a business executive in order to become a writer; that is, to leave a masculine occupation for one that had "feminine meanings." "Bill Paulsen . . . sought desperately to enter the managerial ranks of industry" which to him "represented in part a validation of his manliness."

"When the splitting of power and weakness takes an extreme form," Levinson concludes, "a man regards any sign of weakness in himself as intolerably feminine and dangerous." Extended to separate thought from feeling, this fear downgrades the value of emotion until it "requires a man to be a kind of thinking machine. To be truly masculine, he must devote himself to his occupation in a highly impersonal way. He can allow himself a narrow range of 'manly' feelings related to assertiveness, rivalry and task attainment. But he is not permitted feelings that involve dependency, intimacy, grief, sensuality, vulnerability. Such feelings are associated with childishness and femininity."[8] Another Yale psychologist, Seymour Sarason, concurs, but adds an additional problem to those faced by leaders dealing with the emotions that come to all humans—the problem of *isolation*. Impersonal leaders dare not show weakness. They cannot, must not, "lay all their cards on the table." Uneasiness and anxiety have to be kept private, from that hard-nosed board of directors, those ambitious vice presidents. Lack of trust inevitably invades the relationship between leader and followers until it becomes, says Sarason, "a form of mutual deception."[9]

If women and the others of the weak are reckoned as being incapable of making high-quality decisions by reason of their emotionality, a rejection of feeling seems to impale the powerful on the other horn of the dilemma. They are barring themselves from the interior realm where a self can be renewed and refreshed as it recognizes the positive, relational value of feeling; as it finds there a basis for self-trust and consequently trust of others, even of strangers from a different background. It is in this interior world that we test the information that we have been vigilantly gathering, test it for authenticity and reject it if we find it false. Learning the world within relationships as we do, we validate what we perceive by our own responses as compared with those of others; but unless we can reach and trust our own responses, we have no standards for judgment. We do not have to agree with the reactions that other folk express: we may find them wrong, or congenial, or odd but interesting, or illuminating and enlarging. But our basis for judging them at all can be only the standards we have accreted over the years and which we feel honestly; not, of course, by shrinking from emotionality but by trying to feel it through, with our thinking minds turned on. In a lifetime, experience of shared emotions grows and gives existence a resonance, so that we recognize the true pitch of feeling and judge events against the notes and scales and chords from the past that sound on in our interior world. A journey there may be a frightened retreat to fantasy, but it can also be—or be instead—a search for the self as part of humankind. Then it leads not to a locked cell but to the experience of community.

Can the great afford to do that? So our leaders ask themselves in our time, when feeling is suspect and coolness, rather than ripeness, is all. But those who deny the reality of their feelings are declaring that part of the self is false. On the evidence of Janis and Mann, of Terkel and Kanter, of Levinson and Sarason, such a denial is still very much part of the masculine mystique for managing the world, and it is costly. If emotions don't matter, how are you to *enjoy* anything? If depth of feeling has to be feared, how can you take pleasure even in mastery, in triumph, or fortunate love? How can the success you have labored for come as a full reward for your efforts, how can it satisfy your hopes if you are afraid to feel it?

To cut women off from action and to cut men off from their own deep emotions is a profound disservice to both. Human beings need to take part in positive action in order to establish their presence in the world, to cast a shadow. But another sort of participation is also needed, one that plunges the self into mutuality, where responses to one's presence declare one's connection and likeness to others. Without this experience, the single mind caught in its nutshell skull can neither enjoy its own perceptions and sensations nor rest secure in its own beliefs, for none of these can be made valid without agreement by other selves. This is what the isolated powerful deny to themselves, fearing that to know oneself a part of some community would diminish the individual self.

Jean Baker Miller's words, set at the head of this chapter, ask women to consider what it is within ourselves that we can trust and use for "making the world different." If we come to believe that's necessary, I've been saying, we will want to revalue not only orthodox goals, but also orthodox methods for acting to reach them. If we act reflexively, however, we'll be all too apt to seize on opposite, negative methods, and what the economists call "contrarian" thought is no more creative than orthodoxy; it walks the same way, on the other side of the street. A new structure of belief on which coherent action can be based is not a reversal of the past. It is a synthesis of used but still-valuable ideas, neglected elements overlooked because they have been downgraded, and truly novel imaginings that spring from interaction with a changing world and prove their usefulness by being capable of development as the experience of incomers enriches the earlier mix. The characteristics Miller has in mind are not the only ones that have been devalued, nor are women the only beings to whom they have been assigned, but the tendency of our society to polarize power and dependence along the lines of sex makes these characteristics symbolically feminine by reason of their distance from the power structure.

We don't want to seize on them as a basis for action, though, just because they are familiar, or even because they have useful life in them still, since they've been neglected by the powerful. They are not sufficient in themselves, for they come from a polarized moiety of ideas and directions, and it isn't the one that's been organized coherently for action. When we look at "feminine characteristics" we don't find an articulated paradigm, but attributes relegated to the shadowed side of a male-dominated world still oriented to male purposes. We should not assume an organic linkage between the discards housed here. Some are crippling. We shall have to judge them, both logically and emotionally, coolly and warmly. "I know we don't want to behave like men," said a friend after we had sat together through a long, expressive, and incoherent meeting, "but do we really have to behave so much like women?" The condition we should aspire to is not idealized femaleness, but unpolarized humanity. At present, however, that means restoring the social balance by giving more weight to neglected character traits which have indeed (but not by logical necessity) been placed in the shadowed realm designated powerless, emotional, and feminine.

Let us begin with emotionality itself, since we've surveyed the negative effects of denying one's feelings. What are the positive aspects of accepting and using feelings? Even our present value system finds them useful. Translated into directions for proper female behavior, the expression of emotion serves a needed social function. Women monitor the emotional temperature of existence. In any situation that lies outside the ordinary give-and-take of life, we're expected to weep or cry out in fear or shrink away in horror, and by these reactions to give a lead to others. Female intuition estimates that a reaction is required and supplies one that serves as a guide for men, for whom intuition is suspect and emotional expression inappropriate, but who will now be able to identify the situation and avoid embarrassing mistakes. In addition, by expressing emotion publicly, women inaugurate social rituals that maintain relationships.

It would appear that decision-makers are tacitly relying on the females around them to collect information on the emotional context of life, which gets into their judgments. The division of labor by sex thus sustains, and is sustained by, that between thinking and feeling. Also sustained is the hierarchical rank given the two. Men can get on with the important work of cognition, do math and science, create logical philosophic constructions, develop technology, and deal with the brute facts of the physical world. It's on this basis that they have established their right to govern. Women, meanwhile, take on the sex-appropriate job of mediating personal relations and managing everyday details of social intercourse. The secondary place of feelings must be made perfectly clear, however, and so limits are set on female emotionalism by the use of labels like "hysteria" that mark the boundary where dangerous feelings might get out of hand.

This division of labor is reflected in the overall organization of our society, for polarization operates through the value system of our structure of beliefs as well as by the straightforward assignment of importance to gender roles. In our cash-conscious world, higher wages are paid for cognitive male skills as opposed to female personal services, which always command less of a return and in marriage go for nothing. The division isn't perfectly logical; nothing is. Management of personnel, which requires some sense of human reactions, is an acceptable male activity and brings a fair price. Even so, it is never rated as high or paid as well as the financial management of money and materials. We can see that it's not regarded as acutely sensitive because it serves as one of the entry-points for token incomers. Another entry-point is public relations and advertising, an area where feminine flair and intuitive emotional understanding of how to please an audience are valuable. At the same time, hard selling to commercial outlets or dealers rather than to the general public is reserved for white males, and so are purchasing materials and dealing with other business entities. The whole industrial, commercial, and professional structure, in short, downgrades human interaction through emotional understanding and conjoint feeling as over against cognitive analysis, the results of which factor in another masculine element because they tend to produce confrontation. Since the ranking of status is sex-linked, elementary determinations of hierarchy are predictably fortified by "the way things work."

It will surprise no one to discover that the other feminine traits that Jean Miller sees as being useful for social change also fall into the emotional, relational area. Briefly, they include the ability to accept one's own vulnerability and confront a sense of personal weakness without being overcome by shame and blanking the knowledge out of consciousness. The male mystique takes such awareness to be masochistic or cowardly: it is called wallowing in weakness. And it can be, when it catches body and mind in a vicious circle where stigma is accepted and its acceptance fixes the unworthy in their place. But it can also be a realistic and necessary first step in working one's way out of hurtful weakness and oversensitivity. To a creature caught in a trap, a long, hard look at the trap is a logical and realistic approach to escape. The exploration of weakness, so evident in recent literature by women, can be seen as part of this process. It's an assessment of where one's been that really couldn't be undertaken if one felt condemned to stay there forever. To acknowledge weakness is not the same thing as choosing it. It relates rather to the common condition of humanity and so opposes polarization.

Second on Miller's list is the emotionality that we've already considered. Third is the pleasure women feel in helping others learn and develop their own capacities. This is a function of the traditional mothering role, but fathers who take a hand in child-raising know that it extends across sex lines. Miller suggests that good therapists use such skills when they facilitate the recovery of their patients without overinterpretation. There is a subtle boundary to such facilitation, and Winnicott, like Miller, emphasizes the importance of letting the patient discover his or her own road to improvement. Teachers and mentors too can play this role but, once again, it is not that of directive model molding a protégé. It is a relationship, rather, that clears and shields a space for free growth of an independent individual: a relationship sufficient in itself, which doesn't demand more. This is certainly not the whole of what parents do, but as children mature, it approximates the ideal situation: a processual, changing situation, once more, not one that can be held to a static form.

The ability to encourage development while respecting the individual stature of the learner brings us to Miller's fourth attribute, women's "greater recognition of the essential cooperative nature of human existence"[10] and with it the sense that acting together means getting as well as giving. In spite of frequent lip-service paid to "team play," men are very strongly directed by social norms toward seeking individual rewards, as the analysts of power examined in the last chapter indicate. Leadership, personal achievement, isolated success whether altruistic in intent or blithely immoral, this is the goal; and with it goes an element of contest, not cooperation. Last and greatest of these capacities for change is the unused creativity of those whose abilities are not bound to active support of the status quo.

Of course these feminine virtues are not produced by special gifts of saintliness or generosity built into the X chromosome; they are human assets which have, over the centuries, fallen into women's hands as and when the powerful found them inconvenient. They have remained there because, once they were labeled "feminine," they came to be regarded as inappropriate for male use. We need not, we should not, be proud of possessing them. What we have done is simply to preserve a useful part of the repertory of human behavior. Thus, if women are less prone to be swept away on undercurrents of belief in our own moral superiority, if we hesitate to exaggerate the role of parent into a general compulsion to prescribe goals for others, it's through no virtue of our own. Seldom has our experience lifted us to a level where we could practice that kind of behavior. Abstract principles are defined *for* us, not with our help. In intercourse with others we expect to question rather than to state, and questioning is by definition a reciprocal process. Even when some authority has been part of the female role, within the mothering function, the goals to be passed on to the young don't derive from our experience. They are aims and norms of masculine-oriented societies. If there is good news to be found in our separation from the power to define, it lies in the distance at which we stand from traditional concepts and axioms of governance. Since these premises fit female existence only loosely, they allow women to be more open to change in those areas where we can trust ourselves to act.

In the same ambiguous way, the low ceiling placed on women's ambitions spares us from traumatic shame if we fail in male endeavors. No one is inwardly surprised or outwardly ridiculed if outstanding achievement is not her destiny. "Fame is the spur," wrote Milton, which leads men "to scorn delight and live laborious days," but women have had to get on without help from glory as an adjunct to the Protestant Ethic, living out our laborious days both deprived of and exempt from the impetus of its spur. Deprivation is not pleasant, but exemption saves us from fantasies in which accouterments of fame get mixed up with one's ego identity and begin to usurp the place of practical goals. There are other reasons, too, why fame is a less addictive drug for women. Even those who do achieve a share of it are very apt to be still involved with every-day details of living, anchored in pragmatics and continuingly aware of the presence and feelings of others. Moreover, the traditional female role prescribes modesty, where the male mystique invites braggadocio, and no woman alive has grown up without learning the lessons of the traditional role, even when determined revolt against it follows. Finally, those few women who have become truly famous have made their mark in professions where acclaim offers practical benefits, not just ego-massage. As has also been the case with minority achievers, successful women have tended to be performing artists or professionals who know how to turn fame to good personal account, as a means of gaining higher fees, a choice of roles, better working conditions. For women, that is, fame remains a *means* as well as being a desired end, still part of a process taking place in a very actual world. It's valued, but in a way that's skeptical. Don't be too sure about it, whispers the first power of the weak. You may have earned it, but that's no guarantee that you'll keep it.

These feminine attributes may be useful for making a different world, but the world won't be remade simply by changing the way we rank them as character traits. They have to be put to work. What they offer is a basis for reassessing the world of action and for tapping the power of the community by unorthodox means, for unorthodox ends. We can see that ideals of individual achievement through competitive drive and aggressive confrontation have grown less and less attractive and less and less capable of engendering an atmosphere of hope for the future. Indeed, medical science now reports that stressful social situations in which competitiveness is sharply aroused can produce not simply anxiety but actual physical damage and sometimes death by heart seizure. A series of articles on "The Age of Anxiety" in *The Wall Street Journal* recently detailed the effect on male managers and executives of living with emotions that could not be faced or resolved. Thus, the drive to land a man on the moon took its toll of workers at Cape Kennedy:

> Dr. Robert S. Eliot, a cardiologist now at the University of Nebraska, and several colleagues found a high rate of divorce and alcohol consumption as the workers raced to complete their mission, knowing that once a successful moon landing had been made, the space budget would be reduced and they would lose their jobs. "In short, the project demanded an ever-increasing, if not frenzied pace of produce with the ultimate reward of nearly inevitable dismissal," note Dr. Eliot and Dr. James C. Buell. . . .[11]

And in addition, the researchers observed "an unusual number of deaths, apparently from heart attacks, among the relatively young space-center workers." The rate ran 50 percent higher than normal, and peaked at the point of heaviest layoffs. How could male rationality ignore the toll taken by the linkage between team success and personal risk? One wonders. But it did, to the point of denying, to those who were suffering natural emotional strain, the simple human relief of sharing it. Action to confront the problem couldn't be taken because no one dared admit that there was a problem: to fear an uncertain future was unmanly.

Women are certainly not immune to stress, but female behavior patterns tend to be different. Some six weeks after *The Wall Street Journal* delved into the painful histories of anxious NASA personnel, *The New York Times* reported on "epidemics" of stress that seep through plants where unpleasant working conditions are the rule: boring, repetitive work timed to assembly lines and accompanied by high noise levels. "Assembling electrical switches, packing fish [and] punching computer cards" were given as examples.[12] That sort of job is very often "manned" by a woman who needs the work badly and who puts up with such conditions because she lacks training. The causes of stress are different from those that plagued the men at NASA, but the pressure is the same.

Women seem to react differently. Instead of bottling up anxiety and irritation, they act out their feelings in terms of physical symptoms—headaches, dizziness, visions of blue mists, perceptions of bad smells and tastes —and the symptoms are promptly picked up and shared: hence "epidemics." The sharing is important. The problem may still be defined as "hysteria," but if half a factory floor is hysterical, management gets the idea that something ought to be done about it. In fact, the old diagnosis is now passé, and the National Institute for Occupational Safety and Health has begun to look for external causes. A clinical psychologist, Michael Colligan, who is attached to the Institute, suggests that the women who suffer from such "psychogenic" illnesses are, quite simply, making a statement about their situation: "This place makes me sick."

It would appear that they're doing so in a more productive fashion than the men who keep their feelings private because they see them as being unmanly. The women's behavior delivers a message, a many-voiced one at that, and recommendations from the Institute respond. They're so ridiculously obvious that the reader is pained to discover that they're necessary: vary work assignments, allow breaks for chat and personal contacts, try to clarify the structure of authority so that two superintendents aren't laying down contradictory rules: that is, introduce the smallest elements of responsive relationships into the work situation. No one has yet dreamed, it seems, of suggesting that psychological needs are important enough to influence machine-based schedules, just that some minimal attention be paid to the workers' humanity, since "mass psychogenic illness" costs money. But at least the female reaction, overt and shared, has done something to improve working conditions.

We can find other evidence of a backlash from repressed emotions in a very different area. The explosive growth of do-it-yourself religious cults appears to be a spontaneous reaction to the secularization of society that has taken place in this century, and perhaps longer. The importance, the central place, of established religion in our Western society has been declining inexorably. Churches empty and close, and the pronouncements of the clergy win media space only when they refer to political issues or inflammatory social questions, so that the church (any church) comes to be seen as a lobby whose function it is to promote its own ends in a secular world. Its image as a bridge to the sacred for the community is all but lost; it does not even offer an opiate to the people any more. Secularization has been promoted, if not induced, by separating the expression and sharing of emotion in public from the business of life. It was not just the data of cognitive, scientific knowledge that cast down established religious dogma, it was the accompanying devaluation of feeling in favor of rational process. Religion became the business of women as emotion fell into the feminine realm, and the expression of community through religious ritual was downgraded, while the rule and the role of reason was enhanced. We can observe this process going on throughout the nineteenth and into the twentieth century in the Western world as church attendance and church work were more and more felt to be women's concerns.[13]

Eventually such separation becomes polarization; here too reason and emotion are no longer complementary, but opposed. Now it's obvious that today's proliferation of cults and revivalist sects illustrates a need for community and for some systematic, accepted way to express pent-up feeling; but the division between reason and emotion is now so extreme that only those who are willing to disavow the value of cognitive thought are able to join hands and share emotions by means of deeply felt religious activities. This sets up a painful dilemma, and it's not one that will easily pass away, for our society cannot and will not create its own great new myth until the separation between mind and emotion has been healed, so that the whole force of a bonded community can pour into the act of creation. That day is still far off, and what it may bring (if indeed it ever arrives) is beyond any capacity to imagine the future that our experience provides. Today, judging objectively, we can only say that the connection with the sacred, which Durkheim held to arise from the emotional experience of the individual within society, has slipped beyond the reach of our contemporary elite. Whatever else this means, it denies them the strength that true believers can muster. For better or worse, the Establishment is secular-minded and committed to skepticism, rationality, and cognition in principle—whether or not it lives up to its commitment in practice. In practice, indeed, the Establishment is aware of the explosive effects that ensue when bottled-up emotions break out to express themselves in violence. These effects have now begun to reach shock stage. But our leaders seem no more capable of reasoning back to the origins of Jonestown than NASA was when stress began to take its toll of the men who worked at Cape Kennedy—in spite of all their commitment to rationality. Something more is needed.

I am not suggesting that women should set about creating a new religion; for one thing, such movements are not made, they grow. But there are more roads than one to mutuality, and others are less demanding than that enforced by a creed that, like all creeds, must declare its truth to be universal. These routes may not be as easy to follow as the short step to community offered by a direct explosion of personal emotion for, unfortunately, when the distinction between thinking and feeling is exaggerated to make these elements of interior life contradictory instead of complementary, it shakes our grip on symbolic language, which lies so close to the roots of human community. The symbolic language of a widely practiced religion and widely known sacred texts has vanished, and with it the rituals and festivals where individuals joined in expressing their shared humanity and affirming the significance of their lives. There does, however, remain the symbolic language of the arts. That too has been strained and weakened, but there are signs of life in many places, nonetheless. Because art is essentially pluralistic and defiant of dogma, and always willing to speak the vernacular, it is able to survive and spring up in many new forms.

It's true that the idea of art as a road to community has a queer sound in today's world, a world as material as it is secular, and one that obsessedly turns out counterfeit symbols and metaphors in the service of the competitive drive to sell that is built into our method of distributing the goods and services we produce. Of course that sets off a devaluation of symbolic language, a low road of discreditation where creativity exhausts itself to turn out trademarks, logos, singing commercials, and the subtle styling of "designers' products" which declare that the purchaser is in the know; where the compression and intensity of lyric poetry feed into advertising headlines. Now, it certainly isn't the intention of advertisers and merchants to devalue symbolic language. They would very much like their slogans to carry the significance of poetry; but since the message is irretrievably trivial, the medium suffers too.

Nor, I think, do those who take the high road of criticism and cognitive interpretation at all mean to devalue the symbolic languages that have become a subject for academic investigation. They would regard their work instead as raising art to the level where it has become worth analysis, discussion, and research and is not merely something to feel and respond to in the dailiness of life. Of course symbolic language isn't sacred. There is no reason why it should not be taken as a field of study. But in a culture where (male-linked) rational discourse is valued more highly than (female-linked) communication of emotion, we must ask how deeply the active agent, criticism, can respect the subject of its inquiry. Thinking about techniques of expressing emotion by means of art can be very valuable; internal criticism, conscious or not, is essential to creation. But if the two things are separated too sharply from each other, there is a risk that not only will the difference be accentuated, but that they will be marked superior/inferior. In our culture, contest and competitiveness are ranked high, they are held to be masculine traits, undeveloped in women and possibly undevelopable, but closely related to the quick-thinking, hard-reasoning male mind. Competition, to this mind-set, takes the area of contest as less important than the achievement of besting someone else, as a (male) professor of psychology kindly explained to me. That is, it thinks less about doing something better *in relation to the work to be done* than simply in doing better, and being seen publicly to have done so. It would seem to be here that fame and achievement get tangled.

Overvaluing criticism probably hurts critics more than it does artists, but of course it takes a toll on both. Creative work is never going to be completely understood or explainable by cognitive analysis; something is always going to slide through the grid. As long as what slides through is not lost, not kept from the general public, that's tolerable. But when work is lost, chains of communication are broken as well. This has happened hurtfully to women artists: Ellen Moers and Linda Nochlin have written of the weary effort demanded of writers and painters who have had to begin all over again, without a reservoir of experience to call on, each generation forced to pioneer off into a trackless thicket if it wants to find its own emotional landscape. Hurtful too is the difficulty that the conscious, cognitive mind has in seeing the extraordinary in the ordinary. A minor effect of this is that artists from minorities or the female sex are included in the traditional canon only if they are extraordinary. Even more unfortunate is the encouragement given critical thought to divide extraordinary creative production from everyday inventiveness and see it as different, even opposed; not just to draw a line between talent and genius (which is risky enough, especially for contemporaries) but to set a barrier between them. One begins to feel uneasily that when reason sets out to define the world, it moves inexorably toward polarization, losing touch with the sense of community that shared feeling speaks to.

When Jean Baker Miller describes creativity as a characteristic highly developed in women but also essential to humanity as a whole, she is echoing D. W. Winnicott and his understanding of the term as the ability to deal with events by involving one's capacity to innovate, test, imagine, discard, through a process that involves self with exterior circumstances, within transitional space. For Winnicott too, creativity is essential to human existence. When our society divides high art or great and luminous scientific insight from the ongoing practices of artisanship or group enterprise, of curious interest pursued to greater comprehension, it distances the extremes of achievement from their roots. Polarized thus, the extremes are cut off from their sources and must live on air or dry up, while the normal, usual kinds of inventiveness which grow out of responsive feeling for what ordinary reality requires are downgraded.

It's a commonplace that our culture is plagued by the tendency to judge art in all its forms, fine arts and popular too, in terms of money value. No doubt that's deplorable; but the usual reasons given for deploring the situation aren't much better. They tend to carry art off into another realm where it doesn't belong, an empyrean, where it exists as a mystery to be honored in awe by the learned and sensitive. Only these mandarins can weigh its value. Judging art in terms of how much it will bring in the market may be ignorant, but at least it leaves it in touch with the world as a whole. After all, every enterprise today is liable to be judged in terms of money; and good art is probably better able to survive and surmount this kind of judgment than any other element of life one can think of. Art carries its own value within it, it always commands an audience by alternative ways. It addresses and evokes authentic feeling, moving from artist to audience and from audience to artist—sometimes more easily than at others, of course, for symbolic language not only creates links but is facilitated and heightened by those that exist already. This communication of emotional truth is its essential nature even when material values come into the picture. Like fame, they direct viewers to look at this remarkably expensive painting or sculpture, they suggest we read, or listen to, some praised or popular composition; but once the viewer begins to look, another channel of communication opens at once. What the artist knows about feeling, refined by her own critical ability to whittle away falseness, conveys an intense and comprehensible message that is larger and more vivid than rational verbalization.

Within a group, communications of its own experience are a powerful factor in developing community. If art is now thought of as an investment, a thing, instead of a vibrant message—well, that is another symptom of failing creativity in our present system of social relations. Minority groups create their own binding works of art, often in styles and even forms unknown elsewhere. The terrible uncertainties of the young pour out and seek resolution or at least authentication here. Women's isolation from each other has made it harder in recent times to hear and read messages in a common language, but increasingly poetry and fiction are creating a network of symbols, through which individual minds can discover and name the puzzling events and memories that fell out of consciousness because they could not be identified in traditional speech. For art is a framework, a kind of living trellis, on which public dreaming can shape itself, as the instrument of creativity—the artist—is fed by the response of the audience, so that the process becomes a multivocal conversation. Out of this grows a coherence of symbolization, a language that is constantly refreshed from the interior world of emotion, and tested publicly by the response it evokes. Public and private come together in a community of individuals.

To the symbolic language of art we can add the expressive language of public, political demonstration, which can serve as a kind of loose ritual where joint purpose is illustrated, and felt. Both are easier to handle and more responsive than creeds or ideologies, whose highly structured directives can be profoundly supportive in bad times but are less open to inventive amendment. Art and political demands are rooted in a reality of feeling, and if feelings are diverse, these symbolic languages will reflect the variations without insisting that they confront each other in a contest for dominance. Epic and legend, poetry and fiction, inspire emulation but they don't demand imitation, and so new interpretations that suit changed circumstances can call on, and feed into, old wit and wisdom. Add a new verse to an old song, and those who sing it aloud through the streets will remember ancestral courage and pride but will not be bound to copy archaic deeds.

The title of this chapter, "Impractical Politics," carries a charge of irony. The Establishment may indeed hold that the ways of behavior, ways of knowing, methods of action that they have judged "dysfunctional for success" are just that, whether the world changes or not. And yet they do not act as if they were fully convinced of it. Many of the psychologists and sociologists cited in this chapter are not only aware of the difficulties that men fall into when they trap themselves in polarities that deny them access to their own emotions, they actively counsel efforts to accept the importance of feelings. True, emotionality is pretty generally regarded as dangerous and especially as tending to extremes. Even those who see it as a problem that should be faced find it hard to imagine that it might be a positive asset. For a nice guy to end in first place instead of last still has overtones of a "Man Bites Dog" story.

Just the same, if we take a moment for a small exercise in disbelief, we may well ask ourselves, Are these impractical politics really useless? Take the matter of confronting vulnerability.

There is a strongly argued analysis which derives Franklin Roosevelt's hold on the mass of the governed from his experience of crippling illness, vulnerability overcome but always present, undeniable, unforgettable, acted out whenever he appeared publicly. More generally, if vulnerability is such a drawback, why have generations of politicians cast back to poverty-stricken childhoods, hardscrabble farms, log cabins, menial labor? Add to the experience of poverty that of known, remembered, shared danger in wartime service: John Kennedy's back injury as well as the much-publicized story of his heroism; Hitler's time in the trenches; De Gaulle's exile; Mao and Chu Teh on the Long March to fortress sanctuary in western China; Castro, hunted rebel leader in the Sierra Maestra—out of such confrontations with vulnerability have grown strong links between successful political leaders and their constituencies.

To be in touch with and expressive of his emotions did not disqualify Winston Churchill from power. Hubert Humphrey's emotionality came to seem rather shallow to some, but it was widely honored by others, and so even more was the deep involvement of Lincoln in the struggle of his time, where his emotional understanding of the ordeal of the nation recognized the dignity of those who suffered by letting his own suffering be seen. And as for relying on individual achievement rather than cooperation in order to reach the political heights—brilliance may occasionally bring appointment to high place, but nothing keeps officials in power except a respondent constituency, a coherent group, which declares this leader (appointed or elected) to be its representative. Gratitude felt to a political mentor? It can't be exacted, but when it's spontaneous it endures in the form of continuing affection and respect. Even when it's self-serving ("He was like a daddy to me," Lyndon Johnson used to say of Roosevelt—and Sam Rayburn too), it gives the served self a reach back into the past and a grasp on what was politically good and useful. As for the strength of symbolic bonds, expressed in song and story and jokes and laments—well, the most practical politicians address ethnic groups in their own languages if they can, bite ceremonially into blintzes, don Indian war-bonnets, march in St. Patrick's Day parades, call on the Pope (who had his picture taken wearing a sombrero during his visit to Mexico in 1979), and seek out the ancestral homes where they smile at the camera with their arms about the shoulders of any kinfolk who can be unearthed.

Impractical politics, that is, are politics of *community*. Where it appears useful to appeal to common interests, these symbolic gestures are used even by those who think them cheap. They are still effective and so they have a place in the repertory of politicians who are otherwise committed to hard-driving competition. In fact, these methods seem to be assigned very much the status of those feminine virtues that are used by other (male) human brings when nothing else will do. Like creativity, the politics of community have been smirched by commercial exploitation, and dignified masculine rationality finds that embarrassing. Symbolic political acts not only elicit emotions; because they do it so well they have been copied by merchants as a way of selling goods. So when they are recopied by campaign managers, they are seen less as a confirmation of common interest between governors and governed than as a method of "selling the President."

And yet, like creative invention, they work in spite of the dirt that sticks to them, in spite of the adulteration that invites mockery and revulsion. Something is still alive. It is a sense of the fundamental value, the necessity in human existence, of community. Only within a group that knows and feels such a connection, however fragmented and subliminal it may be, can practical politics of contest and confrontation safely take place. Without a surrounding, sustaining, cooperative body politic, contest isn't practical, it's lethal.

When a public community dissolves in distrust—not the wary, defensive distrust and disbelief of the governed, but the racking and crippling self-doubt of the powerful—it is time to build other communities. They will be small, insufficient, suspicious of each other and prone to make silly mistakes, out of ignorance and lack of experience. But they will be creative, and they will be sensitive to falseness. As their experience grows, so will their capacity not to be foolish. No one knows what they may create. Perhaps they will, or one or another will, turn out to be the source of a whole new order that can heal the widespread sense of isolation and alienation we live with today. Perhaps they will simply teach their members how to shore up, and reform, the existing system so that it becomes minimally responsive to those it rules, enough so to keep it staggering into the future. In any case the procedure is the same: once the weak lay hands on their powers and weave individual doubts into joint resistance, the political process moves them toward positive action and starts teaching the courage to improvise and undertake the action necessary, practical or impractical. Probably both.

CHAPTER 19

Impractical Politics II: Doing and Daring

For who would bear the whips and scorns of time,
The oppressor's wrong, the proud man's contumely,
The pangs of disprized love, the law's delay,
The insolence of office, and the spurns
That patient merit of the unworthy takes. . . ?

Hamlet, *Act III, Scene I*

Thinking about action, for those who make up the category of the governed, begins in everydayness and grubby details, a confrontation with the minutiae of vulnerability which have not changed much since Shakespeare listed them. The weak bear them better than did the Prince of Denmark, who saw the alternative as a bare bodkin, its use deterred only by fear of the nightmares that haunt the sleep of death. To the ruled, these things are the conditions of life. Any heroism we can summon to face them is bound to be utilitarian, based on survival techniques, not princely and suicidal gestures. Experience teaches that such daily pangs exist to be endured, not altered. So when something happens, when we find ourselves forced into serious consideration of change, we begin where we are. Only in extreme conditions are martyrs granted the agonizing opportunity to make large dramatic statements. When, in their daily lives, the weak start to bargain for change, they begin in a push for small advances or with dogged attempts to resist attacks on a shaken community. Poor people's movements take place in the dark, and if they are eventually noticed by the powerful, they're described according to axioms of an intellectual culture not native to them. If they survive and resist cooption, they can still be taken in charge by the Establishment's intellectual opponents, who simply reverse the orthodox axioms. For the polarization of a society can negate creativity by posing an either-or choice even to its rebels: Fall in with the One Right Way, or act by its opposite.

In time, inevitably, movements for change that are developing an impetus of their own begin to formulate original world views which are oriented to actual circumstances as experienced by their members. In doing so they are responding to anomalies that have got too big to be ignored and glossed over by the world explanations of current social mythology. Often, of course, one system of revolutionary doctrine disputes with others, for challenges to old paradigms can come from many quarters. Always they must go through the preliminary phase in which they rid themselves of old doctrines by contradicting them, and so reflect them still. All those who try to think forward, after all, have grown up in a universe of discourse which operates by rules and constructs that are shaped to the causality and the logic of the culture into which they're born. Our logic proceeds by exclusion, discrimination, paired opposites; and the symbolism of art, which mingles essences, is a bit suspect. We prefer to recognize dialectic oppositions that are combined consciously into a synthesis. That, we feel, is the right way to reason, or so say our mainstream philosophers. The chance for deep and far-reaching change comes only when those among us who have been left out of the process of governance, whose experience has never counted, start to ask, "What is still being left out?" What have thesis and antithesis overlooked, both of them, so that their synthesis remains deficient? Are they not both employing the same sort of reasoning in order to talk to each other? Does the resolution they arrive at not itself exclude the pluralism that can support a greater creativity, where things that had not been foreseen and ways of knowing that had not been imagined might spring to life?

If we have to attack the One Right Way in only one way, it's a severe limitation. What's more, it's false to daily reality. Opposition is based on experience of the oppressor's wrong, the law's delay, and all the rest of Hamlet's banes, and it therefore comes in all shapes and sizes. In time these opposing reactions will no doubt shuffle themselves together into some sort of program with various priorities—but in a truly pluralist system, priorities don't have to shape up into a single queue: different respondents can deal with them simultaneously in different ways. At the level of existence, that's just what happens; and there, it seems to me, is where creativity first operates, far from theoretical dichotomies and dilemmas. Intentionally or not, these often work out as distractions from the business at hand. Reform or revolution? Progress within the system or attack from without? Surely before we plunge into discussion we want to ask, "What is the system? Where does it end?" For the Social Revolutionaries in tsarist Russia, working "outside" was a process controlled by the secret police, and FBI reports from the 1960s tell of revolutionary cells in which agents were prime movers toward dissident action. Legendary "social bandits," hailed for robbing the rich to give to the poor, sometimes turn out to have had their private deals with regional magnates, while tales of their exploits siphoned off anger and kept the countryside quiet. Beginning at the other end, efforts at simple reform have built into major movements whose consequences were revolutionary in many senses.

To recognize creativity in the data of dailiness is no easy task; people continue to do what they understand to be expected of them. But these data test expectations and theories too, shifting them unconsciously to incorporate lived experience. For many today, orthodox interpretations of the world and its workings are baffling because the strategies they provide don't mesh with what is really happening to us. They don't explain what seems to be going on, or offer identifying roles that we can accept as suitable to the selves we know. Trying to make a fit between self and role is wearing, expensive of energy that might otherwise be used in the outside world. Meaningless work, contingent connections to others, leave people in a quandary that recalls the confused children who find it so hard to declare a sure identity by saying "I." Perhaps we should judge the search for a trustworthy self, which got the seventies labeled as habitat of the "Me Generation," against this background. Efforts to establish a more certain sense of identity aren't evidence of egotism, hedonism, or rejection of community; they are more likely to signify attempts to get a handhold on a shifting and foggy reality. How can you intervene in events when you aren't sure who is intervening? How can you persist in a purpose unless you know how committed this persistent person is to that purpose? How can you enter into friendships, or take on obligations? It may well be that the male fear of feeling is, in part anyway, a defense against simple confusion over what it is that one feels. If you can't be sure of that, it's hard to imagine what other people are feeling. We see this confusion expressed, I believe, in our tendency to prize sincerity as if it were rare; and to prize it, moreover, without going on to ask what a sincere person is sincere about.

Uneasiness over feelings and even identity is not confined to the governed, though it's probably easier for them to admit it. Perhaps it has always existed to one degree or another, but the secularization of our society may well have worked to increase it. Today it's hard for the elite to take seriously the idea that personal strength and solidity, which are derived from the sort of established religion that elites of the past assumed to be a necessary part of society, are intellectually convincing. Religious belief is tainted with emotionalism, and so our top people tend to replace it with agnosticism mixed with some rational philosophic system. As long as reasonable physical control over existence provides a comfortable life, such demi-creeds are sufficient —for top people. In the case of "other ranks," they may not be. Control over existence is a great deal more chancy among the governed. Events press them harder, are less predictable and often less pleasant; and rational philosophy is a singularly poor opiate for the people.

The revival of evangelism is one response to the need the governed feel for an authority to which they can appeal and find strength in the fashion of our ancestors. But the schism within our society between mass, popular culture on the one hand and high, intellectual-elite beliefs and behavior on the other affects religion as well as art. So, while a revival of evangelism may satisfy emotional needs among ordinary folk, it does nothing to heal the split between cultures. The elite is not moved to join the humble in a common religious body; indeed, devotion is a mark of class apartheid. I don't mean to suggest that our upwardly mobile ancestors expressed devoutness as a means of getting ahead, though I daresay some did; simply that a religious community once existed in which weak and powerful mingled and met. Today, as always, individuals find support in religious faith, but the practices of religion seem to have very little connection with the operations of the rest of society. When a religious body takes a public stand today, it tends to be a reactionary one, a stand that's perceived objectively as running counter to the standards of intellectual respectability. Now, as I've been saying, the intellectually respectable elite can be as thoroughly mistaken as the next conglomerate body about any matter; but it is in charge. In our time, then, a breach exists between the devout and the people in charge, with the result that religion has little to do with the structure of operations in the world of events.

The governed understand that. Consequently, those who want something more or something different from the satisfaction of emotional need have to invent means other than religious precepts to deal with the world of events, and to strengthen themselves for the effort. One approach comes out of their experience of the rubs and flaws in daily life. Can they be dealt with according to received ideas, and if so, how? There is a whole body of self-help literature and popular psychology that has sprung up to answer these questions, which in the past might have been left entirely to prophets and preachers. The high price our society places on cognition and education, however, has produced an extra-academic school of self-improvement. The governed too would like to make high-quality decisions and process information vigilantly. We find this urge reflected in the books and training courses that offer to teach the ruled how to increase their capacities for action by assertiveness training, by developing transactional skills, by learning to marshal their ideas in an orderly way, and by speaking up in public.

There's nothing new about this. Books of etiquette and manners, addressed to the upwardly mobile, go back for centuries and offer historians invaluable information about the concepts, the priorities, and the behavior of our ancestors. We still publish them today. But another component appears in one segment of contemporary self-help literature that sets it apart from the recipes for getting on, pure and simple, that we glanced at in the last chapter. These manuals set great emphasis on *feelings* as well as on cognitive skills; possibly because the consolations of religion are not now mingled with ongoing existence in a functional way. At any rate, self-improvement now includes ways to communicate better, understand others and their needs, and create and sustain "meaningful relationships."

I put that phrase in quotations because it stands as a landmark of breakdown in class communication: a bit of jargon taken over from popularizing psychologists, or sociologists, now worked to death and repulsiveness. And yet, it stands for something that is deeply felt (or it would not have been overused) and far from ignoble—if it could only be described in more noble language. But that, of course, is exactly the problem: How are the governed to convey what they feel? How are they to find a language in which to speak truly and fully? They get no help, on this point, from the educated, who have offered no substitute to express the desired human connection in which warmth, friendship, affection give important and rewarding continuity to shared existence. The ruled need their own poets as well as their own rebellious thinkers, but the split in our culture still imposes its standards and distorts the vernacular.

So banal language as well as simplistic approaches plague the literature of self-improvement and seem to cheapen the needs that have called it forth. And yet a number of these books describe perfectly sensible techniques for practicing new sorts of behavior in a class where peers observe, criticize, applaud, and advise, and for trying out these lessons in public encounters. The intention is to make actions more comprehensible and more effective and to improve understanding of the doings of other people; to help the insecure find a place on the map of the world and then to settle in and assure both place and self by taking a hand in what goes on there. No doubt we should all have learned how to do this when we were small; but if we didn't, why should we not learn now? Assertiveness-training courses are called by another unlovely name, but they recommend ways to get rid of the clumsy submissiveness that overtakes many of the governed in public, and supply opportunities for practice. Pupils act out daily problems that worry them, some of them casual, some connected with work, some personal and intimate: How do you return a purchase that isn't satisfactory? How do you say "No" to an urgent acquaintance in need of a loan? Or start a conversation with a stranger? How do you ask for a raise? How can you best deal with rebellious children or find out what's on the mind of a resentful wife or husband? And so on and so forth.

The simplistic thought in this literature and the banality of its language trivializes the whole matter in the eyes of the powerful, the educated, the well-and-easy-mannered who have been made free of a larger world. But the problems discussed are real. Some of them grow out of the split in our culture between high and low, but others stem from the polarization of thought and feeling. Mass culture is less apt to worry itself about that polarity; which is another ground for high culture to think it unworthy. The literature of self-improvement is certainly concerned about emotional relations as well as productive thinking; which doesn't stamp it as creative, Heaven knows, but at least it doesn't falsify the lives of the governed. They see it as offering lessons in how to meet and cope with the stumbling-blocks that are met with every day—the influence of office, the proud man's contumely, and even, with luck, the pangs of disprized love. None of these are trivial if any casual public encounter can turn into the occasion for shaming, for exposure, for stigma.

A primary and central fact reflected in these books is that the weak are hampered in social relations at *all* levels from minor to profound and intimately personal, and that any collision may be traumatic. Social drop-out is one answer; another is the formation of small colonies with special interests, where stock-car racers, motorcycle gangs, breeders of fighting dogs, can meet and form relationships meaningful enough to warm their lives. But the large political process loses them.

If it loses the ambitious learners who want to take a hand in the workings of the world, it suffers. But while our complicated polarities last, the power granted the powerful to define situations, to put forward interpretations of events, establish logical connections between this datum of experience and that and so institute a system of causality and operations, all of it constructed from know-how limited to one sex and one class—this power creates a universe in which the ambitious governed lose their way. Lewis Carroll's imagination set Alice adrift, at one point in her travels, on the other side of the looking-glass, in a territory where nothing had a name. If nothing has a name that you can attach to it with certainty, you can't even ask for directions, let alone help; it's impossible to say what you need or where you want to go. In the universe of the powerful, the governed need to learn what names to use (i.e., *not* "meaningful relationships"), what categories or what levels of importance events belong to, simply in order to orient themselves: to know how lost they are.

To the extent that the literature of self-improvement acquaints the governed with accepted public rules for managing the external world, it has a real value. The experience of the weak will still be at variance with that of the powerful, but primers of standard social procedures explain and identify some of the categories of existence as defined by the powerful. They are not simply engines of cooption either, though they may look and read like it. But "knowing the ropes" is a necessary prelude to action in the world where those ropes are guidelines. Whether in the end one wants to break rules or keep them, it's useful to know them.

A learning situation like this casts back to childhood. The permanent status of "child" is all too readily assigned to the weak, but if we think of learning as a dynamic process, we are reminded that children can grow up and leave behind the role assigned them. Learners are refusing to be finished. They are choosing to enter a process of resocialization where they can try out new ways of doing and accept emotions because they can be tested as a form of play. They are learning the norms of a world they didn't make; but they are also acting on a decision of their own, they are expected to call on their inventiveness for setting up stressful situations, and for imagining ways to cope with them, and they do this in a social setting, not alone. Even if what one learns is standard procedures, the experience of choice and the small-change use of creativity are strengthening in themselves. So is the chance to take oneself seriously enough to work and plan for a changed future, even if what one begins by changing is oneself; for the future that's imagined is one that can be influenced by this self.

And for the weak there is, in addition, particular value to this kind of adult play just because taking part in it defines the line between play and seriousness. We have looked at the way in which seeing life as a game can trivialize both the self and the world. If, being weak, one comes to believe that everything one does is inconsequential, play and serious activity get hopelessly mixed up. The confusion of gestures, which don't have consequences, and actions, which do, is inhibiting: if one can't tell them apart, one will hesitate to use either. To define play for oneself by playing makes a start. It can set off a process of habituation through which behavior that's reasonably appropriate, reasonably comprehensive to others, replaces behavior that isn't. The intent may be for self-improvement only, but a real change in the self inevitably affects any relationship in which that self is involved. When the upwardly mobile revalue themselves, they make waves whether they intend to or not.

So let us not dismiss offhand the familiar American impulse to change oneself as a way to changing the conditions in which one lives. True, it is not enough; real change comes only through joint, purposive action. But behind the urge to self-improvement there lies the urge to change, and that bespeaks dissent with the way things are arranged. Changing yourself is not evidence of knowing your place and choosing to stay in it. Something is unsatisfactory, and the self-changer isn't resigned to it. If and when self-improvement fails to bring new conditions, many self-changers may give up; but some will not, and in that case they may well be pushed to more searching questions. Unconscious distrust may now surface, as standard procedures, laboriously learned, fail to deliver on their promises. Some, again, will stop here in resentful disillusion, but others may go on to take the steps beyond dissent toward coming together.

Moreover, the lessons in interaction that self-improvement teaches can be useful beyond the obvious techniques they provide. To the timid, these sessions are also lessons in courage: in how to disagree and speak up and hold to a point in the face of argument. Just because they're taught in the most ordinary way, by practice, habituation, rote exercises, they help the weak to lay hands on courage without sheering off from a quality associated with the powerful. And, to put it at its simplest and briefest, the weak do have to learn to be brave. Or, better, they have to learn to be *brave in a different fashion.*

For there is indeed a kind of courage that's very familiar to the weak: endurance, patience, stamina, the ability to repeat everyday tasks every day, these are the forms of courage that have allowed generations of the governed to survive without losing ultimate hope. The knowledge of one's own vulnerability, the choice of restraint in the face of provocation, the ability to hear oneself described as unworthy without accepting the stigma as final—that takes courage of a high order. We do not want to lose it, simply to supplement it, for it's still a source of strength when the time comes to be patient no longer, when direct confrontation with the powerful for independent aims must be risked if not sought. The weak who come, or are driven, to autonomous action, which is by definition unexpected and out of character, soon discover that once is not enough. A single public act is easily ignored. A short series may be observed, but misinterpreted. An event must be repeated again and again if it's to be understood; and if it isn't, it will not have the result that's expected. There is nothing so valuable as endurance, patience, and stamina when one must do, over and over, the self-same deed before this knock on the door of public attention is heard. The courage of the weak sustains persistence for positive goals when it is used positively, just as it supports resistance when that is the only possible aim.

But for decisive action, something else must be added: bravery, daring, risk-taking in public. These, to the weak, seem to be beyond their means; this is the courage of the powerful. The risks the weak face are laid on them by the decisions of others which affect their lives at a slant. That would appear to be truest of all for women, whose situation is, as ever, extreme. Not only has the Second Sex been denied easy access to fields where daring and doing are appropriate, as have other groups of low-status folk. Women have also been given a specific role, that of supporter, whose duties are absolutely opposite to the role of initiator. In addition, the circumstances of life have very often operated to isolate us from each other as well as from the world of action.

And the last two factors reinforce each other. Current norms of middle-class respectability place a "normal" woman in a nuclear family where she is the only adult female. The age of the nuclear family—that is, the length of time during which most households regularly consisted of only parents and children—is a matter of some debate among demographers and social historians at the moment. Certainly the shorter life span of our ancestors must have limited the number of grandparents alive to provide a third generation, and create a stem, or an extended, family. This is rather less important than it sounds, however; whether or not three generations, plus aunts and uncles, often lived under the same roof, parents and children lived, in the past, in closer contact with kin than we do because they were much more apt to inhabit the same small community: sisters and cousins and brothers, uncles and aunts and the occasional grandparent, were nearby and easy of access. Alliances with them could form and affectionate intimacies develop. So could furious family feuds. Contrariwise, today's pattern of mutuality is based on couples. That guarantees that the chief relationship where intimate sharing of life between adults occurs will also be a locus of competition and contest.

We know that family patterns are shifting and family roles changing as men cease to be sole breadwinners and women to be homemakers only, whose main task is handling the expressive, emotional side of things. But we are still affected by earlier visions of the female role, which recommended timidity and passivity to middle-class wives and daughters as demeanor that would please husbands and fathers. For them, endurance, patience, stamina, daily tasks daily done—this was the courage they needed and the courage they used.

But is it the only kind of courage that women have used and been praised for using? It seems not. In peasant cultures, for example, students tell us, women were a good deal more active. They often dominated family relationships, directed economic activity within the household when that was a good proportion of all economic activity, and even handled family funds. Forceful widows and heiresses sometimes achieved the status of head of the household and were counted and even named "honorary males."[1] In such settings some of our foremothers did indeed act decisively, take their own risks, and dare to provoke public opinion.

Now, let us be clear. They were supported in such actions by their role and status *within a family or clan,* and when they undertook praiseworthy action, these deeds could be understood as assisting the interests of family or clan. Of course the matrix of kinship held almost everyone tight—except for the luckless, rootless vagabonds, poorest of poor. It held women tightest of all. To think of herself as set apart and individual must have been all but impossible for any female creature, or else a nightmare of displacement. Nor were women grouped together in convents encouraged to think of themselves as a community that was not also part of a larger, more powerful whole, a clan of church folk, dominated by the great male hierarchy. Any action, then, for such a woman would have tended to be undertaken in a context of family bonds. Nonetheless, if we distinguish between action as action and the purpose for which it occurred (as we might also do with the useful techniques that the governed can learn from self-help programs, even those whose aims are ostensibly so limited), we do get a view of women who acted decisively and bravely, on their own. That is good news and we can be grateful. Women need a sense of the continuity of existence and a reach back to roots as much as the next man, for honored memories validate behavior that is new for an individual by establishing examples from the past. Today, when women are increasingly impatient with the inhibitions that more recent traditions of timid feminity have laid on us all, when we are eager to recover the history that's been dropped because it doesn't fit current expectations, this memory from the past is strengthening.

But at the same time we had better not forget the bad news. Women's acts of courage are praised only when they affirm woman's proper role—supporter—and her proper sphere—the family. Undertaken elsewhere, they carry an aura of strangeness and deviance and raise questions that can't be answered within known postulates. Women who defy conventions are frightening, now as in the past. They are and have been redefined in monstrous roles: witches and succubi, castrators and destroyers. Doing manly deeds is permissible if they are done for womanly aims and within the limits of the female image; and that means, done for someone else, not for this creature's own selfish purposes. The peak of admiration and also the occasion where the most extreme daring can be accepted is reserved for women who demonstrate their courage as a function of mother love—devoted, sacrificial, and by definition defensive even when its deeds are savage.

The deepest, most universal perception of woman's proper and essential nature is her image as mother. Here is where the omnipresent dogma that women have a duty which is also a special sex-related capacity for support and sacrifice begins: in the preverbal memory-traces that retain the extreme vulnerability every infant feels as it comes to know—and to love and fear simultaneously—the hugely powerful, hugely needed parent figure that is later identified as female. It seems evident that the denial of vulnerability that the masculine mystique and the values of patriarchy demand from men stems from this primary relationship. To confront that old dependence is terrifying; dealing with it is beyond the reach of reason and logic, and so it carries a magic menace: Suppose it should happen again? The threat hinders men in acknowledging the feelings of human weakness that all humans know. It also directs them to defend themselves by binding women into a position where they cannot challenge those who claim adult power. Could they defend adult power against the mythic mother if she should reappear?

How can women get out of this trap? Must we accept, as an immutable force, the image of ourselves as inevitable mother-giver-supporter, ideally good and experientially too threatening to be allowed individual freedom? That would be very bad news indeed, for it would compel us to live by the rules of a world that's entirely mythic, existing as masked figures to whom any autonomous active life is refused. Fortunately, there is also a real world, of actual events, full of living human creatures. True, it's influenced by mythic beliefs and most strongly by those that incorporate male fears; and we shall help ourselves most effectively if we confront the vulnerability that the intrusion of myth into actuality lays on us. Once aware of this, we can try to act in ways that lessen mythic pressures, even as we take account of their existence and understand their origin in early magic.

Curing such fears and banishing such myths won't be accomplished by magic. We, in turn, need to begin a program of resocializing those who harbor them by adjusting the data of the external world: by persistently, insistently establishing wider and more various identities for ourselves in a kind of self-improvement with a social purpose; by acting according to our needs and desires as we understand them, by building realistically on the changes in society that have already taken place, and by disentangling ourselves from the false manners that declare we are secondary, abnormal creatures whose knowledge of life will never be applicable to human quandaries.

In order to find a female nature that we ourselves originate and describe, women will have to look at the whole range of our experience, including the past, and we will want then to discriminate among the elements of history so that we can profit from the good news without being overwhelmed by the bad. We can certainly use the intuitive knowledge of feeling that has been described as feminine when we do that, for it will distinguish between falseness and authenticity. But there's no reason at all why we shouldn't employ also those human character traits now labeled masculine. Logic and close reasoning will help us sort out useful techniques and unbind them from goals that are not desirable in the world today. The whole process can be an opportunity to learn wholeness: the use of logic and feeling together instead of in opposition. In judging our past we shall gain practice in dealing with the present. Episodes of courage that supported others establish our ability to act bravely. The bonding to family that called courage forth suggests that a bonding of other sorts, with other beloved humans, will strengthen the impulse to be brave. Special skills that women have developed can be used in different ways. Political wives used to congratulate themselves on their value as campaigners for their husbands; now there are women in politics who can and do use these abilities for themselves. Academic wives who shared in research, in writing and editing their husbands' scholarly works, were pleased when they were rewarded by a dedication. Now they may be recognized on the title page as coauthors, or they write their own books. We are, to use a properly feminine metaphor, picking up some of the dropped stitches of the past. As we reknit our history, we glimpse new patterns that differ from the familiar legends of our time.

The isolation from mainstream activities that has been typical of women for so long is not exclusive to us, of course. All of the weak have been cut off from a range of relationships, and the easy, casual meetings that the self-confident powerful take for granted are not easy for the maladroit governed who enroll in assertiveness-training courses and join encounter groups. The weak are unwelcome in many places, and know it. The distancing of women is most intense of all and the need to maintain it greatest. What is worse, our encounters with the powerful are very often on a one-to-one basis, so that the support of group relations and approval must be incorporated in the self, as the assurance of being trustworthy; worthy of one's own trust as affirmed by the group.

But just as our experience can be instructive for other segments of the weak, theirs can help us. The impractical politics of community have been tried in other times and places, and men committed to contest have dreamed for eons of peaceful Utopias. True, they have consistently neglected to consider the means and methods by which human beings can reach that happy state through daily, repeated acts that shift society away from unnecessary confrontation and recall common interests until we learn to use contest within the ties of community without risking disruption. As that happens, the divergence between the two parts of society that I have been calling the powerful and the weak would lessen, and the pressure to assign everyone to one or the other of such polarized positions would decline. A widening choice of identities, a freer range of behavior invites invention, and would offer the opportunity to augment and vary the political process, so that interaction became both more general and more natural; more "daily."

This may sound like a Utopian dream itself, but it does not ignore process and dynamics. In the course of this book we have already come across some instances where the One Right Way to govern the community was defeated by alternatives. Alternate procedures differ from Utopian goals just because they are procedures, not ends; and as procedures they can deploy the powers of the weak in ways that are best suited to those powers. Those of us alive today who do not despair of the future are pretty much aware that we need variant methods as well as new goals. There is something to be learned from past experience in a work of salvage and revaluation. That's an enormous task, of course. I can do no more than hint at possibilities; and at the same time urge that we do not romanticize the alternatives we come on. It isn't enough to seize on something different. Let us be as practical as Evans-Pritchard's Azandes, who judge their magicians by the efficiency of their spells in the everyday world.

Take the communes of the sixties. Those that foundered first, I think, failed because they had no positive common purpose. Such a purpose holds institutions together through an ongoing intentional sequence of action in which all the members participate. The communes that came into being simply as refuges from an unpleasant larger world tended to dissolve quite rapidly.

The longest-lived communes of all, of course, have been and are religious communities. The common purpose of worship and work is maintained here by a rule, often very strict and apparently hierarchic. But in the classic Christian religious communities, at any rate, hierarchy and strict rule exist along with affirmation of the common lowliness of humankind compared to the all-powerful and beneficient Spirit whose worship is here maintained. This introduces into the structure a very strong element of antistructure. The novice is subject to rule, she must accept the direction of those above her, but the Mother Superior is also subject to rule and, in the eyes of Heaven, is "superior" only in the temporal condition of mortal life, not for eternity. Moreover, rituals regularly declare the egalitarian humility of all ranks of the hierarchy.

In secular organizations, some kind of similar factor of antistructure can be included. Psychologist Seymour Sarason, writing out of his experience of establishing institutions in urban areas, with the altruistic intent of promoting the ability of the poor (mainly black people) to deal with practical and psychological problems, notes the relative success of those that took this tack as compared to those where a strong leader exercised authority. Where structure was loose, where jobs were more or less exchangeable and thus comprehensible to all, where scheduled meetings of the whole staff regularly discussed past errors and alternative ways of doing things, much was accomplished. Where leaders clung to privacy in order to demonstrate their superiority and feared to reveal their worries and problems because they were supposed to "know best," they and the rest of the organization suffered. Sarason's study of some of these institutions, *The Creation of Settings,* reads almost like a handbook of what not to do; but it is better seen as a firmly realistic confrontation of vulnerability—and recommendations therefrom. Sadly, the worst danger that plagued these innovative systems came from other experts in the field who found it difficult to the point of impossibility to accept these deviations from the One Right Way.[2]

The use of a particular alternative technique for gaining political and/or economic ends is discussed at length in a work I've already cited, Gene Sharp's *The Politics of Nonviolent Action.* Sharp documents nearly two hundred cases where group action, for a strongly felt common purpose, has employed nonviolent means. These are, of course, instances of contest and confrontations sometimes maintained over long periods of time. But the very fact that the people who undertook a confrontation with a powerful Establishment dared to forswear the use of violence indicates that they recognized the existence of contest as a political process that occurs as part of a relationship, within an encircling community. There are two parties to the quarrel; but there is also present some broader audience that may find itself becoming participant in the dispute, and whose participation can be encouraged if blood is not shed—at least by one party. Sharp does not dwell on this factor particularly. He is more interested in the mechanics of using the powers of the weak to gain practical ends in "impractical" ways. In the cases he records, the weak were not always successful, but they were effective: that is, they made their points, their goals were understood, both by their opponents and by the "resonant mass" of the surrounding populace, and if they failed they sometimes set in motion a process that brought results over a longer period.

Sharp is very clear that these methods of contest work because they exert force within a relationship, and what it is that they do or threaten:

> The central political implications of our analysis point to control of political power . . . by withdrawal of consent. It is control, not by the infliction of superior violence from on top or outside, not by persuasion, not by hopes of a change of heart in the ruler, but rather by the subjects' declining to supply the power-holder with the sources of his power, by cutting off his power at the roots.[3]

Not only does nonviolent action challenge the purposes of the powerful, it attacks traditional means of enforcement, for it *redefines* the means that can be used for effectual governance by insisting that change can come from below, and without the necessary use of physical force: protests, boycotts, demonstrations, strikes, mutinies, picketing, teach-ins, walk-outs, marches, and more announce determined opposition by techniques that contradict the assumptions of the official police and military. Power, say the maxims of governance, depends on armed might. Nonviolent activists don't just reject these principles verbally, they act out their rejection and with it the substitution of a new definition, declaring that the nature of power is relational. This is a strong statement, for nonviolent protest is anything but passive. Refusing cooption, it also refuses cop-out by demonstrating repeatedly that consent is being withdrawn from the programs of rulers and submissiveness is at an end. It both requires courage and teaches it by sheer necessary habituation to handling tricky and dangerous situations. It also demands and encourages creativity, for not only can this form of struggle shift the perceptions of the powerful; it also "brings changes . . . to the nonviolent group itself . . . changes [that] are especially associated with a new sense of self-respect, self-confidence, and a realization of the power that people can wield in controlling their own lives."[4]

Nonviolence and terrorism have this in common: in each the governed make a dramatic, gestural appeal to the wider community to rejudge the world-description of the Establishment. Terrorism exaggerates accepted techniques of force-against-others in order to announce that the system maintained by the powerful is false: state violence is no more legitimate than terror. The significance of "murder" and "execution" should be reversed. Nonviolent activists may aim at reform instead of revolution. The point of attack for them is change by means of changed techniques, which question the inevitable dependence of social structures on physical force. A muted form of martyrdom is brought into play, so that the protesters risk having force used against themselves instead of using it against others, and thus demonstrate the weight and sincerity of their conviction and its ability to bring strength to the weak. The contest itself can strengthen participants— as Martin Luther King, Jr., declared during the bus boycott in Montgomery, "A once fear-ridden people had been transformed. Those who had previously trembled before the law were now proud to be arrested for the cause of freedom." Equally it can confuse opponents; when Polish troops were brought into East Germany to crush the 1953 uprising there, their officers refused to fire on German workers, and even Russian troops "sometimes proved unreliable."[5] This kind of reversal of stance within an ongoing contest reflects the sense of a surrounding reality, greater than contest, and enclosing both opponents within a community. Soldiers who refuse to fire are responding to a felt relationship with the other side. In the same fashion, activists who attempt to reason with the enemy (as Gandhi did) assume and assert that the other side can comprehend the rationale that is put forward and may conceivably be influenced by it. In our own modern history, the growth of industrial unions during the nineteen-thirties and forties illustrates the effectiveness of nonviolent economic action when the political process, shaken by depression and then by war, was open to intervention from below. So the drama which the nonviolent play out takes place within a community that is not inescapably polarized.

On the face of it, this seems to make the use of nonviolent methods of protest appealing to women. Our training for physical confrontation has been almost nonexistent, and a few lessons on how to resist rape will not change a long tradition of compliance. The feminine body image is still strongly concentrated on appearance, not activity. Sports-minded young girls are, even now, much rarer than their brothers. Aside from these negative directives against active physical contest, there are positive reasons for turning to other ways of managing disagreement and hostility. Our understanding of womanhood teaches us concern for cooperation, for negotiation so that common interests may be discovered that will allow both parties to arrive at some workable compromise. We are also more ready, both for positive and for negative reasons, to risk violence by others and make our points by endurance and repetition, rather than to employ force against others.

Using techniques for change that come naturally has great advantages for any group that is starting out to seek change. But it also has a serious disadvantage which has to be taken into account whether we act on it in the end or not in any particular case. *Nonviolence may suit women too well.* In the first place, it fits the traditional picture so neatly that it may deliver a very ambiguous message to the world at large. Nonviolent protest is not, in fact, passive—as Gene Sharp is at pains to point out. It may very well require more courage to face and endure attacks by opponents without retaliating during public demonstrations than to reply in kind. Nonviolent activists are risk-takers who make behavioral statements that contradict the doctrines and the practices of the powerful and that can be even more upsetting than "normal" violence. These statements can be misinterpreted because they do use a different language of behavior, they may be labeled crazy, but if the Establishment is also perceived as a little crazy by the mass of the community, the nonviolent have a chance to make their points. The fact that they are doing something strange arouses curiosity. Bystanders want to know what they are up to.

The problem for women acting alone is that nonviolence is perceived as being much less strange when they use it; it is "typically feminine" to refrain from the employment of force; and the moment that any procedure can be labeled feminine, it loses significance. Female nonviolence is at variance with the standard procedures for active public protest—but it varies *in the standard feminine way.* Women are behaving in the manner that's expected of them—at least negatively. True, they aren't submitting without protest, but their protests are delivered via behavior that falls within the feminine image. Like the anger of the stigmatized, which is taken as normal for people in their unfortunate positions, nonviolent action by women can merit sympathy for what they suffer—and be pretty much ignored.

This reception of nonviolence leads to a second disadvantage. It elicits a certain amount of approval from men, on a contingent basis: congratulations on "not being strident," on avoiding radical statements, on being reachable by reasonable male arguments—these appeal to women's sense of cooperation and willingness to negotiate progress. It is less easy to see that this approval also has the effect of supporting the status quo: powerful males are still asserting their power, though this time they are doing it by commending the non-ugly bits of the feminine ferment who don't shout stridently, or act in rude, unfeminine ways. Now, women are still close enough to traditional training—we have all received a good deal—to be sensitive to male approval, even when it's superficial. Even if it is promptly rejected, it can awaken old inhibiting reflexes on the one hand and equally inhibiting anger on the other, the immediate negative response that provokes someone who has been told she is pleasantly nonstrident to shout at the top of her voice, if not—like Goering on hearing the word "culture"—to reach for a gun. And there is a very obvious component in such approval of the ancient doctrine of power, "Divide and rule." If some women can be persuaded that they will advance their cause by employing feminine methods (as these methods are understood by men, of course, not by any means as feminists see them), then they may turn away from those who use other techniques for change.

I am not suggesting that the misinterpretations which may attend women's use of nonviolent action mean that we should turn away from it. Far from it. But if we are to use this technique well, *we have to consider the misunderstandings that it may provoke and work to counter them.* The problem here is communication, not just with allies, or just with opponents, but with the public at large. Let me cast back to the example supplied by the English suffragettes: they opted to use violence against property (not against people) at a time when an agreement with the sitting Liberal Government to introduce a Votes for Women bill had not been kept, and when violence against imprisoned feminist hunger-strikers, by forced feeding, had become a matter of course. Not only were the militant suffragettes being denied access to normal political channels, the force of the state was turned against the moral protests attempted through hunger-strikes. Nothing they said appeared to be heard. So they threw rocks through the plate-glass windows of Bond Street shops, and shook and shocked the country.

Was the attention they won worth the horror expressed at their conduct? I am myself inclined to think that it was. British politicians are experts at outsitting their opponents on a heap of piously made and easily broken promises in a style defined as "muddling through." Suffering *by* women was not enough to move them. They needed a shock, and female violence provided it. What should have followed, but did not, was a campaign to explain the suffragettes' aims in dramatic fashion; a campaign aimed less at their own backers or at the Government than at ordinary citizens, men and women. It's easy to say that now, of course, and probably impossible to have done it successfully then. Those very brave women acted within the limits of political knowledge available in a world strongly shaped by a male mystique of Empire and of Victorian morality. Just the same, the purpose of protest has to be changing the minds of enough people so that the cause one presents gets to be seen as conceivable, then as possible, then probable, then normal and desirable. That's no guarantee of success, but without that purpose made clear, there's really no chance of success at all.

Today as then, women—like all the governed—are faced with the task of inventing a language of behavior that is based on authentic feeling; but for it to be a useful language, the fundamental requirement of a language has to be met. That is, it must deliver messages accurately over quite a wide range of meaning, and be comprehensible to its viewers and listeners. Those viewers and listeners are women, in the first place. But the general surrounding community ought to be able to follow them too, for it will only be supportive if it can do so. Such understanding, among both groups—insiders and outsiders—can be greatly enhanced by the growth of comprehensible reference points—and the arts are vital here, in their discovery, creation, and communication of symbols of lived and felt experience. Women's culture has been thin, in the past, because so much of our existence has seemed interesting only to ourselves; it is talked about in private, in intimate speech; and public discourse has more or less had to be made in adaptations of masculine rhetoric. We very much need a culture and a behavioral language that will let us speak easily, accurately, and understandably in public as well as in private. Until we have such an instrument, it will be hard to make our thoughts clear without having intentions and meanings confused and garbled by traditional symbology.

My point here is this: the status of woman as object and as other is going to influence the way women are perceived when they begin to act for themselves. The strategies they use will be evaluated according to traditional expectations of female behavior; and techniques for change that have the advantage of being natural and appropriate for use by women carry the disadvantage of confusing the audience, if they are read as simply feminine gestures. I have taken violent versus nonviolent action as an example, but many others exist: women act intuitively, they are overly emotional, they fail to support their impulsive acts by coherent, structured institutional frames, to name a few. Indeed, we do not want to react by bolting back into male patterns of behavior; but when we use strategies that seem natural and familiar, we also want them to carry a message that we are using them for purposes that are new, that are authentically our own.

I think we need to analyze our own intentions too, for the overtones of old images are hard to erase from memory. The transitory power that is part of the experience of raising children is hard to give up, and the techniques of assertion-by-right-of-motherhood are all too easy to use in situations where they don't belong. Then they can reinforce the myths that male fears of the dominant primary parent have created. Another aspect of the traditional female role invites token women to behave, in a business setting, as if it were social; to show themselves as pleasing, compliant, or seductive. Natural as it is to use such familiar relational forms, they serve to maintain the old masculine-feminine polarity. We need to adapt such behavior to circumstances, so that gentle firmness and the capacity to get on with people cease to present themselves as feminine virtues and are seen instead as human capabilities.

Other symbolic behavior that recognizes the demands made by denied or repressed emotions or brings forward the value of cooperative joint action really needs to be adjusted only by raising its value and affirming its public importance. Arriving at a new image for women is thus a subtle task: the creation of an ordinary heroine, as large as life but no larger, open to emotion, responsive to the human environment, practical in action, rationally aware of the unique worth of intuitive knowledge, and able by swift insight to step back from what feels false and foolish in mechanical logic applied where it doesn't belong, in emotional life.

In a parable or a *Utopia,* we could dream her up at once and set her to work changing the world. As it is, we shall have to go to work ourselves, in the hope that the process of change and struggle will change the selves of women toward billions of individual versions, none of them exactly what we imagine because they will incorporate in themselves what we cannot foresee: descendants of the present, ancestors of the future.

CHAPTER 20

Inventing the Future

The epigraph for this chapter has not yet been written.

Whenever they begin to move beyond resistance and inchoate rebel-lion toward positive, purposeful action, the weak approach the limits of their old status. I have not been happy using that name for the governed majority of humankind; "weakness" is not a characteristic that anyone would rush to claim. I've used it, nonetheless, for two reasons. First, I have not been able to find a better name, one that doesn't divide the ordinary, varied mass of people within itself, or else limit this mass by laying some false attribute on it. Second, I find in the term "weak" an exemplary quality. That's how the powerful see the situation. This is their definition, and as long as they are permitted the power to define things, their definitions are a significant part of the situation. In a polarized society, everyone will be labeled as either weak or powerful by the segment of society that does the labeling.

Symbolic of the future to be invented will be a new name for what I've been calling "the weak." It will take into account both variety among us, and movement within the flow of actual events. It will not deny some capacity for governing to the governed, or some measure of strength, force, insight, and decisiveness to the humble. Indeed, by refusing to accept a static polari-zation within society, it will allow increasing flexibility to the great. But such a redefinition will do more than simply blur confrontation, it will signal the recognition of potential partners within a community, groups that may differ but which may also find common goals. Most important of all, it will testify to the existence of a community that is strong enough to contain differences.

As things stand now, the weak are tagged with a name that conveys a stigma; and, in addition, those who protest against the label find that they are taken to be competing for the other position—power, as the powerful understand it. We have to see this as an impoverishment, almost a denial, of choice. Multiplex, burgeoning life is presented as if it were one of those True-False tests, to be graded by an archaic computer not even programmed for multiple-choice responses.

Where does the impulse to divide the world in two arise? Why do we think so often in binary terms: "Light or dark?" "Yes or no?" "Right or wrong?" "Nature or nurture?" and with Lévi-Strauss in his analysis of myth, "Raw or cooked?" Either-or thinking is very common throughout the world. One source of such "dual symbolism" is certainly the rightness and leftness of our two hands; anthropologist Rodney Needham has edited a collection of essays, *Right and Left*, that illustrates the prevalence of this symbolic opposition. But the reader need not go far in this collection to discover that rightness and leftness are associated not only with Sky as opposed to Earth, or North against South, Cold versus Hot, Dry versus Wet, and so on. They also symbolize the sexes, Yang divided from Yin. "The opposition of the right (male) and the left (female) hands may be seen in many everyday Kaguru practices which clearly indicate the association of the right with cleanness, strength, auspiciousness, and the left with uncleanness, weakness, inauspiciousness," writes Professor T. O. Biegelman, on the beliefs of a Bantu-speaking people of Tanzania. And as the Kaguru think, so think their neighbors the Gogo, and the Nuer, and the Nyoro, and the Lugbara; so think the Chinese and the Arabs; so thought the Greek philosophers Parmenides and Pythagoras. Right and left, male and female, clean and unclean, strong and weak, the duality is sometimes elaborated, but the sexual connotation is constant.

Does this mean that a polarized world not only derives from the duality of sex—but must continue to do so, since there are indeed two sexes? Let us not scare ourselves with mythic terrors. It's not sex itself that feeds this idea but the unequal assignment of value and importance to masculine and feminine gender. If anatomy were just anatomy, who would care any more than we now care about red or dark hair, blue or brown eyes? Taste and private pleasure might favor one or the other, but that would be personal. Let anatomy be defined as *destiny*, however, and as every child learns that lesson, so she or he learns that her fate and her identity are set on an either-or course, boys over here, girls there, and no other choice, nothing else between or above or around or below. Two sexes, two hands, two patterns of existence.

And two ranks in the hierarchy of power, which still keep their connection to gender even though, in our world, the links to rightness and leftness have vanished.

Women have been thinking long and hard about the reasons for the continuing linkage of gender to status. We have, in a way, accepted our own social contract or, rather, a more or less either-or agreement to a position that took more than it gave, but did give something and which was, for eons and ages, not only enforced but apparently validated by the circumstances of external life. The position we agreed to, however, was based on a definition that did not originate with women: it is that woman's most essential quality is her capacity to bear children. Now that is the view from outside. To any woman, her essential quality is simply her own integrated identity, her "indwelling" (as Winnicott calls it) in her own body, and the inner psychic reality that forms the base for all her ongoing relationships; which is simply to say that she shares the essential quality of being human. What we agreed to under the old bargain, however, was the central significance, for women, of the role of mother and, moreover, of that role as interpreted by the male makers of myth. So "mother" is another word that needs redefinition.

Why did that happen? Since there are, by definition, no records from prehistory to consult, we have to proceed by informed guess or, to speak scientifically, by estimate and hypothesis. It would appear that there were physical reasons for women to accept the old definition, and with it the old social contract, in that long-ago time when it was evolved. Pregnancy could not be controlled with any certainty; there was no way to feed babies that could replace, or supplement, the breast (though one woman's breast could substitute for that of another); nor were there medical defenses against the diseases of childhood. Replacement of the stock, among scattered hunting-foraging groups often threatened with disaster, depended on close mothering during infancy and early childhood. The clustering of women with their children put them into a bounded social category, but it also permitted mutual help. Such clustering occurs among prehuman primates, where it also permits mobile adult males to protect the slower-moving group of mothers and young.

The question of physical mobility further reinforced the concept of women and children as a group within the larger society. How far can a woman carry a two-year-old? How far can a four-year-old walk? Those are perfectly reasonable questions, but once they are asked, they promote the idea of a division by gender. This affects the kind of productive labor assigned or allowed each sex. Women who forage and gather plant food often kill small animals too. They often, it seems from studies of still-existing hunter-gathers, go quite far afield. But the presence of children prohibits the group's participation in big-game hunting. We are here looking at the beginning of a division of labor by gender, and also of space: women carried on their activities closer to camp.

We should also take account of the effect of bodily size and strength. Human dimorphism is not as extreme as in some other species, but it appears to show up in the earliest hominids. It gives men an edge in muscular power; not just in the case of violent confrontation, though of course it does that, but also in terms of dividing heavier work from lighter, during the long centuries when work power was muscle power. We know that these divisions were never complete and that they often differed from people to people, but they tended to set a pattern, and the pattern joined with the association of women and children together to limit the type of work women did and bound the space in which they did it. Among some pastoral peoples, where climate and the nature of the land allow a mix with agriculture, this works out to a pattern in which men and older boys go off, sometimes for months, with the herds while women and little children stay at home and cultivate the crops. Women were, and are, also called into service in male activities; but they are expected to serve there as assistants, not principals. In time, women and children took on the aspect of a joint class that had to be looked after, and men came to be seen as responsible caretakers, who deserved the dominance they assumed. This is shorthand, of course; women's place and work has varied widely, and some have enjoyed dignities and asserted authority, as allowed by the circumstances of life and the opportunities that could be exploited. But these are the physical conditions that underlay the old contract, and which made it hard to imagine alternatives.

Within the terms of the contract, the structure of character that we think of as feminine was shaped; and this, too, is a term that needs redefinition. Redefinition doesn't mean a break with the past, it means a new look at it. Women have always managed to do some bargaining inside the old contract, sometimes well, sometimes less effectively and from poorer positions, and have learned a good deal about negotiations by doing so. The settlements we've been able to win are one-sided, and sometimes extremely onerous. But the courage of endurance, vitality, hope, and ingenuity has never been killed off; and these qualities have won some advantages, and in good relationships they have given birth to affectionate partnerships and mutual respect. The true overlap of humanity can prevail over sex division, and it has always allowed some marriages and friendships and kin-connections to thrive where the usual axioms of male-female difference are forgotten and other premises invented, spacious enough for real coming together. Unfortunately, these divergent relationships don't much affect the behavior patterns expected by orthodoxy; they are data not generalized from. Women have not been able to call such relationships anything *but* fortunate; which means out of the ordinary. Looking ahead at our own lives when young, or thinking for daughters, we have not dared predict such good fortune. The letters and journals and memoirs that we have from the past record warnings, not hopes: don't expect too much, do your best to put up with things, think how much worse off you might be.

Stoic acceptance, then, is what mothers have tried to teach daughters in order to save them from despair; and often things have been better, in one way or many ways, so that the hard lessons were disproved and did serve to make reality seem easier than it might have been. If women have got on with less hope than men, it's partly because of such provisions to squeeze it out of the rock of existence: to derive good news from bad news itself.

Assigned particular tasks, women have learned to do them well and to take pride in work well done, and, kept in woman's place, to find joy in loving friendships with each other. There has been good news, good, strong lives have been led, and they should not be undervalued by women no matter how they are defined by the powerful.

But we can't forget those definitions which base our essential being, and the activities proper for us, in the mother role; not as we see it, but as it is laid down for us by the powerful male elite. What makes us unique, we are told, what is always present in the way that we are perceived, the root of necessity which gives us an identity, is that we bear children. And of course we do; we can't quarrel with the fact; but we can question the interpretation of the fact. What does our childbearing role mean, specifically in a society that is dominated by people who don't bear children? It certainly doesn't mean what it would in a society of equals, in the future that we invent.

But until we do, we are caught in the old contract, where motherhood is the essential characteristic defining the whole being of women. That makes us very important, we are told. In fact, procreation is so important that *its control cannot be left to women.* For woman-as-mother holds the key to the whole future of the race or the nation, tribe or city, to the endurance of a man's heritage, to the passage of his possessions to his offspring, to his very place in the human stock. So important are we as mothers, in fact, that we really shouldn't try to do anything else.

In this vision the individuality of any woman is diminished compared to the significance of the function she can serve as childbearer. So central is the identity bestowed by the mother role that we can't get rid of it even when we are not fulfilling it. A childless woman does not become an honorary male, free to do the world's work. On the contrary, her condition has usually been seen as a defect, and even now, in some societies, barren wives can be set aside by their husbands. Women's own perceptions of identity now include much more than motherhood; indeed, they must always have reached beyond it; but as yet this has not done much to change the social contract, where gender identity still blends with power identity.

Personal prehistory plays a part in reinforcing this definition of women. All humans learn our gender identity by means of another polarity, that of big and small, parent and infant. Differences in power are clear. Big people are in charge, little people aren't. Today, as ever, most of the close and regularly present big people are female. The others may be there from time to time, but they tend to come and go. Mothers are the first power figures we encounter. As time passes, that power appears to wane, in the real world of experience, but preverbal memories remain. So the male need to control the future by controlling the childbearing, future-creating sex is complicated by a sense of early dependence on that sex. Those memories contribute to the masculine urge to bind women-as-mothers to privacy and apartheid, for the mythic power inherent in the definition might become overwhelming if it came to be combined with ordinary human force, drive, and effectiveness. Gender roles provide a barrier against the seizure of double power by women; thus, declaring the supreme importance of motherhood actually works to keep women in a subordinate place.

Once again, the question is not about fact, but about the significance and the interpretation of fact. When men say, and women agree, as many undoubtedly still would, that the mother role is central, essential both for the individual and for society, what does that mean? What did our mothers and foremothers think when they were told to center their identities here? What do the women who agree feel in private, below the public acceptance of this honor? Love for their children, certainly, and pleasure in seeing them grow, pride in their accomplishments; but is this the most significant aspect of their whole lives? What is the psychological effect of founding the core of your identity in something that lies outside the self, bound up in a service relationship that has a terminal date in actual practice though not in affection? What sort of identity will remain when the active function is finished? When, like the NASA engineers at work on the moon-shot, you have worked yourself out of the job that defines you?

These speculations, I repeat, have nothing to do with the joys and the aches, the rewards and the anxieties of *actual* mothering, which can be great or may not be, like everything else in life. My question has to do with the outcome of accepting a dictated status *that is contingent.* If the mother-function is central, how can a woman be central to herself? How does the image awarded her fit into her own mental and emotional contours? Does it override them? Can she consider her natural drives and desires as trustworthy (whether or not they can be satisfied, which is another question)? Or must she stand at a little distance from her own needs, unable to be sure that her *a priori* perceptions communicate a world that's really there, forced to displace her feelings and to doubt the immediacy of intuitive knowledge? Has she, have we all, been legislated into a state of altruism and enforced saintliness without having had a chance to vote on the proposition? "To be a true woman," Simone de Beauvoir wrote in *The Second Sex,* "she must accept herself as Other."[3] Does Otherness stem from Motherness?

If this is the case, we are looking at an overlap among social perceptions of Woman as Other, the mothering role, and the condition of actual powerlessness combined with feared mythic power, all of them reinforcing each other. By association, then, powerlessness takes on an aura of Otherness; so that women's condition is extrapolated to the whole body of secondary human beings, whose differences of class or race or nationality or religion or language or custom or dress acquire a symbolic character. "Not like us," say these symbols. "Incomprehensible. Unpredictable. Threatening—what will they do next?" Physical variations are seized on and exaggerated as evidence of difference, and if none exists, some external sign is invented. We've seen how this emphasis on difference prevents the powerful from making use of the experience of the weak in a practical way. Psychologically the menacing presence of these strangers, ignored in the waking world, can surface in public nightmares of oppression and genocide. But the mythic threats projected onto these deviant others, and then avenged, go on to awaken mythic guilt. May not the powerful have to pay, someday, for being powerful? May they not lose their magic connection to power, just as the mythic mother did? Power is changeable, chancy, labile, sometimes there, sometimes not. Do they dare to be sure that they own it? For how long?

Of course they don't own it, since power is not a thing to be owned. But if you believe that it is such a thing, losing it becomes a possibility to fear. That fear, I think, is one reason for the dark projections of a catastrophic future that are so widespread, in our dual society. The present powerful, being committed to polarization, expect that any new deal will overturn the one that set them in authority; that the last shall be first and the first last, role reversal everywhere, men as slaves, women as masters, in a revolution of contradiction. Within the nightmare-ridden mind, great Mother-goddesses take shape in a universe returned to infancy, where myth-shrouded figures punish and cherish at their own unknowable will. As the erstwhile powerful feel reality skidding out of control, they imagine some ambiguous, perilous, Utopia-Dystopia where Fate and the Sphinx, the Norns and the Sybils, hold sway. Rational orthodoxy knows better, but that doesn't sweep away all the shreds of nightmare that drift through the rational world and darken relations there.

Do women too develop, or accept, such revenge-fantasies? A good deal of repressed anger has certainly appeared in recent writing, and it can be found in some that is not so recent. Any impression of the aims or direction of this anger is just that—an impression; but judging impressionistically, women's anger appears to come out of the past, but to aim at a future not of revenge, which would reproduce the past in reverse, but of freedom, independent action, and the creation of something new. If the world were indeed limited to the old rules, then I think we would be seeing more retaliatory fury than we are. What keeps it relatively minor is hope, hope that has found some realistic roots. As long as opportunities and options increase, women's energy moves toward them, and vengeance doesn't seem worth spending time on. Some of the most bitter estimates of sex-repressions date back to writings of the nineteen-twenties and thirties; one might guess that the retreat from suffragist action of earlier years has something to do with this mood. It is reminiscent of the stirrings of Nazism in the twenties, among

Germans who had begun to climb into the middle class during the war years, and were then thrust back to a lower status. This, it appears, is the sort of experience that engenders dreams of revenge—all that one can hope for in a world that refuses alternatives.

Women do see alternatives now to a life of minimal survival, although optimism certainly isn't secure; it comes and goes, tentative though not timid. We are wondering how much we can trust our own judgment of the data of reality in the face of a surrounding atmosphere tinged by male frustration and anger. And yet our lives do tell us, over and over, that old physical limitations laid on women have disappeared, that machines do the work that muscle power used to do. They tell us that mothering may have taken up almost the whole of active life for women of past centuries, but not now. The obligations of child-raising largely remain with us, but we can *choose* when to take them on, if we want to take them on at all. The once-mysterious male parent is now more ready to become a part of the regular process. And so what used to be inescapable duties that defined the female being have turned into adjustable options, within the social framework. The joy of mothering can be shared, and if there isn't any joy, the mothering had better be shared.

These changes offer grounds for hope. They also bring home the need for redefinition. As the old myths wear thin and we see behind them a shifting landscape, we understand that the secure identity they gave us is fading. It was not created by women; it was crippling. But it was there, and without it, how are we to think of ourselves? Who is it who hopes and dares to plan? Who is it who must act and create? Who is it that we will invent? We ask these questions, as do all the no-longer-weak who want, at last, to define themselves—neither deviants, nor goddesses, nor menacing nightmare shapes, but simply human creatures, differing individually on a foundation of likeness.

What has changed in the world out there and what now forces redefinition on all of us is something we know so thoroughly that we take it for granted. In the last couple of centuries the human race has learned how to exploit and administer the physical world for our own ends. That is unique and unheard-of power, and we do well to hesitate and wonder in the face of such enormous shifts in the conditions of existence. So far, human creatures have exploited the world better than we have administered it, and we know it; which is a step toward wisdom, for recognizing limitations (vulnerability) is a necessary stage on the way to finding remedies. But the symptoms of panic manifested by the powerful men who rule our world aren't healthy. They seem to deny reality instead of searching through it for remedies, to

refuse to look at limitations instead of trying to assess them. Rational planning declines into ramshackle solutions based on archaic conditions. Women
are enjoined to solve social problems by acting as if we all lived in the
eighteenth century, while the twentieth rolls swiftly by. Science and technology have achieved an enormous amount, by way of dominating the physical
world, but the emotional rewards of this all but miraculous achievement
don't seem to be rewarding enough. By no means do they offset the flaws and
insufficiencies that are also there.

I don't doubt that a good deal of rational, useful cognitive effort is going
into planning repairs; and yet it seems curiously fragmented, one part disconnected from another. One gets the feel of a social mythology in process of
breaking up. Some of the parts—some of the sections of the paradigm—are
still fertile and usable; but they don't hook on to each other. And in the gaps
between, a miasma rises. The polarized universe is coming apart, but we are
not getting pluralism within a community, we are simply getting confusion.
As a result—and indeed as an effort to imagine a connecting pattern—magic
solutions are offering themselves for real problems. We can see these most
readily in the public communication of art: science-fiction dreams are everywhere, in which humans are redeemed from their difficulties by mysterious
forces that intervene from somewhere outside, and yet are closely related to,
and thoroughly knowledgeable of, our internal hopes and desires. They are
dream-answers: new versions of the *deus ex machina,* salvation by spaceship
full of benevolent magical creatures, the Messiah in the flying saucer.

The force of such fantasy is complicated by our uncertain hold on the
symbolic language of art, which makes it hard for us to be sure what is fact
and what is fiction in our complicated world. The new knowledge developed
by science and technology lies, most of it, beyond our capacity to judge it
for ourselves; that too blurs the line between fact and fiction. Take a simple
example: it's scientifically possible to clone a viable individual if you are
working with some amphibian species. How far, in the animal kingdom, does
this possibility extend? Does a book that declares it to have been done with
human animals immediately proclaim itself to be fiction, or will the reading
public buy it as being fact? The ordinary reader certainly doesn't know where
experimentation may stand at any given moment any more than most of us
could explain the workings of machines that we use every day. If we go by
our own experience, they might as well function by means of magic spells.

Our puzzlement is understandable, but it has the unfortunate effect of
increasing the apparent incomprehensibility of scientific knowledge, already
complex enough; and this is knowledge whose function lies in exactly its
factual accuracy. Underlying all scientific paradigms is the basic value that
they can be repeated, that rules hold true no matter who applies them if
conditions are met. By confusing our genres, we are substituting fictional

plausibility for the hard-edged reliability of fact. So we open the door to magic. The earthly dangers and difficulties that go along with our physical transformation of the world, and the social effects of that transformation, are none of them going to yield to magic solutions; but if we can't tell fiction from fact, how are we going to know? Why should we not appeal to intergalactic angels against our contemporary demons, just as our ancestors did, in the troubled ages they lived through?

In early medieval Europe, when the ordered structure of Roman power was merely a fading memory, popular literature came alive with miracle tales. "Society had . . . little earthly hope to offer"; wrote Erich Auerbach, "the prospect of a better order of life here below had all but vanished. The world was beset by famine, plagues, natural catastrophes, and aimless brute force. In such a world visions and miracles were indispensable."[4] In such a world, at any rate, disaster could not be reversed or averted by scientific planning. So Hope put on its magic cap. The pope himself, Gregory the Great, compiled a book of miracles designed to comfort and instruct the lowly, "the Dialogues, in which the supernatural continually, even on seemingly trivial occasions, takes a hand in everyday life."[5] They were read and recounted for a thousand years.

How familiar it all sounds—except for the thousand years. Our apocalypses are promised sooner. But where the psychological analogy is all too evident, the underlying facts differ. The causes of our disasters are the causes of our achievements: we have made them ourselves. And so they can be analyzed, they can be attacked, and if they can't all be remedied, perhaps we can find alternatives. What we don't need is angels, even delivered by spaceship; they will only distract us.

Nor do we want to reverse the drives that transformed the physical world and head back to the handloom and the hoe. Our need is to redirect the powerful creative urge that got us where we are, so that it can work to remedy the mistakes we have made. They are mistakes, but they were made in the course of enormous advances. This surge of invention has accommodated the external world to human needs, interpreted many of its laws, manipulated the "aimless brute force" that beset our ancestors, and dominated it in important ways. It is a very positive force, and it has brought great good things—the end of drudgery and slavery as inevitable aspects of existence, relief of sickness, lengthening of life, harvests bountiful beyond the wildest dreams of the past, and a base of fundamental data whose potentiality we have hardly begun to tap.

The trouble with this great drive to conquer and exploit the natural world lies in one circumstance: it does not include any self-limiting system. That means that it isn't complete in itself. It requires control and—short of miracles, magic, and fantasy—control can only come from the human environment; from acknowledging and strengthening a community that surrounds, and should contain, the urge to mastery, for this is the only force that can direct it toward cooperation.

By dividing the world into two, into males and females and, by extension, into powerful and weak, we have let go the unity of life that limits any thrust to domination. The drive to achieve, the urge to lay hands on the decisive powers of the mighty and to plan and govern well for others, all this is invaluable—as long as it is held in place within the human context. It is this context that the powers of the weak address and invoke. They express, and they continually reconstitute, the underlying awareness of community both as a limiting factor strong enough to tame vainglorious ambition and as a source of creative potential. Out of this creativity will come our new definitions, our new social contract.

How to do that? All the wisdom of patriarchy, and there's a great deal of it around, tells us that recognizing the equality of women is a very minor event. We have good reason to distrust this opinion, however, in the degree of resistance that even our moderate contemporary advance has brought forth. And if women are indeed the central body within the category of the weak, granting equality to us sets many things in motion. It means a revaluation and a reactivation of all the characteristics and qualities within all the areas of life that have been designated part of the female sphere of influence and beyond, to the whole territory of the weak.

Historians no longer speak of "dark ages." The Renaissance, which bridged medieval and modern times, is not now considered a unique blooming, but part of a process of development. Just the same, something happened; it happened by way of contact of cultures between Europe and the Moslem world during the Crusades, it happened through the reacquisition of classical learning, it happened as the age of exploration doubled the extent of the known world, it happened as new classes of people thrust their way into the political process, and as curious natural philosophers began to ask questions about the physical world which they then put to practical test. Now, an exploration of the obscure territory of the weak is going to differ in many ways from earlier ages of exploration; for one thing, the people who live there will be part of it. Romantic dreams of mastery, projected outward, and supported by superior armament, are not going to overwhelm the native population. But there are likenesses in the extent and the possible rewards of the two experiences.

The future we are going to invent starts here. Many women shelter an underground, half-articulate sense of possibility, of bountiful opportunity waiting not so much for individuals or even women as a sex, but for women as alerted forerunners of all humanity. It is very likely the ground for our resistance to male despair, and for our current relative indifference to dreams of revenge. But even those who feel hope most steadily and securely are wary as yet about reaching out too fast and too greedily. That's not only because burned children fear the fire, though they certainly do. It's also because female experience has taught us a sense of process and growth; these seeds of the future lie so deep in the feeling mind that we hesitate to force them.

We know too that in a bleak climate ideas for change that aren't understood will be unwelcome; and we have to understand them ourselves before we try them out on others. We need time to feel our way into the implications of change, time to acquaint ourselves with our own capacities, which have been undervalued for so long, time to learn to trust them and try them out. We have begun, for sure, but we don't yet know how great our resources are, and there are times when we hesitate to accept as true our own estimates of strength. For we are still timid, still unready to believe we know enough to challenge the structure of orthodox belief, even when we do deeply mistrust its dicta. Part of the vulnerability that we know how to face and to live with is believing that it really does make us so vulnerable that we cannot influence affairs as we would like. We still devalue our abilities, as current mythology tells us we should, even though we are aware that we devalue them and with them our outside-the-conventional-framework knowledge. There is a journey that we have to make into self-knowledge, and as we do it we must share with each other what we find in order to make it useful and to trust it; only then will we be certain that we can articulate it for others; for women first, for those of the weak besides ourselves who are our natural allies, and at last for everyone. It has been a long time, after all, since the dominant forces of society thought seriously and practically about the impractical, necessary value of community, or about those "feminine virtues" that need redefinition. We need the strength that will let us both articulate discoveries and insist on the dignity of old matters and qualities, long cast aside. Otherness has diminished us, and until we can shed it, it threatens to falsify the knowledge we offer to feed new paradigms. It is not enough to change the internal image of women, but only an authentically changed self-sense can support us in acting to change the world outside. Reciprocally, our ability to do that reinforces self-confidence. Creativity comes out of confidence and daring, and they enlist the stamina and persistence and endurance we shall need for our task of exploration.

I think of that task as drafting a new map of the world to a different projection—polar, perhaps, instead of Mercator. Of course it's a map with four dimensions, since it will factor in the time-process and allow us to chart the effects of change; a map of the future, but not one that lays out a fantasy or a miracle tale. Its reference points are here and now. They are the anomalies that "normal" procedures and policies can't deal with, the questions that can't be answered because they're based on inaccurate paradigms; questions that parallel the "crisis-provoking problems" that Thomas Kuhn sees as leading to scientific revolutions, which also draw new maps of knowledge.

Some of these anomalies our male-oriented society calls "women's issues." That seems to mean matters that women ought to resolve themselves, as they had to do in the settled past, when no one else was ever asked to worry about them: women used to do the housework without complaining about it, and take the wages they were offered, and raise children to respect their elders and betters, look after their own embarrassing female complaints and abort themselves if the need arose without making a song and dance about their rights, and fade into a pious old age with a fan and a rocking chair. No doubt all that is now out of date; but if women want to do these things differently, why can't they get on with the job by themselves? Women's issues, they say, are the province of women.

Other anomalies are admitted to be of general concern, but they are just as difficult. In fact, they may be related to the shifts that restless women have set about making in their lives, but they spill out into the rest of society, and so women can't be asked, or trusted, to cure them; only blamed for failing to prevent them. "Juvenile crime" falls in this category, and so do "problems of aging." Our social mythology holds that the young and the old ought to be cared for by women—women-as-mothers, women-as-dutiful-daughters.

Other insoluble and troubling questions are so general that no one thinks of them as being related to gender divisions. In fact, no one really likes to think about them at all: the isolation of individuals in urban settings, boredom, alienation, purposelessness, work-as-burden, violence . . . On the map we use now, these landscapes of disorder are scattered about, unconnected to each other; which I take as a sign of the map's inaccuracy.

Suppose, as a sketch for a new attempt, we group them all together, at the center of our chart. Start with the daily encumbrances of life as lived by the weak, not the terrifying doomsday visions of disaster and despair with which the powerful frighten themselves into immobility, but the obstacles we stumble over so often that we would take them for granted—if we could. Other segments of the weak will have different perspectives, but the cracks in our world seem to point to a central focus. I shall consequently use the view that we get when we start with women's lives and with the litany of familiar difficulties, so often repeated, so often ignored.

How do you manage to keep a job and run a house? How do you do that and raise a family too? How do you do those things if you're the only adult around? What happens if you get sick? If a child gets sick? If a child gets *really* sick, so that you are trying to earn the household's living and make a normal life for the healthy ones and care for a sick child all at the same time? What happens when you lose your job?

What happens when you're fifteen years old and poor and pregnant?

What happens if you're forty-seven and your husband leaves to get a divorce and you haven't worked for pay since you were twenty-two? What happens if your live, present, crazy-drunk husband beats you up and breaks your jaw? What happens if one of your children vanishes—into jail for robbery with violence? onto the streets? into thin air? What happens when they cut back the school-lunch program and your food stamps barely cover what you need as it is?

What happens if you're lucky and better off and ambitious—can you get a job that isn't deadly routine? Can you get promoted in it? Can you train for a profession, and how much remedial work do you need now because your high-school advisor naturally assumed that you'd get the usual sort of job for a few years, and then get married? And if yes, some people certainly can do all this, then—how many? Suppose you're one, and you get a good job which, like most good jobs, demands time, and then you get married, like a "normal" professional person with a good job except that "normal" means "male," and have a family, also like a normal professional person and even a normal human being except that normal still means male, and there you are, where we started: How do you manage to keep a job and run a house and raise children, but this time the job needs long hours and some travel? And you like that job, maybe you more than like it, maybe you find that it's where a continuing, centered self, an active and primary person in touch with the ongoing world of events, has been born and started to grow into something besides the traditional female identity—which you don't want to lose either. How can male "normal" be stretched to make room for a woman inside the definition? How can you reconcile pleasure in what you do outside with tiredness and a sense of guilt that shadows the pleasure you might feel inside—if you weren't loaded down? And these are the nicest, simplest, least complex, run-of-the-mill problems that female people find they are coping with, for better or worse. What good is a map where not a trace shows up?

The old map was drawn to match the old bargain, in which women and children and the work women did all went together. But now they have been spun apart, as if caught by some madly accelerated process of continental drift. We have been accepting the fragmentation too, *as if* it really were the result of geologic forces that can't be controlled, but of course it's not. Social changes caused the breakup. They can't be reversed simply and easily, if at all; but other changes can be set in motion to counter the results. If kinship networks have weakened (and that is both good news and bad, for sometimes they were hideously restrictive), well, other sorts of networks can be invented. The governed have invented a fair few: co-ops and unions, consumer-protection groups and neighborhood organizations to fight city hall, opponents of nuclear power and people's lobbies, and so on and so forth. On the main political battlefields they don't seem very significant, and they are quickly opposed by other contentious groups. Many of the latter look like the real thing, but aren't; they're façades for this or that entrenched organization. But entrenched organizations work by the old paradigm. Their efforts intensify "crisis-provoking problems," and so they will continue to manufacture their own opposition; in time that opposition will stop being so insignificant.

What's exciting about that very cautious, overly moderate statement is just this: the timing isn't up to them, it's up to us. We can affect the lives we lead in major, public ways. The problems that have marched into woman's place and upset our lives are overall human disruptions, and we know more about them than anyone else in the world. We know we need a new map and a new, adjusted society to match it; and each will influence the other. We can never forget the obscure half of existence, the emotional female sphere, and so we shall not be caught in the foolishness of trying to solve difficulties without reference to the human environment. The lip-service paid today to vital questions—the future of the family, gender identities, building communities, creating new urban settings, adolescent violence, exploitive pornography, and all the too-familiar topics for high-level one-week conferences—it will never deceive us. If you live with such crises you grow expert in telling lip-service from constructive efforts at change.

Distrust, the first power of the weak, is already ours. Defensive groups have formed, and women are learning how to move beyond them, the ugly ones included. Increasingly we will have to concern ourselves with the extensions of those female issues where our rebellion began, with the anomalies and crises that a polarized society breeds. To be effective here we shall have to ask the kind of questions that come out of dailiness: Why must we leave our children in order to earn a living that can keep, or help keep, our families? Why are children isolated from the adult world? How can we change residential patterns so that work and living can get mixed up together again, but in ways that don't exploit either adults or children? How can our system of education be redirected to the realities of adult life and needs? And how can work itself cease to imitate the worst of past drudgery and boredom, and reacquire some of the pleasure that craftsmanship used to afford—and in a realistic, everyday way? Technology can certainly do a lot more for us than pollute our living space, jam it up with traffic, and uglify our cities. How do we get it to start?

Talking about problems—about, shall we say, building community—is terribly easy, and useless if we stop there. We need to build it, not to talk. But in fact any job that we undertake as a group with a common interest builds community. We come together and lay out plans, we try them and some work and some don't and we try to find out why—these are daily endeavors, not beyond the powers of the weak even when we still think of ourselves as weak. And they are exactly the efforts that will help us frame our new map, in terms of alliances and relationships, in terms of bargaining and negotiation and political processes, sometimes with friends, occasionally with enemies who turn up on our side for a space of time. A *New York Times* story out of Chicago recently reported on precisely the matter of building community: "Activist Neighborhood Groups," ran the headline, "Are Becoming a New Political Force." Unstructured, firmly refusing to tie in with any political party, nonpartisan, nonideological, "the neighborhood lobby has succeeded in winning a series of laws and regulatory changes intended to combat what the activists view as the mindless ravages on residential areas of big government and big business." These groups are inventions of the governed who are taking a hand in controlling the conditions of life. Like activist women's groups, they are building-blocks of the future. They deliberately refuse unnecessary structure. Concentrating on minutiae instead of grandiose plans means that they know what they want and aren't distracted. They don't offer solutions. They do offer techniques; and practice in breaking into and changing the political process; and asking the right questions, plus not taking "No" for an answer. They are exemplars from which the weak can learn. Women are not only prominent among them, they also manage to override racial divisions and involve both old and young.

So the fragmentation of the old social structure, which has brought much dislocation and pain, is also perceivable as a loosening up of strictures. "Bonds" can immobilize as well as support. The spontaneous coming together of people who see their common interests as more important than their different status in traditional society is an example of the creativity of the governed at work. Like neighborhood organizations, women's networks are everywhere and they grow in variety all the time. The Boston Women's Collective devotes two chapters of its book on parenting, *Ourselves and Our Children,* to a discussion of how to use conventional family services and how to invent new ones. Work-related groups proliferate, and women who have found their way into macro-politics as well as local activities count more and more on having a female constituency. The black minority is ahead of us here, and other minority groups are growing.

Very often this pattern is described by the powerful as divisive. It can be, the boundaries of such groups are sometimes too tight and too hard to penetrate; and they do indeed have "special interests" at heart. But the special interests of the people are what governance should take into account; and when it doesn't, the native human potential for invention and intervention comes into play. The more such groups can accomplish, the less defensive they will have to be about their specialness, the more ready to join others in larger social campaigns. Then a wider sense of community may reawaken.

Is that a Utopian dream? Any attempt, here and now, to imagine it conceptually certainly would be. But those who would be coming together for such purposes would know firsthand, and not just in their heads, not as lip-service, what community experience is, because they come together into communal groups through their own activities. They have lived through the process, and they know that community grows out of efforts to get things done, not by dreaming up and discussing ideals. It isn't theory, it's action that sets us off and keeps us going in the enterprise by which we create a livable future out of the muddled present; or at least try to do so. If we are to tap the reservoir of evolutionary change to be found in the unused potential of the governed, it will be by testing it in action. For the world changes not only through leaps in insight by the famous; the leaps come out of the social context, and technical skill and daily use of know-how are the substance of social context. The scientific exemplars of which Kuhn speaks tied data together in brilliant new interpretations, but the data came out of a matrix of knowledge that was already in place. Without that matrix, the significance of these discoveries would not have been understood, and they probably would not even have been made.

Inventing the future—metaphorically, drafting a map that will fit it—is an active process of learning and collaboration. It begins where we are, in trouble. It takes that trouble seriously, sees it as exemplary, paradigmatic, of what will have to be tackled one way or another. If, like Martin Luther King, the governed have dreams, they are dreams that are shaped by the troubles we know and that impel us to set about overcoming those troubles. I have tried in this book to talk a great deal about techniques and very little about ends. My reason is that I believe that we may accomplish so much more than we can yet imagine that laying down goals is a bad idea; it limits us and it may misdirect our energies. What women and the rest of the weak can bring to the active world can't possibly be laid out ahead of time: we simply don't know what may naturally develop from responding positively and inventively to the changes that are already going on, and how these responses will then call forth other changes. I have never, myself, read a *Utopia* that seemed to approach even distantly the size and the vitality of the human world. The past was full of surprises; the present is astonishing (as well as frightening); who knows what the future may be?

Let us begin our map, then, in dailiness and distress and think out from there, inking in new bits of territory as they establish themselves in relation to the anomalies and crises with which we start. It isn't enough to have an idea that gender division and the subjugation of women underlie the polarization of society, and to be sure in one's own mind that our climate of pessimism results from misguided definitions of power. We need to understand how these things work in detail, how the power structure frustrates its own aims and denies its own maxims with such pigheaded obstinacy, and how to set about ending these tangles and binds. To change ourselves, to change relationships, to change the world—all these work together and can't be separated, and all of them will supply us with new data, as we update our chart.

New though it must be, however, I like to imagine it incorporating a few features dating back to a time when play and poetry and metaphor were not excluded from serious business. Our map should take account of excitement and adventurous hopes, and jokes too, so that androgynous angels can trumpet away at each corner and chubby cherubs puff out their cheeks to waft along adult armadas. Let us greet the animal kingdom, with leaping dolphins, a spouting whale, and a wary cat in a tree, and recall the ancient labels that identified the land of the Amazons, or Prester John's kingdom, in order to bear in mind all the area still to be explored. It will not be a map confined to marking the boundaries of nation-states or other existing entities based on power relationships; those areas will be redrawn so often that dotted lines will do very well. Instead, let it take note of weather patterns, of mountains and valleys, of roads, and all the other networks of communications and language areas. No, let us not lay out a planned and structured Utopia, but work toward a map of uncertain prediction connecting to memory, a map of promise, a map of possibility, of an unbounded future that will not be limited by

an end . . .

Notes

Epigraph to book, page v

Turner, *Image and Pilgrimage in Christian Culture,* p. 251.

Chapter 2

1. Rose, *The Conscious Brain,* p. 145.
2. Griffin, *The Question of Animal Awareness,* p. 5.
3. Ibid.
4. Goody, *Questions and Politeness,* introduction.
5. Bartlett, *Remembering,* p. 204; cited in Langer, *Mind,* vol. 1, p. 5.
6. Langer, "Speculations on the Origins of Speech," in *Philosophical Sketches,* p. 47.
7. Minturn and Lambert, *Mothers of Six Cultures,* p. 23.
8. Erikson, *Childhood and Society,* p. 194.
9. Piaget, "Mental Development of the Child," in *Six Psychological Studies,* p. 9.
10. Winnicott, *Playing and Reality,* p. 89.
11. Ibid., p. 65.
12. Fantz, "The Origin of Form Perception."
13. Irwin, "Infant Speech."
14. Goody, *The Domestication of the Savage Mind,* p. 47.
15. Weber, *Peasants into Frenchmen.*
16. Solzhenitsyn, *The Gulag Archipelago, III,* p. 101.
17. Goody, *The Domestication of the Savage Mind,* p. III.

Chapter 3

1. Arieti, *Interpretation of Schizophrenia,* pp. 316, 317.
2. Erikson, *Identity, Youth and Crisis,* p. 103.
3. Ibid., p. 122.
4. Curtiss, *Genie: A Psycholinguistic Study of a Modern-Day "Wild Child."*
5. Winnicott, *Playing and Reality,* p. 2.
6. Ibid., p. 6.
7. Rutter and Schopler, eds., *Autism: A Reappraisal of Concepts and Treatment.*
8. Schachtel, "Focal Attention," in Coser, ed., *The Family: Its Structure and Functions,* p. 389.
9. Rock, "Repetition and Learning," p. 143.
10. Schachtel, "Focal Attention," p. 389.
11. Gombrich, "Illusion and Art," in Gregory and Gombrich, eds., *Illusion in Nature and Art,* p. 210.
12. Ibid.
13. Piaget, "Mental Development of the Child," in *Six Psychological Studies,* pp. 12–13.

Chapter 4

1. Durkheim, *Moral Education,* pp. 67–8.
2. Erikson, *Childhood and Society,* p. 418.
3. Bettelheim, *The Empty Fortress,* p. 63.
4. Winnicott, *Playing and Reality,* p. 51.
5. Winnicott, *Therapeutic Consultations in Child Psychiatry,* p. 380.
6. Ibid., p. 392.
7. Ibid., p. 394.
8. Glasser, "Prisoners of Benevolence," in Galen et al., eds., *Doing Good: The Limits of Benevolence,* p. 107.
9. Bettelheim, *Truants from Life,* p. 48.
10. Ibid., p. 55.
11. Ibid., p. 78.
12. Ibid., p. 295.
13. Ibid., p. 292.
14. Bettelheim, *The Empty Fortress,* p. 235.

Chapter 5

1. Dodds, *The Greeks and the Irrational,* p. 102.
2. Kumin, "The Appointment."
3. Mack, *Nightmares and Human Conflict,* p. 36, quoted from Foster and Anderson, "Unpleasant Dreams in Childhood," pp. 77–84.
4. Mack, *Nightmares and Human Conflict,* p. 203, quoted from Hawkins, "A Review of Psychoanalytic Dream Theory," pp. 14–25.
5. Mack, *Nightmares and Human Conflict,* pp. 119–21.
6. Ibid., p. 124.
7. Ibid., p. 127.
8. Machiavelli, "The Prince," in Gilbert, *Machiavelli: The Chief Works and Others,* vol. I, p. 58.
9. Ibid., p. 15.
10. Spence, *Emperor of China,* p. 29.
11. Ibid., p. 31.
12. Ibid., p. 30.
13. Winnicott, *Therapeutic Consultations,* pp. 55, 83.

Chapter 6

1. Sharp, *The Politics of Nonviolent Action,* p. 8.
2. Davis, *The Problem of Slavery in Western Culture,* pp. 67–8.

Chapter 7

1. Taken from John Locke, *Two Treatises on Government,* as transcribed in Peter Laslett's edition, Cambridge: Cambridge University Press, 1960.
2. Janis and Mann, *Decision-Making,* p. 238.
3. Spence, *Emperor of China,* p. 9.
4. Aries, *Centuries of Childhood,* p. 63.
5. Reedy, *The Twilight of the Presidency,* pp. 22–3, 168–9.

Chapter 8

1. Homans, *English Villagers of the Thirteenth Century,* p. 342.
2. Spence, *Emperor of China,* p. 43.

Chapter 9

1. Weber, *Peasants into Frenchmen,* p. 29.
2. Weimer, "Magic in Brazil."
3. Laing, *The Divided Self,* p. 38.
4. Winnicott, *Playing and Reality,* pp. 68–9.
5. Ibid., p. 69.
6. Durkheim, *The Elementary Forms of the Religious Life,* pp. 236–7.
7. Ibid., pp. 464–5.
8. Ibid., p. 495.

Chapter 10

1. Evans-Pritchard, "The Morphology and Function of Magic," in Middleton, ed., *Magic, Witchcraft and Curing,* pp. 18–19.
2. Ibid., p. 19.
3. Wilson, "Nyakyusa Ritual and Symbolism," in Middleton, ed., *Myth and Cosmos,* pp. 161–5.
4. Lévi-Strauss, "The Sorcerer and His Magic," in *Structural Anthropology,* pp. 167–8.
5. Arieti, *Interpretation of Schizophrenia,* p. 436.
6. Wilson, "Nyakyusa Ritual and Symbolism," p. 162.
7. Ibid., p. 165.
8. Makarius, "The Crime of Manabozo," p. 663.
9. Ibid., p. 664.
10. Ibid.
11. Ibid., p. 665.
12. Ibid., p. 668.
13. Ibid., p. 660.
14. Ibid., p. 669.
15. Ibid., p. 670 (italics added).
16. Ibid.

Chapter 11

1. Emerson, "Power-Dependence Relations," p. 32.
2. Ibid., p. 34.
3. Weber, "The Nature of Charismatic Domination," in Runciman, ed., *Max Weber: Selections in Translation,* p. 229.

Chapter 12

1. Genovese, *Roll, Jordan, Roll,* p. 293.
2. Hanawalt, "Violent Death in Fourteenth- and Early Fifteenth-Century England," p. 317.
3. Rudé, *Europe in the Eighteenth Century,* pp. 62, 64, 65.

4. Thompson, *The Making of the English Working Class*, pp. 306–307.
5. Ibid., pp. 194, 424.

Chapter 13

1. Sakharov, *My Country and the World*, pp. 29–30.
2. Bettelheim, *The Informed Heart*, p. 131.
3. Crankshaw, *The Shadow of the Winter Palace*, p. 169.
4. Ibid.
5. Lewin, "The Social Background of Stalinism," in Tucker, ed., *Stalinism*, p. 112.
6. Ibid., p. 113.
7. Lenin, *State and Revolution*, p. 23.
8. Medvedev, *Let History Judge*, p. 399.
9. Ibid., p. 400.
10. Smith, *The Russians*, pp. 452–3.
11. Sakharov, *My Country and the World*, p. 46.
12. Ibid., p. 3.
13. Morrison, "Books," p. 33.
14. Amalrik, *Will the Soviet Union Survive Until 1984?*, pp. 62–4.

Chapter 14

1. Hobsbawm, *Bandits*, p. 43.
2. Engel and Rosenthal, ed. and trans., *Five Sisters: Women Against the Tsar*, p. 227.
3. Ibid., p. 226.
4. Beradt, *The Third Reich of Dreams*, p. 62.
5. Ibid., p. 74.
6. Ibid., p. 87.
7. Solzhenitsyn, *The Gulag Archipelago I*, pp. 3–4.
8. Ibid., p. 414.
9. Solzhenitsyn, *The Gulag Archipelago II*, pp. 602–603.
10. Bettelheim, *The Informed Heart*, p. 139.
11. Solzhenitsyn, *The Gulag Archipelago I*, pp. 515–17.
12. Bettelheim, *The Informed Heart*, pp. 111–15.
13. Ibid., p. 136.

Chapter 15

1. Palmer, *The World of the French Revolution*, pp. 48–9.
2. Auerbach, *Literary Language and Its Public in Late Latin Antiquity and in the Middle Ages*, p. 62.
3. Engel and Rosenthal, ed. and trans., *Five Sisters*, p. xxxiv.
4. Wheeler-Bennett, *Friends, Enemies and Sovereigns*, pp. 103–104.
5. Solzhenitsyn, *The Gulag Archipelago III*, p. 297.
6. Price, "The Strategy and Tactics of Revolutionary Terrorism," p. 59.
7. Hobsbawm and Rudé, *Captain Swing*, p. 17.
8. Crankshaw, *The Shadow of the Winter Palace*, p. 298.

Chapter 16

1. Anonymous, quoted in Auden, *A Certain World,* p. 227.
2. Kanter, *Men and Women of the Corporation,* p. 209.
3. Goffman, *Stigma.*
4. *The New York Times,* February 11, 1979.
5. Hardwick, *Seduction and Betrayal,* p. 192.
6. Carling, *And Yet We Are Human,* pp. 54–5.

Chapter 17

1. Kuhn, *The Structure of Scientific Revolutions,* 2nd ed., pp. 5–6, 68.
2. Korda, *Power: How to Get It, How to Use It.*
3. McClelland, *Power: The Inner Experience,* p. 260.
4. Ibid., pp. 257, 258.
5. Ibid., p. 266.
6. Ibid.
7. Turner, *Image and Pilgrimage in Christian Culture* (as in epigraph to book).
8. McClelland, *Power,* p. 263.
9. Ibid., p. 266.
10. Burns, *Leadership,* p. 15.
11. Ibid., p. 425.
12. Ibid.

Chapter 18

1. Miller, *Toward a New Psychology for Women,* p. 124.
2. Janis and Mann, *Decision-Making,* p. 11.
3. Ibid., p. 15.
4. Terkel, *Working,* pp. 407–408.
5. Kanter, *Men and Women of the Corporation,* p. 48.
6. Ibid., p. 49.
7. Levinson et al., *The Seasons of a Man's Life,* pp. 232–3.
8. Ibid.
9. Sarason, *The Creation of Settings and the Future Societies,* p. 217.
10. Miller, *Toward a New Psychology for Women,* p. 41.
11. *The Wall Street Journal,* April 5, 1979.
12. *The New York Times,* May 29, 1979.
13. Douglas, *The Feminization of American Culture.*

Chapter 19

1. Fél and Hofer, *Proper Peasants;* Ladurie, *Montaillou: The Promised Land of Error.*
2. Sarason, *The Creation of Settings.*
3. Sharp, *The Politics of Nonviolent Action,* p. 47.
4. Ibid., p. 807.
5. Ibid., p. 675.

Chapter 20

1. Needham, ed., *Right and Left: Essays on Dual Symbolic Classification,* p. 135.
2. de Beauvoir, *The Second Sex,* p. 262.
3. Auerbach, *Literary Language,* p. 102.
4. Ibid., p. 96.

Bibliography

Included in this bibliography are some books, not specifically cited in the text, which have nonetheless pervaded and enriched the context of the argument developed here. Some are becoming classics of feminist thinking. Others provide remarkable insights into the daily experience of women, past and present. Still others record and discuss processes of crisis and of breakdown occurring at earlier stages of Western civilization, moments when structure was endangered or overthrown, when old paradigms were stretched, rigidified, or recreated. Like extreme conditions, these eras were testing times, times when powers of the weak were called upon for survival. Survival once achieved, it appears that the strengths of the governed majority are forgotten or remembered only as a disturbing and anomalous phenomenon— even as a potential threat. The appeal of Marxism as an ideology is surely due in part at least to its revaluing of the governed; but until the ancient division of labor, status, and power between the sexes is healed, no attempt to cure the ills of society by overcoming class differences can be successful.

Amalrik, Andrei. *Will the Soviet Union Survive Until 1984?*. New York: Harper & Row, 1970.

Aries, Philippe. *Centuries of Childhood*. New York: Vintage Books, 1965.

Arieti, Silvano. *Interpretation of Schizophrenia*. New York: Basic Books, Inc., 1974.

Auden, W. H. *A Certain World*. New York: The Viking Press, 1970.

Auerbach, Erich. *Literary Language and Its Public in Late Latin Antiquity and in the Middle Ages*. Bollingen Series LXXIV. New York: Pantheon Books, 1965.

Bartlett, F. C. *Remembering*. Cambridge: Cambridge University Press, 1932. (Cited in Susanne Langer, *Mind*, vol. 1. Baltimore: The Johns Hopkins Press, 1967.)

Beradt, Charlotte. *The Third Reich of Dreams*. Chicago: Quadrangle Books, 1966.

Bettelheim, Bruno. *The Empty Fortress*. New York: The Free Press, 1967

———. *The Informed Heart*. Glencoe, Illinois: The Free Press, 1960.

———. *Truants from Life*. Glencoe, Illinois: The Free Press, 1955.

———. *The Uses of Enchantment*. New York: Alfred A. Knopf, Inc., 1976.

Boston Women's Health Collective, The. *Ourselves and Our Children*. New York: Random House, 1978.

Burns, James MacGregor. *Leadership*. New York: Harper & Row, 1978.

Canetti, Elias. *Crowds and Power*. Compass Edition. New York: The Viking Press, 1966.

Carling, F. *And Yet We Are Human*. London: Chatto & Windus, 1962.

Cohn, Norman. *Europe's Inner Demons*. New York: Basic Books, Inc., 1975.

Crankshaw, Edward. *The Shadow of the Winter Palace*. New York: The Viking Press, 1976.

Curtiss, Susan. *Genie. A Psycholinguistic Study of a Modern-Day "Wild Child."* New York: Academic Press, 1977.

Dangerfield, George. *The Damnable Question: A Study in Anglo-Irish Relations*. An Atlantic Monthly Press Book. Boston: Little, Brown & Co., 1976.

Davis, David Brion. *The Problem of Slavery in Western Culture*. Ithaca: Cornell University Press, 1966.

de Beauvoir, Simone. *The Coming of Age*. New York: G. P. Putnam's Sons, 1972.

———. *The Second Sex.* New York: Alfred A. Knopf, Inc., 1953.

Deregowski, Jan B. "Pictorian Perception and Culture." In *Scientific American,* November 1972.

Dinnerstein, Dorothy. *The Mermaid and the Minotaur.* New York: Harper & Row, 1976.

Dodds, E. R. *The Greeks and the Irrational.* Berkeley: University of California Press, 1951.

Douglas, Ann. *The Feminization of American Culture.* Alfred A. Knopf, Inc., 1977.

Durkheim, Emile. *The Elementary Forms of the Religious Life.* New York: The Free Press, 1965.

———. *Moral Education.* New York: The Free Press, 1961.

Emerson, Richard. "Power-Dependence Relations." In *American Sociological Review,* February 1962.

Engel, Barbara Alpern, and Rosenthal, Clifford, ed. and trans. *Five Sisters: Women Against the Tsar.* New York: Alfred A. Knopf, Inc., 1975.

Erikson, Erik. *Childhood and Society.* New York: W. W. Norton, Inc., 1963.

———. *Identity, Youth and Crisis.* New York: W. W. Norton, Inc., 1968.

Evans-Pritchard, E. E. "The Morphology and Function of Magic." In *Magic, Witchcraft and Curing,* edited by John Middleton. Garden City, N.Y.: Natural History Press, 1967.

Fantz, Robert L. "The Origin of Form Perception." In *Scientific American,* May 1961.

Fél, Edit, and Hofer, Tamás. *Proper Peasants.* Chicago: Aldine Publishing Co., 1969.

Foster, J. C., and Anderson, J. E. "Unpleasant Dreams in Childhood." In *Child Development* 7(1936):77–84.

Fussell, Paul. *The Great War and Modern Memory.* New York: Oxford University Press, 1975.

Genovese, Eugene. *Roll, Jordan, Roll.* New York: Pantheon Books, 1974.

Glasser, Ira. "Prisoners of Benevolence." In *Doing Good: The Limits of Benevolence,* edited by Willard Gaylin, Ira Glasser, Steven Marcus, and David Tothman. New York: Pantheon Books, 1978.

Goffman, Erving. *Stigma.* Englewood Cliffs, N.J.: Prentice-Hall, 1963.

Gombrich, E. H. "Illusion and Art." In *Illusion in Nature and Art,* edited by R. L. Gregory and E. H. Gombrich. New York: Charles Scribner's Sons, 1973.

Goody, Esther N., ed. *Questions and Politeness: Strategies in Social Interaction.* Cambridge: Cambridge University Press, 1978.

Goody, Jack. *The Domestication of the Savage Mind.* Cambridge: Cambridge University Press, 1977.

Griffin, Donald R. *The Question of Animal Awareness.* New York: Rockefeller University Press, 1976.

Hanawalt, Barbara A. "Violent Death in Fourteenth and Early Fifteenth Century England." In *Comparative Studies in Society and History,* July 1976.

Hardwick, Elizabeth. *Seduction and Betrayal.* New York: Random House, 1974.

Harris, Anne Sutherland, and Nochlin, Linda. *Women Artists, 1550–1950.* Los Angeles: Los Angeles County Museum of Art, 1976.

Hawkins, D. R. "A Review of Psychoanalytic Dream Theory." In *The British Journal of Medical Psychology* 39(1966):85–104.

Hobsbawm, Eric. *Bandits.* New York: Delacorte Press, 1969.

———, and Rudé, George. *Captain Swing.* New York: Pantheon Books, 1968.

Homans, George C. *English Villagers of the Thirteenth Century.* Norton Library Edition. New York: W. W. Norton, Inc., 1975.

Irwin, Orvis C. "Infant Speech." In *Scientific American,* September 1949.

Janeway, Elizabeth. *Man's World, Woman's Place.* New York: William Morrow and Co., Inc., 1971.

Janis, Irving, and Mann, Leon. *Decision-Making.* New York: The Free Press, 1977.

Kanter, Rosabeth Moss. *Men and Women of the Corporation.* New York: Basic Books, Inc., 1977.

Korda, Michael. *Power: How to Get It, How to Use It.* New York: Random House, 1975.

Kuhn, Thomas. *The Structure of Scientific Revolutions.* 2nd ed. Chicago: University of Chicago Press, 1970.

Kumin, Maxine. "The Appointment." In *The Privilege.* New York: Harper & Row, 1965.

Laing, R. D. *The Divided Self.* London: Penguin Books, 1965.

Langer, Susanne. "Speculations on the Origins of Speech." In *Philosophical Sketches.* Baltimore: The Johns Hopkins Press, 1962.

Lasch, Christopher. *The Culture of Narcissism.* New York: W. W. Norton, Inc., 1978.

Lenin, V. I. *State and Revolution.* New York: International Publishers, 1974.

Le Roy Ladurie, Emmanuel. *Montaillou: The Promised Land of Error.* New York: George Braziller, 1978.

Lerner, Gerda, ed. *The Female Experience: An American Documentary.* Indianapolis: The Bobbs-Merrill Co., 1977.

Lévi-Strauss, Claude. "The Sorcerer and His Magic." In *Structural Anthropology.* New York: Basic Books, Inc., 1963.

Levinson, Daniel J.; with Darrow, Charlotte N.; Klein, Edward B.; Levinson, Maria H.; and McKee, Braxton. *The Seasons of a Man's Life.* New York: Alfred A. Knopf, Inc., 1978.

Lewin, Moshe. "The Social Background of Stalinism." In *Stalinism,* edited by Robert C. Tucker. New York: W. W. Norton, Inc., 1977.

Locke, John. *Two Treatises on Government,* edited by Peter Laslett. Cambridge: Cambridge University Press, 1960.

Lynd, Helen Merrell. *On Shame and the Search for Identity.* New York: Harcourt, Brace and Co., 1958.

McClelland, David C. *Power: The Inner Experience.* New York: Irvington Publishers, Inc., 1975.

Maclean, Fitzroy. *Escape to Adventure.* Boston: Little, Brown & Co., 1951.

Machiavelli, Niccolo. "The Prince." In *Machiavelli: The Chief Works and Others,* vol. 1. Durham: Duke University Press, 1965.

Mack, John. *Nightmares and Human Conflict.* Boston: Little, Brown & Co., 1970.

Makarius, Laura. "The Crime of Manibozo." In *American Anthropologist,* June 1973.

Medvedev, Roy. *Let History Judge.* New York: Alfred A. Knopf, Inc., 1971.

Miller, Jean Baker. *Toward a New Psychology for Women.* Boston: The Beacon Press, 1976.

Minturn, Leigh, and Lambert, William W. *Mothers of Six Cultures.* New York: John Wiley & Sons, 1964.

Moers, Ellen. *Literary Women: The Great Writers.* New York: Doubleday & Co., 1976.

Morris, John. *The Age of Arthur: A History of the British Isles from 350 to 650.* New York: Charles Scribner's Sons, 1973.

Morrison, Philip. "Books." In *Scientific American,* May 1978.

Needham, Rodney, ed. *Right and Left: Essays on Dual Symbolic Classification.* Chicago: The University of Chicago Press, 1973.

Palmer, R. R. *The World of the French Revolution.* New York: Harper & Row, 1971.

Piaget, Jean. "Mental Development of the Child." In *Six Psychological Studies.* New York: Random House, 1967.

Pipes, Richard, ed. *Revolutionary Russia.* Cambridge, Mass.: Harvard University Press, 1968.

Pomeroy, Sarah B. *Goddesses, Whores, Wives, and Slaves: Women in Classical Antiquity.* New York: Schocken Books, 1975.

Price, H. Edwards. "The Strategy and Tactics of Revolutionary Terrorism." In *Comparative Studies in Society and History,* January 1977.

Reedy, George. *The Twilight of the Presidency.* New York: World Publishing Co., 1970.

Rich, Adrienne. *Of Woman Born: Motherhood as Experience and Institution.* New York: W. W. Norton, Inc., 1976.

Rock, Irwin. "Repetition and Learning." In *Scientific American,* August 1958.

Rose, Steven. *The Conscious Brain.* New York: Alfred A. Knopf, Inc., 1973.

Ruddick, Sara, and Daniels, Pamela, eds. *Working It Out.* New York: Pantheon Books, 1977.

Rudé, George. *Europe in the Eighteenth Century: Aristocracy and the Bourgeois Challenge.* New York: Praeger Publishers, 1973.

Rutter, Michael, and Schopler, Eric, eds. *Autism: A Reappraisal of Concepts and Treatment.* New York: Plenum Press, 1978.

Sakharov, Andrei. *My Country and the World.* New York: Alfred A. Knopf, Inc., 1975.

Sarason, Seymour B. *The Creation of Settings and the Future Societies.* San Francisco: Jossey-Bass, Inc., 1972.

Schachtel, Ernest. "Focal Attention." In *The Family: Its Structure and Functions,* edited by Rose Coser. New York: St. Martin's Press, 1969.

Sharp, Gene. *The Politics of Nonviolent Action.* Boston: Potter, Sargent Publishers, 1973.

Smith, Hedrick. *The Russians.* New York: New York Times Book Company, Quadrangle, 1976.

Solzhenitsyn, Alexandr. *The Gulag Archipelago.* Vol. 1, 1973. Vol. 2, 1974. Vol. 3, 1978. New York: Harper & Row.

Spence, Jonathan D. *Emperor of China: Self-Portrait of K'ang-hsi.* New York: Alfred A. Knopf, Inc., 1974.

Stern, August, ed. *USSR vs. Dr. Mikhail Stern.* New York: Urizen Books, 1977.

Stone, Lawrence. *The Family, Sex and Marriage in England, 1500–1800.* New York: Harper & Row, 1977.

Terkel, Studs. *Working.* New York: Pantheon Books, 1974.

Thompson, E. P. *The Making of the English Working Class.* New York: Vintage Books, 1963.

Toynbee, Arnold J. *A Study of History.* Oxford: Oxford University Press, 1934, 1939.

Turner, Victor. *Dramas, Fields, and Metaphors: Symbolic Action in Human Society.* Ithaca: Cornell University Press, 1974.

———. *The Ritual Process: Structure and Anti-Structure.* Chicago: Aldine Publishing Co., 1969.

———, and Turner, Edith. *Image and Pilgrimage in Christian Culture.* New York: Columbia University Press, 1978.

Weber, Eugen. *Peasants into Frenchmen.* Stanford: Stanford University Press, 1976.

Weber, Max. "The Nature of Charismatic Domination." In *Max Weber: Selections in Translation,* edited by W. G. Runciman. Cambridge: Cambridge University Press, 1978.

Weimer, Joan. "Magic in Brazil," unpublished paper.

Wheeler-Bennett, John. *Friends, Enemies, and Sovereigns.* London: Macmillan & Co., 1976.

Wilson, Monica. "Nyakusa Ritual and Symbolism." In *Myth and Cosmos,* edited by John Middleton. Garden City, N.Y.: Natural History Press, 1967.

Winnicott, D. W. *Playing and Reality.* New York: Basic Books, Inc., 1971.

———. *Therapeutic Consultations in Child Psychiatry.* New York: Basic Books, Inc., 1971.

Woolf, Virginia. *A Room of One's Own.* New York: Harcourt, Brace & Co., 1929.

Yglesias, Helen. *Starting: Early, Anew, Over, and Late.* New York: Rawson, Wade Publishers, Inc., 1978.

Index

abnormality, *see* deviance
Abraham and Isaac, 144
absolute power, 123, 187–201
academic excellence, 237
accidie, 129, 130
action, *see* organization for action
Acton, John Emerich Edward
    Dalberg-Acton, Lord
  dictum on power, 91, 111, 132
    and failures in relationship, 264–5
    and inadequacy of power, 126–7
    and ordered/disordered uses of power,
      88
    and (the) supernatural, 123
    and tyranny, 186
    and (the) weak, 148
Adams, Henry, 91
adult-child relationship, 49–50
  see also mother-child relationship
adult play, 291
Aesop, 92
Affirmative Action programs, 236, 237,
    238, 239
age as determinant of status, 28, 29
aggression, expressed in dreams, 70–1
agoraphobia, 169–70, 171, 173
altruistic leadership, 259–64, 297
Amalrik, Andrei, 198–9
ambition, 275–6
amorality of power
  in dictionary definitions, 88
  of the weak, 157
anatomy as destiny, 7–9, 150–1, 245,
    305–307
  see also gender differences
anger
  repressed, 61–2
  of (the) weak, expressed through the
    Church, 129
  of women, 310–11

animals
  communication, 39
  in dreams, 76–9
  in legends and fairy tales, 128
anxiety
  and dreams, 66–7, 68–9, 205–206
  effect on children, 50–1
  as male phenomenon, 253–4
  see also fear; stress
apathy (political), 173–4, 200
  among English working class, 178
  see also "cop-out and drop-out"
arbitrariness, *see* prediction
Arendt, Hannah, 237
Arieti, Silvano
  Interpretation of Schizophrenia, The, 36,
    46, 140
art
  and community, 279–82
  and dreams, 66
  and emotions, 279–82
  judged by commercial value, 281
  and symbolic language, 279–82, 286,
    302, 312
Asev, Yevno, 231–2
assertiveness training, 289
astrology, 124, 125
astronomy, 124, 125
Auerbach, Erich
  Literary Language and Its Public, 220,
    313
authentication of person, 46, 47, 131
  see also self-esteem
authentication of power
  in child's language, 41
  by (the) weak, 72–3, 111–14, 162–7, 170
  withdrawal of, 107, 114–15, 162, 172, 183,
    227, 298–9; *see also* disbelief
authority, *see* power
autism, 40, 42, 50

A NOTE ABOUT THE AUTHOR

Elizabeth Janeway is the author of *Man's World, Woman's Place* and *Between Myth and Morning,* as well as six novels and four children's books. She is a director of the Author's Guild and a trustee of Barnard College. She and her husband, the economist and author Eliot Janeway, live in New York City.

A NOTE ON THE TYPE

The text of this book was set in a computer version of Times Roman, designed by Stanley Morison for *The Times* (London) and first introduced by that newspaper in 1932.

Among typographers and designers of the twentieth century, Stanley Morison has been a strong forming influence as typographical adviser to the English Monotype Corporation, as a director of two distinguished English publishing houses, and as a writer of sensibility, erudition, and keen practical sense.

Composed, printed, and bound by The Haddon Craftsmen, Inc., Scranton, Pennsylvania.
Typography and binding design by Virginia Tan.